Cars for Comrades

CARS FOR

The Life of the
Soviet Automobile

COMRADES

LEWIS H. SIEGELBAUM

Cornell University Press
Ithaca & London

First published 2008 by Cornell University Press
First printing, Cornell Paperbacks, 2011

Printed in the United States of America

Library of Congress Cataloging-in-Publication Data

Siegelbaum, Lewis H.
   Cars for comrades : the life of the Soviet automobile / Lewis Siegelbaum.
      p. cm.
   Includes bibliographical references and index.
   ISBN 978-0-8014-4638-2 (cloth : alk. paper)
   ISBN 978-0-8014-7721-8 (pbk. : alk. paper)
   1. Automobile industry and trade—Soviet Union—History.   2. Automobiles—Soviet
Union—History.   I. Title.
   HD9710.R92S54   2008
   338.7'62922209470904—dc22
                                    2007037036

Cornell University Press strives to use environmentally responsible
suppliers and materials to the fullest extent possible in the publishing
of its books. Such materials include vegetable-based, low-VOC inks
and acid-free papers that are recycled, totally chlorine-free, or partly
composed of nonwood fibers. For further information, visit our website
at www.cornellpress.cornell.edu.

Cloth printing   10 9 8 7 6 5 4 3 2 1
Paperback printing   10 9 8 7 6 5 4 3 2 1

contents

tables

preface

On an overcast May morning in 2006, I opened the curtains to let some
light into the room I had rented in the center of Moscow. I had arrived the previous night and was trying to get my bearings. As my eyes adjusted to the
light, they fell on a very large, predominantly off-white automobile, a Chaika
(Russian for "seagull"), nestled among some poplar trees that were only beginning to turn green. Droppings from the overhanging branches and other
detritus had discolored its body paint, suggesting the old car had been there
a long time. Returning wearily to my apartment in the days that followed, I
often looked into the courtyard and the beached whale of a car. Occasionally,
I saw someone sweeping the pavement around it, but that was all. And then,
one afternoon while chatting with someone at the opposite end of the courtyard, I was startled by a loud roar. Turning to look, I saw that "my" Chaika had
come back to life.

This sorely neglected car struck me as an apt symbol of Russian attitudes
toward their automotive past. This book is a history of that past, a biography
of the lives of the Soviet automobile. To some, the very idea of such a book
seemed quixotic. "That will be a very small book," quipped one citizen of
Moscow. And in our alumni magazine, a college classmate offered "Nada to
the Lada" as a fitting title. Indeed, the automobile and Soviet Communism
made an odd couple. Unlike some other modes of transportation—trains, airplanes, tractors—cars had rarely served as icons of the Soviet march to the
bright socialist future. As an object of individual desire, the car—in effect
a mobile private space—had always existed in tension with the collectivist
ideology of the Communist Party. Not until the 1970s could one say that the
automobile revolution had occurred in the USSR. Even then neither cars nor
the complex infrastructure needed to support them dominated the landscape
as they did in the United States and other Western countries. But the desire

for car ownership knew no bounds, and efforts to fulfill that desire would intensify the social, economic, and political contradictions that beset the Soviet system.

It is precisely the apparent incompatibility of cars and Communism that prompted me to write this history of the Soviet automobile. It offers the opportunity to approach the Soviet period from a de-centered perspective—neither from above nor from below but from the side, where politics and labor, the economy, the arts, and international relations all commingled. To study cars in the context of Communism is at the same time to study Soviet Communism in the context of cars. It is to de-center Soviet history in a geographical sense by taking us to places not otherwise encountered—to towns and districts of cities built specifically for auto manufacturing; along roads, projected as well as built, in city centers and in remote regions of the country; and to garages, filling stations, and camping sites. Initially the exclusive prerogative of comrades, cars eventually became available to a broader spectrum of the Soviet public. This "democratization" process was not accompanied, however, by a corresponding expansion of services to keep automobiles going, at least not legally. While the care and feeding of cars collectively consumed more and more time and space, Communism was withering and dying in the land of its birth. Wonderful and strange it is, therefore, that, aside from buildings erected in the Soviet era, nothing reminds one so much of those decades as the aging Volgas, Ladas, Moskviches, and Chaikas increasingly consigned to the scrap heap but occasionally showing the capacity to roar back into life.

PURSUING the Soviet automobile took me down some strange paths and not only of the metaphorical kind. Little had I suspected before deciding to write this book that reading car magazines, watching low-brow Soviet movies from the 1950s and '60s, and prowling around the courtyards of Soviet-era apartment buildings could be considered research. One of the pleasures of doing research on a vastly different subject is making new acquaintances. Among those whom I am particularly happy to have met are Corinna Kuhr-Koroleva, Andrei Miniuk, Boris Shpotov, and Mariia Zezina in Moscow; Tatiana Adaevskaia, Vladimir Iamashev, Max Mikhailovskii, Leonid Pakhuta, Nadezhda Rumiantseva, and Alexander Efimevich Stepanov in Togliatti; Alain Blum, Yves Cohen, and Patrick Fridenson in Paris; and Bob Argenbright, Tracy Nichols Busch, Andrew Paul Janco, Steve Meyer, Andrey Shlyakhter, and Olga Velikovskaia, who are spread out across the North American academic archipelago. Their generosity and other kindnesses are greatly appreciated. I also am happy to acknowledge institutional support from Michigan State University's Department of History, the International Research and Exchanges Board (IREX), the École des Hautes Études en Sciences Sociales in Paris, the Université de Toulouse—Le Mirail, and the Netherlands Institute for Advanced Study in the Humanities and Social Sciences (NIAS). And to Marcie Cowley for being a particularly conscientious and effective research assistant; to Susan Reid, Meredith Roman, Steven Harris, Jim Heinzen, and my colleague and friend Lisa Fine for passing on citations they thought would be (and were) useful; to Sarah Jane AcMoody for applying her cartographic skills to the map that appears herein; Vadim Cherkassky for cheerfully answering numerous queries about Soviet automotive jargon; Corinna Kuhr-Koroleva for recounting her experiences as a female driver in Moscow and for assisting me in obtaining permission to include artistic reproductions; and Leonid Veintraub for introducing me to the cornucopia of videos about cars and drivers available at the Gorbushka (the music and electronics bazaar in Moscow), I express profound gratitude.

Then, there are those without whose help the completion of this book would have been inconceivable. Bob Edelman was a confidence booster whose enthusiasm about the subject proved infectious. Diane Koenker, who got serious about the project before I did, gave me incredibly perceptive criticisms and steered me in the right direction at several stages. Cornell University Press's director, John Ackerman, is the best editor I ever have encountered and the best imaginable. He improved the manuscript immensely. So did Candace Akins, the Mozart of manuscript editors. Finally, Leslie Page Moch knows more than anyone else that nothing in this book came easily, but she nonetheless made the process a lot easier in all kinds of ways. None of these people bears the slightest responsibility for errors contained herein. They are mine, all mine.

glossary

AMO Avtomobil'noe Moskovskoe Obshchestvo or Moscow Automobile Society

ASMR Automobile and Farm Machinery Workers Union of Russia

Avtodor Society for Cooperation in the Development of Automobilism and Road Improvement

Avtograd Auto Factory District; Auto City

avtomobil' any motor vehicle, car or truck or bus

avtoprobeg auto rally

Avtostroi Automobile Construction Trust

AvtoVAZ *see VAZ*

AZLK Automobile Factory of Leninist Komsomol (*see also MZMA*)

GAI State Automobile Inspectorate

GARF Gosudarstvennyi arkhiv Rossiiskoi Federatsii (State Archive of the Russian Federation)

GAZ Gor'kovskii Avtomobil'nyi Zavod or Gor'kii Automobile Factory

Glavdortrans Board of Road Transport

Gosplan State Planning Commission

Gulag Main Administration of Labor Camps

GUPVI Main Administration of Prisoners of War and Interned Personnel

Gushosdor Main Administration of Highways

GUTAP Main Administration of the Auto-Tractor Industry

IaAZ Iaroslavl' Automobile Plant

KamAZ Kama Automobile Factory

kommissionyi magazin state commission [second-hand] store *krai* territory or region on the periphery

MDC machine road stations

MKAD Moscow Ring Road

MVD Ministry of Internal Affairs

MZMA Moscow Factory of Small (displacement) Automobiles (*see also AZLK*)

NAMI Scientific Automotive Institute

Narkomput People's Commissariat of Transportation

NKVD People's Commissariat of Internal Affairs

OAO Otkrytoe aktsionernoe obshchestvo (Open Joint-Stock Company)

Osoaviakhim Society for Cooperation in Defense, Aviation, and Chemical Development

podvig self-sacrificial act of generosity

raion **(plural, *raiony*)** regional district

RGAE Rossiiskii Gosudarstvennyi arkhiv Ekonomiki (Russian State Archive of the Economy)

Sotsgorod Socialist City

Sovnarkom Council of People's Commissars

STO Council of Labor and Defense

STOs service stations

TGA Upravlenie po delam arkhivov g. Tol'iatti (Togliatti State Archive)

trudovaia povinnost' labor service

TsAGM Tsentral'nyi Arkhiv Goroda Moskvy (Central Archive of the City of Moscow)

TsIK Central Executive Committee of the Soviets

Tsudortrans Central Administration of Highways and Unpaved Roads

TsUGAZ Central Administration of State Automobile Factories

UAZ Ul'ianovsk Automobile Factory

VAD military automobile road

VATO All-Union Automobile and Tractor Association

VAZ Volzhskii Avtomobil'nyi Zavod or Volga Automobile Factory

Vesenkha (also VSNKh) Supreme Council of the National Economy

ZAZ Zaporozhskii Avtomobil'nyi Zavod or Zaporozh Automobile Factory

ZIL Zavod im. Likhacheva or Likhachev Automobile Factory (formerly ZIS)

ZIS Zavod im. Stalina or Stalin Automobile Factory (formerly AMO)

Cars for Comrades

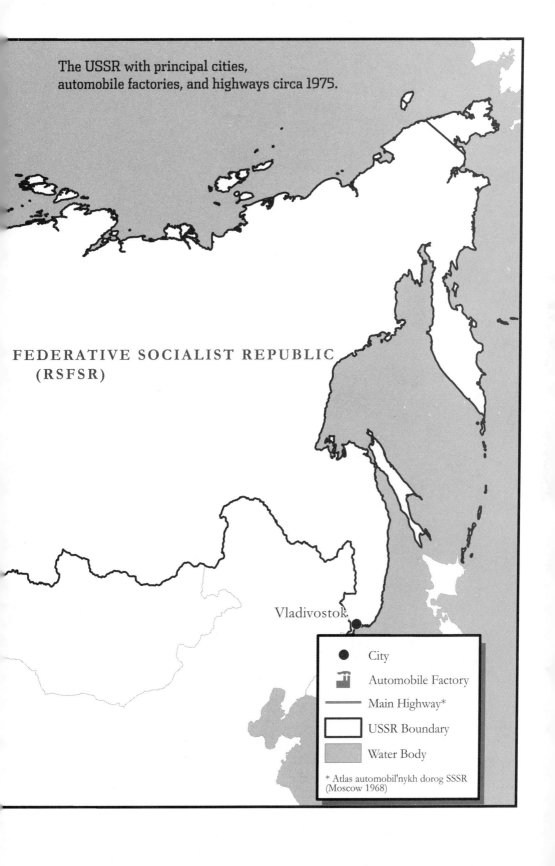

The USSR with principal cities,
automobile factories, and highways circa 1975.

FEDERATIVE SOCIALIST REPUBLIC
(RSFSR)

Vladivostok

City
Automobile Factory
Main Highway*
USSR Boundary
Water Body

* Atlas automobil'nykh dorog SSSR
(Moscow 1968)

Introduction

> The current literature has almost no grasp of the global reach of the
> car...except in matters of production and destruction. There is no
> sense that the car might be a different cultural form or experience
> among different groups.
>
> DANIEL MILLER, *Car Cultures*

In April 1929 the International Labor Organization in Geneva received a
rather unusual request. It came from Sir Percival Perry, chief of the Ford
Motor Company's European operations, which was based in London. Sir Percival wanted the ILO to undertake a systematic study of "how much a Pari-
sian, German, etc. worker would need to expend if his general standard of
living was to be approximately equivalent to that of his Detroit counterpart."
At the time, Henry Ford, the world's most revered entrepreneur, was keen to
expand his company's production operations in Europe as he pursued his
dream of creating the Universal Car. The company already operated assembly plants in Antwerp, Copenhagen, and Cork. In 1928 Ford broke ground
for a factory in Dagenham, England, that was to be "the Detroit of Europe."
It also had plans for Istanbul, Rotterdam, and Cologne. While expanding his
network of factories, Ford also sought to replicate abroad the wage he paid
his workers in Detroit. Edward Filene, the Boston department-store magnate,
acknowledged the boldness of Ford's vision in the telegram announcing his
pledge of $25,000 to the research project: "If [Ford] can help to bring about
the same changes in Europe, it will mean higher wages, lower prices, greater
total profits, and higher standards of living in Europe and as a result greater
world prosperity and an enormous impetus to world peace."[1]

Today, the notion of a U.S. automaker setting up factories abroad to raise
foreign workers' standards of living to that of Americans seems incredible and
must have raised a few eyebrows at the time. Still, the ILO agreed to conduct
the inquiry. Its investigators spent over two years compiling and assembling
data from more than a dozen countries. The problem was that by the time
the English-language edition appeared in December 1931 its representation of

the Detroit-based standard of living "belonged to another time."[2] The Great Depression had hit Detroit with considerable force. Most of the workers interviewed in 1929–30 were now unemployed.

Ironically, it was just then that Detroit began to serve as the standard against which to measure car factories and towns farther to the east. "Detroit but without Ford" read the headline in a Soviet newspaper reporting on a technical assistance agreement with the Ford Motor Company that would make possible the construction near Nizhni Novgorod of an integrated plant and alongside it a town to accommodate fifty thousand people. *Pravda* used virtually the same words to describe a renovated auto factory on the Moscow River within sight of the Kremlin. Soviet journalists were not alone in making the analogy with America's quintessential auto city. American reporters dubbed the new Nizhni Novgorod auto plant "Soviet Russia's new Detroit" or simply "Communist 'Detroit'." The reference eventually became detached from its referent. As recently as 2001 readers of the *Detroit News* were informed that Togliatti, the mid-Volga town that had ballooned with the construction of the Volga Automobile Factory (VAZ) in the late 1960s and early 1970s, "calls itself 'Detroit on the Volga.'"[3]

The Detroit being invoked bore little relation to the actual city on the straits between Lake St. Clair and Lake Erie. The imagined Detroit was an industrial colossus of assembly plants, metal and machine tool shops, proving grounds, and other automobile-related facilities, whose seemingly limitless production of automobiles was Promethean. Soviet imaginations conjured up a city of auto-mobility, of masses of forged, pressed, and stamped metal relentlessly moving along conveyor belts and gradually assuming the materiality of motor vehicles. Soviet hearts beat faster to the notion that a city could be built on Soviet soil to rival "the greatest centre of manufacturing in the entire world," the place whose "implacable assembly lines" symbolized the miracle of mass production.[4] Soviet breasts swelled with pride that their auto towns could do without the great magician-organizer of the imagined Detroit, Henry Ford.

Soviet attitudes toward Ford-the-entrepreneur were mixed, as they were elsewhere in Europe, though perhaps for different reasons.[5] But "*Fordizatsiia*" and "*Fordizm,*" terms widely used in the 1920s interchangeably with "American tempo" and "American efficiency," were a different story. What Ford had wrought deeply impressed Marxist theoreticians, the technical intelligentsia, the cultural avant-garde, and ordinary readers of mass-circulation popular science journals.[6] No less so than their counterparts in Weimar Germany, these groups exhibited an abundance of "technological optimism," that is, an identification of industrial technology with regularity, reliability, and material abundance. In both countries people assumed that what Ford had invented in Detroit could easily be installed—indeed, perfected—by a socialist society that would protect its workers from overexertion and fatigue.[7] Even the less flattering version of Detroit and Ford that the Soviet press subsequently presented—workers being laid off, stick-wielding goons breaking up union rallies, the unemployed succumbing to hunger and despair—did not so much negate the earlier positive associations as underscore that a *Soviet* Detroit would achieve Fordist productivity while avoiding the "anarchy" of the market.

The Detroit of Soviet imagination had little to do with the actual city in Michigan, but Soviet Detroits were real places. They consisted of factories containing tens of thousands of workers, managers, and other personnel engaged in the production of automobiles and the cities (or in one case, an urban district) in which those factories were located. Real as they were, the Soviet Detroits also led an imagined existence. By virtue of being Soviet, the towns, their workers, and their products had to be represented as no worse than—or at the very least in the process of catching up to and overtaking—their equivalents in Detroit. They were in this sense what the literary theorist Vladislav Todorov has called "allegorical figures of industrialization," with the allegory extending from the heroic construction of the factory to the labor in the factory that constituted "the poetic completeness of the factory itself."[8]

Soviet automobiles thus were born amid dreams of a technological utopia. Their most celebrated attribute lay not in their intrinsic design or performance, still less in the physical mobility, privacy, and freedom they afforded, but rather in the assembly-line technology associated with their production. Indeed, as the quintessential consumer item of the twentieth century, they presented some problems for an ideology that subordinated consumer goods to "social" needs. Automobiles were the reason for the construction of a "Socialist City" in the Soviet Russian heartland and later, in the 1960s and '70s, a new auto town on the Volga, but they did not figure prominently in the designs for those cities or in the lives of the auto workers.[9] Ideological hostility to personal consumption had abated by the latter decades. Still, plans for the mass production of a Soviet "people's car" generated as much enthusiasm for the plant and its lengthy assembly line as for the vehicle itself.

Yet, the automobile inspired other kinds of dreams even in the Stalin era. "Visionary town planners" such as Leonid Sabsovich envisioned large numbers of working hands, freed by collectivization, building a network of roads that would eliminate the contradiction between town and country "almost completely" in five to eight years. In keeping with socialist principles, individual ownership of cars would "not be needed," but driving a car was something that "a majority if not all toilers" would learn, and those newly constructed roads could accommodate "millions and tens of millions of vehicles."[10] The "disurbanist" theoretician Mikhail Okhitovich described his version of the future city as "not a city, but a new type of settlement" consisting of a collection of houses each of which would be "a standardized, motorized, easily transportable, small and hence inexpensive structure."[11] Like RVs?

Another vision of the future, more about roads than cities, came to Valerian Osinskii, a prominent Bolshevik and erstwhile member of the party's Left Opposition, who did more to give life to the Soviet automobile than anyone else. In November 1928, just as the whirlwind of Stalin's Socialist Offensive was gathering pace, Osinskii published a letter that purported to have been transmitted back from the twentieth anniversary of the October Revolution in November 1937 by H. G. Wells's time machine. Addressed to a "dear friend," it describes a journey to Voronezh along the Moscow—Khar'kov highway, laid with asphalt only two years before (that is, in 1935) and so smooth that the only sound heard was the whish of tires. As his car leaves Moscow it passes suburban buses and the intercity line from Khar'kov. Outside Tula he comes across new garden settlements with roads covered by ground slag that resembled asphalt when pressed down by a vehicle's wheels. In the city itself the schedule of the holiday's festivities is broadcast from a helicopter, the announcer's voice amplified a hundred million times.[12] Much given to campaigning for a Soviet "automobilism," Osinskii proclaimed several months later that "our century...is the century of electricity and the automobile," that the automobile would destroy the barrier between town and country, and that if the United States was a nation on wheels, then "we are a class on wheels, the most revolutionary class in history, the class that forged an 'iron party,' and a class that will travel to socialism in the automobile."[13]

Some dreamed of roads to socialism—metaphorical and real—while others imagined obtaining or at least riding in cars. These dreams predated Soviet times, but the association of the automobile with dynamism made it a natural for modernist writers of the 1920s to indulge their fancy by actually owning a car for their own amusement—or that of a loved one. They, along with outstanding workers and lottery winners, were among the very few who had the opportunity. Members of the party elite and the upper echelons of the state bureaucracy had access to cars for their "personal use." Residents of major cities, of course, encountered cars generally in their capacity as pedestrians. Some of them, seeing limousines with curtained windows that shrouded high officials of the party and state, came to associate cars with dark, even ghoulish, happenings. Adolescent boys, by contrast, tended to idolize the automobile, or at least they were encouraged to do so by children's magazines, newsreels, and newspaper reports of long-distance endurance rallies.

One might regard Osinskii's dreams as bombast, part of the utopianism of the age that within a few short years would turn into a search for wreckers and enemies of the people—a group that would include Osinskii himself. But the longing among Soviet citizens for the perils and pleasures of driving a car on the open road is not so easy to dismiss. At first inchoate, it lodged itself in the collective subconscious, waiting for a time when it could assert itself with considerable force.

From their birth in the 1920s and for many decades thereafter, Soviet automobiles were distributed, not sold. The overwhelming majority consisted of trucks, long on ruggedness and short on comfort. Essentially the property of the state, they had institutional homes in the armed forces and in the commissariats of internal affairs, heavy industry, light industry, and agriculture and among regional and municipal administrations. But even these vehicles could be appropriated for other purposes. They needed drivers who, although subjected to regulations of one sort or another, had considerable freedom, too, especially when they got out on the road. For the state, the principal function of trucks was to carry produce from state and collective farms to railheads or depots. For rural dwellers in need of getting to town or some other location too far to walk, trucks could serve as surrogate omnibuses, and as alternative sources of information and sociability.

Even in its formative stage, therefore, the Soviet automobile was hard to control; its use and the dreams it inspired tended to deviate from prescribed norms. Of mixed parentage, its hybridity extended to other dimensions, and that is why I have organized this inquiry into the life of the Soviet automobile along three axes: foreign and domestic; public and private; and continuity and change. The arc traced here extends from fantasies of time transcendence and other compensatory dreams inspired by auto technology to something approaching a consumer society, or at least one informally accommodating to the needs of mass-produced and consumed automobiles. It is an arc that in some ways coincides with that of Soviet modernity and in others deviates from it. We can plot its trajectory along the three axes.

The Soviet automobile was more cosmopolitan than is portrayed in nationalistic narratives. The factories producing cars and trucks were "Soviet Detroits" not only in that the architecture and lay-out of the shops were similar or that a lot of the machinery was identical to what one would find at River Rouge, Hamtramck, or Flint. Among those who worked at AMO (Avtomobil'noe Moskovskoe Obshchestvo or Moscow Automobile Society) and GAZ (Gor'kii Automobile Factory), including a few who served as directors, were "re-emigrants" who had done stints in the Motor City. Detroit also came to the Oka and the Moscow rivers in the person of engineers and skilled workers, some because their company sent them, others for the adventure, and still others because of political sympathies. Both the Detroit factories and the Soviet enterprises were modern technological marvels in their time, symbols of the achievements of their respective political systems and ways of life. Both pioneered or made important contributions to incentive systems that had the similar objective of encouraging diligence and discipline.

The vehicles themselves were derivative of models designed in Detroit and elsewhere in the West but adjusted for Soviet climatic and road conditions. They included what once had been basic lines in Ford's repertoire, luxury limousines from General Motors and Packard, and, decades later, Fiat's "car of the year." During World War II American cars and trucks helped the Red Army and stayed on to help administer the Gulag. Meanwhile, "trophy" cars captured from the German enemy gave wheels to Red Army officers in retirement, and one model served as a prototype for a car named for Moscow's residents. How to interpret this degree of dependence on Western automotive technology and design? As the sincerest form of flattery, an indication of a congenital weakness, or as a more interactive process involving not only donors and recipients but brokers too?

Although some models retained their Western origins more closely than others did, all somehow managed to look Soviet. Is that because they embodied the Soviet cultural ideals of logicality, functionality, and (stodgy) predictability, or did their very presence on the streets of Moscow and other Soviet cities help to define the meaning of "Sovietness"? Given the very limited opportunities for consumers to express their preferences, was the power of engineers and designers enhanced as compared with their Western counterparts? Is this why those professions became precarious under Stalin?

When it came to infrastructure and particularly roads, foreign influence was indirect. Military preparedness served as a major impetus to highway construction in the 1930s with (ironically) Fascist Italy's autostradas and Nazi Germany's autobahns providing the models and convicts providing the labor. On secondary roads, the main source of labor—peasants performing corvée—was right out of the Russia of old. Later in the 1930s and '40s, prisoners of war and Red Army units shared the burden. Shirking, low-quality work, and high-cost road maintenance—features of unfree labor everywhere—were endemic to Soviet road building. Change is evident too in the form of mechanization that enabled regional administrations in postwar decades to professionalize road maintenance operations and even introduce a bit of esprit de corps among maintenance crews. Yet, no matter how many additional kilometers of road got paved or at least graded, complaints about roadlessness, a condition lamented since tsarist times, persisted. Such was the result of rising expectations associated with the expansion of automobile ownership.

The analytical categories *public* and *private* should be understood (at least) in the Soviet context neither as mutually exclusive nor antagonistic but rather in a dynamic tension, sometimes reinforcing each other and often producing symbiosis and hybridity.[14] The life of the Soviet automobile substantiates this general point. From before the dawn of Soviet power, cars were contested property—requisitioned by the Imperial Russian Army during World War I, refused to the Provisional Government's prime minister as he desperately searched for a means of escape, acquired from the Americans for this very purpose, seized by the Bolsheviks to provide a means for their leader and his comrades to travel around Moscow and its environs, and driven across the border to escape the Bolsheviks' clutches. The contingency of automobile possession was evident in their liability to conscription in the case of emergency and, on at least one occasion, their obligatory trade-in. Private (or "personal") ownership theoretically was guaranteed by the 1936 Constitution, but only after the war did the state set aside a portion of new cars for purchase by individuals. Even then, professional drivers—to say nothing of the traffic police—barely tolerated "enthusiasts." But gradually the balance shifted, though not without some detours for ideological reasons.

The major turning point in the life of the Soviet automobile came with the mass production of cars at the VAZ plant in Togliatti. In 1972, two years after the first Zhiguli rolled off the assembly line, the Soviet Union produced more cars than trucks for the first time. By 1974, when VAZ reached its capacity of 660,000 cars, car output hit the million mark nationwide. Turning points and revolutions always bring unanticipated consequences. Although there was nothing new about shortages of fuel, spare parts, and garage space—this was, after all, the Soviet economy—the dimensions of those shortages and the social weight of those seeking these items vastly expanded. The state's attempt to manage desire involved it in a whole series of compromises and concessions, a Faustian bargain with heterodox (if not actually private) economic activity it ultimately could not win. Underground markets and semilegal arrangements proliferated. Servicing one's car absorbed a considerable amount of time, became a major topic of conversation at work, and a major reason for skipping work. Nobody, it seemed, could keep pace with the seemingly eternal combustion engine. In the final years of the USSR desire had become demand.

The more time one spent in and with one's own car the less there was for performing other functions, whether social, professional, or otherwise.[15] Such time was essentially private, spent either by oneself or with mechanics, parts suppliers, or other car owners, the vast majority of whom were men. Gender in the form of male bonding turns out to have been an incredibly important dimension of car ownership in the late Soviet period. This gendering of time had its spatial equivalents; garages, make-shift auto parts bazaars, and the interiors of cars themselves served as refuges from the crowded conditions of apartment dwelling.

Could it be said that a distinctly Soviet form of "automobility" was emerging in the last decades of Soviet power? Closely identified with the work of British sociologist John Urry, the concept of automobility has been defined as a "hybrid assemblage of specific human activities, machines, roads, buildings, signs and cultures of mobility" encapsulated in the notion of the "car-driver." It is said to comprise "an ideological or discursive formation, embodying the ideals of freedom, privacy, movement, progress, and autonomy."[16] Movement and progress certainly fell within the orbit of officially endorsed Soviet values, but freedom (of an individual kind) and autonomy were more problematic. Even after the mass production of cars had signaled the abandonment of ideological objections to private car ownership, such accoutrements of "car-driver" mobility as limited-access highways, motels, dependable road clearance and repair, and a host of other features of the "roadscape" taken for granted in the West remained at best rudimentary in the USSR.

Yet, if we are to take seriously the notion that "automobility intersects with the contextualizing matrix of the nation," we must grant the existence of a Soviet automobility, not despite but because of the lack of conveniences.[17] This would be to acknowledge, notwithstanding variations from one Soviet republic to another and differences between urban and rural conditions, a nationwide Soviet car culture replete with "specific human activities...roads, buildings, signs and cultures of mobility." Such a culture sustained the general disdain for wearing seat belts. It included traffic police punching holes in driver's licenses to indicate infractions, drivers paying bribes to settle fines, adorning the cars transporting a bride and groom with dolls or toy bears and bunting and balloons, the removal of windshield wipers and side-view mirrors from parked cars to prevent their theft, and many other distinctive practices.

Some of them survived the collapse of the USSR and others did not, but they all originated in and were constitutive of a Soviet sociocultural environment. The automobiles born in the USSR thus can be identified as Soviet not only because of where and how they were produced and who got to use them but how they were used. For students of material culture, this inquiry into the life history of the Soviet automobile should defamiliarize an object long associated with twentieth-century industrial capitalism. For students of Soviet history, it should defamiliarize certain narratives based on the paramountcy of centralized political power and the centralized system of resource extraction and redistribution.

A FEW words are in order about methodology and terminology. To try to assess the role(s) of automobiles in the USSR, I paid particular attention to sources from different media—memoranda and correspondence by party and state officials, technical literature, guidebooks, mass-circulation newspapers and magazines, memoirs, belles-lettres, and movies. The approach throughout was to remain sensitive to what made automobiles Soviet, something that was only possible by thinking comparatively. But to think comparatively was to run the risk of employing alien standards, a risk that is all the greater given the hegemonic influence of Western and especially American cars. Fortunately, the literature on cars and car cultures in the West is itself far from monolithic or uncritical. Its heterogeneity plus my immersion in Soviet discourses helped me to detect the creeping imperialism of Western standards.

Auto mechanics is, among other things, a language not easily mastered by the neophyte. Not pretending to have more than an amateur's acquaintance, even in English, I have tried to the best of my ability to render terms from the Russian in their nearest English (or American) equivalents. One term, though, requires special attention, namely *avtomobil'*. From its introduction into the Russian language at the end of the nineteenth century until the end of the Soviet period, the term meant—to cite the *Great Soviet Encyclopedia*'s first edition (1926)—"a self-propelled apparatus intended for the conveyance of people and goods on roads."[18] In other words, it applied to both cars and trucks (and in certain contexts other motor vehicles too). The proper way of specifically referring to a passenger car was as a "light automobile" (*legkovoi avtomobil'*) and, especially during the middle of the century, either an "automobile with small cylinder capacity" (*malolitrazhnyi avtomobil'* or more colloquially, *malolitrazhka*) or a limousine (*limuzin*), a term that earlier in the century denoted a "closed" car or sedan. By the 1960s, cars were known more popularly as *mashiny,* a word that, depending on the context, could also mean machine or mechanism. Trucks were first known as "goods auto-mobiles" (*gruzovye avtomobili*) and only somewhat later as *gruzoviki*.

The changing definitions of these terms are one of the elements of the history of the phenomena to which they refer. Nevertheless, to try to avoid confusion, I have employed "automobile" throughout in the generic sense (that is, as a synonym for motor vehicle). I use "car" only when referring to passenger cars. As for other kinds of vehicles, such as motorcycles and tanks, though their history is rich, I leave them to other historians.

chapter 1

AMO–ZIS–ZIL–AMO–ZIL

Detroit in Moscow

"Руки в масле, жопа в мыле—мы работаем на ЗИЛе"

"Hands in the oil, ass in the soap—we work at ZIL," chant of
Torpedo-ZIL soccer fans

On a peninsula jutting into the broad and winding Moscow River just a
few kilometers to the southeast of the Kremlin stands a dense complex of
soot-stained buildings—an automobile factory. The factory, known today as
AMO-ZIL, celebrated its ninetieth anniversary in 2006. It is the longest-lived
of Russian automobile plants.

Founded in 1916 as the Automobile Society of Moscow (AMO), the enterprise retained its name for several years after the October Revolution of
1917. In 1923 the Moscow bureau of the metalworkers union insisted on
adding Ferraro to the enterprise's name, in honor of an Italian anarchist trade
union leader brutally murdered by the Fascists in December 1922. That gesture toward internationalism and solidarity on the left lasted for approximately two years after which the factory officially became the "First State
Automobile Factory, formerly AMO," although everyone continued to call it
just AMO. In 1931, on the completion of the enterprise's renovation, it was
honored with the name of the Stalin Factory, better known as ZIS (Zavod im.
Stalina). It remained thus, with its main office at Auto Factory Street (Avtozavodskaia) 23, throughout the industrialization drive, the state terror of the
late 1930s, and other momentous events induced by Stalin. The ZIS appel-
lation survived Stalin's death by three years. But in 1956, within months of
Nikita Khrushchev's denunciation of his former boss, the enterprise took the
name of its recently deceased director, Ivan Likhachev. Periodically modern-
ized thereafter but somehow increasingly showing its age, ZIL (Zavod im.
Likhacheva) reverted to AMO-ZIL in 1992, the year following the demise of
the USSR.

The factory stamped its identity onto the cars and trucks it produced. They bore no other name than that of the enterprise itself. But what sort of identity did the factory have? Clearly, it was Soviet. The enterprise's geographical proximity to the corridors of power in the Kremlin and Red Square parade ground and the use of its limousines in state functions of the highest order suggested a close, symbiotic client-patron connection to the system's center of political power—the conflation of Detroit and Washington. "What is good for the country is good for General Motors, and vice versa," GM's president, Charles Erwin Wilson, famously remarked in 1953. A Soviet Charles Wilson might likewise have argued that what was good for the USSR was also good for AMO–ZIS–ZIL. But "Soviet" could mean different things at different times, and that was true of the factory too. Its makeover in the First Five-Year Plan, dispersal during the Great Patriotic War, postwar reassembly, post-Soviet near collapse and accompanying name changes were part and parcel of the often violent ruptures and transformations experienced by the country in general.

AMO

AMO owed its existence to the Imperial Russian Army's ever-expanding need for motor vehicles during World War I. One of five private companies that received such contracts from the Main Military-Technical Administration in February 1916, it was the only one created for that very purpose. AMO represented a logical extension of the Riabushinskii family's business activities that had begun two generations earlier with textile manufacturing and branched out into banking and newspaper and book publishing. Essentially a child of the Riabushinskiis' Moscow Bank, the company was directed by the Riabushinskii brothers, Sergei and Stepan, along with another member of the bank's board, the engineer A. I. Kuznetsov. The circularity of the Riabushinskii connections did not stop there. The president of the Moscow Bank, Mikhail Riabushinskii, served on AMO's board, while Kuznetsov was a member of the Moscow War-Industries Committee that yet another Riabushinskii brother, Pavel, chaired.[1]

The urgency of the army's need for vehicles dictated a tight schedule. The contracts with the five private firms called for construction of the necessary facilities to be completed by early October and production to begin no later than March 7, 1917. AMO was quick off the mark, purchasing sixty-four hectares of land from a railroad magnate, P. P. von Derviz, on which to construct its factory.[2] The area, known as Tiufel Grove, was the very same where Nikolai Karamzin set his late eighteenth-century sentimental tale "Poor Liza" about a peasant lass abandoned by her aristocratic lover. It lay within sight of the fourteenth-century Simonov monastery, described by one historian of Moscow as "probably the premier monastery anywhere in Russia."[3]

The once-bucolic character of the area had disappeared by the end of the nineteenth century. In the vicinity of the AMO construction site one could find the city's slaughterhouse (built in the 1880s), a boiler factory, a pipe works, a chemical plant, a leather works, and the area's largest enterprise, the Belgian-owned factory Dinamo.

Just to the north, beyond the railroad line forming the boundary between the Simonov and Rogozh districts (*raiony*), was another factory founded in the 1880s, the Guzhon (Goujon) steelworks, renamed Sickle and Hammer (Serp i Molot) in 1922. In time, these three enterprises—Dinamo, Sickle and Hammer, and AMO–ZIS–ZIL—would be joined by others, notably the Kaganovich ball-bearing plant (GPZ-1) and Automobile Factory of Leninist Komsomol (AZLK). From 1928, this densely integrated industrial zone got to call itself the Proletarian District.[4] Moscow was too large, diverse, and politically central to be a Soviet Detroit, but in function, appearance, and poor air quality, its Proletarian District came close.

Construction on the factory began in July 1916 and, according to a report sent to the War Ministry at the end of August, proceeded "in brilliant order." The company managed to meet the October deadline. Rather than designing and building a brand-new vehicle, its directors decided to obtain from the Turin-based firm Fiat the right to import components for its one-and-a-half-ton trucks, known as Fiat-15 TER, and to assemble them on site. The trucks already had proved themselves quite serviceable in the off-road conditions of Europe's African colonies, a testing ground in more ways than one for World War I. AMO thus anticipated being able to produce fifteen hundred vehicles a year, more than twice the number any of the other automobile factories could provide.[5]

Other aspects of the project did not go nearly so smoothly. Purchases of machinery and equipment from abroad, primarily from the United States, were delayed by difficulty obtaining foreign currency. Shipped by sea, supplies waited outside Russia's few ports, which were inundated with other freight. The overthrow of the tsar in February brought no relief. A memorandum in July 1917 reported that only 15 percent of the equipment had been installed and that 50 percent was still in transit.[6] Disputes over layoffs and pay further disrupted work. In May workers resorted to the Russian equivalent of tarring and feathering by carting the factory's director, Dmitrii Bondarev, and his assistant, Sergei Makarovskii, out of the factory grounds in wheelbarrows. In July, they temporarily seized the factory. Released by the War Ministry from its contractual obligation to assemble trucks, the company stumbled along with nothing to show for its efforts except the maintenance and repair of a few hundred vehicles imported from abroad or rescued from the front. On August 15, 1918, ten months after the Bolshevik seizure of power, the Soviet government's Supreme Council of the National Economy (VSNKh) decreed the enterprise to be the property of the Russian Soviet Federative Socialist Republic (RSFSR).[7]

What began as a cozy family business arrangement with visions of combining patriotism and profits turned into a fiasco. Faced with the state's urgent demand for vehicles, AMO's administration initially looked to foreign supplies. But their inaccessibility threw the company back on its own limited resources and the ingenuity of its workforce. Workers, though, held the administration hostage. Eventually, the enterprise collapsed and had to be reinvented—a syndrome that would be repeated in the future.

The Supreme Council placed AMO under the authority of the Main (after February 1921, Central) Administration of State Automobile Factories (TsUGAZ). Like Lebedev, Russian Renault, Putilov, and other nationalized enterprises, it received assignments to repair tractors, motorcycles, tanks, trucks, and anything else that had a motor and moved. Moscow worked on Cleveland's progeny—in 1919 alone, 250 three-ton trucks built by the White Company and shipped to Russia during World War I made their way to AMO's shops. Cannibalizing parts from different kinds of vehicles, AMO's workers came up with a variety of White-AMO "mutants."[8] Work was sporadic, though, and according to one source, workers who didn't drift off to other enterprises or engage in hooliganism at the expense of the nearby Simonov monastery and its garden spent much of their time turning out cigarette lighters and pots and pans that they would take to outlying villages to trade with peasants for food.[9]

To the factory's Bolsheviks, such activities smacked of workers' lack of consciousness. This they attributed either to the recentness of workers' migration from the villages or the influence of the Bolsheviks' erstwhile political rivals, the Mensheviks and Socialist Revolutionaries (SRs). Members of those parties along with "nonparty" socialists did unusually well in factory elections, beating out Bolshevik candidates for the trade union committee and district and city soviets during the early 1920s. Still, since workers elsewhere in the city were also absconding with consumable and exchangeable materials, scouring the surrounding countryside for anything edible, and otherwise playing hooky, the elemental desire to stay alive rather than rural origins or political heterodoxy seems a more obvious explanation.[10]

These, the Civil War years (1918–21), were years of hunger especially in Russia's major cities. Dwindling supplies of food, fuel, and habitable housing meant dwindling energy for work and, ultimately, a dwindling population. Moscow's declined by nearly half between 1917 and 1920; Petrograd's fell by two-thirds. Industrial production stood at a mere 20 percent of what it had been on the eve of the war. As for auto production, none of the factories that had received advances from the tsarist war ministry in 1916 managed to turn out a single vehicle. Why not just close up shop?

Just when things seemed to be heading inexorably in that direction, AMO's would-be saviors arrived: a cooperative association (*artel*) of 123 Russian-American "re-emigrants" boasting of having worked at the Ford Motor Company's Highland Park factory.[11] Their talk of "assembly-line methods" and "mass production" persuaded the highest Soviet organs to approve their takeover of the factory, which occurred in May 1921. Arthur A. Adams (1885–1969), who before leaving New York in November 1920 had served as head of the Soviet Russian Information Bureau's Technical Department, assumed

the position of director. Adams had led a very peripatetic existence. Born to a
Russian Jewish mother in Sweden, he studied explosives at the naval school
at Kronstadt, where, he later claimed, he joined the Russian Social Democratic Workers' Party. Arrested for his participation in an illegal strike, he
was banished to Olonets Province in the Far North, but he later escaped and
went abroad. He eventually arrived in Canada and enrolled at the University
of Toronto. In 1917, he crossed the border into the United States to escape
conscription, but he soon entered the U.S. Army's officer training program.
How three years later he wound up working for the Information Bureau is
unclear. Nor is it obvious what qualified him to serve as director at AMO.[12]

In fact, neither Adams nor his fellow re-emigrants had much success at
AMO. Even before the takeover, political and union activists, fearing for their
own authority, voiced objections. Rumors circulated that Riabushinskii, then
living in France, had sent them and that they were "concessionaires" intent
on extracting profits. "Here come the 'gentlemen' all dressed up and we're
starving," a re-emigrant engineer overheard someone muttering on arriving
at the factory. In some ways, the new administrators fulfilled workers' worst
expectations. At a meeting with workers Adams reportedly laughed at their
"Riurik methods" (a reference to the Norse chieftain who became Russia's first
ruler in the ninth century) and promised to "smash them." The imposition
of "American methods" resulted in the closure of the factory during the first
half of June 1921 and the dismissal of hundreds of "superfluous, unskilled or
semi-skilled workers." A month later, absenteeism averaged 54 percent among
workers and 27 percent among other employees. No wonder Mensheviks and
SRs remained popular. In May 1922, TsUGAZ returned the previous director, Vladimir Tsipulin, to the factory, now in the capacity as chief engineer,
but he apparently did not get along with Adams and the other "Americans."
Adams, for his part, claimed to have introduced some improvements such
as "more cultured conditions" in the cafeteria (including plates and knives)
and the construction of housing, but he admitted that on the whole he was
"unsuitable for the position of director" and had "suffered through those
three years."[13] By August 1923 Adams was gone, replaced by Georgii Korolev,
whose "rather coarse and harsh" demeanor was more "in the manner of a
worker" (*po-rabochemu*).[14]

Less than a year later, the ascendant Joseph Stalin lectured the comrades
at Sverdlov University about the necessity of bringing "American efficiency"
to bear on "Russian revolutionary sweep."[15] Synonymous with both "Fordism" (assembly-line production) and Taylorism (the scientific organization
of labor, in its Russian version), "American efficiency" was exactly what the
re-emigrants tendered. But it turned out that importing Detroit to Moscow
required more than these veterans of U.S. factories could deliver. It required
more mundane things like precision instruments, regular deliveries of supplies, careful training of personnel, adequately educated workers, and enough
food and housing to meet their needs. Stalin warned his audience about the
danger of American efficiency "degenerating into narrow and unprincipled

practicalism" if it were not combined with Bolshevik élan. But he didn't say how such élan would compensate for these deficiencies.

Perhaps the cart was being put ahead of the horse, perhaps not.[16] What officials at TsUGAZ wanted was neither carts nor horses but automobiles. Releasing funds to the new administration at AMO, they ordered the servicing of hundreds more White trucks as well as the fabrication of the Fiat-type models.[17] Now, as the seventh anniversary of the October Revolution approached, workers stayed in the factory round the clock, sleeping in the body of the vehicles they were assembling. On the evening of November 1, 1924, they all held their breaths as the first of the ten AMO F-15 trucks rumbled into life. Six days later, all ten, appropriately painted red, made their way past the Dinamo factory and the Moscow Auto Club's headquarters to Red Square where party and government leaders "greeted them ardently."[18]

This too represented a syndrome—the recognition of technological backwardness compared to the "advanced capitalist countries" and the organization of a transcendent act involving personal sacrifice and fortitude *pour encourager les autres.* Such "compensatory symbolism" predated the revolution. It also could be detected contemporaneously in other countries' sponsorship of far-flung expeditions and analogous acts of individual bravery. But the Bolsheviks' emphasis on the "mastery" of technology and on forcing the pace of events (or really, time itself) made the practice ineluctable.[19] Almost inevitably, the Herculean effort to demonstrate revolutionary "sweep" was followed by exhaustion, if not of supplies then of energy, and tended to obscure rather than clarify the problems to be overcome. It also could induce a search for blame.

Yes, the four-cylinder, 35 hp F-15s were the first Soviet-made trucks— though not the first motor vehicles, an honor that belonged to Armored Tank and Automobile Factory No. 1's Prombron S24–40 cars from 1922.[20] And yes, production did increase thereafter, reaching 366 in 1926 and 451 the following year. By January 1928 when the first issue of the automobile journal *Za rulëm* (Behind the Wheel) appeared, its front cover displayed a photograph of the one-thousandth F-15 turned out by AMO. If early versions lacked an electric starter, lights, and a horn, later models contained these items along with improved disc brakes, a rear wall to the driver's compartment, and other improvements. The truck performed successfully in several experimental rallies, including the All-Union rally of 1925 in which it "quite seriously competed with foreigners."[21]

But how impressive was this? In 1926, over four million automobiles were produced in the United States, Italy turned out sixty-five thousand, and even little Austria managed to put five thousand new Steyrs and other autos on the road. AMO's original owners, the "big bourgeois" Riabushinskiis, had promised to deliver fifteen hundred a year beginning in 1917. Absent the revolutionary upheavals of that year, they might have succeeded, and who knows how many they could have produced by 1928? AMO and the auto industry in general were still paying for the revolution ten years later.

On Lenin's insistence, the Soviet government had adopted a New Economic Policy (NEP) in 1921 that included the stabilization of the ruble as a means of encouraging international trade and the acquisition of foreign technology by other means as well. Some sectors of the economy thereby benefited, but the fledgling automobile industry was not among them. AMO seemed congenitally incapable of securing an adequate supply of machines and other materials for itself. The State Automobile Trust (Avtotrest), successor to TsUGAZ, simply lacked the clout to enforce fulfillment of orders within the country or to obtain the necessary foreign currency to buy equipment abroad.[22] Leading personnel came and went. Korolev resigned as AMO's director in September 1925 in favor of F. I. Kholodilin. The technical director, Tsipulin, lasted only another two months.

Then, in December 1926, Ivan Alekseevich Likhachev (1896–1956) arrived at AMO to take over from Kholodilin. Like his predecessors, Likhachev was a "red director," a party man whose appointment—at age thirty—did not necessarily reflect technical competence so much as loyalty to the party's agenda. He had joined the Bolsheviks in 1917 while a soldier at the front. After the October Revolution, he served in the Cheka (secret police) and the Moscow trade union apparatus before coming to AMO. Unlike Kholodilin and the others, Likhachev remained director of the factory for a long time—a quarter of a century—interrupted only by a brief and unremarkable stint in 1939–40 as commissar of medium machine construction. Five times the recipient of the Order of Lenin and twice of the Order of the Red Banner of Labor, Likhachev was honored in death as well by the interment of his ashes in the Kremlin wall.[23]

So large does Likhachev loom in the history of AMO–ZIS–ZIL that it might be written in terms of before, during, and after his directorship. His tenure coincided with Soviet industrialization, a turbulent—and for not a few of his counterparts, lethal—process. His survival retrospectively conveyed to him the aura of a Soviet patriot, wise to the need for importing foreign technology but not a slave to it, confident in the advice and potential of "our specialists" and thus able to tell Henry Ford that "for the time being the paths of our automobile and tractor builders lead to America, but I am convinced that soon the road will turn in another direction—toward the Soviet Union."[24] Likhachev, in short, upheld Soviet amour propre.

The trick was to know at what point "the road will turn" and, in the meantime, on what kind of foreign technology to rely and how to obtain it. The triangular affair involving AMO, the Automobile Trust, and the Arthur J. Brandt Company of Detroit, Michigan, represents a less happy alternative to the deal with Ford discussed in the next chapter. It is a cautionary tale in the perils of technology transfer on the cusp of industrialization. It also was a psychodrama for three dramatis personae—Likhachev; the Automobile Trust's director, Mark Lavrentevich Sorokin; and the engineer, Arthur Brandt—among whom only Likhachev emerged with his reputation intact.

The story opens in January 1928 when the Soviet government approved in principle the construction of a new automobile factory in Moscow capable of producing ten thousand vehicles a year, and the expansion of AMO to raise its productive capacity to four thousand. Which vehicles and with what kind of machinery? The stuff of a blizzard of bureaucratic reports, these questions drove a selected group of engineers and administrators (among them Sorokin) abroad, first to Germany and Great Britain and then to the United States.[25] Sorokin knew his way around the United States, having studied engineering at Cornell University and working for a time in Pennsylvania. He also was fluent in English. Brandt began pitching his proposal to Sorokin in September 1928, and by December the two reached a tentative agreement. Brandt would head a group of American engineers that would supervise the factory's reconstruction and refitting; the factory would gradually phase out production of the F-15 in favor of a larger 2.5-ton truck modeled on a prototype from the Autocar Company of Ardmore, Pennsylvania. The agreement, envisioning an annual rate of production of twenty-five thousand units, thereby superseded plans for the construction of a new factory in Moscow.[26]

Sorokin returned to Moscow where he set up a commission to oversee the project, appointing himself as head. Although he did inform AMO's party bureau about these developments, Likhachev and his technical staff deeply resented their exclusion from the commission. They also had substantive objections to the choice of vehicle and the reconstruction plans that Brandt had brought with him to Moscow. The Moscow City Party Committee ignored their objections, however, and on May 24, 1929, Sorokin and Brandt formally signed a technical assistance agreement. The agreement called for "manufacturing 25,000 2.5-ton trucks per year in one shift working seven hours...and further expansion to produce 50,000." Brandt's company assumed responsibility for providing "all the parts and details necessary for installation of equipment for the making of jigs and fixtures for the new model and a managerial control system." The total cost approached $12.5 million.[27]

Complications with fulfillment of the contract arose not long after Brandt's return to the United States. At first, Brandt had difficulty extracting from Autocar the complete set of blueprints for the truck to be built at AMO. Then, AMO's engineering staff discovered discrepancies between the dismantled model and the blueprints sent by Brandt. For his part, Brandt's representative complained to Sorokin about delays by Amtorg, the company set up by the Soviet government in 1924 to handle Soviet-U.S. trade, in placing orders. These, he claimed, made it "impossible to get machines and equipment delivered...in time to meet the working schedule originally set." The American engineers came, saw there was little for them to do, and left. Likhachev, who in the meantime had been complaining to all and sundry about these problems, eventually had his moment of sweet revenge when he addressed a meeting of the Politburo on January 25, 1930, reportedly delivering a "fiery speech" to which members listened with "great attention."[28]

The tide turned in favor of Likhachev, who replaced Sorokin as head of the reconstruction commission. Sorokin also lost his position as head of the Automobile Trust when the Politburo abolished the institution, vesting administrative responsibility for the development of the automobile industry in the All-Union Automobile and Tractor Association (VATO) under the Supreme Council of the National Economy. Brandt's withdrawal of personnel in protest against Moscow's revision of the reconstruction plans precipitated the annulment of the contact, with Sorokin humiliatingly dispatched to the United States to tie up loose ends.[29]

The affair had no obvious lessons other than the need for exercising more care in the selection of technical assistance "partners." For all their dissatisfaction with the Autocar prototype and Brandt's plans for reconstruction, Likhachev and company came up with a very similar model, the AMO-3, and only slightly modified the factory's design.[30] Rigging up an assembly line to produce automobiles and doing without hydraulic presses, metal-forming machinery, and other equipment from abroad was simply out of the question at this point. Hence, Likhachev's departure to the United States on a shopping expedition not long afterward and his encounter with Henry Ford.

Putting the affair in larger context, of the 170 technical assistance agreements that the Soviet Union entered into with foreign firms between 1923 and 1934, it abrogated thirty-seven (22%). A retrospective memorandum from the Commissariat of Heavy Industry's Foreign Department identified four reasons: the inability of the firm to fulfill its obligations; adventurism on the part of the firm; the inability of the USSR to use the technology provided; or Soviet mastery of the technology by other means. It listed Arthur J. Brandt as an "adventurer."[31] Politically, the affair played itself out against upheavals in the Moscow party organization that resulted from the removal of successive leaders (Nikolai Uglanov, Karl Bauman) in less than eighteen months. What Likhachev undoubtedly learned—if he did not know it already—was that attaching oneself to a high-ranking patron in good odor with Stalin increased one's maneuverability among other middle-ranking functionaries. In Grigorii ("Sergo") Ordzhonikidze (1886–1937), commissar of Worker-Peasant Inspection and Politburo member, Likhachev found such a patron. Ordzhonikidze, who on several occasions took a solicitous interest in AMO, arranged for Likhachev to address the Politburo at a critical moment in the affair.[32]

Finally, while nobody lost his head (or life) over the affair, it proved a turning point in the careers of the two Soviet principals as well as the Moscow automobile industry. Likhachev presided over a second round of expansion and the production of authentically Soviet-made trucks and limousines, with his factory becoming the apple of the Kremlin's eye. Sorokin never again held a leadership position of any prominence. Toiling as an assistant director of VATO, he became an ardent exponent of the tractor-trailer. He also served briefly on the party's Central Control Commission in 1934 and as director of an agricultural implements factory in the city of Tula. A recently published necrology of Muscovites executed and buried anonymously in the outskirts of the capital between 1936 and 1941 indicates that Sorokin, whose real patronymic was Moiseevich, was arrested in December 1938, tried by a military tribunal in July 1941, and shot the same month.[33] The source, unfortunately, does not provide an explanation for the execution.

ZIS

Catching up to and overtaking the advanced capitalist countries in all kinds of ways but especially industrial production was what the Soviet Union was about once it embarked on its course of forced-pace industrialization in the late 1920s. And by golly, they were going to demonstrate that they could do it—"storm the fortress," in the parlance of the day—no matter what. But surely they would have to make an exception of automobile production. After all, Ford alone was churning out a million cars a year before the Soviets had made a single one. In 1927, during their first meeting, Sorokin showed Likhachev a diagram of automobile production throughout the world. The United States was represented by a twenty-eight–story skyscraper. Britain, Germany, France, and Italy appeared as one-story houses. The USSR was not even a little cottage but only a tiny square and occupied last place with a total automotive fleet of 15,300 vehicles.[34] Output over the next few years remained paltry—1,450 in 1928–29 and 5,888 in 1929–30.

The rebuilding of the AMO factory to accommodate shops with gigantic presses, precision-cutting dies, casting and other machinery that sent their products to the assembly shop's main conveyor belt changed all this. The new AMO, child of the First Five-Year Plan for industrialization, was reborn as the Stalin Factory (Zavod im. Stalina or ZIS), the "largest truck factory in the world." Party leaders and representatives of other "giants" of the automobile and tractor industries—the Stalingrad Tractor Factory and the just-built Khar'kov Tractor Factory, the Iaroslavl' Automobile Factory and the soon-to-be-completed Nizhni Novgorod Automobile Factory—attended the celebrations held on October 1, 1931. Greeted with loud applause, the new chair of the Supreme Council of the National Economy, Ordzhonikidze, noted that "the director of one of the world's mightiest trusts [Alfred P. Sloan Jr.], the American General Motors [Corporation], said that no other factory in the world can equal its equipment." The factory's newspaper quoted an American engineer (identified only as "Taylor") as complimenting his hosts for having "built a factory that is equipped according to the last word of technology and can proudly stand in the ranks of the largest automobile factories of America."[35] Three weeks later the first AMO-3 trucks rolled off the assembly line. With a six-cylinder 66-hp engine and a carrying capacity of 2.5 tons, the AMO-3 was considerably larger and more powerful than the AMO F-15. By the end of the month 75 had been produced; by December, 508; in April 1932, 1,404; and in September, 1,422.

"The USSR Ploughs Its Fields with Its Own Tractors and Rides in Its Own Automobiles," proclaimed the headline at the top of an entire page of *Pravda* devoted to the accomplishments of the country's three tractor factories (Stalingrad, Khar'kov, and Red Putilov) and three motor vehicle factories (Nizhni Novgorod, Iaroslavl', and Moscow). The pride and optimism conveyed in the corresponding articles nearly jumped off the page. Meanwhile, U.S. car makers were struggling. As Politburo member Lazar M. Kaganovich told celebrants at ZIS's opening, production of cars in "much-vaunted America" was falling sharply—from 620,000 in April 1929 to 416,000 in August 1929 to 224,000 a year later, and, by August 1931, to only 70,000. In October 1932, three years into the Great Depression, *Pravda* was reporting that "disintegration (*razval*), panic, and demoralization" were sweeping the Ford Motor Company. Its workforce had plummeted from 120,000 to 15,000, and its factories were operating at a mere 6 percent of capacity. One cartoon depicted Ford cursing the AMO truck and Khar'kov tractor that roar past him as he sits helplessly by the side of the road in a swamp labeled "crisis"; another showed him at the wheel of the 1932 model which, with skulls instead of headlights affixed to the front bumpers, hurtles down a steep hill. The caption reads: "Ford has taken to producing new models, lowering the wages of workers, and exercising all his powers of inventiveness to hide the real situation."[36]

The cartoon under the headline about the USSR ploughing its own fields displayed a banner flapping in the wind as the AMO-3 truck to which it is attached races along, its driver waving to his counterpart seated in a SKhTZ-15/30 tractor. The banner reads: "When we sit the USSR in a car and the muzhik on a tractor, let the esteemed capitalists try to catch up to us. (Stalin)"

"The First Automobile Factory named Stalin and the Khar'kov Tractor Factory named Ordzhonikidze are not the Last but the First in the line of Giants that we are building and will build," *Pravda*, October 2, 1931. Cartoon: "Who Is Going Where?" Ford with his top hat in the swamp of crisis watches in frustration as an AMO truck and a tractor from the Khar'kov factory roll by.

Рис. К. РОТОВА.

Banner text: КОГДА ПОСАДИМ СССР НА АВТОМОБИЛЬ, А МУЖИКА НА ТРАКТОР - ПУСТЬ ПОПРОБУЮТ ДОГОНЯТЬ НАС ПОЧТЕННЫЕ КАПИТАЛИСТЫ". (Сталин)

"The USSR Ploughs Its Fields with Its Own Tractors and Rides on Its Own Automobiles," *Pravda*, December 19, 1932.
Cartoon: Banner reads, "When we sit the USSR in a car and the muzhik on a tractor, let the esteemed capitalists try to catch up to us." (Stalin)

And underneath the cartoon, this news: "The Five-Year Plan assumed production of 91,000 tractors, but in fact in four years 105,850 tractors were produced." An even more astonishing fact followed: "In 1932 the USSR will have caught up to the USA in tractor output." According to the accompanying table, tractor production in the United States dropped from 229,000 in 1929 to 50,000 in 1932; that of the USSR rose from a little over 3,000 to 50,250.[37]

Could the day be far off for automobiles? Perhaps not, but in the meantime, Soviet propaganda had another message: "Formerly we had no Soviet automobiles, but we have them now."[38] The fact that these powerful totems of industrialization were being manufactured in the USSR, in Soviet factories, with Soviet workers producing them, outweighed the non-Soviet origins of the models and machines and the gap in output.[39]

Who could know that in the long term the criteria would change to the point where Soviet gains would seem insignificant if not irrelevant? The story up to that point was the one Lenin had articulated in 1918: "without machines, without discipline, it is impossible to live in modern society."[40] In this story, AMO occupied the honored role of the Soviet first-born (*pervenets*). But no sooner had AMO transformed itself into ZIS than GAZ (Gor'kovskii Avtomobil'nyi Zavod) was up and running in Nizhni Novgorod. GAZ's capacity for producing 140,000 trucks and cars per year—nearly six times as many as at ZIS—made it the real Soviet giant. ZIS thus became known more for the quality rather than quantity of its products. For example, the six-cylinder ZIS-5 truck (known popularly as the "three-tonner") it introduced in 1934 earned superior marks compared to the GAZ-AA. Its extremely well-designed engine could use low-octane fuel and could go much longer without servicing than any other vehicle at the time. Drivers achieved the status of "one hundred thousanders" (*stotysiachniki*) by chalking up at least 100,000 km between

ZIS-5, workhorse of the Red Army during the Great Patriotic War. From the Lomakov Automobile Museum, Moscow. Author's photograph.

"capital repairs" during and after the war. The ZIS-5 also handled easily even in the worst weather and road conditions, and plenty of both existed where the truck went. It continued to be produced with modifications up to the mid-1960s, long after the execution—on trumped up charges—of its designer, Evgenii Ivanovich Vazhinskii (1889–1938).[41]

Not long after the introduction of the new model, the factory underwent a second bout of reconstruction to raise annual capacity to seventy thousand trucks and ten thousand passenger cars plus assorted parts. The workforce, numbering some twelve thousand in 1934, would rise to forty thousand by the time the expansion was completed in 1938.[42] The reconstruction involved quadrupling the size of the factory grounds largely through the acquisition of land in Kolomenskoe to the south of the Moscow River; hiring thousands of construction workers from other projects; building entirely new stamping, pattern-making, body, fitting, and tool-making shops; and vastly modifying the existing foundry shop. Likhachev did not spare himself. As one of the construction bosses recalled years later, he appeared at the site even on Sundays, concerning himself with everything from arrangements for feeding the evening shift to the laying of water pipes that connected the new buildings to the river.[43]

ZIS employed over a thousand people in the mid-1930s to deal with workers' alimentary and housing needs. Typical of large urban-based factories, it had its own state farms in nearby districts to supply produce to its cafeterias, shops, and other distribution points. But both the amount of supplies and the facilities for their distribution were woefully inadequate. During 1932–33, the leanest of years, employees from ZIS's housing and food department (ZhKO) organized rabbit breeding to help offset the shortage of meat. One pensioner later remembered potatoes being cultivated on land strewn with building materials for the new body shop.[44]

Even before the more than threefold increase in the number of workers at ZIS, the housing shortage had reached catastrophic proportions. The Moscow city archive contains a copy of an undated letter approved by fifty-seven hundred workers at shop conferences concerning the situation. The letter, addressed to Politburo members Kaganovich, Valerian Kuibyshev, and Ordzhonikidze, requested additional funds for housing not in anticipation of an expanded workforce but to accommodate those already on the books. Of seven thousand workers surveyed, only three hundred lived in the vicinity of the plant, six to seven hundred lived within five kilometers, three thousand were scattered across the rest of Moscow city and oblast, and the remaining three thousand had "no housing at all." In desperation, the factory's housing department leased dormitory and barrack space from such organizations as the Moscow Metro construction project, the Academy of Sciences, and the Gulag.[45]

By the end of the second reconstruction, dozens of two- and three-story apartment buildings, some of brick but most of timber, stood in Kolomenskoe, or "Kolomengrad," as a pensioner referred to it. The task of accommodating all the workers, however, proved Sisyphean. Hastily erected barracks housed both families and single people. Rooms of forty-two square meters squeezed in fifteen unmarried people; those of twenty-one square meters were home to six or seven. A housing official also recalled that Likhachev—the *seigneur de domaine*—liked to visit the Kolomenskoe settlement, "especially barrack No. 38 where women lived."[46]

A group of engineers under Vazhinskii meanwhile was designing and testing a new vehicle, the ZIS-101. The enterprise's first passenger car—and a luxury car at that—it was not, however, the first of its kind in the USSR. That honor went to the Red Putilovets-L [for Leningrad], the "Soviet Buick," ten of which that factory turned out in time for the May Day celebrations of 1933. It planned two thousand more for 1934, but because orders for tractors and tanks trumped cars, the Commissariat of Heavy Industry cancelled its order and gave the task to ZIS.[47] What a beast the ZIS-101 was! It weighed over 2.5 tons, some six to seven hundred kg more than analogous foreign models. Equipped with an eight-cylinder 120-hp engine that itself weighed 470 kg, it got less than 4 km to the liter (26.5 liters per 100 km, compared to the GAZ-A's 12). Fittings included synchronized transmission, thermostatically controlled heating, a radio, and a window separating the forward from the rear seating. Vazhinskii described it as "like the best American models [such as the] Buick and Packard." Indeed, it boasted American materials. Chassis and body stamping machinery came from the Budd Manufacturing Company of Philadelphia and were installed under the supervision of Budd personnel at a cost of $1.5 million. An additional half-million dollars bought ZIS sheet metal presses from the Hamilton Foundry and Machine Company of Ohio.[48]

On April 29, 1936, ZIS employees drove two cars, one painted black and the other cherry red, to the Kremlin for inspection by Stalin and other members of the Politburo. The political elite's involvement in decisions about the model's appearance (Stalin supposedly advised a change in the insignia on the grill) made sense in terms of the car's role as the flagship automobile of the Soviet state in the late 1930s.[49] But it also possessed symbolic significance in the production process, as if Stalin's grant of approval had become the final stage in the planning and design of automobiles. By the time production ceased in July 1941, some 8752 (a figure that includes the modified 101A and 102 convertible) ZIS-101 limos had been turned out. Although not quite up to the original expectations of 10,000 *a year*, it was more than any other limousine the factory would ever produce.[50]

Aside from chauffeuring the party and government elite and emblematically representing the USSR abroad (the Soviet pavilion exhibited it at the 1937 Paris exposition and the diplomatic service used it extensively), the car saw limited service as a taxi and as an ambulance. Mikhail German—whose father, Iurii, was a prominent writer and owner of a "Gazik" (GAZ-A) and then an "Emka" (M-1)—recalls that the much larger ZIS-101 seemed "as long as a tram, literally springing out of the pages of the journal *USSR in Construction,* lacquered and magnificent." "It even smelled festive," he adds. "Everyone desperately wanted to 'roll up' in a ZIS. Children, if they got a chance to ride in a taxi, pleaded with their parents to pass up other cars for the opportunity to take the longed-for limousine: ZIS taxis were rarities and cost a little more."[51]

Alas, like the Stalinist state itself, the ZIS-101 looked more impressive the less one knew about its inner workings. In 1937 three mechanics from the Commissariat of Heavy Industry's garage sent an open letter about the car to the factory. Of the fourteen in their care, four had to be sent back to the factory because of a knock in the engine, possibly caused by defective crankshafts. The letter also reported broken spring valves after only a thousand kilometers of driving, incorrect mountings of pinions, faulty electrical systems, damage to brake drums caused by the wearing out of a plastic bracket on the boot, speedometers that fluctuated between 20 and 60 km/h when the car was doing 40, stuck fuel gauges, turning indicators that discharged the battery, and radios that did not work at all in eight of the cars. Fuel consumption averaged 28 liters per 100 km. A chauffeur with twenty-six years of experience unfavorably compared the result he obtained (30 liters per 100 km) with the Lincolns (22.5 liters per 100 km) and Buicks he previously drove.[52]

The ZIS-101 (and its successor, the 110 to be discussed below) came closer than any other Soviet car to the general significance ascribed to the automobile by Kristin Ross: "the central vehicle of all twentieth-century modernization." "In the middle of this century," she writes, "the automobile industry, more than any other, becomes exemplary and indicative; its presence or absence in a national economy tells us the level and power of that economy."[53] Few economies could be more "national" than the Soviet Union's in the sense of functioning (or being intended to function) as an integral, even autarkic, whole. None has been more closely identified with national power. The cars ZIS made for transporting the state's leaders quite literally embodied the relationship between the Soviet national economy and state power at a time when the state was at its most ambitious, insecure, and therefore destructive.

The dynamic tension between ambitiousness and insecurity exploded into the Great Purge of 1936–38. This extraordinarily tragic phenomenon consisted of overlapping patterns and cross-currents of repression against "enemies of the people" carried out by the People's Commissariat of Internal Affairs (NKVD) in the name of purifying Soviet society. Certain categories of people (for example, former political enemies, members of their families and their associates, diasporic nationality groups, recidivist criminals, ex-kulaks, military and technical personnel possessing strategically important information) were particularly vulnerable. Hundreds of thousands of them were executed, and millions were sent to special settlements and labor camps. Engineers working in auto plants such as ZIS could not have felt very secure during these years. Indeed, Vazhinskii was not the only victim. Among others, former technical director Tsipulin and assistant chief engineer E. G. Ainshtein did not survive for reasons we can only surmise. Likhachev did survive despite the death by suicide of his patron, Ordzhonikidze, in February 1937. He was more fortunate in this respect than his counterpart at GAZ, Sergei Diakonov, whose execution in 1938 came in his fortieth year.

Production of the 101 ceased on July 7, 1941, two weeks after the Nazi invasion of the country and two weeks before the first aerial bombardment of the factory grounds. Many workers left for the front; others formed home-guard units. Going over entirely to military production, the factory stepped up its output of the all-terrain semi-Caterpillar ZIS-22M, adapted for military transport the ZIS-5 truck, and accepted orders for other war-related materiel. As the front moved perilously close to Moscow, the State Defense Committee decided to put into effect its plan for evacuating the city's key factories. ZIS's evacuation began on October 15, the day the factory shut down entirely. Preliminary scouting had identified four sites in the Middle Volga and Urals regions to which machinery and personnel would be evacuated: Ul'ianovsk—tool, steering, frame, assembly; Miass—motor, gearbox, foundry; Shadrinsk—carburetor, woodworking, and tool and die-casting; Cheliabinsk—cold-stamping of parts for chassis, motor, body and frame. Convoys of trucks and trains began departing for these destinations on October 16. In all, over fourteen thousand people and 12,800 pieces of equipment arrived safely.[54]

Part of the vast shift of the Soviet Union's industrial base eastward, the evacuation could not have been nearly as smooth as the factory's official history claims. Both memoirs and historians' accounts speak of panic, dastardly deeds, improvisation, and heroism elsewhere in Moscow, and there is no reason to believe that ZIS's evacuation was any different.[55] Two of the factories set up as a result of the evacuation eventually became full-fledged automobile plants. The Ul'ianovsk Automobile Factory (UAZ) started producing GAZ-AA trucks in 1944 and later added jeeps. The Miass factory (UralAZ) turned out ZIS-5B trucks on which it mounted Katiusha rockets. Not until 1962 did UralAZ shed ZIS from its name and that of its products.[56]

In January 1942, after the Soviet counteroffensive achieved success in the battle for Moscow, the State Defense Committee ordered the restoration of automobile production at ZIS. The ZIS-5B trucks that the factory started turning out in June lacked headlights and proper paneling, but otherwise they served the army well for the remainder of the war. But still during the war, while the battle of Stalingrad raged on and the blockade of Leningrad continued, even though victory remained in the balance, another task consumed the factory's planning department and its designers—a new passenger car of the highest class. That car, which debuted on the morrow of victory in August 1945, was the ZIS-110. *Pravda*'s David Zaslavskii explained retrospectively why the state had commissioned this car in the midst of war. It symbolized the "firm and quiet confidence" that "prevailed in Moscow, in the Kremlin." Even though "the world did not yet know that Hitlerite Germany would be destroyed, Stalin knew." His "gaze...was fixed on the future." Just as "one must think about war during peacetime," so was it important to think "about peacetime in the midst of war." Thus, the car, "the first-born of the newborn Soviet peacetime industry," represented Stalin's "historical perspective on the Motherland's postwar development."[57]

Zaslavskii, one of the party's key ideologues under Stalin, must have had his master in mind when he referred to the car as "handsome, wise, and powerful." He described its lines as "regular and severe," (*pravil'nye strogie*) and its quietness and comfort as simply "amazing." Its 600 cc eight-cylinder engine, the most powerful installed in a Soviet car up to that point, enabled the ZIS-110 to achieve speeds of up to 140 km/h and with less expenditure of fuel (25 liters/100 km) than its predecessor. With independent front-wheel suspension, front and rear axle stabilizers, and power windows (all firsts for a Soviet car), the ZIS represented the Cadillac of the Soviet automobile fleet.[58]

Cadillac or Packard? Soviet designers had several models with which to work in their efforts to reproduce or better American limousines. As a token of the wartime alliance, President Roosevelt arranged for the delivery of two 1942 Cadillacs and three Packards dating from 1941–42. Two were Clippers, the first streamlined Packards, and the third was an eight-seater touring car in the 180 series. What Stalin really wanted, according to General Vlasik, director of the Kremlin's garage, was one of those prewar Packards, perhaps a Packard 8. ZIS's chief designer for light automobiles, Andrei Nikolaevich Ostrovtsev (1902–88), and his crew labored for more than three years to get it right, eventually settling for a reproduction of the Packard 180 with some stylistic modifications.[59]

Whether they employed Packard body dies or fabricated their own is the subject of dispute among automobile aficionados, with Russia's leading expert unequivocal in asserting the latter.[60] This carping about the location of a particular car on the domestic-foreign axis reflects the symbolic significance accorded to the vehicle, which in the case of the ZIS-110 was—and remains—immense.[61] More than any other, the ZIS-110 represented the Soviet state on wheels. In the material sense, its components came from a broad range of enterprises—seventy-three in all—scattered throughout the country. These included processing plants that supplied cork padding for interior panels and—fittingly for a product at this point in Soviet history—the Gulag-run Sokol'niki labor camp that furnished some of the leather upholstery. When it came to distributing the finished product, Moscow received favored treatment as it did in so many other respects. Of the seventy-one vehicles assigned by the middle of 1946, thirty-eight remained in the Soviet capital. Kiev got seven, Leningrad three, and Minsk, Riga, Tallinn, Kishinev, Kaunas, and Petrozavodsk received four each.[62]

Between 1945 and 1958 ZIS sent forth 2,083 units, including small numbers of armor-plated (ZIS-115) and convertible (ZIS-110B) versions. The armor-plated model, completed in 1947, went into production just after the U.S. atomic bomb blasts at Hiroshima and Nagasaki. The car was a "bunker on wheels," a real colossus. With added layers of steel and seven-centimeter-thick Plexiglas windows, it weighed more than seven tons and required special wheels and tires to bear the additional weight. ZIS only made a few dozen, most of which it dispatched directly to the Kremlin. Stalin reputedly had five of them at his disposal, using a different one every day as a safety precaution.[63]

During these early cold war years, the state's security apparatus subjected key institutions such as ZIS to extraordinary surveillance. Jews, disproportionately represented among the country's technical as well as cultural intelligentsia, received more than their share of attention especially after "more and more members of the Soviet intelligentsia—now branded inescapably with biological ethnicity—began to consider themselves Jews" and assert that identity.[64] Paradoxically, the more faithfully Jewish individuals had served the state, the more of a threat they posed. That was why, in 1948, the Ministry of State Security (MGB) arrested and otherwise disposed of so many members of the Jewish Anti-Fascist Committee. But matters did not stop there. In 1950, the minister, V. G. Abakumov, identified Aleksei Filippovich Eidinov as the principal link between the Jewish Anti-Fascist Committee's activities on behalf of Zionist organizations abroad and Jewish administrative and technical personnel at ZIS where Eidinov had worked as an assistant director. Eidinov himself allegedly passed secret technical information about the ZIS-110 to the U.S. ambassador, William Bedell Smith, during Smith's visit to the factory in 1947. As a result, the MGB took into custody forty-eight employees of the factory, of whom forty-two were Jewish. Boris Mikhailovich Fitterman (1910–91), who had worked on Ostrovtsev's team designing the ZIS-110 and

Jews

received a Stalin prize in 1946 for his efforts, figured among these victims of the "ZIS affair." Eidinov was executed.[65]

Jews at nearby Dinamo and at the Iaroslavl' truck plant also suffered during this anti-Semitic convulsion. But those at ZIS experienced the heaviest blow precisely because ZIS was the flagship auto factory, the one whose insignia was most readily identified with the USSR. The enterprise's name, physical proximity to the Kremlin, and prestige derived from its products made it a source of Soviet national pride. Two things jeopardized that pride in the immediate aftermath of the Great Patriotic War: "cosmopolitanism," which is to say the attribution of national achievements to foreign inspiration, and internal enemies, which is to say at this juncture "rootless cosmopolitans."

All this was rather disturbing from the point of view of Likhachev's reliability. After all, he bore the responsibility for the appointment of all these "Jewish nationalists." He had hosted Ambassador Smith's visit to the factory, showed him the ZIS-110, and received an invitation to view the embassy's new Cadillac. Called to the Kremlin, Likhachev was confronted by the rather formidable troika of Georgi Malenkov, Lavrenty Beria, and Nikita Khrushchev, all members of the Politburo. In his memoirs, Khrushchev could not recall Eidinov's name and referred to Likhachev as "minister, I think, of automobile transport," which would not be the case for another three years. He did remember, though, that faced with the "incontrovertible evidence" of the confessions of Eidinov and others, Likhachev fell into a swoon, was revived with water, and sent home. Removed in April 1950 from his position as director of ZIS, he was reassigned to direct a small aviation factory. It could have been a lot worse. Khrushchev surmises that Likhachev escaped from more serious punishment because of Stalin's fondness for him. "Likhachev had been a favorite of Sergo [Ordzhonikidze]," Khrushchev recalled, "and Sergo always called him 'likhach.'" Stalin, exercising a prerogative of power, also began to call him "likhach." To a Russian speaker, the nickname is entirely appropriate. "Likhach" translates as "1. (*obs.*) driver of a smart cab. 2. (*pejor.*) road-hog. 3. bold, daring fellow."[66]

Likhachev labored in obscurity for the next three years. But on Stalin's death, he was elevated to minister of automobile transport and highways, a new position within the Soviet constellation of ministries. He thus inherited much of the road construction administration and facilities that the security organs had shed at the insistence of the new minister of internal affairs, Lavrenty Beria. Meanwhile, Likhachev's successor at ZIS, Konstantin Vasil'evich Vlasov, struggled to fulfill the targets that the Fifth Five-Year Plan (1951–55) laid on the factory. The assignment of a broader range of products complicated the task. In addition to motor vehicles and agricultural machinery, ZIS assumed responsibility for production of such articles of domestic consumption as refrigerators and bicycles.[67]

Many early American car manufacturers, including the Duryea brothers, also produced bicycles. And as General Motors's president, William Durant, once put it, cars and refrigerators were essentially the same item: metal boxes with motors inside. Perhaps, but GM's ownership of Frigidaire did not encumber its production of automobiles. ZIS's top administrators claimed that absent the burden of producing domestic appliances, they could double vehicle output. Unfortunately, while the ZIS-151 truck—an all-wheel-drive vehicle intended for the military but particularly popular with collective farm administrators—failed to reach its planned target for 1953, the factory surpassed quotas for bicycles and refrigerators: a million "Progress" bicycles by November 7, 1954; one hundred thousand refrigerators by September 17, 1955.[68]

The factory also fulfilled its "socialist obligations" by sending hundreds of cadres to the Virgin Lands of northern Kazakhstan and the Altai region, training 550 Chinese technical personnel, and dispatching its own specialists to assist with the construction of the First Automobile Works in Changchun in China's northeast province of Jilin. The Chinese connection proved to be one of ZIS's more durable legacies. The Changchun factory officially opened on October 15, 1956, when it began producing CA10 trucks, the Chinese equivalent of the ZIS-150. In 2001 the organizer of the Changchun International Automobile Fair jointly sponsored by the First Automobile Works and the Changchun municipal government claimed that half a million residents of the city worked for the auto or auto-related sectors and that "people in Changchun are confident they will build the city into China's Detroit."[69]

ZIL

By October 1956 ZIS was no longer ZIS. All over the Soviet Union factories, cities, streets, canals, and other objects that had borne Stalin's name officially lost it as a result of Khrushchev's "secret speech" at the Twentieth Party Congress in February 1956 and the subsequent de-Stalinization campaign. But in actuality the name changes rarely happened before 1961 when, by resolution of the party's Twenty-Second Party Congress, the once-mighty leader's remains were unceremoniously removed from the Lenin mausoleum. In Communist Eastern Europe, the story was the same. Alone among cities bearing Stalin's name, only the Polish Silesian town known since 1953 as Stalinogrod reverted to its original name, Katowice, in 1956. Poland, though, as Poles never tire of emphasizing, constituted something of a special case. Was ZIS a special case? Symbolism may not have been everything, but when it came to the name of the factory—and the cars—serving the Kremlin, it counted for a great deal.

An opportune moment to rename the factory arrived in 1956 courtesy of its longtime director and loyal servitor of the Soviet state to the end. On June 24, 1956, Likhachev died suddenly of a heart attack, having just turned sixty the week before. Two days later, by a joint resolution of the Central Committee of the Communist Party and the Council of Ministers, the factory was renamed ZIL in his honor. In the USSR, scientific and academic institutes sometimes commemorated illustrious figures in this manner, but not factories. The change came well into the production runs for the 150-series trucks, the 155 city bus, the diesel-powered intercity 127 bus, and the 110-series limousines. But the team under Ostrovtsev had only just begun to design the 111, successor to the quintessentially "Stalinist" ZIS-110.

The two cars bore certain similarities. Like its predecessor, the ZIL-111 took a Packard (the 1955 Caribbean) as its inspiration/model. They rested on identical chasses. They also shared several of the same engineers. But the new car incorporated some of the advancements in automotive technology that had occurred over the intervening years. Its V8, 6,000 cc. 200-hp engine with single camshaft was more powerful, getting 4,200 rpm instead of 3,600. At 2,605 kg it weighed slightly more (by 30 kg) than the ZIS-110, but it also had greater acceleration, taking twenty-three seconds to reach 100 km/h from a stationary position compared to the twenty-eight seconds it took the ZIS model. It reached a maximum speed of 170 km/h, a figure that compared favorably to 140 km/h for the ZIS.[70] All in all, the new car was less ponderous, sleeker, and more modern in the way that much of the Soviet Union would be in the post-Stalin era.

ZIL displayed a prototype of the car in late 1956 at Moscow's Disneyland, the All-Union Exhibition of the Achievements of the National Economy (VDNKh). It debuted along with a model of a Sputnik and other wonders of Soviet technology at the 1958 Brussels Expo. But did it represent Soviet technology? One contemporary car maven whose website is prone to fractured English contends that in styling and technique the ZIL-111 was "brutally copied from American models"; it was "'born in the USA,' not in Russia" and would fit very well "in a museum about the fifties in America alongside a juke-box and a photo of Elvis, or in a drive-in."[71] Elvis aside, the model that the 111 most closely resembled was the 1955 Packard Caribbean, whose specs indicate a V8 engine with dual carburetors producing 275 hp, push-button transmission, and self-leveling suspension, giving the car "the best combination of handling and ride among full-size American cars." "Brilliantly restyled by Dick [Richard A.] Teague and his design crew," the Caribbean was intended to rescue Packard from a series of poor management decisions including its ill-fated merger with Studebaker. However, in the estimation of two car-design specialists, certain flaws (noisy hydraulic lifters and a tendency to spring leaks from blown seals) cost the company "an immeasurable amount of good will among long-time marque loyalists." Whether the "brutally copied" Soviet version suffered from the same faults probably would have been known only to a few of the mechanics in the Special Assignments Garage.[72]

The factory produced no more than a dozen units of the original ZIL-111, including the 111A (with air conditioning) and the 111V convertible used for parades and conveying heroes such as Yuri Gagarin after his return from the cosmos in April 1961. The second series commenced in December 1962 with a model (111G) equipped with four headlights instead of two, a slightly longer and heavier body, air-conditioning, and a more plush interior. These machines and their successor, the even more powerful ZIL-114 that premiered in 1967, were "presidential," the exact Soviet equivalents of the Lincolns and Cadillacs that transported U.S. presidents Kennedy, Johnson, and Nixon in motorcades throughout the country and abroad. This close association with the Kremlin at a time when the USSR was at the pinnacle of its world power reinforced the connection between the enterprise at Avtozavodskaia 23 and the Soviet state.

ZIL embodied in many ways the quintessential Soviet industrial enterprise of the post-Stalin era, representing the state's priorities and serving as a microcosm of what the system offered its working-class citizens. Beginning in 1959 its production facilities underwent a fourth bout of renovation, the third having occurred just after the war. The main objective of the renovation was to accommodate production of the ZIL-130 and 131 trucks, replacements for the 150 and 151 series. The ZIL-130 started rolling off the assembly line— nearly two years behind schedule—in the fall of 1964, followed in 1967 by the more rugged three-axle all-terrain 131. These became the most durable of ZIL's vehicles, the bread and butter of the entire enterprise, serving the agricultural and military sectors respectively for decades to come.[73]

The enterprise itself, to use Kenneth Straus's terms, served as both "social melting pot" and "community organizer" for tens of thousands of recent migrants from the countryside. In this respect, it played a role not unlike that of the Ford Motor Company's Sociological Department of the second decade of the century. Just as Ford hoped to transform southern and eastern European immigrants into sober, law-abiding patriotic U.S. citizens, the party, Communist Union of Youth (Komsomol), and trade union apparatuses at ZIL worked on inculcating Soviet values among newcomers to the factory.[74] At first, they enjoyed only modest success. Workers fortunate enough to be housed in an enterprise-owned apartment confronted not only overcrowded conditions but also the unfamiliarity of modern conveniences. One former housing official later recalled that newly laid pipes had to be dug up and replaced because nails from the wood used to heat the buildings and the stoves punctured them, having been flushed down the toilets.[75] But the experience of moving into a new apartment after living for several years in wooden barracks or other makeshift quarters established a pattern that repeated itself in succeeding generations. In addition to housing, ZIL provided other facilities that contributed to the acclimation of peasant migrants to their new urban environment and, from the party's standpoint (if not their own), their acquisition of "culture." These included, by 1940, cafeterias and buffets throughout the enterprise, a well-staffed medical complex and clinics, kindergartens and nurseries for two thousand children, and the spectacularly modern Palace of Culture that served the entire Proletarian District.[76]

Housing construction resumed after the war, not all of it close to the factory. A retired housing office accountant recalled that workers who signed up to live in a suburban dormitory located some thirty-five kilometers from Moscow received a bed and mattress, pillows, covers and towels, a bedside table, heating, hot water, a radio, and a table and chairs. These he described as "privileges." Standards began to rise though. By 1960 another former housing employee was writing that Kolomenskoe had become hard to recognize. It had asphalt sidewalks and streets, planted rows of trees, a cinema, a hospital, two pharmacies, five schools, a "splendid" covered market, six food stores, two department stores, and assorted other buildings.[77] This commenced the beginning of the real boom that coincided with the factory's renovation. Between 1959 and 1965 the factory added some 270,000 square meters of living space for ZIL workers and their families, all with hot water, gas, stores in the buildings, and transportation nearby. And this was not all. As of 1966, the enterprise contained a state-of-the-art hospital with five hundred beds and a staff of 614 physicians and nurses; ran resorts in Yalta, the North Caucasus, and Moscow Oblast; owned a ten-thousand-seat soccer stadium; and operated an indoor swimming pool and other modestly salubrious facilities.[78]

Since further expansion of the ZIL plant was not an option, ZIL's director, P. D. Borodin, responded to the demand for increased volume by establishing branch facilities elsewhere in the country. In 1967 he created the Urals Auto Parts Factory (UZAZ) in Sverdlovsk-44 (today, Novoural'sk) to provide parts for the ZIL-157 all-terrain 6 X 6 and ZIL-164A trucks. The plant, renamed the Urals Auto Motor Factory (UAMZ) in 1976, gradually diversified, producing not only engines but various parts for the diminutive Zaporozhets and the even smaller children's pedal car, the "Ant." ZIL also established affiliates in Riazan' (truck assembly), Serdobsk in Penza Oblast (rear axles), Iartsevo in Smolensk Oblast (diesel engines), and elsewhere. By 1971 seventeen affiliates officially constituted the ZIL Production Association; in 1974 the Smolensk Auto Assembly Factory joined the association, becoming responsible for transmission production.[79]

In the Soviet administrative-command economy, bigger really did mean better.[80] The larger the enterprise the more resources it could command, and ZIL, a very big enterprise, commanded a great deal. In 1940 it employed about thirty-nine thousand people. After the war, employment leveled off at about forty-three thousand, but this figure does not include those working at the other factories within the production association, who numbered as many as fifty thousand. The salad days of the enterprise, the 1960s and early '70s, saw ZIL as "the spearhead of the automobile industry and a model of economic and social success." That was when "visiting foreign dignitaries saw the country through the prism of this sparkling showcase," and Muscovites living elsewhere in the city knew that if they needed an article of clothing—a fur hat, for example—they could get it at stores in ZIL's vicinity. No wonder "people from the provinces lined up to get a job at the factory, attracted in particular by the idea of obtaining the *propiska* or Moscow residency permit."[81] These people belonged to the generation of postwar migrants to the cities, a generation whose childhood years were often filled with hardship.

An ageing Muscovite woman described one such family with eleven children to a reporter from the United States in the early 1970s:

> [They] are all grown up and married and have their own children. They are still working-class families, but they live much better than their parents. Each now has his own apartment. Small. One or two rooms. But with conveniences—a stove, maybe a refrigerator. One has a car.
>
> Those eleven children have become forty to forty-five people now, including all the grandchildren. They get their subsidized passes through the trade unions for summer vacations. They work in different factories—one at a food enterprise, one in an electrical power plant, one at Likhachev Automobile Plant, the others in other factories. They all know how much better they live now than during the hungry years of the war and after the war.[82]

The luster started wearing off this version of the Soviet dream by the mid-1970s. The deterioration of ZIL's facilities plus the rise in standards and expectations resulting from past improvements acted as solvents. Whereas for the middle generation an apartment anywhere in Moscow seemed like a blessing, their children evidently thought otherwise. According to surveys from the late 1970s, residents identified the southeast as the most "reviled quadrant" in the city. Air pollution resulting from the concentration of heavy industry reached higher levels than anywhere else in the city. As the prefab mass housing hastily erected in the early 1960s by ZIL and AZLK aged rapidly, it became "some of the most unappealing in the city."[83] An investigation of birth weights among infants in different parts of Moscow conducted in the early 1980s found the Avtozavodskaia District around ZIL at the bottom.[84] The district resembled a hard-bitten industrial town in the U.S. rustbelt, minus the ghettoization of people of color. That came too with the recruitment first by AZLK and then ZIL of hundreds of limited-contract workers from Uzbekistan and, eventually, Vietnam.[85]

As ZIL stagnated, effort, energy, and personnel went elsewhere. In truck production the action moved to Naberezhnye Chelny in the Tatar Republic where, with great fanfare, the giant Kama Automobile Factory (KamAZ) began turning out vehicles in 1976. Since bigger meant better, KamAZ's heavy trucks with carrying capacities in excess of ten tons garnered more prestige than ZIL's smaller models. As long as the Soviet and East European military and agroindustrial complexes continued to order and consume them, ZIL had little incentive to change the formula. Its limousine line did undergo some moderate alterations. A scaled-down version (ZIL-117) with a shorter wheel base appeared in the early 1970s and was followed in 1977 by the first of the 4,000-series cars. These powerful (315 hp) vehicles embodied in their own way the USSR of the 1980s: they were bulky (3.3 kg), unwieldy, profligate in using resources, and, well, funereal.[86] When in March 1989 nine out of ten voters from Moscow's national-territorial district chose Boris Yeltsin as their representative to the Congress of People's Deputies, his Communist Party opponent, Evgenii A. Brakov, was, appropriately enough, the director of ZIL.

Postscript: AMO-ZIL

During the first post-Soviet decade, ZIL's existence hung in the balance. It hardly could have been otherwise when its primary customers—the armed forces, agriculture, and industrial concerns—all suffered from a slashing of state funding and were downsized. In surviving the upheavals of the post-Soviet Russian economy, the company once again seemed to lead a charmed existence. Although far from universally beloved, it nevertheless had enough support in the right places to get by with a few minor adjustments.

ZIL was the first automobile firm and among the first large enterprises to be privatized after the collapse of the Soviet Union. In September 1992 its name officially became AMO-ZIL (Open Joint Moscow Company—Likhachev Works), a revival of the original company's initials, though not the name. Employees collectively received the right to 50 percent of its shares; the other half went unevenly to the public, management, and the municipalities where AMO-ZIL had plants. The "public," of course, included commercial enterprises, one of which, the trading firm Mikrodin, cashed in on the bargain-basement price offered for the company's shares. For a mere five million dollars, Mikrodin obtained a 30 percent controlling stake. At the same time, the firm suffered a blow to its prestige when President Yeltsin, breaking with the tradition established by Stalin, replaced the ZIL limousine with a Mercedes as his official car.[87]

Mikrodin's asset stripping and director Brakov's failure to restructure in the face of dwindling demand proved more substantively damaging. With many workers furloughed or working part-time, AMO-ZIL seemed heading for closure, until Moscow's mayor, Iurii Luzhkov, stepped in to relieve it of the cost of maintaining its vast housing and social facilities. Moscow further increased its role in the enterprise in April 1994 when a shareholders' meeting—AMO-ZIL's first—chose a member of the city council, Aleksandr Vladislavlev, as chairman of a new board of directors. Vladislavlev then called on the federal government to freeze or delay debt repayment and went in search of international backers to pump badly needed funds into the company.[88] In April 1996 Luzhkov effectively deprivatized the company by arranging for the city to buy back Mikrodin's shares, making it the company's largest shareholder. He also required all city departments to purchase ZIL vehicles. Even Yeltsin got into the act in February 1998, swapping his Mercedes for a ZIL.[89]

Back from the brink, AMO-ZIL entered into talks first with Volvo and then Renault for joint ventures to produce heavy trucks. Under the agreement with Renault, the Moscow firm would assemble bodies from Renault-made parts and manufacture its own engines. Nothing seems to have come of this deal, which at least one observer considered "risky for Renault" from the start.

Still, at the beginning of the twenty-first century, the picture looked brighter. The company at last shed its refrigerator line and, with its "Bychok" line of vehicles (starting with ZIL-5301), broke into the expanding small-truck and minivan markets. The Bychok, a name allegedly picked by Luzhkov that means bull calf or steer, debuted in 1995. Although not without its shortcomings—difficulty starting in temperatures below minus 15 degrees Celsius, the most expensive parts of any ZIL vehicle—it gradually gained in market share against GAZ's less obviously macho Gazelle. By 2003, AMO-ZIL's dealers were selling over thirteen thousand, and experts were predicting at least double that number within a few years, assuming that the engine could be brought into conformity with European Union emission standards.[90] For a company that, according to Vladislavlev, "never had to sell anything before," this wasn't bad.

Perhaps as a legacy of the paternalist nature of Soviet industrial relations that ZIS-ZIL exhibited with especial clarity, the workers have been less prone to engage in job actions than their counterparts at other major automobile factories. A rare protest meeting in 1996 against wage arrears reportedly "broke up in confusion" after "the company director explained that there was no money available" and that demands should be addressed to the government. Workers more recently have been characterized as having "lost their self-confidence...and self-esteem," feeling "crushed, with no future, and uncertain of everything."[91]

Most of these workers presumably are, or have been, supporters of ZIL's soccer team, Torpedo-ZIL, whose origins go back to 1924. Supporting Torpedo, however, became complicated in the post-Soviet era, when the company sold and repurchased it—with corresponding alterations of the club's name—several times. In other respects, the situation at AMO-ZIL is uncertain at best. Foreign correspondents seized on what looked like the cessation of limo production in 2003 to wax smug about "the end of the road for the limo loved by Kremlin dictators." Every now and then, though, one of the old mastodons would pop up somewhere in the world to evoke emotions about the Soviet Union that were a little more complicated: in Moscow, where someone offered for sale an armor-plated ZIL-41052 used by both Gorbachev and Yeltsin, describing it as a "piece of priceless history"; in Kiev, where the minister of defense reviewed troops while standing, Soviet-style, in the backseat of a ZIS-110 convertible; at the Havana airport where a gift to Fidel Castro from Leonid Brezhnev was waiting to take Jimmy Carter into the city in May 2002; and in Genoa during the G8 summit of July 2001 where Vladimir Putin dusted off a black ZIL-111 convertible from 1963, "a marvel of gleaming chrome, white-walled tyres and leather upholstery...a symbol of the days when Soviet power was at its height." As one diplomat who was present at the occasion opined, "Perhaps Putin is deliberately stressing the continuity of Russian history by emphasising one of the more enlightened periods of Soviet rule."[92] Perhaps so.

chapter 2

GAZ, Nizhni Novgorod–Gor'kii–Nizhni Novgorod

> Communism created ultimately effective aesthetic structures and ultimately defective economic ones. . . . Factories are not built to produce commodities. They produce the united-working-class-body. They are allegorical figures of industrialization. Industry represents the leading metaphor of party ideology and factories are the works of this ideology. They result in a deficit of goods, but an overproduction of symbolic meanings. . . . They are the poems of communist ideology.
>
> VLADISLAV TODOROV, *Red Square, Black Square: Organon for Revolutionary Imagination*

> Sure it breaks down, but you can always fix it. It will be sad when there are no longer Volgas on the streets of Moscow.
>
> ANATOLY SAFAROV, chauffeur, quoted in the *Times* (London) online edition

"The old village of Monastyrka huddled together on the left bank of the Oka, a dozen or so kilometers from 700-year-old Nizhni Novgorod. Decrepit willows and poplars stood, like sentries, next to its earthen izbas [peasant huts] and plain houses. . . . A grove of oaks moaned in foul weather above the river's mirror-like surface."[1] A monastery—or at least a village that probably used to be one—and a grove of trees. Where have we encountered them before? But of course! Tiufel Grove on the outskirts of Moscow in what would become the Proletarian District.[2] Nizhni's equivalent to Moscow's Proletarian District originally was known as Socialist City (Sotsgorod), and then, from 1932 formally called the Auto Factory District (Avtozavodskii Raion). Its equivalent to—and rival of—AMO–ZIS–ZIL was the Nizhni Novgorod Automobile Factory.

Built during the First Five-Year Plan (1928–32), the factory also underwent name changes. In 1932, to honor the famous writer, Maxim Gor'kii, a native son whose return to the Soviet Union the previous year constituted a major propagandistic coup, Nizhni Novgorod became Gor'kii. The factory followed suit, becoming the Gor'kii Automobile Factory or, in common parlance, GAZ. But as Gor'kii had become a place, GAZ, like other Soviet enterprises and institutions, had the right to honor an(other) individual. In 1935 it exercised that right by augmenting its name with that of Viacheslav Molotov (1890–1986), chairman of the Council of People's Commissars. The successor to the factory's first car, the model A, was the Molotovets-1, abbreviated simply as M-1, or in popular speech, "Emka." But, just as Stalin's name would disappear from the Moscow auto factory, GAZ dropped Molotov's in 1956. One cannot help noticing in both cases the onward march of Soviet history reflected in nomenclature: the substitution of terms inherited from tsarist (or even earlier) times with revolutionary ones; political and cultural leaders honored (or indulged); acronyms supplanting the referents; and more anodyne names replacing the disgraced ones.

The history of GAZ and the city built to accommodate its workers is infinitely richer. The version told here is that of a Soviet Detroit on the Oka where dreams of technological utopia were inspired in part by Americans. It is a story of the heartland where peasants came directly from the "deep forests" to work and live in Socialist City, where the auto industry's version of Stakhanovism began, and where many managers and the engineers had their careers—and lives—prematurely terminated through arrest and execution. It is a story—like that of Detroit—of the glory years after the war when cars were named after the victory that seemed so unlikely in 1941, after the mightiest of rivers into which the Oka flowed, and after the birds flocking along its banks. Finally, it is a story of the effects of political implosion and the impact of a globalized auto industry, a story of painful adjustment and transformation to the point where in some respects GAZ resembled less its former Soviet self than it did contemporary Detroit.

Dreams

Erstwhile member of the Left Communist and Democratic Centralist factions within the Communist Party, former head of the State Bank and assistant commissar of agriculture, director of the Central Statistical Administration, and a leading official in the State Planning Commission (Gosplan), Valerian V. Osinskii (1887–1938) was one of the more mercurial of Bolsheviks.[3] He also thought big. In 1925–26 he spent several months traveling by car in the United States, visiting not only major metropolitan areas such as New York and Detroit but the back roads (for there was little else) of Alabama and Texas.[4] Already an automobile enthusiast, Osinskii returned to the USSR even more convinced that the country needed its own auto industry.

An auto industry and what else? What about the metal for the bodies, the magnetos and spark plugs for the electrical system, and the rubber for the tires? What about the capital for building the factory (or factories) and purchasing machinery? What about competing needs? Were passenger cars or even trucks more important than tractors? When it came right down to it, did the Soviet Union really need an automobile industry quite as immediately as Osinskii believed? Judging by the initial drafts for long-term (five-year) industrial development put together by Gosplan, the answer seemed to be no.

Such lack of enthusiasm provoked Osinskii to go public with his case. In July 1927, he published a series of articles in *Pravda* provocatively titled "The American Automobile or the Russian Cart?" The articles used the "automobile" and the "cart" both literally and metonymically. They reported on the tremendous stimulus automobiles gave to the U.S. economy and their enhancement of its military capabilities, contrasting these developments with the retardation of economic activity in the USSR resulting from its reliance on "the Russian cart." The Soviet Union, Osinskii argued, was caught in a vicious cycle of its own making: proverbial Russian backwardness made the establishment of an automobile industry seem inappropriate, but the absence of an automobile industry perpetuated that condition of backwardness. To break out of the cycle required the determination to invest in technological transfer essential for mass production of automobiles. Instead of the "wretched" 10,800 Gosplan envisioned after five years, Osinskii called for "at least 100,000 per year." That, however, would only be the beginning. Thinking (or dreaming) further into the future, he called for "every worker and peasant in a car within not more than ten to fifteen years!"[5]

The articles turned out to be the opening shots in a debate that continued partly in the press and partly behind the closed doors of Gosplan, the Supreme Council of the National Economy, and the Politburo of the Communist Party's Central Committee. The case Osinskii made provoked all manner of objections: the country lacked sufficient demand because peasants couldn't afford cars and wouldn't know what to do with them anyway; investing in an automobile factory of such large capacity constituted a waste of precious resources; we should avoid concentrating the production of all components in one factory and instead produce each item in a different place; given how relatively inexpensive American cars are, it makes more sense to import them; the car is a "bourgeois carriage" inappropriate for Soviet socialism. In his replies to each of these objections and others contained in letters to the editor Osinskii stuck fast to his original position.[6] He also lobbied the Politburo—successfully. On September 1, 1927, it approved "Comrade Osinskii's proposal" to create a permanent commission on technical and scientific relations with the United States under its auspices. The commission initially consisted of four individuals: the commissar of foreign relations, Boris Chicherin; the former chairman of the Central Cooperative Union and head of the Soviet trade delegation in London, Lev Khinchuk; the director of the All-Russian Oil Syndicate, A. P. Serebrovskii; and Osinskii, who acted as chairman.[7]

Finally, Osinskii's call for a voluntary society or public (*obshchestvannaia*) organization to promote automobile production and transport inspired the

formation of the Society for Cooperation in the Development of Automobilism and Road Improvement (Avtodor). The organization attracted technical
specialists, professional drivers, auto enthusiasts from the Moscow Automobile Club, and a smattering of the cultural intelligentsia, who lent their name
and fame allegedly in hopes of landing a car in return. It sponsored two
debates on (what else?) the American automobile versus the Russian cart,
hosted a series of conferences, and organized other activities.[8]

Osinskii's maximalist position benefited from the upward revision of targets in successive drafts of the First Five-Year Plan, from the dismissal by
Stalinists of those who warned against the trend as "rightist deviationists" and
other indications of a general leftward lurch in the Kremlin. Osinskii himself
kept up the pressure. In April 1928, as news of negotiations to build a state-of-
the-art automobile factory began to circulate, he was campaigning for "another
factory capable of producing not 100,000 vehicles a year, but 500,000."[9] Later
in the year, he traveled to the United States again, this time to discuss a possible joint venture with the Ford Motor Company. Ford seemed receptive, but at
this point, Soviet bureaucratic politics intervened not so much as a Left versus
Right division as competition for resources among different projects. Moscow's
Automobile Trust, just then pursuing a parallel course of negotiations with the
Brandt Company, complicated things further. From Osinskii's standpoint, Sorokin's coup of lining up Brandt to help AMO turn out 25,000 Autocars a year
represented at best a diversion and at worst the kind of "handicraft" (*kustarnyi*)
approach he had railed against in "The American Car or the Russian Cart."[10]

One of the losers in these highly competitive games was the NAMI-1,
the fruit of collaboration among a twenty-six-year-old designer, Konstantin
Sharapov; the future chief engineer at GAZ, Andrei Lipgart; and several engineers from the Scientific Automotive Institute (NAMI). They assembled the
first version of this small, lightweight passenger vehicle at Moscow's Spartak
factory, and road tested it in May 1927, just two months before Osinskii's
denigration of the "Russian cart" appeared in *Pravda*. In the fall of that year,
it entered into serial production. What was wrong with this car, the first to
be manufactured on Soviet soil since the Prombron back in 1922? Nothing, except the handicraft nature of its manufacture and its excessive cost of
production.[11] The NAMI conceivably might have been adapted for mass production elsewhere in the country, but instead it became the road not taken.
Discussions resumed with Ford as well as with General Motors. For reasons
not clear from the documents I have seen, GM dropped out of consideration
at some point, leaving Ford as the company to bring Detroit to the Oka and
thereby fulfill Osinskii's dream.[12]

In choosing Ford, VSNKh was hardly contracting with an unknown quantity. Ford began advertising and selling Model Ts in Russia in 1909, and
continued to ship modest numbers of both cars and trucks through the years
of the world war and civil war. Better known, though, was its Fordson tractor, described by the French historian Yves Cohen as "one of those machines
that changed the world." The Fordsons were purchased through Amtorg on

credit. By 1926, Soviet fields were being ploughed by some twenty thousand of them, and Leningrad's Red Putilovets factory was replicating them (without a license). As already noted, many of the re-emigrants employed at AMO had worked at Highland Park where Fordsons were made. By 1929 some Russian graduates of the Henry Ford Trade School, which started admitting about fifty annually in 1926, were working at Red Putilovets.[13]

"For the Bolsheviks," wrote one (unsympathetic) foreign observer in the middle of the decade, "industrialized America became the Promised Land."[14] Nobody represented industrialized America better than Ford. Both his autobiography and collection of self-help nostrums went through numerous editions in Russian translation, and many Soviet citizens attributed near magical powers to his principal industrial innovation, the moving assembly line.[15] Despite its origins in capitalist enterprise, Moscow considered it, like Frederick Winslow Taylor's principles of scientific management, an ideologically neutral technique that could serve the cause of communism just as it had served capitalists.

The technical agreement with Ford was signed on May 31, 1929, in Dearborn by VSNKh's deputy chairman, Valerii Mezhlauk, and the president of the Amtorg Trading Company, Saul Baron. Ford's vice president, Peter Martin, and Henry Ford himself cosigned for the company. The agreement called for the company to produce "a detailed plant layout and working project for the construction and equipment of an assembly plant and body shop of sufficient size and capacity to assemble one hundred thousand automobiles per year of the type of Ford model 'A' car and Ford model 'AA' truck in two daily shifts of seven hours each." The arrangement obligated the Soviet side to (1) purchase through Amtorg parts and subassemblies amounting to a total of seventy-two thousand vehicles (minus tires) over a period of four years; (2) receive from Ford all necessary patents, specifications, and technical personnel; (3) send up to fifty students per year to receive instruction and work at the River Rouge plant; and (4) pay for all costs including packing and freight charges.[16] Over the next several months VSNKh signed additional contracts with the Austin Company of Cleveland, Ohio, for the construction of the plant and the workers' city, and with dozens of other American and European firms and Soviet enterprises for the provision of construction equipment and materials.[17] To oversee the project, VSNKh appointed a special trust, which it called the Auto Construction Trust (Avtostroi). The name also applied to the entire project and the location of the building site.

The Politburo's decision to locate the factory about eight miles downriver from the old fortress city of Nizhni Novgorod represented a triumph for the regional party organization, whose first secretary, Andrei Zhdanov, exulted that it would stimulate the industrialization of the upper Volga.[18] The largest automotive plant in Europe, it would consist of three million square feet of floor space divided among a foundry, spring shop, forge shop, pressed-steel shop, machine-and-assembly shop, power station, warehouses, and other buildings spread out over an area of 242 hectares. The buildings would be made of reinforced steel and concrete with wood-block floors, and they would be surrounded by reinforced concrete highways.[19] In advance of the main production plant, the contract provided for the erection of two small prototype assembly plants in Nizhni (No. 1) and Moscow (No. 2). The contractors hired the American architectural firm Albert Kahn, Inc. to build them. Kahn, well-known in the United States as the architect of Ford's River Rouge plant and the Fisher Building in Detroit, already had been commissioned by Amtorg to supervise the design and construction of the new tractor factory at Stalingrad. Before its sudden departure from Moscow in May 1932, Kahn's firm would produce drawings and calculations that reputedly were used in "more than 530 plants" and that had an influence that "may have been exponentially greater."[20]

The point of the two prototype plants, each equipped with Ford tools and dies, was to give Soviet auto builders practice in assembling knocked-down models shipped from the United States. No sooner did plant No. 1 come on line in February 1930 than the first Model A assembled in the USSR appeared to great acclaim. The Moscow plant, completed in November 1930, became the basis for the KIM (later, AZLK) factory that produced the Moskvich.[21] By May 1933, four years into the contract, VSNKh (in actuality, Avtostroi) purchased a total of 36,069 vehicles, or just over half of the seventy-two thousand for which it contracted in 1929. Ford's records show that by 1935 the company had received $18.1 million, which was more than half a million short of expenses associated with the production and shipping of the cars.[22]

Responsibility for construction of the main plant rested with the Austin Company. Although less experienced than Kahn at building auto plants, Austin had boosted its reputation by having completed General Motors's Pontiac Six factory ("the world's largest and most efficient automobile plant" of its time) in only seven months in 1927.[23] Its interest in the Soviet plant was piqued by a visit of its executive vice president, George Bryant, to the USSR as part of a delegation from the Russian-American Chamber of Commerce. Austin reached terms with VSNKh on August 23, 1929. The company conducted surveying and site clearance during the fall and winter, with construction scheduled to start on May 1, 1930.[24]

Historians have evaluated the Ford contract in rather different ways. Antony Sutton, perhaps confusing the United States with Nazi Germany, claimed that by giving the USSR the capacity to produce military vehicles, the deal had contributed to U.S. "national suicide." Boris Shpotov by contrast asks, "Did the Soviet Union overpay Ford?" He concludes that both sides benefited from the deal—Ford, after all, managed to unload a sizeable contingent of aging models and provide additional work for its machine-tool shops just as the Great Depression was radically reducing demand elsewhere—but that "the USSR for understandable reasons received incomparably more advantages from cooperation with the capitalist firm."[25]

Whether it knew what to do with these advantages was another matter. Some may have been convinced of the correctness of this path because it was

shorter, but others writing about the construction of GAZ emphasize the coun-
terproductiveness of the haste. "The failure to achieve planned results," in
the view of the historian Kurt Schultz, "was a direct consequence of the political decision to demand progress on every economic front at once, which
in turn created an environment deadly to the rational pursuit of plans."
As Schultz characterized the process: "Improvisation replaced planning....
Bureaucracies at the center and in the field...took on all of the characteristics
of sovereign, independent states...alternately negotiat[ing] and warr[ing]
over men, money, and materiel." Avtostroi was at war with Metallostroi, the
trust that VSNKh chose to build the factory. VATO (All-Union Automobile
and Tractor Association), the agency that had replaced the Automobile Trust,
intervened to try to sort out the mess, but it was unsuccessful. Then VSNKh
took a stab. It dispatched commission after commission to investigate and reorganized the chain of command, but "little came of it." The Council of Labor
and Defense (STO) tried its hand, but with the same meager results.[26]

Schultz's assessment echoes what Allan Austin, one of twenty Austin
Company engineers at the construction site, was writing to his father, Wilbert, president of the company. "I wish we had a simple criterion by which
to judge the efforts we put forth on this job," he complains in a letter of
November 5, 1930. "Here every principle of economics and workmanship
seems upset, and the results are most confusing."[27] Neither Schultz nor Austin could know that Osinskii had to fight for the life of the project within the
Communist Party Central Committee. On December 18, 1930, he complained
that the Council of People's Commissars (Sovnarkom) had slashed funding
for 1931 from the R 192 million that VATO (which he chaired at the time) had
requested to R 94 million. This he contrasted with the largesse with which
Sovnarkom treated the Stalingrad Tractor Factory.[28] So many wars to fight!

The attempt to realize Osinskii's dream of a leap forward in automobilism
appeared to induce nothing so much as chaos and confusion. As party boss
Zhdanov reported to Molotov on August 30, "Each building site falls under
the crossfire of all manner of instructions, advice, and demands on the part
of three organizations....The organizational muddle at the present time
has...reached absurd lengths."[29] In such circumstances, the raising of the
plant's annual production target from 100,000 to 130,000 and then 140,000
vehicles seems like proof of either supreme optimism or lunacy. It is worth
asking, though, whether some other logic might have been involved in the
hasty construction of the plant and parallel projects throughout the country.
Perhaps, as Moshe Lewin put it, the "superstructure" was "rushing ahead."
That is, industrialization as envisioned in the First Five-Year Plan gave the
state the opportunity to engage in a "particular dynamism," encouraging it
"to go all the way through to a full blossoming of a new model" that Lewin
identifies as "coercive acceleration and stage skipping."[30] Is it possible, therefore, that the inevitable failure to achieve planned results was, if not exactly
intended, then at least the stuff of what further dreams were made, and that
the only criterion to judge effort was more effort? Could this have been the

Soviet/Communist answer to the dynamism of capital(ism) summed up by Marx as "Accumulate, accumulate! That is the Moses and the prophets!"?[31] Maybe this is why Vladislav Todorov considers Communist factories as "allegorical figures of industrialization" and "poems of communist ideology."[32] In this case, one of their unheralded poets was Boris Agapov, special correspondent at the auto factory's construction site for the Commissariat of Heavy Industry's newspaper, *For Industrialization* (Za industrializatsiiu).

Agapov wrote many articles exposing the rampant bureaucratic wrangling and bungling. The one published on August 2, 1930, under the title "Off the Road" (*Po bezdorozh'iu*) was no different from the others in that it too documented shortages of materials and workers, shoddy work, and other deficiencies at the construction site. It roundly criticized the men in ties, "the most powerful people in Nizhni Novgorod," for not knowing what was happening or what to do. Dripping with sarcasm, it asked the "highly esteemed managers and engineers of Metallostroi" and "respected Moscow leaders" if they were aware that the plant had to be built in fifteen months and that workers had to be assisted by machines. It condemned the limitations on recruiting workers and other "*narkomtrudnosti*" (a pun on the Commissariat of Labor and the word for difficulties).[33]

But it also contained a vision or dream of the factory's future, glimpsed on the blueprints where "General Plan of the Auto Plant at Monastyrka" was written in Russian and in English:

> I see one hundred and forty thousand machines...four in a row...com[ing] from the assembly shop, the biggest shop in Europe, one and a half kilometers long.
>
> I see them shudder at their first touch with the hard ground on leaving the conveyor for the first time. The pressed steel building, spring shop, forge shop and woodworking shop, electric station, tool and die forge shop, warehouses and garages are planned in rows, collecting and reflecting the sun's rays in their glass walls. They are situated parallel to the river.

Here in miniature we have the industrialization drive of the late 1920s and early 1930s—the tempo, the chaos, the shortages, and the dream of a more orderly "planned-in-rows" sort of existence. Nineteen-thirty just may have been the most tempestuous, chaotic, and dream-inducing year of the five. It was when, according to Stalin, collectivizers had gotten themselves "dizzy with success," when *tekuchka* (labor turnover or just wandering) reached its height, when social purging—the removal of individuals with the wrong class background from positions in the state apparatus, the legal and other professions, and the schools—reached its zenith, when the party "unleashed" avant-garde visionaries, and when "it seemed to many Communist intellectuals...that Engels' prophecy of the withering away of the state was already being realized."[34]

In Agapov, the dream of total transformation of human existence had a particularly articulate spokesperson. Walter Chrysler, one of Detroit's giants, once wrote, "There is in manufacturing a creative job that only poets are supposed to know."[35] Agapov was a poet of manufacturing. Just six years before reporting from Avtostroi, he had cofounded the Literary Center of Constructivists with erstwhile fellow poets Kornelii Zelinskii, Vera Inber, Il'ia Sel'vinskii, and others. A summary by Victor Terras of the center's "Declaration" certainly rings true for the Agapov of 1930: " 'Soviet Westernism' and 'Americanism,'...progress in terms of a rational technological utopia. Their positive values were speed, precision, intensity, and expediency." The only difference was that the architectural plan on which Agapov gazed had replaced poetry, providing "the way to transform the world into a manageable structure and an instance of the triumph of technology over nature":[36]

> Among the forests and parks is the new city [*novyi gorod*]—it is not Novgorod, but rather the City of Socialism. Like flowers in beds, there are rectangles everywhere. Every rectangle is a combination composed of a clubhouse, nurseries and kindergartens, cafeterias, libraries, bathtubs and showers working around the clock. At the end of the city are playing fields and green parks. Its buses and stores, dining halls and pavements, gardens and sky are not spoiled by soot and smoke. It is a city without chimneys and kilns, lit by electricity and heated by steam. I cannot imagine the town otherwise than it has been drawn in the architectural plan.[37]

The Hungarian historian Sándor Horváth, in commenting about "the first Hungarian Socialist City" of Sztálinváros, wrote, "Rulers have dreamed for [*sic*] time immemorial of creating cities from nothing or shaping civilization from the wilderness."[38] The Soviet city of socialism, or socialist city (sotsgorod), was an artifact of the First Five-Year Plan (1928–32) that has been likened to Tommaso Campanella's early seventeenth-century utopian City of the Sun.[39] Born from the frenzy of destroying old institutions, it represented a conscious effort to create ex nihilo a new urban landscape. "The socialist city" would embody what avant-garde architects and urban planners had been discussing for at least a decade and visionary social(ist) thinkers for far longer than that.[40] It would be distinguished by its commitment to communalism, gender equality, collective education of children, and public health and hygiene. It would be devoid of bourgeois deformations like shops (as opposed to "distribution points"), private apartments, personal property, and tall buildings, thereby destroying the distinction between the public and the private. Socialist cities, so named usually in connection with the construction of a major industrial enterprise, sprang up in many parts of the country during the 1930s. But no matter what their location, they all would—to cite Agapov again—"appear as a leap into the future" where life would be lived "in new ways, unseen in human existence." Only then, he added,

> when we will be standing on the turret of the workers' club, will we remember the rutted roads, the engineers' disputes, the plywood barracks, the backward workers, the newspapers' trepidations, the shortages of materials, the failures,

the hitches, and the moments of despair like people remember a difficult childhood, severe training, and war from which they emerge victorious.[41]

From dreams of leaping forward to the bureaucratic foul-ups that inevitably followed from trying to realize those dreams, to the dreams of their supersession, the Soviet Union had entered into a cycle both rapturous and vicious. By this measure, the only way of breaking the cycle would be to give up the dreams. The massive celebration occasioning the completion of the main buildings on November 1, 1931, suggested otherwise. A globe encircled with the slogan (in Russian and English) "There are no such fortresses that cannot be taken by Bolsheviks" formed the tribune on which speakers stood. *Pravda* proudly reported that Russian and foreign tourists attending the ceremonies "refused to believe that fifteen months earlier the ground on which the factory stood had been swampy land covered with small bushes." It also noted that similar factories erected by Ford in Canada and Germany had taken five years to build.[42]

The comrades pressed on. By late January 1932, they had the assembly line up and running. But no sooner had a few score AA trucks made it to the end than a lack of coordination caused the whole operation to seize up. Suppliers had failed to provide specialized steel, expected imports had not arrived, and machinery malfunctioned. A mere ten vehicles issued forth in February, followed by 136 in March. On April 2, 1932, G. K. Ordzhonikidze, recently appointed commissar of heavy industry, visited the factory—not for the first time—and ordered a halt to production to sort things out. The foreign press had a field day reporting "Mass Output Fails; Soviet Plant Halts" and "Russia Closes Big Auto Plant: Too Many Bosses." In July a new wrinkle surfaced in the form of rivalry between two groups of engineers: on the one hand, the "Russian Americans" such as L. A. Merts, who had worked for two-and-a-half years in the United States, and on the other, those who previously worked at AMO and Stalingrad Tractor and who looked to the chief engineer, V. G. Lapin, as their spokesman. That same month, Stepan S. Dybets, the factory's first director who had spent ten years in the United States before returning to his homeland in 1917, was replaced by Sergei S. Diakonov; in September, the party organization received a new secretary. Output meanwhile slowly but inexorably rose, from 360 in June to 775 in July and over a thousand during September. Still, as Schultz notes, "the facility at Nizhnii-Novgorod never lived up to Osinskii's dreams. Not until 1937 would the entire Soviet automotive industry produce the 130,000 units that had earlier been expected from Nizhnii-Novgorod alone."[43]

The parallel process of peopling the "city of socialism" followed a course not unlike that of another Socialist City, actually a district of Magnitogorsk, the city of steel "behind the Urals." There, "everything had pointed toward success." But because "most energies, materials, personnel, and money were riding on industrial construction" the housing construction plan for 1932 reached an abysmal rate of fulfillment of 10 percent and remained "well below

Entrance to the Socialist City, Avtostroi. Courtesy of the Western Reserve Historical Society, Cleveland.

50 percent" for the following year.[44] John Scott, the American who lived in Magnitogorsk's Socialist City for much of the five years he worked at the steel plant, described it as "not really a very good example of a Socialist city to put before the population. The houses were... arranged in long rows, like military barracks, and were all of the same matchbox-on-edge shape." Soon, the Socialist City disappeared in favor of the Kirov District.[45]

At the Avtostroi site construction also got off to a splendid start. In January 1930, the regional trade union council's presidium hosted a meeting in the Palace of Culture in Kanavino (a district just to the north of the construction site) at which representatives of Avtostroi presented to assembled "comrades" a preliminary plan. The city would be built, they were told, "so that workers would have the best living conditions, and the old way of life in which women were chained to the kitchen and the laundry would be destroyed.... Everyone will work, men in the factory, some women there as well, and the remainder in supplementary enterprises." The audience peppered speakers with questions about food preparation and living space, and "many comrades warned Avtostroi not to choose dark, cheerless, barracks-like types of housing."[46] They clearly were interested.

A few weeks later, the situation no longer looked so good. The local press reported that—just as at Magnitogorsk—Avtostroi had changed its mind several times about the location of the city, and that in the eastern zone a "whole series of structures that had been built before the arrival of the blueprints will need to be torn down and rebuilt." Turnover of workers was becoming a problem too. Meanwhile, Austin Company engineers in Cleveland were experiencing difficulties in satisfying Avtostroi. This too had its parallel with Magnitogorsk, where another Cleveland firm, McKee and Company, was responsible for designing and supervising the construction of the giant steel mill.[47] On April 11, 1930—just weeks before official groundbreaking was scheduled—the *New York Times* reported that Avtostroi considered Austin's plan "entirely unsuitable to Communist conditions of life." It went instead with a design consisting of two overlapping rectangles with circular ends, like oval tracks, that a team of eighteen architectural students from the Moscow Higher Technical School had submitted to a Soviet architectural competition. One of the rectangles was tilted at a 45 degree angle from the other, which ran perpendicular to the riverbank, and both were separated from the car plant

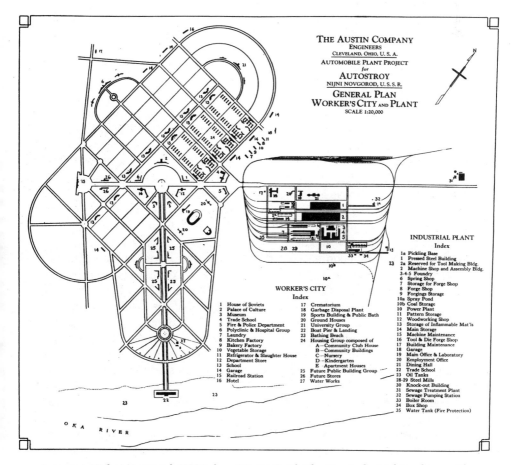

Autostroi, Nizhni Novgorod, USSR, from Martin Greif, *The New Industrial Landscape: The Story of the Austin Company* (Clinton, N.J.: Main Street Press, 1978), 106.

by service facility buildings.[48] As Agapov's description of the blueprints suggests, the main residential zone consisted of rectangular-shaped superblocks, each accommodating one thousand residents.

Allan Austin noted in an article he eventually landed in the *New York Times Magazine* that the plan reserved two-thirds of the blocks for family apartments and one third for "community houses." It is clear from his descriptions that the family apartments were really communal (*kommunalki*) in that families would live in one room of twenty square meters, sharing a kitchen and bathroom with two other families, a "plan generally followed in the cities at the present time." The community apartments offered communal living of a "higher" sort in which "groups of three or four young men or women [would] work, study and live together" as a commune. Most activity would occur in the "clubhouse," which Austin described as "the nerve center" fulfilling "all social, educational, recreational and gastronomic needs of the adult population." Children would be housed in nurseries and kindergartens intended to serve as "actual, full-time home[s]...with eating and sleeping quarters, and a staff of child specialists and nurses in charge." This "new scheme of life," he added, "is frankly admitted by the Soviets to be experimental." Austin, who "had been raised in affluent surroundings...was eager to follow his father and his grandfather in the family construction enterprise" and who was accompanied by his young bride on the trip, was remarkably nonjudgmental.[49]

The experiment, like many ventured at this time, never had a chance to be implemented. The demand for housing was so great that construction workers and future autoworkers moved into the buildings even before their completion. Harry Miter, the American supervisor of construction, wrote in February 1931 that "these buildings will have lots more people living in them than the buildings were designed for." He soon complained to VATO's office in Moscow of "very poor" sanitary conditions, which he feared would lead to "a serious epidemic of sickness" in Socialist City. "There are workers' cots in rows in the halls, people camped in the laundries, each with a primus," wrote a visiting American reporter in June. A Soviet critic writing in December 1931 noted that the occupants of the first block faced "a difficult situation with respect to water, heating, and sanitation," that the workmanship was poor, and the lack of food dispensaries required residents to go as far as the relocated village of Monastyrka. A former resident of the building opposite the Central Club recalled that it presented a "depressing (*unyluiu*) picture: a long corridor with identical doors, several kitchens and washrooms—and that was it for conveniences."[50]

As far as living space was concerned, two and three people were occupying rooms of nine square meters intended for one. Indeed, the 14,411 people living in the new buildings had at their disposal an average of five, not nine, square meters. At least they had more than the 3.34 square meters cited by John Scott as the average in the Kirov District of Magnitogorsk for 1937. Although "unacceptable for the auto factory," it exceeded the norm in Nizhni

Novgorod. Paved streets and sidewalks did not exist "because there was no organization to care about this." And "where green plantings had existed they have been destroyed."[51] The salubriousness of the city had been sacrificed to the factory's construction, concluded the leader of one of many groups formed to investigate living conditions on the eve of the production of the first automobile. He added: "At bottom, there is not a single completely furnished building in 'the Socialist City.'"[52] His use of quotation marks said as much as the entire report.

As crowded and otherwise unpleasant as living in these buildings was, conditions compared favorably to the two-story apartment buildings and one-story barracks that also went up at this time and, although intended as temporary accommodation, lasted for decades. This is why "the more skilled the worker was, the greater the chance he would be living in a brick or standard-frame building," as opposed to wooden-frame and barracks accommodation. The amount of average living space continued to fall. As of March 15, 1932, it was below four square meters; by December 15 it had reached a low of 2.5, after which it improved (to between 4.2 and 5) thanks in part to the resettlement of "a significant number of residents who had nothing to do with the factory."[53]

The project's insatiable demand for labor produced overcrowding. *Nizhegorodskaia kommuna* reported in July 1930 that although some ten thousand workers were already on the site, the project needed an additional 5,400. An American visitor in September 1930 found "hordes of people" at work. A year later, he reported "greater hordes of people," though also "floating labor," which he attributed to "more than a trace of nomadic instinct." The Komsomol had just "mobilized" three thousand members but needed to organize an additional two thousand into its "shock divisions." At this point, the site contained its maximum number of people, forty thousand, of whom a reported 40 percent were women "engaged in all but the very heaviest of construction work."[54] Another foreign visitor—the Avtostroi site having become something of a tourist attraction—noted that boats brought as many as five thousand *subbotniki* (people devoting their days off to such projects on a supposedly voluntary basis) every day, and that *lishentsy* (people deprived of their civil rights because of their "alien" social identities) also found employment, although without necessarily revealing their true status. They overwhelmingly performed manual labor with simple tools: crosscut saws and axes for carpenters, "little stretcher-like devices" for two people to haul dirt, and hods for carrying mortar and bricks. The hardships, the unpredictability of deliveries of materials and even money to pay wages resulted in a turnover rate of 135 percent in 1932, but the effort persisted until the buildings were occupied and functioning, more or less.[55]

One way of telling the story of the construction of GAZ and Sotsgorod is to emphasize its contribution to the rapid industrialization and urbanization of the USSR. Indeed, between 1927–28 and 1932 the number of workers employed in metalworking factories in Nizhegorod Oblast more than doubled, increasing from 34,250 to over 77,000. Thanks to the influx of peasants from the surrounding region and of construction workers from farther away, the recorded population of Nizhni Novgorod rose from 241,000 on January 1, 1928, to 451,500 five years later. The figures roughly correspond to Detroit's between 1900 and 1910 at the dawn of the U.S. automobile age.[56]

The workers who experienced these dizzying changes "came out of peasant villages [and] hadn't seen anything more complicated than a wheelbarrow or pitchfork" up to that point. "Even if they graduated from the local FZU apprenticeship school," added Victor Reuther who encountered them on and off the shop floor in the early years of GAZ's existence, "this was an incredible leap in a few years." After laughing about how easy it was for ordinary American workers "going over there" to appear as if they were engineers (because "the whole regime almost worshipped technological advance"), he added, "But as I look back upon it, the whole nation took a quantum leap in an incredibly short time."[57]

This recounting of Avtostroi's construction underscores the "peculiar factor of haste" that Moshe Lewin considered crucial to an understanding of the entire political system's transformation.[58] Inspired initially by techno-utopian fantasies of modernity and justified thereafter in terms of national security, the mania to outpace time developed a dynamic that was self-perpetuating—at least to the point of exhaustion. Remarkably, though, when Richard Cartwright Austin, Allan's son, visited Nizhni Novgorod in the late 1990s, he discovered that "nearly all of the apartment buildings erected for the Workers' City in 1930 and 1931 remain standing and useful." It is not clear whether this was a testament to "vision," "persistence," and "workmanship by Russians and Americans together" as Austin graciously suggested or the persistence of low standards of housing in a provincial Russian city.[59]

Adventures

There is another story embedded in the construction of the GAZ and Socialist City, or rather, another way of constructing the story. It has a stronger foreign, and particularly American, slant. As should already be clear, Americans were intimately involved in the building of both the factory and the city, in reproducing "Detroit" in the land of the Soviets. But what did they think about their involvement, both at the time and later, and what did others think of them? This is a different sort of question from whether or not the American contribution was crucial to the development of a Soviet automobile industry.[60] It is an inquiry into the mentalities of those whose lives willy-nilly became entwined with the making of a Soviet Detroit.

Charles Sorensen, a long-time associate of Henry Ford and his director of production, got involved early. He handled negotiations with Osinskii and other Soviet officials in Dearborn in 1928 and in Moscow the following summer. He includes an account of these meetings, his visits to the AMO and Putilov factories, and his tour of the site for the new car plant in a chapter of his autobiography, "Russian Adventure." The chapter also refers to tractor troubles in Britain, unsafe Model T brakes that caused problems in Germany, and a more pleasant stay in Warsaw, but Russia is the only country where he—and by extension, the company—had adventures. Allan Nevins and Frank Ernest Hill's company history, published the year after Sorensen's autobiography, gives the same characterization.[61]

What did they mean? Ford was hardly the first American company to do business with "the Soviets." Alcoa, General Electric, Standard Oil, and other well-known firms already had signed either concessionary or technical assistance agreements, and many more were lining up to join them. It may have been a way of signaling the strangeness and even political danger of this "marriage of convenience," as Hill and another coauthor later referred to the deal. For his part, inveterate anticommunist though he was, Henry Ford explained his policy in characteristic homilies such as "Russia is beginning to build" and "It is my duty to help any people who want to go back to work and become self-supporting."[62] Wilbert Austin, equally sanguine about his company's involvement, told the Cleveland City Club (to "spontaneous applause"), "I do not believe we are being disloyal to the United States in helping Russia to better her own conditions and get ahead."[63] It was not so much the companies, and still less their eponymous founders, that experienced adventures in Soviet Russia as the people sent there by companies to carry out the work.

In reference to foreign workers in Soviet Russia, Andrea Graziosi notes that "the year, 1930...was a turning point," for it was then that the Communist Party's Sixteenth Congress decided to admit "foreign engineers, foremen, and skilled workers" to further the cause of Soviet industrialization.[64] The Austin Company sent some twenty engineers to supervise construction of the auto factory and the new city that would accommodate its workers. Allan Austin, just three years removed from engineering school, was, at twenty-five, the youngest among them. His letters leave little doubt that his sixteen-month stay was stressful, notwithstanding the relative comfort of the stucco cottage he occupied with his wife, the provision of cooking and maid service, access to (Ford) automobiles, and the company of fellow residents of the American Village (dubbed Austingrad by its inhabitants). The unfamiliarity of Russian practices alternately fascinated and puzzled him, but the bureaucratic turf wars, the vagaries of building and food supplies, and the harshness of the climate caused Allan periodic bouts of infuriation and depression. "The job is trying our patience a good deal these days," he wrote two weeks into construction. "Russians make promises recklessly, and usually forget about them.... They are among the world's greatest talkers and get correspondingly little done.... It is the dickens of a job to get anything done as you want it." He admitted to "disgust" and "ragged nerves" and that "the effort to control my temper takes more effort than anything else I do."[65]

His generalizations about "Russians" were tempered by the extraordinary differences among the people he met. He seemed to have had little direct or personal relations with the thousands of laborers, although he did note that women were performing all sorts of jobs that in the United States were reserved exclusively for men. But he was in daily contact with the female interpreters and the project's engineering and managerial staff. Among the latter, relations were particularly cordial with "Mr. Makarovsky," Avtostroi's man on the spot in Socialist City, and Makarovsky's wife, a former opera singer.[66] After his return to the United States, Allan Austin resumed working at his father's firm and eventually succeeded him as president. Asked in 1976 about his time in Russia, he replied, "It was strange because when we left it was just like dropping a curtain behind us and that was the end of the whole episode."[67]

Also reproduced in Richard Austin's book are letters that Harry A. Miter, project superintendent, sent to Avtostroi and VATO. These by their very nature were more peremptory, but even so, Miter appears to have had no stomach for the difficulties he and his fellow engineers had to endure. On one occasion, even his personal Buick rebelled, filling his mouth with mud as he tried to extricate it from a sea of the substance. So frequently was he out of sorts that at one point Allan lamented that the "beautiful disposition of his has undergone a remarkable change," adding, "I hope it is not permanent."[68]

There is no record of what Soviet workers thought of the Americans, but Shpotov has found an interesting document in the Soviet archives that gives some indication of displeasure at a higher level. Dated December 27, 1930, it is a memo from G. I. Gertsenberg, a VATO agent, expressing anger at the Austin men for having caused "alarm and noise about packages with Christmas tree decorations." It goes on to assert that the Austin people were "insolent and irresponsible," that their complaints were "mostly false," and that they behaved as if they were living on "conquered land."[69] A more trenchant critique of the Austin Company is contained in a memo assessing VATO's dealings with Ford, Austin, and Brandt. Noting that Austin was "a firm of the contractor type that never had undertaken planning of a serious structure before," it gave poor marks for its designs of building interiors and to its engineers for their unwillingness to calculate precisely the quantity of materials used and how they could be economized.[70] Hardly could work cultures clash more.

Gertsenberg's memo mentions only one Austin man by name—neither Allan Austin nor Harry Miter, but rather D. H. Kempler. Nearly half a century later, David Kempler could recall the minute he set foot in Russia. "The air changes," he told an interviewer in 1976. "It is typically Russian...definitely an odor of change caused by unwashed bodies, excrement. There's no sanitation whatsoever." Still seething about "the most exasperating people in the world," he added, "after all, they were Communists." "Do you know how they got manpower?" he continued. "They would go into a village and take the whole damn village and bring them down to the job sites and say, hey, you are working here. This is your job....Some of them died like flies. But nobody cared. It was their life. It was expendable."[71]

Foreign workers who from various parts of the world and for various reasons wound up helping to build the auto factory had different experiences. A hardy band of mostly Finnish Americans from Hoboken, New Jersey (where Dybets had worked on the docks) were so thrilled with socialist competition as a form of worker cooperation and so appalled by the "bourgeoisie's" claim that it amounted to forced labor that many requested permission to remain in the USSR, their new "proletarian homeland." To be sure, by 1932–33 millions of people were dying "like flies" elsewhere in the Soviet Union—mostly in Ukraine as a result of the collectivization-induced famine—but by this time the Austin people had returned home along with dozens of others who had come from abroad to help build the new factory and the new city.[72] Several hundred foreign engineers and skilled workers, of whom about half were from the United States, took their places. They included the Reuther brothers, Walter and Victor. Although Walter had worked in the River Rouge tool room until October 1932, he was not among the thirty skilled workers whom Ford sent to Gor'kii in partial fulfillment of the company's contractual obligations with the Soviet authorities. Rather, like many others with industrial skills and socialist sympathies, he went on his own initiative because he was curious about the USSR and felt he could be useful. He and Victor arrived in December 1933 and took up work in the not-quite-yet-completed tool-and-die shop, where, for the next twenty-two months, they instructed workers in die molding.[73]

The Gor'kii adventure of the Reuthers seems to have been typical of foreign workers' experiences in the USSR during the first half of the 1930s.[74] Like most, they lived a somewhat privileged existence, being housed in the American Village (officially known as the Ruthenberg Commune after one of the founders of the CPUSA, Charles Ruthenberg) and having special access to scarce goods. They also, like "almost all foreign workers [who were almost all male] lived with Russian women." Of the two it was Walter who formed the stronger attachment, living for "five happy months" in the American Village with a local woman identified by Victor as "Lucy." Like many, the Reuthers initially were shocked at the prevailing poverty, the shortages of just about everything, but especially of shoes, meat, and fresh vegetables, and the poor quality of clothing and housing, too. As for the work, they chafed—not uncommonly—at the lack of safety precautions, the extensive use of piece-rate payment and "speed-ups," the patently nonvoluntary nature of the *subbotniki,* and the general political repressiveness.[75]

The overwhelming majority of foreign workers who returned to their native countries reportedly were disillusioned with "Stalinism," "repudiating the equation 'socialism = Soviet Union.'" This may be, but it was not the case with the Reuthers, at least not immediately.[76] Earlier biographers claimed somehow to know that on leaving the Soviet Union in 1935 Walter "had many private reservations about the benefits of the 'classless society' and the 'rule of the proletariat,'" and that the brothers "were not totally disillusioned." But Nelson Lichtenstein is on firmer ground in asserting that "the Reuther brothers, and especially Walter, returned to the United States as committed and vocal defenders of the Soviet Union to an extent quite extraordinary among foreign workers who came back to the West in the mid-1930s." That in his steady rise to leadership first of the United Auto Workers Union (UAW) and then the Congress of Industrial Organizations (CIO), Walter became increasingly, indeed "obsessively," anti-Communist is not in dispute. But the claim that his observations and experiences while wearing the white apron of a skilled technician at GAZ put him on this path is simply not credible.[77]

Ups and Downs

During the eighteen months the Reuthers worked at GAZ they witnessed not a few triumphs. Victor claimed that the factory made "phenomenal progress" in turning out dies. He also noted the increase in Model A production from the "pitifully small" number when he had arrived to an average daily output of 130 during 1934. In March of that year both Dybets and Diakonov, as well as the factory's party secretary and its technical director, chief engineer, and other GAZ notables received the Order of Lenin from the Central Executive Committee of the Soviet government. And, even as GAZ celebrated the production of its one-hundred-thousandth vehicle in April 1935, its engineers were working on prototypes of a new five-seated passenger car, the M-1.[78]

Машину ГАЗ „приспосабливают" к местным условиям.   Карикатура бригады художников МОССХ на автозаводе

Delegates at a conference of GAZ users note the necessity of "reconstructing" the cars as a result of careless assembly and shortage of parts. Caption reads "A GAZ auto 'adapts' to local conditions." *Za rulëm*, no. 2 (1934).

Popularly known as Emka, or even more affectionately, "Emochka," the GAZ M-1 had an enclosed body derived from the 1933 Ford V8 Model 40. GAZ's engineers strengthened the suspension system on account of the rougher roads—or no roads at all—the car was likely to encounter, and disc wheels with larger tires replaced spokes. But the most significant alteration was beneath the hood. According to one aficionado's website, "The team of GAZ designers and engineers, headed by the talented specialist and manager A. A. Lipgart...completely refused to copy the American example....Thus, instead of a V-8 from the American analogue, a 4-cylinder engine, already then in production, was significantly modified and boosted from 40 h.p. to 50 h.p." This assertion of Soviet technical innovativeness echoes GAZ's official history, which lauds the team's "creativity" and "energy" and singles out the engineer A. V. Pshenisnov as a "magician of motors." It does not, however, match what other sources have to say. When asked in January 1935 how the car would differ from Ford's latest model, the chief engineer, A. S. Ivanov, responded that "almost everything except the body and motor is changed." According to a post-Soviet assessment, the engineers, not wanting "to venture into complicated production," undertook "a small modernization" of the four-cylinder engine, raising its capacity by 10 horsepower. According to another, "GAZ unfortunately was not able to master the V-8 engine" and thus copied the Ford BB flatbed truck engine.[79]

The "surprisingly unpretentious" sedan that ran on the lowest octane gas— even kerosene would do, it was said—won plaudits for Lipgart and his team of engineers, though not before "Sergo" (Orzhonikidze) "captiously examined" one of the prototypes and complained that its external finish was of poor quality. The first M-1s emerged from the assembly line in March 1936 to great acclaim. Their production, after all, depended on the installation of new equipment—indeed a second assembly line—without the help of foreign specialists. "Not justified," crowed GAZ's official history, "were the overseas oracles according to whom the Soviet people would learn to make a car only after 25 to 30 years." The vehicle did suffer from a few "infantile diseases" such as a shimmy at high speeds, which was all the more disconcerting because of the unreliability of brake cables. But it underwent frequent modification—an experimental model from 1938 sported a six-cylinder engine that subsequently powered the GAZ-11 and many other vehicles—and the Emka continued to be turned out for another five years. GAZ produced 62,888 in all, of which 27,000 (42%) appeared in 1938. The army was the main customer. By the outbreak of the war, it possessed some 10,500, and until Ford GPs and Willys MAs and MBs arrived courtesy of the Lend-Lease Act, the M-1 served as the main vehicle of staff officers.[80] Its less happy associations are discussed in a later chapter.

Soviet technological nationalism reached its apogee with the Stakhanovite movement of the mid-1930s. Here, at last, was a means to assert productivity breakthroughs ("only in the land of socialism"); exert pressure on both managers and workers elsewhere to apply the new methods of production (and correspondingly raise quotas); and give the party, the trade unions, and other "transmission belts" something around which to campaign. No sooner had word spread of Aleksei Stakhanov's feat of mining more than one hundred tons of coal in a single shift than analogues began popping up in other industries. None, except Stakhanov, received as much official adulation as GAZ's own Aleksandr Kh. Busygin. In fact, autoworkers who consistently overfulfilled their quotas were more often known as Busyginites than Stakhanovites. Born "deep in the forests" of the Nizhegorod region in 1907, Busygin had arrived at Avtostroi in 1930, semiliterate at best. Like so many others recruited to help build the factory, he stayed on afterward, graduating from greaser to steam hammer operator and eventually brigade leader. By mid-September 1935, thanks to the extraordinary preparations of the blacksmith shop's personnel, his brigade was chalking up over a thousand crank shafts per shift, or several hundred more than its quota, and that sufficed to catapult him to fame.[81]

Soon Stepan Faustov, Fedor Velikzhanin, and others were competing against—and outperforming—Busygin's shift, and the "movement" spread to other jobs and shops. Komsomol member Alla Generalova and her fellow shift-worker Anastasiia Striukova outdid each other producing pistons—first 3,800, then 3,990, then 5,000 in a single shift, and who knew where it would end? On December 5, 1935, less than three months into the "highest stage of socialist competition," the recorded number of Busyginites stood at 3,605. Thanks to Busygin and his imitators, a year-end report on the factory noted that "the old technical norms were superseded and left far behind."[82]

Party leaders approved and did everything to encourage the expansion of this bacchanalia of record breaking and rate busting because, by their lights, every blow of the hammer was a blow for socialism—or at least it kept workers out of trouble. The reasons for workers' participation are less obvious. Coercion or the threat thereof cannot be ruled out, though except in cases of overt resistance or attempts to sabotage the movement, coercion was more likely to be in the form of assignment to poorly paid tasks or mandatory overtime than criminal prosecution. As industrial sociologists pointed out a long time ago with respect to rate-busting behavior in North America, the ludic dimension of shop floor competition should not be overlooked. But it is hard to avoid the conclusion that many Busyginites—like their counterparts elsewhere in the country—initially viewed the movement as an opportunity to ensure themselves of supplies, get ahead, and even make a name for themselves. In short, these workers internalized the Soviet formula for respect and success.

And why not? Arriving home a few days after his record stint, Busygin found a "small present" from GAZ's assistant director: a box of apples, three kilos of meat, ten kilos of flour, and packages of butter, sausage, cured sturgeon, pirogi, and chocolates. Accompanying the present was a letter addressed to Mrs. Busygin asking her "to care for your husband so that he has sufficient rest to repeat his shock work every day." The good woman promised to do just that, evidently not minding the intrusion. Like many Stakhanovite notables (*znatnye liudi*), Busygin and his family received a new apartment from his employer. Soiuzkino devoted a newsreel episode to the "housewarming" (*novosel'e*) to which, it claimed, the "entire community of the Molotov Automobile Factory" gave "special attention." He received an M-1 automobile too. He may have been unique, though, in having an entire block (in Socialist City) named after him. By the end of 1937, eight hundred Stakhanovite families resided there. Generalova quite possibly was among the beneficiaries. She relates in her little autobiography, written "above all for women to tell them about how I found the path to happiness," that after she had become a Stakhanovite, director Diakonov bestowed on her a bicycle, a phonograph, and a furnished apartment. GAZ's provision of the apartments was evidently part of a standard policy in the automotive and tractor industries where, according to the Soviet historian V. A. Sakharov, "Stakhkanovites were given first preference in the allocation of living space."[83]

In November 1935, Busygin was whisked off to Moscow to meet the great leaders and participate in an all-Union "conference" of Stakhanovites. Then it was back to Nizhni. But not back to the smithy, for Busygin had become too famous to be wasted on his former job. Nominally an instructor in his technique, he spent at least as much time traveling to ceremonial events such as Maxim Gor'kii's funeral and, in the important capacity of expediter (*tolkach*), seeking supplies of steel for GAZ. He also was utilized by higher authorities in their never-ending search for unutilized capacity. At Ordzhonikidze's prompting, he turned up in June 1936 at a session of the Commissariat of Heavy Industry's council to report on the "sad" condition of machinery at GAZ and problems with shop-floor organization. Few managers would have appreciated this kind of attention. GAZ's representative at the meeting, Boris Sokolinskii, did his best to explain that "if previously we were able to repair equipment once every six months, now...our punches don't last a single shift." The Stakhanovite speedup, in other words, was placing an unbearable burden on machines and the repair shops.[84]

Ordzhonikidze was a demanding but also understanding taskmaster. Thanking Busygin and his fellow Stakhanovite Faustov for coming forward, he cited the extenuating circumstances of both GAZ and ZIS undergoing reconstruction ("even Ford stops the factory when a new model is being prepared"). He also took the occasion to strongly reject the inference that problems with the application of Stakhanovite methods were due to sabotage by engineering-technical personnel: "Some saboteurs! They are not saboteurs, but good people—our sons, our brothers, our comrades who are entirely and completely for Soviet power."[85] But trouble was brewing from other quarters. In October, Lazar Kaganovich was informing "the Boss" about a meeting of the Politburo at which members quizzed GAZ's director, Diakonov, about complications in the production of the M-1. "It turned out," he wrote to Stalin on October 12, "that a number of important parts are indeed different from Ford parts: the wheels, the steering wheel, springs, shock absorbers, the frame, the air filter, and others." Diakonov assured the party bigwigs that all could be accommodated within the design of the vehicle, but they wanted an independent technical analysis from the Commissariat of Heavy Industry. Not only was production behind schedule but defective parts, including engines, clutches, transmissions, and rear-axle assemblies, were getting into the assembly line, resulting in "a number of accidents" in Moscow. "We gave Diakonov a tough talking-to," Kaganovich reassured Stalin, and the regional party boss, Eduard Pramnek, also received "harsh criticism" for deflecting the blame to supplier plants. More interference from the Politburo followed early in 1937.[86]

Unfortunately for those held responsible, these problems were occurring just as momentum gathered for the Great Purge. In February 1937, Ordzhonikidze died, and all those sons, brothers, and comrades lost their chief patron and protector. The hand of the NKVD fell heavily on technical-engineering personnel in general, and GAZ was not spared. Gone by the end of 1937 were the chief engineer, Ivanov; the head of production, Slutskii; the supervisor of the tool-and-die shop (the Reuther brothers' boss), Bondarchuk; the head of the wheel shop; the assistant director for supplies; the chief electrical engineer; the head of the machine shop; the head of administration for contiguous production; the head of the nonferrous foundry; the head of the planning department, and others. Boris Sokolinskii, who had created the conditions for Busygin to set his record only to be called on the carpet for failing to keep up with the destruction of punches by GAZ's leading Stakhanovite, figured among those "others."[87]

Through it all, Diakonov continued to serve as director, defending GAZ and the reputation of its new product. The reason, he insisted in *Pravda,* that the paint job on so many M-1s had faded was not the factory's fault but rather that of Moscow's garages, where sandpaper, soda water solution, and other "alchemic" methods were employed to clean the cars. To the extent problems with the model persisted—two-thirds of the windshield wipers and speedometers that had been installed ceased to function after as little as five thousand kilometers—the suppliers were to blame. Diakonov remained at large until early 1938 when he received a sentence of ten years' confinement without the right of correspondence for his role in a "right-Trotskyist organization." Party people fared little better. The NKVD came for A. S. Zashibaev, the party committee secretary; his assistant, Osipov; the district committee (*raikom*) secretary, Ashin; and the leader of the Komsomol, V. Sorokin. Among the dreamers, Agapov was not arrested; he continued writing about the wonders of technology and the poetry of science well into the 1960s. Osinskii was not so fortunate. He and his twenty-five-year-old son, Dima (a designer and engineer who worked for the Commissariat of Defense Industries), were arrested on October 13, 1937. At the time, Osinskii was serving as director of the Academy of Science's Institute of the History of Science and Technology. He languished in prison for nearly a year but was executed on September 1, 1938, in his fifty-first year.[88]

Was there any logic or pattern to the arrests at GAZ? Many of the arrested engineers were Jews, and of some three hundred Communists at the plant who were arrested, "not less than forty" were Jewish, but how do these figures compare to the general population of engineers and Communists at GAZ? A high proportion of those who had spent time in the United States either as emigrants before the revolution or as students in Dearborn were arrested. When Sergei Diakonov's son was asked whether his father's friendships with foreigners—including Ford—had incriminated him, he replied, "Yes. Without question." Later he added that "since he was accused of spying for foreign governments, his . . . open relationship with the American workers, with the German workers, with the Finnish workers, probably served to incriminate him." He also noted, perhaps not without a touch of irony, that Diakonov was picked up in an Emochka and taken away.[89]

The people who interviewed Diakonov's son were primarily interested in hearing about "Yanks" and whether their relatively privileged living conditions provoked anti-American resentment. But popular anti-Americanism did not cause the Great Purge any more than anti-Semitism did. What is consistent throughout the now vast literature on this, the darkest episode of Soviet history, is the official xenophobia—the fear of foreigners and those who had had contact with them. So much the worse for the foreigners who remained in the country to become Soviet citizens, like Sam Herman and his children, including Victor (who didn't "escape" until decades later in 1974), and the hapless Schutzbündler, the group that had fled Austria after the failure of their uprising in 1934 and were recruited by GAZ. They actually started disappearing in 1935, before the Great Purge began.[90]

"Russia in the 1930s was a deep bog," writes Andrea Graziosi, "and nearly all the foreign workers who stayed there after 1933–34 disappeared in it." By this measure, the Reuthers were fortunate to leave when they did. So was John Scott, who left in 1938 with his Russian wife, Masha, although not before informing a U.S. Embassy official inter alia of the sorry fate of Finnish, Polish (Jewish), German, and Bulgarian refugees.[91] By the late 1930s, even foreign visitors were something of a rarity. Among them were the Austin Company's George Bryant and Harry Miter, who visited GAZ in August 1939. Two days before the Nazis invaded Poland, Miter wrote to Phil Davis and his wife (who had been part of the Austin contingent) that they had "just returned from Autogorod Workers City [aka Socialist City] and were dumb founded" to discover that "it had been tremendously increased" to 120,000 people, that is, twice the number originally intended. Most of the apartments built since their departure were taller—six to eight stories. Miter also commented that the streets were paved, flowers were in profusion, and the people looked better.[92]

Unfortunately, this is all he reported. Other sources testify to material and aesthetic-cultural improvement in striking contrast to the prevailing image we have of this period, which is of victimization and dread. We learn from a post-Soviet architectural review of Nizhni Novgorod that among the newer apartments mentioned by Miter was a seven-story concave building designed by the workshop of the Vesnin brothers, the Soviet Union's leading construc- tivist architects. Completed in 1937, the building sported "light, elegant col- onnades" supporting an overhanging cornice. It faced Prospect Zhdanova (since renamed Molodëzhnyi Prospect), just up the street from the "Mir" cinema, built in 1934. Not far away on Prospect October stood a handsome department store (1936–38) with rounded façade and a massive complex of residential buildings containing three- and four-room apartments. Being quite capacious, the rooms could fit an entire family into each of them.[93]

What Miter and Bryant thought about the factory, or even whether they received a tour of inspection, is unknown. GAZ too, having undergone ex- pansion, was almost unrecognizable. Aside from an enlarged woodworking shop and die-casting, machine-assembly, and smithy buildings, the factory encompassed by 1939 a new wheel assembly division that served not only GAZ but other auto factories as well. The tool-and-die shop occupied an enormous amount of space and contained nearly twenty-five hundred sepa- rate pieces of equipment. Even larger was the body shop, reputed to be the largest building "not only at Avtozavod but in Europe." The whole ensemble constituted an enterprise-city with a workforce of over forty thousand and an output of 140,000 vehicles in 1938. In addition to the M-1 and its stan- dard line of trucks, the factory was producing cars, pickups, and trucks that converted hard fuel to gas (*gazogeneratory*), a three-axle variant of the AA, an all-terrain vehicle with Caterpillar wheels (GAZ-60), and a dump truck (GAZ-410). The nearby plant where the Model AA was first assembled in 1930 (from 1939, the independent Gor'kii Bus Factory) produced buses, and GAZ opened a truck assembly facility in Rostov-on-Don. It also issued quite a few experimental off-road vehicles with military application such as the GAZ-11 and GAZ-61. The latter, a product of the legendary designer Vitaly A. Grachev, would serve during the war as an alternative to the M-1 in trans- porting commanding officers. It had four-wheel drive, a 76-hp motor, and a weight distribution that enabled it to climb hills up to an angle of 38 degrees. A famous photograph shows a GAZ-61 convertible climbing the steps of the recently built River Station (Rechnoi Vokzal) just beyond Moscow's north- western boundary.[94]

In the last years before the war, GAZ's production profile shifted. Accord- ing to the enterprise's annual report for 1940, vehicles made up 76 percent by value of all goods produced in 1937 but only 50 percent in 1940. Mean- while, the share of auto parts increased from 14 percent to nearly 33 percent, and that of other goods including such items as bed frames, children's tobog- gans, and toy trucks rose from 2 to 11 percent. In monetary terms, vehicles produced in 1939 were valued at R 709 million as compared to only 475 million in 1940.[95] It is now clear that the decline in vehicle production re- sulted from a diversion of steel and other strategically significant items from civilian to military commissariats and thence to their respective enterprises. Lacking the necessary ingredients, "GAZ was forced to retrogress from mass flow production to low-volume production, incurring large losses." It also was forced to cut its workforce from some forty-four thousand at the beginning of 1940 to thirty-five thousand by year's end.[96]

GAZ, of course, was not alone. The output of motor vehicles throughout the country declined from 211,000 in 1938 to 145,000 in 1940. The steel diverted from car and truck production was going into the making of tanks—230 of which were being produced every month in 1940—and other armored fighting vehicles. But, of course, the Red Army needed cars and trucks too. Between June 22, 1941, when the Axis powers invaded Soviet territory, and the end of the World War in August 1945, roughly three of every four vehicles produced in the Soviet Union—or 184,000 of a total of 245,000—went to the Red Army. GAZ accounted for more than one hundred thousand vehicles, including MM and AAA trucks, Caterpillar half-tracks, ambulances, staff cars, jeeps, and armored cars, many of which were designed by GAZ engineers working under Grachev. The factory also supplied about twelve thousand T-60 scout tanks and T-70 light tanks, nine thousand self-propelled guns, and tens of thousands of mortars and shells for the Katyusha rocket launcher.[97] As throughout the country, it was mainly women who produced these instruments of war at GAZ. Having made up close to 40 percent of the enterprise's workforce before the war, women were in the majority by the end of 1941 and remained so at least through the duration of the war.

Of the vehicles GAZ produced during the war, the GAZ-67 jeep stood out as the real workhorse. Russia's premier auto historian, Lev Shugurov, notes that its payload capacity of 800 to 1,000 kg was 18 percent greater when operating in the lowest gear than the "well-known American jeeps of that time, the Willys MB and Ford GPB." These foreign models also exhibited less lateral stability because of their narrower wheel base. Shugurov praises the GAZ-67's "simple" engine for being able to run on any kind of gas and, at an octane level of 66, consuming a modest 18 liters per 100 km.[98] At least one web-based source contends otherwise. "There is universal agreement," it claims, "that the GAZ-67 was harder to maintain and less reliable than the American jeeps made available for sale to the Russians under Lend Lease....Many things on the GAZ were lacking. The brakes were weak and hard to repair. The fuel consumption was very high, and in hard conditions the GAZ could consume a half liter of fuel per km."[99] That is 50, not 18, liters per 100 km.

Beginning in November 1941 workers at GAZ assembled Dodge, Chevrolet, and Studebaker trucks that arrived in kits on railroad flatcars.[100] In this manner, Detroit (or South Bend) and Nizhni Novgorod were linked in one more-or-less continuous process of production, transportation, and assembly. Assembly activity continued until November 1944 when Soviet military authorities transferred personnel and equipment to the Daimler-Benz plant in Minsk (the future Minsk Automobile Factory, MAZ) that the Nazis had set up after occupying that city and that the Red Army had recaptured. This facility's appropriation scarcely compensated for the destruction the

Luftwaffe had wrought. On the night of June 4, 1943, and for nearly every night throughout the rest of the month and into July, GAZ was subjected to aerial bombardment. Over fifty buildings reportedly sustained damage, some beyond repair. Quite a few people were killed including the head of the smithy, some Stakhanovite notables, and antiaircraft crews stationed on the roofs of several buildings. But unlike ZIS, GAZ held its ground. "What the fascists destroyed at night, people rebuilt during daytime," the official history noted. Assembly of Lend-Lease trucks went on in the open air. Komsomol brigades, experienced workers, party agitators—all into the breach! The heroes finished restoring the factory before the end of October 1943, one hundred days after the beginning of the bombing.[101]

The Glory Years: First Phase

"The victory is slight, but let it be 'Victory.'" Thus did Stalin legendarily reply to GAZ's director, Ivan K. Loskutov, when asked whether the passenger car shown to him in the Kremlin could be called "Pobeda." The date was June 19, 1945, and the Allied victory in Europe was little more than a month old. The car, officially designated GAZ M-20, was a bit older, having been conceived in 1943 in the aftermath of victory at Stalingrad. GAZ had an experimental version ready by November 1944, but engineers debated whether to equip it with a six- or four-cylinder engine. Evidently, the issue remained unresolved by the time of the official inspection by the exalted

The fruits of victory: Moskvich and Pobeda, Moscow (2006). Author's photograph.

inhabitants of the Kremlin. Stalin allegedly expressed some concern about the fuel consumption of the six-cylinder version, especially as supplies of fuel were not likely to be plentiful for some time. Lipgart's assurance that a four-cylinder variant would be quite adequate somewhat mollified him. At this point, Loskutov broached the question of the vehicle's name. So, Pobeda it was, a victory memorialized in a *Krokodil* cartoon ("War and Peace") in which an engineer, holding a drawing of the car is asked by another, "Why do you have two medals?" and replies, "One 'For Victory over Germany' and the other for this 'Victory'."[102]

Such inspections had become something of a state ritual, and the summer of 1945 provided many: various ZISes, the Moskvich, Iaroslavl' factory's diesel truck, GAZ trucks, and the Pobeda all received their "start in life" (*putevka v zhizn'*) at the Kremlin. Symbolically, they reinforced Stalin's paternal authority. "Comrade Stalin daily follows the development of our automobile industry and technology," readers of a popular history of cars and trucks were assured. "He assists builders with his instructions on the location of new factories, types of vehicles...their design, external appearance, cost of production, and use." The industry's workers "always felt" Stalin's "constant concern and directing role," according to Sergei Akopov, who presided over the industry first as commissar of medium machine construction from 1941 to 1945 and then as minister of automobile production.[103]

The first mass-produced car of the postwar era, the Pobeda, represented a radical design departure from previous models. Its most characteristic feature, the swooping "streamlined" shape of its frameless body, gave it an extremely low drag coefficient of 0.34. The basic design, bearing some similarities to the prewar Opel Captain, would reappear on such disparate autos as the first Kaisers (1946) produced in Willow Run, Michigan, Czechoslovakia's Tatra 600 (1947), and the British Standard Vanguard (1948). Citing these other vehicles, Soviet—and post-Soviet—commentators argued in effect that despite having Stalin looking over their shoulders, Soviet designers were very much part of an international trend, if not setting it. Pride in the achievement was considerable. The Pobeda has retained the special affection of those of a certain age, however, for another reason: it was the first Soviet car that individuals could purchase, if only in principle.[104]

This car, too, unfortunately had its problems. Owing to the discovery of systematic defects in the clutch, muffler, and brake mechanisms, production ceased in October 1948. Loskutov paid for the problems with his job, but Lipgart escaped sanctions and quickly set about rectifying the defects. Production resumed in February 1949, and the few additional changes that GAZ made, such as mounting the gearbox lever on the steering wheel and altering the front grill, the upholstery, and a few other parts, went off without a hitch. The third series of the Pobeda, the GAZ-20V, emerged in 1955. In twelve and a half years, GAZ produced just under 236,000 Pobedas of which 78 percent were sedans, 14 percent were taxis, and the remainder were convertibles. Built to withstand the roughest of conditions, the car was exported to other

Soviet-bloc countries (including China) and to Finland, where one could see them on the streets of Helsinki as late as the 1970s.[105]

The teething problems of the Pobeda behind it, GAZ enjoyed a decadelong string of successes in truck and car design and production that in retrospect made up its glory years. During this period, GAZ continued to do what it did best—keep pace with the state's growing demand for vehicles that managed to appear both distinctively Soviet and up-to-date. What this meant has been summed up in the following terms:

> The first generation of postwar GAZ cars and trucks is distinguishable by the rationality and technological logic of their construction and the balance struck between unity and variety of components and features. The successful resolution of these forms created the recognizable look [oblik] and formed the characteristics of the "GAZ" style that endured throughout subsequent generations of GAZ automobiles: compactness and lightness, simplicity and clarity of logically and functionally worked-out sizes, with a minimally necessary degree of decorative trim.[106]

Aside from the Pobeda, the first postwar generation included the GAZ-51 truck, the most durable of all GAZ's heavy vehicles, and the one luxury car manufactured in Nizhni Novgorod/Gor'kii, the GAZ-M12 (otherwise known as ZIM, the Molotov Automobile Factory). Both these vehicles ran on the same six-cylinder 3.5-liter engine that Lipgart's team had developed for the Pobeda but rejected in favor of the four-cylinder alternative. In the case of ZIM, the factory's engineers modified the intake valve, installed a dual carburetor, and increased the compression ratio to 6.7:1 to raise the horsepower from 70 to 95 and enable it to run smoothly on 70 octane gas. The level of fuel consumption, 18–19 liters per 100 km, was quite respectable for a car weighing nearly 2,000 kg, although the rate of acceleration—thirty-seven seconds to 100 km—compared unfavorably to the twenty-eight seconds for the ZIS-110. The car also featured a frameless body with extremely tight inner seals, a hydro-clutch mechanism, and a curved rear window (all firsts on a Soviet car), as well as interior velour panels and an insignia that bore the image of the antlered deer, the emblem of Nizhni Novgorod since Catherine the Great approved it in 1781.[107]

The car passed the all-important Kremlin inspection on February 15, 1950. Was this when Stalin apocryphally asked why Lipgart had not been punished (presumably for the Pobeda's initial problems), or was it a year earlier when the Pobeda's improved version was presented to him? The sources are inconsistent about this. Whether true or not, the story underscores the precariousness of working in a high-profile position in a high-profile industry. Like writers, car design engineers seemed to have special access to the human soul, or at least their vulnerability to repression implies that Stalin feared they did. Despite having several times received the Order of Lenin and the Stalin Prize, Lipgart could not avoid punishment. In December 1951 he was demoted at GAZ and several months later was sent to the Urals ZIS plant in Miass where he languished as a ordinary engineer until after Stalin's death. Transferred to NAMI in 1953, he spent the rest of his career as its assistant director, retiring in 1969.[108]

The ZIM entered into serial production in October 1950 and remained in GAZ's repertoire for the next ten years. In all, the factory turned out 21,527 units. The car chauffeured mid- and upper-echelon government and party officials who ranked just below the ZIS-driven nomenklatura. It also saw service as a taxi, the cost of which was pegged at one-and-a-half times the rate charged for Pobedas. One wonders how many boys pestered their parents (as Mikhail German had in the 1930s) to pass up Pobedas so that they could glory in the fleeting luxury of a ZIM.

GAZ's glory years coincided almost exactly with the "golden era" of the American automobile industry. "Cars," as Ruth Brandon recently noted, "are one of the two great symbols of the post-war United States—the other, of course, being rock n' roll.... For post-war America, and for all those non-American millions whose imaginations Hollywood formed, the car was desire on wheels." How did cars come to fulfill this role? For one thing, they had become more accessible. Thanks to the long postwar boom, purchasing a car came within range of not only middle-class families but working-class ones as well; not only for dads to drive to work, polish, and tinker with on weekends, but for their teenaged sons to cruise, make out in, drag race, and detail. The banner year of the decade was 1955. In that year, sales of new cars exceeded nine million. Not only accessibility but style made cars desirable. "The stodgy car died in 1955," John Jerome wrote years later:

> All our clinging Calvinist sensibilities of practicality, economy, simplicity, all the cramped guidelines of American Gothic, were junked. We wanted more. We got it: bigger engines, more "zestful" performance, more options, chrome, jazz, sex.... We were building automobiles for the new American voluptuaries. The single central goal was the appearance of luxury, even in the "small" "economy" models.

Every year, Detroit created wonder and excitement. "I was awestruck," recalled Robert Szudarek, a Detroiter, "thinking there would never be a car again that would be better than what I was seeing. The magnificent chrome trim, spinner, hub-caps, two-tone paint, even three-tone paint. Then I would see next year's offering and start all over again thinking this would be the ultimate."[109]

Detroit's magic did not go unnoticed in the Soviet Union. In 1956, the journal of the Ministry of Automobile Production published an article by Konstantin Sharapov, then working at the Academy of Science's Engine Institute, on that year's American cars. The article, replete with graphs, charts, and photographs, evaluated the performance of new engine designs, commented on the new elongated spark plugs, referred to new gadgets such as

Chrysler's record player offering forty-five minutes of uninterrupted music on seven-inch disks, and surveyed experimental cars such as Buick's Centurion, Oldsmobile's Golden Rocket, and Chevrolet's Impala sports sedan. It noted that a major change had occurred in 1953–54—"the substitution of high quality, six- and eight-cylinder straight-line engines by V-shaped engines with overhead camshafts and sharply increased power." The conclusion read in part: "The extreme increase in power of engines and speed of movement connected with the lengthening of the body and decrease in height of the car...severely limits the possibility of using American cars in countries where the extent of good roads and the density of traffic is not so great as in the USA."[110]

Another article noted the same trends, contrasting them unfavorably with the European emphasis on "rationality." "The bodies of American cars are uneconomical," it flatly stated. "Their large overhang on the front and rear axles, the length of the frame, the trunk and rear fins mean that the space occupied by passengers represents only a small part of the total area."[111] Such comments were indicative of the conventional wisdom among automotive engineers when GAZ introduced its signature automobile, the Volga (GAZ-21), in October 1956. Although it could not be acknowledged at the time, the Volga managed to adhere to European standards while simultaneously gesturing

1961 Volga, Moscow (2006). Author's photograph.

toward American styling. The "panoramic windows were typical fifties," remarks one foreign enthusiast. "For American standards the Volga was a small car, only 4 meters and 83 centimeters long. For European standards the Volga was a large car, placed in the upper middle class."[112] It also represented a compromise of another sort: it had to provide a smooth ride on the slowly increasing number of asphalted highways and be sufficiently rugged to traverse the pitches and rolls of the country's still prevalent unimproved roads. This may have been what Lipgart meant when he told a conference of automobile designers and engineers a month before the Volga appeared, "We need autos that are not American and not European but are our own, Soviet, type."[113]

The GAZ-21 went through three series, the third of which coincided with the production of the GAZ-22 station wagon. Early models included such innovative but hard-to-service features as an automatic gearbox and a central lubrication system attached to the front-wheel suspension that tended to distribute oil unevenly and often excessively. Exhibited at the Brussels Expo '58, which awarded it a grand prix, the car was exported to both the Benelux countries and within the Soviet bloc. It also became the principal Soviet entry on the international rally circuit, earning its reputation for ruggedness at least in part for its performance in Finland's Thousand Lakes Rally, Greece's Acropolis Rally, the "For Peace and Friendship" tours through the Soviet Union and Eastern Europe, and others. But its greatest presence was felt on the streets of Moscow and other Soviet cities where it served as the workhorse of urban taxi fleets and as the car in which officialdom drove or was driven to and from work. It is hard to picture Soviet towns in the 1960s without these vehicles gathered outside regional party headquarters and other important buildings. In all, some 640,000 were produced. They were not only the "basic passenger car of the Seven-Year Plan" (1959–65) but truly "symbols of an entire age."[114]

That age coincided with the directorship of Ivan I. Kiselev. As rugged-looking as the cars and trucks that bore his factory's name, Kiselev served as director of GAZ from 1958 to 1983, longer than any other in the Soviet car industry. Indeed, he was the first GAZ director since Ivan Loskutov to last more than two years in that position, the intervening five occupants having left to assume other posts. Kiselev's biography reads like a Soviet success story. Born in 1917 in Kostroma Province, he came to GAZ at twenty and worked himself up from technician to assistant head of the cutting tools shop and then of the motor section. In 1954 he became assistant chief engineer, then chief engineer, and in 1958 director. He had impressive party credentials. He joined the party during the war, and thanks to his position at GAZ served successively on the Avtozavod district committee (*raikom*), Gor'kii regional committee (*obkom*) and central committee. He was a delegate to six successive party congresses beginning with the twenty-first in 1959.[115]

In 1958, when Kiselev took over, GAZ had a workforce of slightly more than seventy-five thousand. Successful Soviet enterprises grew in people as well as in resources and facilities, and that is what happened in subsequent years. By 1965 the workforce numbered 83,350.[116] In the course of the 1960s, GAZ remodeled several shops and built others, including an experimental design department, from scratch. In 1960 GAZ employed the world's first—so the enterprise's official history claims—machine for friction welding steering columns to axles. Kiselev also presided over the introduction of the Chaika, GAZ's answer to the succession of ZIS-ZIL limousines. Inspired (like the ZIL-111) by the Packard Caribbean, the Chaika may have been the most exuberant of Soviet vehicles produced during the glory years. At 5.6 meters long and weighing 2,100 kg, it also was one of the biggest. Its engineers may have been critical of the American penchant for capacious engines and lots of gimmicks, but they did not begrudge the Chaika's 5.5-liter, four-barrel carbureted 195-hp engine that was capable of getting the big bird up to a top speed of 160 km/h; nor did they deny it push-button automatic transmission.

GAZ made a gift of the first Chaikas to the Communist Party in honor of its Twenty-First Congress. They stayed in production until 1978 (when they were replaced by the GAZ-14) for a total run of slightly over three thousand. Many served the diplomatic corps, heads of ministries and departments, and first-party secretaries of the Union republic branches. Khrushchev reputedly preferred Chaikas to the ZILs and made a gift of them to such Soviet luminaries as Mikhail Sholokhov, Yuri Gagarin, and the ballerina Galina Ulanova, as well as to Fidel Castro. Those retired from state service wound up working for Intourist and at wedding palaces where, as a talisman of fecundity, their front grills were festooned with dolls.[117]

Chaika, Moscow (2006). Author's photograph.

The Glory Years: Second Phase

One imagines not only engineers and managers at GAZ but assembly-line workers occasionally enjoying a spin in a Volga, perhaps on an outing along the river via taxi or rented car. It is even possible that they too celebrated weddings in the deluxe embrace of a Chaika. But as far as car ownership was concerned, the glory years were still in the future. During the postwar decades GAZ workers made do with public transportation—the trams, buses, and minibuses that coursed along the main thoroughfares of the Auto Factory District, once known as Socialist City.

Originally intended for fifty thousand people, the district was home to more than 130,000 by 1950 when postwar rubble clearance, necessitated by the Luftwaffe sorties of 1943, ended. Privileged factory employees were fortunate enough to occupy the new buildings along Kirov Prospect and Krasnodontsev Street that exhibited the grand neobaroque style characteristic of late Stalinism; others crowded into the "temporary" barracks that had been part of the residential landscape since the early 1930s; still others rented "corners" or lived in outlying settlements. In late 1955, frustrated over delays in the construction of an apartment building, the head of the factory's pressing shop and the chairman of the union's housing commission mobilized workers to erect the building themselves. This evidently was not the first time workers from GAZ had been assigned to residential housing construction; what was new was the guarantee of a single-family apartment for those who participated. Thus was born the people's construction (*narodnaia stroika*) movement, an interesting nodal point on the public-private axis.[118]

The movement quickly caught on in other shops of the enterprise. In each case, organizers selected workers for construction and apartments on the basis of either their outstanding performance on the job or family need (or a combination of both), they received their regular wage or at least a portion thereof while engaged in construction, and other workers in the section made up the difference by working above their quotas or overtime. Responsibility for locating building materials, financing, and allocating labor rested with councils for housing construction assistance that consisted of representatives from management, the union, the party, the Komsomol, and rank-and-file workers. Apparently with the support of the party Central Committee, the movement spread rapidly to other parts of the country. In June 1957, when the Gor'kii regional party committee hosted a conference devoted to it, representatives from forty-two territorial divisions (oblasts, krais, and autonomous republics) of the RSFSR attended.[119]

The following month, the Council of Ministers issued a decree ("On the Development of Housing Construction in the USSR") that took note of the "huge significance of the initiative by toilers of industrial enterprises in the city of Gor'kii to build apartments with their own means according to the 'method of people's construction.'" This and a subsequent decree of the RSFSR Council of Ministers that specifically addressed the "collective construction of multiapartment and one-apartment individual houses" enshrined the movement in law. Steven E. Harris conservatively estimates that people's construction produced some nine million square meters of housing space per year during the 1958–60 triennium, representing 10-13 percent of all new housing construction during those years.[120]

As far as Gor'kii was concerned, the people's construction method resulted in the erection in various parts of the city of buildings containing eight, ten, and twenty single-family apartments. GAZ's workers labored on a reported total of 376 two- and three-story buildings containing some six thousand apartments. Their greatest concentration was in the Forty Years of October, a settlement that arose on thirty-three hectares of previously undeveloped land in the Auto Factory District. Ironically, the campaign to build separate family apartments by those who would occupy them originated in what a quarter of a century earlier had been one of the prime sites for the great experiment in communal living. That experiment was inflicted on the autoworkers, most of them recent migrants from the countryside, by architects, town planners, and other visionaries who assumed that they knew better than the workers how the workers' lives should be organized. It foundered on an inadequacy of resources, the crush of people needed by the factory, and flaws in the design plan itself.

The volume of people's construction tailed off after 1960 because, so Harris argues, the state became increasingly intolerant of alternatives to its own agenda for factory-based production of prefabricated panel housing and construction of four- to five-story buildings. By this time, the Auto Factory District's population stood at 167,000. Although part of the city, the district for all intents and purposes represented suburbanization Soviet-style. The forest of apartment buildings that stretched back from the Oka for several kilometers symbolized a reduction of ambition compared to the boldness of social engineering crystallized in the Socialist City. Workers would live as families, and the families would live in apartments that they would not have to share with other families. American visitors such as Wyndham Mortimer commented on the immaculateness and comfort of the rooms but, oblivious to the alternative arrangements that had prevailed as recently as a decade earlier, took for granted that parents would be raising their children in their own apartments, and that toilets and bathrooms would not have to be shared with other families.[121]

In 1961, the year of Mortimer's visit, a new Palace of Culture opened its doors. It too represented a reduced vision. Unlike its predecessor from the 1930s, it did not aim to fulfill "all social, educational, recreational and gastronomic needs of the adult population." It did, however, contain a theater seating twelve hundred people, a cinema, dance hall, billiard room, planetarium, restaurant, café, and library. Later in the decade a hospital and swimming pool were added to the district whose population by 1970 was 247,000. But the way of life of the Auto Factory District's residents still differed radically from what prevailed in, say, Oakland and McComb counties whence many white autoworkers fled from Detroit. For one thing, they had very few autos.

In 1970, GAZ introduced its new Volga model (GAZ-24). With a slightly more powerful—although still four-cylinder—engine (ZMZ-402) that got it up to 100 km/h in twenty-three seconds, the new model was a little shorter and more boxy or "European" in its styling. Variants included a taxi, a station wagon, and an export version that came with a Peugeot diesel engine. The GAZ-24 provided the chassis for all subsequent models, ranging from the GAZ 24–10 that differed only in grillwork to the somewhat sleeker and more powerful GAZ-3102 that began production in 1982, to the limited-quantity luxury sedans introduced in the 1990s.

Not rocking the boat seemed to be the objective when it came to the GAZ-24, and in this respect the Volga could well serve as a metaphor for the Brezhnev era. For just as GAZ put out essentially the same austere *barzha* (barge) year after year, so functionaries who rode around in them functioned in an uninspired, mechanical way. With no fear of competition from abroad or within the USSR, GAZ had little incentive other than its engineers' own professional élan to try to make the car more appealing to a different "demographic." Engineers may have been so inclined, but they faced formidable obstacles within the auto-bureaucratic hierarchy, particularly after the mid-1980s when GAZ embarked on a major reconstruction of its truck production facilities in the interests of going diesel.

The overhaul was long overdue. The equivalent of the GAZ-24 in the truck world was the GAZ-53, introduced in 1961 as the main alternative to the ZIL-130. Equipped with a six-cylinder engine, the original version had a carrying capacity of 3.5 tons, was able to reach a maximum speed of 75 km/h—maybe a bit more going downhill—and contented itself with 72 octane gas of which it consumed on average 19.5 liters over 100 km. The modified version (GAZ-53A) sported a V8 engine, got up to 85 km/h, was guaranteed by the head of the assembly shop at GAZ to carry four tons on any kind of road surface, but expended a lot of fuel—24 liters—over 100 km.[122] Production of this model continued until 1992. Like the acrid-smelling smoke of certain brands of cigarettes (or better still, the low-grade unfiltered "papirosi"), the exhaust fumes of a GAZ-53 truck are inextricably connected with the USSR in its last decades.

That these cars and trucks survived on the assembly line for three decades may have had something to do with not wanting to disrupt delivery schedules, parts supplies, and other such arrangements. Or, it could have reflected a lack of incentives compared with what the military offered for new designs and modifications. Whatever the reason, creative car designing in the Soviet Union turned out to be a one-generation affair. Men (and they all were men) such as Grachev, Lipgart, Konstantin Sharapov, A. N. Ostrovtsev, and A. P. Zigel', born in the early years of the century, hitting their stride in the latter half of the 1930s, getting their second wind in the late 1940s and early 1950s, and ending their active careers by 1970, had opportunities that the next generation could only dream about.[123] At some imperceptible point, it seems, interest at the top in encouraging new designs withered, indifference became habit forming, and pretending became a way of life. One of the examples of such pretending is that in 1972, just north of the original Socialist City, a new block of apartments started to go up under the name Sotsgorod-II.

Exchanging Places?

In analyzing the sudden and unexpected cessation of Communist Party rule in East Germany and the consequential liquidation of the German Democratic Republic, Charles Maier notes that "modern authoritarian regimes had been governments based on projects.... Whatever the blueprint, they proposed an activist summons to some new physical or political construction." What seems to have happened to Communist authoritarian regimes is that in the course of the 1970s and '80s "no credible secular projects remained." Maier argues that this was more than merely a failure of imagination. It was a function of the increasingly yawning gap between the ruthless dynamism of the post-Fordist capitalist West and the communist East's inability or unwillingness to move beyond Fordism. The capitalist first world responded to unprecedented increases in energy costs and globally uncompetitive labor and welfare costs by shedding entire mass-production industries and their labor forces and moving toward instantaneity of capital transfers via the electronics and telecommunications revolutions. The communist second world by contrast "shrank from the logic of reform and sought to reaffirm the principles that had guided the Soviet Union since the 1930s." The "decade of delay, in effect, cost the nomenklatura their system. By the end of the 1980s the Communist Party claim to political and societal leadership could no longer be sustained in view of the developmental deficit that had to be remedied."[124]

Maier's analysis provides a useful point of departure for understanding what has happened to automobile manufacturing—the quintessential Fordist industry—in Detroit and its principal Soviet equivalent over the past several decades. Throughout its glory years, Detroit operated on the basis of "annual improvement factors" that pegged wages to productivity growth, life and disability insurance paid by the company, and, eventually, full medical coverage for workers and retirees. The formula resulted in seven to twelve million motor vehicles per year, billions of dollars in profits for the Big Three, and the blue-collar "middle class" of Middle America. When the oil crisis hit in 1973, U.S. carmakers were still churning out lumbering "gas guzzlers." They were slow to adjust, and when the Organization of Petroleum Exporting Countries again sharply raised its prices in 1979, consumers balked. Three years later, Honda started building cars in Marysville, Ohio. Nissan, Toyota, and Subaru followed suit by opening plants elsewhere in the heartland, while Detroit started to outsource, robotize, and downsize its plants. Flint, Michigan, became the most notorious case of a city sustained for decades by one or the other of the Big Three companies only to be abandoned when the going got rough. GM, Ford, and Chrysler emerged from the crisis leaner and smarter, or so they thought. Detroit itself just got leaner and meaner.[125]

By the mid-1980s, with oil prices back down almost to their pre-1973 levels, auto sales rebounded. In the interests of stability, the Big Three opted for long-term contracts with suppliers and profit-sharing arrangements with workers. They also extended job protection. Ford's Taurus, which reached the market in late 1985, turned out to be "one of the leading family cars of its day," outselling Toyota's Camry and Honda's Accord for several years in a row. But Taurus had been "born in adversity," and Ford's executives got ambitious for higher profit margins. As if fuel economy was a bad dream, Ford started turning out an ever-increasing array of expensive sport utility vehicles (SUVs, or 4 x 4s), and Chrysler and GM joined in the exuberance.[126] Foreign manufacturers such as Toyota and Nissan got into the act too, but not nearly to the same extent. They concentrated on increasing their share of the market for compact and medium-sized sedans with considerable success. Aside from attention to quality and clever marketing, Japanese firms benefited from policies that blurred the distinction, both objectively and in terms of perception, between foreign and domestic car manufacturing. In 1983 Toyota entered into a joint venture with GM when they created New United Motor Manufacturing, Inc. (NUUMI) to produce Corollas in Fremont, California. Mazda and Ford joined forces to establish AutoAlliance International (AAI), and Mitsubishi and Chrysler did the same. Thus did Japanese car companies became more American, while U.S. companies continued to look for investment opportunities overseas. "Which decision was better for the U.S. economy," Micheline Maynard asks rhetorically after pointing out that GM shut down over twenty plants in this country in the 1990s and invested more than a billion dollars in new plants elsewhere, while Toyota opened plants in Kentucky, Indiana, and West Virginia valued at over a billion dollars.[127]

In the meantime, the Soviet Union had collapsed, Gor'kii resumed its historic name of Nizhni Novgorod, and a year later, the GAZ production association went private. The sale of shares was not without its irregularities. The auction of privatization vouchers was voided in December 1993 after a special investigating commission appointed by Nizhni Novgorod's governor, Boris Nemtsov, found that GAZ's general director, Boris Vidiaev, had misappropriated state funds to purchase his vouchers. Vidiaev resigned under the cloud of suspicion and was replaced by Nikolai Pugin, who had directed GAZ before leaving in 1988 to serve as the last Soviet minister of the automotive and agricultural machinery industries. Aside from such machinations at the top, GAZ experienced little of the turbulence that afflicted the other major automobile companies in the early post-Soviet years. The Soviet Union was no more, but management and organized labor continued to relate to each other pretty much as before.[128]

As for production and sales, two of the company's primary customers for trucks—the army and collective and state farms—severely curtailed their orders, and individual customers for cars took advantage of the end of import restrictions on used Western European and Japanese models rather than purchasing new Volgas. But Pugin used his connections in Moscow to obtain financing to reequip assembly lines to produce armored vans, pickups, minivans, cargo vans, minibuses, and other commercial vehicles. The shift paid off handsomely. The Gazelle line of vehicles became instant favorites of police forces, security guards, ambulance services, and business start-ups. In 1997, three years after the Gazelle's introduction, 86,300 of them leapt off the production line. This was nearly as many as the number of Volgas. Two years later, GAZ introduced a new line of smaller vans, known as Sobol (Sable). Interested in boosting its share of the market for passenger cars as well, the company secured a $65 million loan from the European Bank for Reconstruction and Development (EBRD) to refine its line of Volgas. In January 1998 it announced a joint venture with Fiat and the EBRD for the production of three Fiat models (Siena, Palio Weekend, and Marea) in Nizhni Novgorod. Roberto Testore, chief executive of Fiat Auto, called the deal "the most important industrial project in Russia today." Projections had the first cars coming in February 2000.[129]

The future definitely looked bright for GAZ and, because the firm loomed so large in Nizhni Novgorod's economy and tax base, for Nizhni too. The city was practically unique in this respect among Russian provincial towns. Aside from Pugin, much of the credit for the success went to Boris Nemtsov. As first deputy prime minister from March 1997, Nemtsov pushed for joint ventures, supported high tariffs on car imports, and allegedly mandated that federal officials ride Volgas, as their Soviet predecessors did, rather than foreign makes. Things were looking up in the Auto Factory District too. Apartments, schools, bakeries, and markets were sprouting in the mid-1990s. The wedding palace built in Stalin's time was reconstructed and received its first nuptials in 1996. The next year, a McDonald's opened on Vedeniapin Street near the Park Kul'tury metro stop.[130]

Then came the financial collapse of August 1998 and the ruble's devaluation. Unable to afford higher prices for imported automobiles, even secondhand ones, Russians turned to domestic models. But GAZ, like other Russian car companies, had difficulty expanding production. In hock to foreign creditors, it had to turn over a substantial proportion of its common shares to Avtobank as collateral for a loan to cover its debts. The situation presented, as one analysis had it, "a unique, but fleeting, opportunity for U.S. automobile producers, suppliers, and distributors to gain a strategic foothold in the NIS [newly independent states] automotive market."[131] GM initiated talks with Togliatti's AvtoVAZ that eventually resulted in a joint venture agreement, signed in June 2001, to produce the Chevrolet Niva 4 x 4. Ford decided to invest $150 million in its own plant located in Vsevolozhsk outside St. Petersburg to produce the Focus, a model already then under production in Valencia, Spain, and Saarlouis, Germany.[132] As the new millennium dawned, it was hard to predict whether these initiatives would bear fruit or, more to the point, whether there was a market for such fruit. But the possibility such ventures would help compensate for sluggishness at home evidently made the risk worth taking.

GAZ meanwhile found itself vulnerable to takeover. In 2000, Ruspromavto, a subsidiary of Oleg Deripaska's Siberian Aluminum (Sibal) group, bought up 26 percent of GAZ's shares. This proved enough to gain control of its board of directors and have Sibal's vice president, Viktor Beliaev, appointed general director.[133] Up to this point, the company had maintained the Auto Factory District's infrastructure of housing, hospitals, child care, recreation facilities, and other institutions and services inherited from Soviet times. It also seems to have maintained a "much calmer socio-psychological situation" among workers than at other auto plants. But with over half of the workforce employed outside production, GAZ was, by the standards of the new globalized economy, terribly inefficient and overstaffed. Total output of motor vehicles in 1998 was 223,000, or a mere two vehicles per worker.[134] Beliaev stayed around just long enough—a year—to push the company in a new direction. Purchasing of parts and sales of vehicles were turned over to a newly created limited liability company, RusavtoGAZ, that abandoned Pugin's heavy reliance on discounted barter arrangements with dealers in favor of cash. The new arrangement temporarily caused dealers to cancel orders and disrupted arrangements with suppliers, including the Zavolzhskii Engine Plant (ZMZ) sixty kilometers away. "Mass permanent layoffs" of as many as 30 percent of GAZ's workforce and benefits reductions affecting all workers followed. In 2001, the new management team started turning over hospitals, educational institutions, and other social infrastructure to the city. In 2002, it quietly shelved the Fiat deal. The Volga 3111, a high-end car with a great deal to offer in luxury, convenience, and styling, nevertheless was withdrawn from

Volga taxi, Moscow (2005). Author's photograph.

production after a very small run, evidently owing to a surge of buying power that drove up the number of imported cars from 362,000 in 2001 to 480,000 in 2002. Only 50,000 Volgas were sold in 2005, and in December of that year, GAZ announced that it would discontinue all Volga production after 2007.[135]

The takeover by Deripaska was only one of many such acquisitions by which Sibal spawned Rusal (Russian Aluminum) and in 2001 itself was folded into the asset management company Bazel (Basic Element). Aside from autos and steel, Bazel "manages" insurance, banking, hydroelectric energy, and timber and pulp interests. Born in 1968, Deripaska represented along with other metals moguls a new cohort of billionaires. Unlike the oligarchs of the '90s, their fortunes were not derived primarily from asset stripping and the diversion of capital abroad, but from transforming their acquisitions within Russia into leaner, competitive operations. As Basic Element's website declares, the company "plans to work in Russia on a long-term basis." The image it presents is that of a responsible firm, one that "is committed to invest for the future of our country and support[ing] various social projects and initiatives" ranging from scholarship programs for "the most gifted students in Russia" to equipping classrooms with computers and providing Internet access, assisting in the development of new technologies in the medical sphere, and rendering assistance to the All-Russian National Military Fund of which Oleg Deripaska is an active member. By 2004, Bazel had managed to reduce the number of workers on GAZ's payroll to sixty thousand, and by February 2006 a further ten thousand had been shed. This represented a decline of over 50 percent in six years.[136]

Bazel does face competition from OAO (Otkrytoe aktsionernoe obshchestvo, Open Joint-Stock Company) Severstal, Russia's second-largest steel producer. Based in the northern city of Cherepovets, Severstal also entered the car manufacturing business in 2000 with its purchase of controlling shares in ZMZ and the Ul'ianovsk Automobile Factory, producer of Russian jeeps and other off-road vehicles. Two years later, it created Severstal-Auto as a holding company for the new automotive division of the Severstal group. Then, in October 2003, Rouge Steel, the fifth-largest steel producer in the United States, announced that, to avoid filing for bankruptcy, it had agreed to be acquired by OAO Severstal. Rouge, located in Dearborn, was founded in 1923 to provide the Ford Motor Company with high quality flat-rolled carbon steel products. In 1989, it became an independent company. Facing what the *New York Times* described as "stiff competition...from foreign rivals," it last turned a profit in 1999.[137] Thus did a Russian company that had emerged from the state-owned steel industry of the former Soviet Union purchase one of the former jewels in Ford's crown. The wheel, it seemed, had turned 180 degrees.

Or almost. Just about two years later, on October 9, 2005, Delphi Corporation, the world's second-largest auto parts manufacturer, filed for bankruptcy. Like Rouge, it had once been part of a Big Three company—General Motors—but had been spun off in 1999. Its assets were reported as $17.1 billion, and it had annual sales of $28 billion ($14 billion to GM alone). With headquarters located in the Detroit suburb of Troy, Delphi was the biggest corporate bankruptcy in Michigan history. A month later, the bleak news got bleaker for Michigan, a state that already had lost more than 220,000 auto-industry jobs in the first six years of the millennium. First GM and within days Ford announced plant closures throughout North America totaling an additional sixty thousand jobs. These announcements came after the United Auto Workers (UAW) had agreed to have its members pay a greater share of their health insurance, thereby reducing GM's health-care costs by $1 billion a year.[138]

Health-care and retirement payments for GM workers and their families were crippling the Big Three, so said the executives. In 2004, GM alone spent $5.2 billion on health care for its 1.1 million workers and retirees, or $1,500 of the cost of each vehicle the company produced. Others pointed to "wounds" that the companies had inflicted on themselves, such as the Job Bank. Introduced in 1984, the employee-development bank was intended to help train or find jobs for UAW members laid off as a result of technology improvements. The program provided for payment of a worker's full wage plus health-care and other benefits. After being renewed in 1990, it developed into a regular feature of Big Three contracts with the UAW. Its estimated cost in 2006 was $1.4 billion to $2 billion. For some of the nearly fifteen thousand workers involved, the program has meant little more than turning up to clock time at classes offered by GM; for others it is a chance to get an education. Among the latter is Tom Adams whose grandfather, Frank Adamec, arrived in Flint in 1910 from what is now the Czech Republic. Adams, an electronic technician, has been in the bank since 2001 and is earning his doctorate in history at Michigan State University. He praises the Job Bank as "doing what it is supposed to do" in his case, "which is to make it so I won't be a burden on society." But as far as GM is concerned, Adams's view is that "they took the Toyota concept of lifetime employment and...create[d] a bureaucracy. That's what GM does."[139] Cradle-to-grave health care, pretend(ing) to work, and bureaucracy. It could have been the Soviet Union. The wheel indeed had turned: Detroit had traded places with Nizhni Novgorod.

Coda

The Auto Factory District had a population of 311,600 at the end of 2003. This represented 24 percent of Nizhni Novgorod's population and was greater than any of the other seven districts of the city. Higher too than any other, with the exception of the central Nizhegorod District, was the average monthly wage of Auto Factory District residents—R6,202. As far as housing is concerned, the district boasted "no narrow or crooked lanes with continuous buildings as is characteristic of very old cities." Rather, the dominant architectural aesthetic was a "precise, regular lay-out of buildings constructed by industrial methods," just as Boris Agapov had dreamed and Alan Austin had helped to build. The amount of dwelling space had crept up from 5.8 million to 5.9 million square meters, or in per capita terms from 17.6 to 18.9 square meters, between 1998 and 2003. This too compared favorably with other districts in the city. Less likely to be the source of boasting was that the number of divorces had averaged 63.1 percent of marriages over the same period and reached as high as 96 percent of marriages in 2003.[140]

"How to sing the praises of the 'gaziks,' the 'Gazelles,' the 'GAZes' and especially the stubborn all-terrain, unsinkable Volgas that inhaled all the virtues of Russian women?" So asks Marina Kulakova, a former GAZ autoworker in her poem of 1996, "Hymn to Avtozavod." She tries. The poem, on one level, is about her contradictory experiences (and feelings about those experiences) of growing up within a stone's throw of the factory, working in it, and then leaving it. On another, it is a bittersweet elegy for the Soviet past. It begins with the observation that for more than half a century mosquitoes from the swamps along the Oka have been feasting on tasty humans who settled "on the land of the small blood-sucking aboriginals." The image is at once humorous and accusatory, casting the car factory as an alien intrusion, perhaps a metonymy for the artificiality of the entire Soviet project. We are then thrust abruptly into the quotidian world of payday when the "majority of the able-bodied population extinguishes its existential melancholy" and "colorfully formulates eternal questions." At this point the poet enters the picture, noting that the "drunken crossroads" of Kirov and Il'ich is the place where she was born, has left forever, but will never be able to leave.

This kind of contradictoriness of position pervades the poem. From her childhood she remembers "flower beds" and "terrifying basements." She recalls standing behind an engine lathe on the factory floor "with endless shavings, like gold, beneath my feet, the smell of machine oil, and noise." The work was hard, but people were nice. She remembers the construction of the housing estates (Northern, Forty Years of October), the teachers' house "white and beautiful," and the books everyone read, noting sardonically that "nobody is building houses for teachers now." And she returns to the challenge and impossibility of writing a hymn to Avtozavod—that "giant, that huge human termitarium, filled with multistory 'garages for people.'" Avtozavod—that "island of the Gulag. That is also you [ty]. Ignorant, sinister, merciless." More memories—the Number 40 bus ("cradle of my youth"), the park with its swings and merry-go-rounds, the children's village ringing with children's voices, and the benches whose fresh coat of green paint was applied simultaneously with the appearance of the same color on the trees to announce the arrival of spring.

In the end, lost in these childhood memories, she can do no more than recite a song from Pioneer camp:

> Along the Oka steamships ply,
> Horns sounding round the bends.
> Avtozavoders—that's our cry.
> We're all from here and we are friends.

Above the Volga expanse,
Above the Oka blue
Stands the town beloved,
Where we live with you.
Our dreams take flight
Our youth—it passes
Today lads and lasses,
Tomorrow—masters.[141]

Not exactly a poem of communist ideology, it is also not so full of symbolic meaning. Just of loss—of childhood, of flower beds, rectangular and otherwise—and of park benches painted green.

chapter 3

VAZ, Togliatti

> The country created the factory, the country created the city, the resources were from the entire country, from every oblast and republic. In essence, this construction project proceeded with the affection and assistance of the entire Soviet people.
>
> V. N. POLIAKOV, founding director of VAZ

> Unfortunately, far from everything planned for the seventies was realized, even ten years later. Perhaps they weren't first-order objectives...but without them, the district lost something in its spiritual development. I don't want to console myself with the thought that such is the fate of all our new "socialist cities"; anyway, that's a separate theme, large and instructive.
>
> S. P. POLIKARPOV, assistant director of VAZ, 1991

> What's good for VAZ is good for Russia.
>
> VLADIMIR KADANNIKOV, general-director
> of VAZ, October 1992

Scattered across the length and breadth of the former Soviet Union are cities with populations ranging from about two hundred thousand to eight hundred thousand that owe their existence or at least their comparatively rapid growth to massive Soviet construction projects. In their mobilization of tens of thousands of construction workers, the harshness of the conditions of work, and the drab uniformity of the buildings erected, these projects were characteristically Soviet. The cities that resulted from them represent one of the more significant, if baleful, legacies of the Soviet period. Among them is Togliatti. Along with its cousin, Naberezhnye Chelny, Togliatti is what might be considered a third-generation Soviet city.[1] The first generation included the signature towns of the prewar five-year-plan era: Magnitogorsk, Komsomolsk-na-Amur, Novokuznetsk (Stalinsk), Severdvinsk (Molotovsk). They were built to expand the country's mining and steel-making capacity or for strategic-defense purposes, and they relied on both the mobilization of young enthusiasts and prisoner labor.[2] Second-generation cities date from the mid-1950s to the early 1960s. This period coincided with the nuclear arms race and led to the creation ex nihilo of cities dedicated to scientific research and the production of fissionable material. Prime examples are Akademgorodok near Novosibirsk, the "nuclear archipelago" of five closed cities in the Urals identified by postal addresses of nearby towns (e.g., Cheliabinsk-70), and a few similarly designated places further to the east in Siberia. At the same time, the Soviet economic engine relentlessly churned its way into ever more remote regions of the country. The cities of Bratsk, founded in connection with the celebrated Siberian dam by that name, and Tselinograd (formerly Akmolinsk, now Astana, the capital of Kazakstan), became hubs of this kind of development.

The third-generation Soviet cities of Togliatti and Naberezhnye Chelny are inextricably connected with motor vehicle production—passenger cars in the case of the former, heavy trucks in the latter. As auto towns, their raison d'être was identical to that of the Proletarian District of Moscow and the Socialist City of Nizhni Novgorod. Yet, their creation during the Brezhnev era set them apart. How, though? At a time when the Soviet Union was experiencing a loss of dynamism, and vigor was the last thing one associated with its aging political leadership, both Togliatti and Naberezhnye Chelny evinced an aura of youthfulness and purposefulness, their populations being among the youngest in the entire country. Did these auto towns reflect the "actually existing socialism" of the Brezhnev era? Were they throwbacks to an earlier era? Or did they function according to a different logic, one that anticipated the company town of the post-Communist era? What was generically Soviet and what was peculiar to their provenance as auto towns? In this chapter I address these questions with respect to Togliatti, approaching its history both from the "top-down" perspective of its national function as the engine of the Soviet Union's push toward mass production of passenger cars and the "bottom-up" experiences of moving to and working and residing in it.

In focusing on Togliatti I do not mean imply that Naberezhnye Chelny is a less interesting place or that its history is identical. Today both cities are dominated by companies that survived the collapse of the Soviet Union, although not without major perturbations. OAO AvtoVAZ and OAO KamAZ are the major employers, provide the lion's share of tax revenues, and engage in a variety of philanthropic activities in their respective home towns.[3] Both cities existed for quite some time—indeed, centuries—before their selection as sites for major investment and population expansion. But only one had an Italian connection.

From Stavropol' to Togliatti

Togliatti, as every Soviet schoolchild used to know, derives its name from Palmiro Togliatti (1893–1964), one of the founding members of the Italian Communist Party (PCI) and its leader for more than two decades up to his death. Naming places after deceased Communists was a tried-and-true tradition in the Soviet Union, expressive of a yearning for "revolutionary immortality," a secular canonization that had turned into a statist rite.[4] The practice included foreign Communists as well, especially after World War II when it helped to strengthen Soviet ties with the "people's democracies" of Eastern Europe. Georgi Dimitrov, the Bulgarian Communist hero of the Reichstag fire trial of 1933 and later general secretary of the Comintern, was honored after his death in 1949 by the renaming of Melekes, a mid–Volga River town, as Dimitrovgrad. One month before Togliatti's death in July 1964, the chairman of the French Communist Party, Maurice Thorez, passed away and soon thereafter, Torez, a mining town in the Ukrainian Donbass, was born.[5] Indeed, as a whole generation of European Communist leaders, born around the turn of the century, was passing from the scene, their names started popping up on Soviet maps. The Romanian Gheorghe Gheorghiu-Dej was memorialized after his death in March 1965 by an industrial town on the Don River in Voronezh Oblast exchanging its name (Liski) for his.

Ironically, both Togliatti and Gheorghiu-Dej (though not Thorez) involved themselves with initiatives that distanced their respective parties from Moscow. The Romanian party had begun irritating the Soviet Communist leadership in the late 1950s by siding with China in the Sino-Soviet dispute and establishing extensive economic relations with Western countries pursuant to its goal of making Romania an independent industrial power. Togliatti had long championed "polycentrism" within the Communist world and reiterated his stance in the so-called Yalta memorandum.[6] This document was published by the PCI on September 5, 1964, just three weeks after Togliatti's death and one week after his name was attached to a Soviet city.

The city chosen to bear Togliatti's name was Stavropol'-on-Volga. Founded in 1737 about one hundred kilometers upriver from Samara (or Kuibyshev as it was known between 1935 and 1991), Stavropol' (in Greek, "town of the cross") owed its existence to the Russian state's provision of a refuge for Kalmyk Buddhist converts to Christianity. It is not to be confused with the other, and larger, city (still) known as Stavropol' that was established in the North Caucasus region in 1785 and is the regional capital. From whom the Kalmyk converts might have needed refuge, and whether, in fact, they understood conversion in quite the same way as their converters are questions left unaddressed in the local guidebooks, textbooks, and their online equivalents.[7] Despite the arrival of successive convoys of Kalmyk converts over several decades, the population of Stavropol' did not appreciably increase. Evidently, at least as many drifted off after arriving as stayed, reverting to the nomadic (and Buddhist) ways of their ancestors.[8]

Organized into a "host" (*voisko*) like the Cossacks, the Kalmyk converts eventually came under the authority of the governor of Orenburg Province. As they continued to resist the delights of agriculture, increasing numbers of Cossack and Russian migrants settled in the area, transforming it into a bountiful grain-growing region. In 1842, Nicholas I abolished the now redundant host, resettling its members in the Orenburg steppe. The town, which had seen little population growth throughout the late eighteenth and early nineteenth centuries, became an uezd (county) seat within Simbirsk Province. By the 1890s, it had about six thousand inhabitants. The arrival of Soviet power in 1917 was registered in Stavropol' without much of a struggle, but the civil war that followed saw the town—and much of the rest of the middle Volga region—under the control of the Czechoslovak legion, the Komuch (Committee of Members of the Constituent Assembly), the Bolsheviks, and other contending forces. The famine of 1921 hit the town particularly hard, leading to a mass exodus and the town's downgrading to village status in 1924.[9]

Not until World War II did Stavropol' experience significant growth. This occurred thanks to the evacuation of several institutions from Moscow and Leningrad including the Red Army's Institute of Foreign Languages. As of 1946, the town, with the status of a raion (district) seat, had a population of about twelve thousand. A migrant who arrived in 1950 later described it as "poorly planned and cheerless. Sand dunes on the outskirts of town, mountains of sand. Ramshackle gray houses. Log huts used as warehouses for grain, maybe three or four brick buildings, a saddle-maker's workshop. Onions in the kitchen gardens. Hardly any trees."[10] The newcomer, a graduate of the Novocherkassk Polytechnic Institute, had been recruited to work on the construction of the Kuibyshev Hydroelectric Station (GES). One of the big projects of the 1950s, it involved damming the Volga to generate more than two million kilowatts of electricity and creating a vast reservoir known as the Zhiguli (formerly, Kuibyshev) Sea. The tens of thousands of workers engaged on the project, many of them prisoners, were housed in rough-and-ready settlements along the river with names such as Floodgates, Port Town, and Apple Gully. Other settlements such as Socialist City (Sotsgorod) and Komsomol'sk harkened back to earlier construction projects and presumably were intended to house the more politically conscious.

The dismantling of Stavropol' and its reconstruction on a site not far from the Komsomol'sk settlement about eighteen kilometers upriver from the hydroelectric station began in May 1953. Engineers relocated three thousand buildings on the eastern shore of the sea. When the station came on line in 1958 the population of the city, now encompassing both the Komsomol'sk and Central districts, already approached seventy thousand. Thanks to the abundance of power and the Khrushchev administration's push for expanding petrochemicals production, substantial synthetic rubber, phosphorus, and ammonia plants opened up in an industrial zone to the northwest of the Central District. Along with standard Soviet prefabricated apartment blocks, administrative buildings, and a few department stores, they gave the city its dull, rather colorless appearance.[11] Why this insalubrious industrial town should have been chosen to honor the leader of the PCI is not exactly clear. Perhaps the fact that Togliatti spent part of his exile from Fascist Italy during the late 1920s and 1930s in the not-so-far-away city of Kuibyshev was a factor. Since that regional capital already bore the name of a prominent Bolshevik, somewhere else would have to do. Much of the ground formerly occupied by Stavropol' was under water anyway.

Looking back from the perspective of 1966, *For Communism* (Za kommunizm), the organ of both the city council (soviet) and the city committee (*gorkom*) of the Communist Party, exulted at how rapidly "our Togliatti is growing and stretching its young but already athletic [*bogatyrskie*] shoulders. Where not long ago was emptiness now stand giant factories and residential districts." But there was more to come. "What struck us first of all," noted Francesco Perucci, a former senator and one of twenty-six Italian Communists visiting Togliatti at the invitation of the Soviet Communist Party Central Committee, "is the enormous scale of industrial and housing construction." "Until recently thick weeds grew here," read a caption to a photo published a few days later. Now "a whole forest of cranes" dotted the landscape.[12]

And then on July 27, 1966, came the news that merited a banner headline: "Yet Another New Construction Project in Togliatti!" This one was to be like no other. In fact, in the history of the whole country only the deal with Ford was comparable. The Soviet government had signed an agreement with Fiat to build an integrated automobile factory in the USSR and had settled on the place named after the Italian Communist. To understand how this deal came about, we must leave Togliatti in eager anticipation and travel back to Moscow—and abroad.

Soviet Cars of the Mid-1960s

"At present," wrote the minister of automobile production, Aleksei Mikhailovich Tarasov, to the assistant chairman of the State Planning Commission in December 1965, "our domestic automobile industry is not meeting the requirements of the economy in terms of production." Translation: we need to produce more cars. There were, he reported, some 2.74 million vehicles in the country, most of them trucks with capacities of 2.5 to 4 tons, and about 30 percent of those were eight or more years old. In terms of passenger cars, the Soviet Union found itself near last place compared to "other countries." At a time when the United States had one car for every 2.7 people, the USSR had one for every 238. The Soviet government had been rather grudging in its release of funds for investment in the automobile industry, he pointed out. Compared with the equivalent of R 12.7 billion invested in the United States between 1945 and 1963, which had resulted in an increase in output of cars from 3 million to 9.1 million, the USSR had invested only R 1 billion over the slightly longer period of 1945 to 1965. Output in 1965—617,000 vehicles—would not even reach the modest figures (750,000–856,000) projected in the Seven-Year Plan approved in 1958.[13]

Why had the Soviet government allowed such a situation to develop in the first place? The standard explanation is that Nikita Khrushchev was ideologically hostile to personal ownership of cars, preferring to expand existing public transportation and develop a car-rental system. Only with Khrushchev's ouster in October 1964 was there sufficient interest at the top to put the expansion of car production and personal ownership on the government's agenda. A comment by Premier Aleksei Kosygin to a session of the State Planning Commission on March 19, 1965, was indicative of the changed orientation at the top:

> You know how staunchly the idea was imposed that there was no necessity in our country to develop the production of passenger automobiles on a large scale. Let all people ride only in buses, so to speak. Everything has been done to deprive even the leaders of big enterprises and economic organizations of the right to use passenger cars. Is this correct? The result has been that many leaders have been compelled to use trucks unlawfully for their official rides.[14]

No doubt there is something to this. Biographical and commemorative literature credits Kosygin not only with changing the orientation of the leadership toward passenger cars but also with smoothing the path toward clinching the deal with Fiat.[15] At best, however, it's a partial explanation. Official ambivalence toward the rapid expansion of car ownership was not limited to Khrushchev and did not end with his ouster. Moreover, ideological objections were only one dimension of the issue. The limited capacity of Soviet roads to bear increased automobile traffic, the limited capacity of the state's budget to accommodate increased spending on consumer goods, to say nothing of the ancillary costs associated with embarking on such a course, also weighed in the balance. Over and above these considerations was bureaucratic politics, no small issue when considering decision making in the USSR. Until the abolition of the system of economic administration that Khrushchev had introduced in 1957, no institutional voice existed at the center of the Soviet government for expanding automobile production. Only with the creation of a ministry of automobile production in 1965 could such a case be made and support solicited from within the Council of Ministers. It is in this sense that change at the top mattered.

Pressure "from below"—popular demand by another name—is unlikely to have played a direct role. Yet, it cannot be ruled out, especially since just such pressure had begun to manifest itself indirectly in the mid-1960s in the findings of Soviet sociologists about leisure-time expenditure and desires, in articles and cartoons in the press about the trials and tribulations of automobile tourists, in popular films about adventures on the road, and in the publication of the first automobile tourism guidebooks. At the very least, the combination of increased savings per capita, longer vacations, and a larger proportion of vacationers consisting of "independent health resort visitors" (*samostoiatel'nye kurortniki*) made it easier for those advocating expansion of car production to make their case.[16] "What could be simpler than sitting in a car and getting on the road?" asked an engineer from Leningrad in a letter to *Izvestiia,* adding "but immediately the tourist confronts problems of sustenance, lodging, and transport that make traveling complicated."[17]

Returning to the case that Tarasov outlined, he actually understated the gap. The 9.1 (actually, 9.3) million produced in the United States referred only to passenger cars. If trucks and buses were added, the figure would rise to 11.1 million. Soviet output for 1965 was indeed 617,000 vehicles, but nearly two-thirds of that figure consisted of trucks and buses. The actual output of passenger cars was just slightly more than 200,000.[18] No matter. Looking to the future, and this was the point of the memo, the minister proposed an increase to 750,000 cars by 1970 thanks to "the completion of reconstruction of existing factories and the construction of a complex of auto, motor, and assembly plants with a general capacity of up to one million cars per year." To achieve this result, it would be necessary to invest R 3.1 billion by 1970, or over three times as much as the industry had received in the previous twenty years.[19] Looking beyond 1970, Tarasov envisioned two new factories for the production of passenger cars. The suggested locations were the Volga region and Belorussia.[20]

What kind of cars would they be? The last all-new Soviet car had debuted in 1960 when the ZAZ 965 ("Zaporozhets"), a minicar weighing a mere 650 kilos, began rolling off the assembly line. Designed and built at ZAZ (Zaporozhskii Avtomobil'nyi Zavod or Zaporozh Automobile Factory) in south-central Ukraine, this "little car that could" had a rear-mounted, air-cooled 26-hp engine and a body resembling the Fiat 600 (a later restyling made it look more like an NSU Prinz 4). Khrushchev, who somehow maneuvered his thick body into the passenger seat for a spin around the Kremlin, reputedly called it a "hunchback" (*gorbatyi*) and considered it an appropriate "car for the working class," like West Germany's Volkswagen or the GDR's Trabant. Whichever class bought the Zaporozhets—one source claims it became the "car for pensioneers [*sic*] and intellectuals," while another cites the practice of giving them to "invalids"—it definitely was among the most proletarian of cars. Thanks to its notorious unreliability and unpretentious appearance, its name inevitably was shortened in popular discourse to "Zapor," which means both a "bolt" or "lock" and "constipation." Also known as "Big Ears" (*ushastyi*) because of its side vents, and "Soap Dish" (*myl'nitsa*), a more endearing description of its overall appearance than "zapor," the Zaporozhets figured in an endless series of jokes in which it confronted and often ironically bested a Mercedes.[21]

Despite being cofeatured in *Three Plus Two,* the 1963 romantic comedy film in which it transported the "two" attractive young women to a remote campsite on the Black Sea coast, the Zaporozhets was not made for extended trips and steep gradients. An altogether different vehicle and more of a man's car was the Volga, specifically the GAZ-21, manufactured at the Gor'kii factory from 1956 onward. With a four-cylinder 70-hp engine and a top speed of 130 km/h, the Volga was somewhat smaller than the Chaika or the ZIL but large by ordinary mortals' standards. It also was, in the view of a young enthusiast quoted not too long ago by the *Los Angeles Times,* "the only beautiful car ever made in the USSR in its entire history."[22] Finally, there was the Moskvich. The 408 model, introduced in 1965, had a none-too-capacious 1360 cc, 50-hp engine, but it also possessed a few notable features including the use of aluminum for the engine and easily removable cylinders (which, considering the temptation for theft, might be regarded as a negative feature). It was produced at MZMA (the Moscow Factory of Small [displacement] Automobiles), the same factory known before the Great Patriotic War as KIM (Communist Internationale of Youth) and from 1967 onward as AZLK (Automobile Factory of the Leninist Komsomol).[23]

It is difficult to reconstruct the thinking of Soviet officials as they grappled with the question of expanding automobile production. The difficulty lies not so much in a lack of documentation as in the rapid pace of technological change, which makes it hard to see the models of that time through their eyes. Nevertheless, it seems safe to conclude that of the three Soviet passenger cars in production in the mid-1960s only one would have been a serious candidate for seating millions of additional Soviet drivers. If the Zaporozhets was too slight, and the Volga considerably more than was required, then, as in "Goldilocks and the Three Bears," the Moskvich 408 was "just right." The only problem with the Moskvich was that it was a terrible car. On December 18, 1965, the board of the Ministry of Automobile Production instructed MZMA's director, Vasil'ev, and chief engineer, Matveev, to take immediate steps to improve the quality of the product. The instructions were based on a report filed five days earlier by the ministry's quality control inspector that detailed a broad range of defects. The report concluded that, while the car was exportable and that many defects had been eliminated, quite a few remained—seventeen, in fact—and they required attention. The factory's leaders promised to fix all seventeen (plus an additional fifteen!), but who knew how they were going to improve the quality of parts manufactured elsewhere in the country? A year later, the board again cited the factory leadership's failure to eliminate the car's defects—now having grown to thirty-five—and both Vasil'ev and Matveev were put on notice that they were being held personally responsible.[24]

None of this precluded expanding production of the Moskvich 408, which is exactly what the ministry proposed to the Council of Ministers in February 1966. "To satisfy the growing demand among the population and in the economy," the ministry envisioned additional facilities that would raise output to two hundred thousand per year by 1975.[25] The ministers approved the proposal, paving the way for an agreement with Renault that involved the modernization and expansion of MZMA and the supply of technology to equip a new plant capable of turning out an additional two hundred thousand cars per year by 1971.[26] The plant was built in Izhevsk, capital city of Urdmurtia. Founded in 1760 as an ironworks settlement, Izhevsk began producing small-bore rifles in the middle of the nineteenth century, and since 1949 has turned out the Kalashnikov rifle. The city is also renowned as the birthplace of the Russian motorcycle industry. Car assembly dates from 1967 when "Izhmash" began producing the new Moskvich 412.[27] Even as production began, however, the news from Togliatti was putting Izhevsk in the shade.

"The Deal of the Century"

The deal with Fiat was a megadeal, the largest of all commercial agreements concluded by the USSR. Fiat, Italy's largest company, was no stranger to this part of the world. In 1916 it had provided the fledgling Moscow Automobile Company with the components for assembling its "15-TER" trucks, the "first swallows" in that enterprise's long line of trucks.[28] Fiat also supplied a good deal of the machinery for Moscow's First Ball Bearing and Metallurgical Factory, a key undertaking of the First Five-Year Plan. Giovanni Agnelli, Fiat's founder and president, traveled to Moscow to attend the opening of the factory in 1932. Elsewhere in Eastern Europe, the Red Flag (Crvena Zastava) factory near Belgrade began producing modified versions of Fiat 600s in 1954 under license from Turin, making it the first arrangement between a Western corporation and an enterprise in a Communist-controlled country in the postwar era.[29] A deal with the Warsaw-based Fabryka Samochodów Osobowych that the Polish government had nixed as far back as 1950 was revived in the less ideologically stringent conditions of 1965. The result was the Polski Fiat 125.

Recent accounts of the big deal tend to emphasize the international political climate as a major factor in the Soviet government's choice of partner. Notwithstanding the achievement of the Nuclear Test Ban Treaty of 1963, relations with the United States were going through a bad patch, largely in connection with the escalation of the U.S. war in Vietnam. This in itself would have made a deal with any of the Big Three automakers unlikely. The fallout over the construction of the Berlin wall and the Soviet campaign against West German "revanchism" appear to have eliminated Volkswagen from consideration. But these negative reasons only suggest why company X or company Y was out of the running (or never bothered to enter the competition). The explanation thus boils down to a process of elimination: Italy provided just the right sort of conditions by virtue of not being involved directly in a cold war controversy.[30] No less important in my view, though, was what Fiat had to offer and how it cultivated a relationship that made its offer hard to refuse.

The architect of Fiat's postwar "Ostpolitik" was Vittorio Valletta, the company's general director. Born into a petit-bourgeois family in 1883, Valletta had a career as a technical-school instructor and professor of banking before joining Fiat in 1921. He rose rapidly in the firm, becoming a general manager in 1928. By 1939, the aging Agnelli appointed him managing director, and in that capacity he saw Fiat through the war years when it turned out vehicles of all kinds for the Axis. Already effectively running the company, "the Professor," as Valletta generally was called, took over as chief executive on Agnelli's death in 1945. His tenure as regent to the heir apparent—Giovanni's twenty-four-year-old grandson, Gianni—was supposed to be short-lived, but lasted until his death in 1966.[31]

Leonid Kolosov, the KGB agent who doubled as an Italian-based correspondent for *Izvestiia,* repeats a story about Valletta that the Soviet writer

Marietta Shaginian told him during her visit to Turin. It seems that the Professor was among those arrested by partisans shortly after the liberation of Turin in April 1945 and sentenced to be executed for his complicity with the Fascist dictatorship. Only the intervention of the Communist Resistance leader, Luigi Longo (who would succeed Togliatti as secretary of the party in 1964), saved him. Like much else in Kolosov's memoir, the story is of doubtful accuracy, though it is possible that Shaginian, who wrote a series of articles for *Izvestiia* that cast Fiat in a favorable light, did relate it to Kolosov.[32] Whatever the case, Fiat's survival as a corporate giant owed a great deal in the postwar years to Valletta's skillful maneuvering among Communist-led workers' councils; the Chase Manhattan Bank and other U.S. creditors, who kept the company afloat via the Marshall Plan; and the Agnelli family.[33]

Valletta's contacts with the Kremlin date from the early 1960s. Initial talks with Khrushchev and Kosygin focused on tractors and the building of a factory capable of turning out four hundred a day. Fiat had long been in the business of producing tractors, and while the USSR previously had relied heavily on the United States for models and technical assistance, no a priori reason existed for continuing such dependence. Indeed, it appears that Kosygin, who visited Turin in the summer of 1962, was quite keen on such a deal. Conversations continued intermittently over the next several years at somewhat lower levels. On Fiat's side, they involved Aurelio Peccei, who had overseen the company's operations in Argentina and would soon found the Club of Rome; on the Soviet side, the key negotiator was German Gvishiani, vice chairman of the State Committee on Science and Technology and Kosygin's son-in-law.

Valletta was careful to keep the Americans informed about his discussions in Moscow, meeting with high-ranking officials of the Kennedy and Johnson administrations at least four times between 1962 and the middle of 1965. On the last of these occasions, indicative perhaps of the extent to which Marshall Plan assistance to Fiat had benefited U.S. interests, he promised to annul any deal that "was not in accord with United States policy." The idea of a tractor factory had been abandoned the previous year, owing both to the technical difficulty Fiat was experiencing in meeting the Soviet specifications and to a change of orientation in Moscow.[34] In its stead, a car factory, perhaps like the Mirafiori plant in Turin that Soviet engineers had visited, emerged as a real possibility. Mirafiori had opened to great fanfare on May 15, 1939 (with Mussolini in attendance). Designed to accommodate twenty-two thousand workers in two shifts, it significantly expanded Fiat's productive capacity during the war. Although seriously damaged by Allied bombing, it was rebuilt between 1956 and 1958, doubling in size and regaining its status as the firm's flagship facility.[35]

In late June 1965 Valletta traveled to Moscow again for talks with Premier Kosygin. A protocol of understanding, cosigned with the chairman of the Committee on Science and Technology, K. N. Rudnev, resulted, according to which Fiat would provide technical guidance in future Soviet automobile production.[36] Then it was off to Washington for another debriefing. The Professor told Secretary of State Dean Rusk that Kosygin now seemed serious in his "desire to reduce his defense costs and, with the resulting savings, shift from the production of armaments and nuclear weapons to more intensive development of consumer goods." The news seemed to please Rusk, who opined, "We could accordingly think of better ways to spend $50 billion each year than for defense." The remark, coming in the midst of the huge buildup of U.S. "defense" forces for Vietnam, was disingenuous. The USSR might cut back on expenditures for MIG fighters and ICBMs, but the United States could not possibly reduce the number of its F (not for Fiat)-series fighters and Minuteman missiles. But if engaging in pieties was how Rusk could support an agreement between Fiat and the Soviets, Valletta was not going to argue. The protocol in any case had no binding authority on either party. Asked by Rusk about the timetable, Valletta replied that only the general aspects had been touched on and that more precise details awaited a Soviet follow-up mission to Turin.[37]

Preparatory to that mission, Tarasov, minister of automobile production, dispatched the director of Moscow's Likhachev Factory, P. D. Borodin, to undertake an onsite general assessment of Fiat's operations. His report, bound in two volumes full of glossy photos, concluded that while the technical level of Fiat's truck production was "significantly lower" than at ZIL's (perhaps a bit of self-promotion had crept in here), the Mirafiori car factory exhibited a "high level of organization and culture of production." Thanks to the installation of the most up-to-date automated equipment and the maintenance of "strict discipline" on the factory floor, output of cars and workers' productivity had risen sharply. Borodin's report described the factory itself as "constructed in the contemporary style with a well-conceived layout...clean [and] uncluttered. The facade of the building is simple and well-formed architecturally. At the entrance to the administration headquarters is a large hall lined in marble."[38] Fiat, in short, had much to offer.

In February 1966 came the official offer for "a factory to produce two thousand mid-sized passenger cars per day in two shifts of seven hours." The car in question was the Fiat-124 that Mirafiori had just begun to produce, albeit at the lower rate of 320 per day. The proposal projected an operation far more efficient than anything yet seen in the Soviet Union. Instead of MZMA's five cars per year per worker, it anticipated each worker turning out fifteen, one more than at Mirafiori. This rate of productivity could be achieved by relying on fewer auxiliary workers and making greater use of automation and computer information systems. At Mirafiori, for example, there were "fifty separate locations in the factory [at which] such machines collect information and transfer it to an interpretive and calculating center....Information is collected and processed not only for the basic production process of assembling cars but for other tasks such as labor accounting and calculating wages."[39]

After the State Institute for Automobile Production (Giproavtoprom) had studied the proposal and reported its findings to the ministry, a substantial

Soviet delegation traveled to Turin in mid-April to engage in almost continuous discussions with Fiat personnel. Aside from engineers, the Soviet mission included Tarasov; his assistant at the Ministry of Automobile Production, N. I. Strokin; and the assistant minister of foreign trade, I. F. Semichastnov. Gvishiani and the vice chairman of Gosplan, V. D. Lebedev, were also present. Simultaneous discussions concerning financial arrangements were led by M. N. Sveshnikov, president of the Bank for Foreign Trade, and on the Italian side by Stefano Siglienti, longtime president of the Istituto Mobiliare Italiano (IMI).[40] From these two sets of negotiations emerged separate protocols that essentially clinched the deal and, according to one recently published account, "demonstrated the Soviet delegation's surprising degree of perspicacity." One was the protocol on cooperation that represented a modified version of what Fiat had proposed in February; the other was the financial agreement that provided terms for long-term credit repayment.[41]

In the meantime, discussions with other Western car firms were taking place. Those with Volkswagen date from May 1966 and proposed building a fully integrated factory capable of producing two thousand cars a day—the same as Fiat—in five years.[42] More or less at the same time, a team of six specialists from ZIL, GAZ, and the Scientific Institute of Automobiles left for France where they inspected Renault's car and truck facilities. This was merely one in a series of steps that would result in the above-mentioned agreement of June 10, 1966, which the cosignatories couched euphemistically as "expanding scientific-technical cooperation" between Renault and the USSR. Whether Moscow ever considered breaking off negotiations in Turin to give all its business to another Western auto firm is doubtful. Nevertheless, there may be some truth to Kolosov's claim that the Italians believed the rumors (which he spread) that Tarasov was prepared to depart for Paris at the drop of a hat to sign an agreement with Renault. It is hard to explain otherwise why, in late April, when negotiations bogged down over the interest rate to be charged to the Soviet Bank for Foreign Trade for credits amounting to two hundred billion lire, the Italians more or less caved in to the Soviet insistence that it could not go above 5 percent.[43]

The ceremonial signing by Valletta and Tarasov, captured in a photograph that appeared on the cover of *Illustrato Fiat,* Fiat's glossy magazine, took place on May 4, 1966. Fiat was to provide all technical assistance and training in connection with the construction of a factory to produce a car that would be "substantially similar to the Fiat types currently in production" but with modifications required by the particular climatic and road conditions of the USSR. Valued at some $900 million, the agreement was "the biggest deal of the century" in the words of Averell Harriman (who had seen quite a few big deals in his lifetime). It certainly was the most expensive single purchase the Soviet Union had made up to that point. Reflecting on it later, Gianni Agnelli, who took over from Valletta shortly after the agreement, said that "for us, [it] represented almost a zero profit operation. But this plan...was very successful in establishing Fiat as one of the biggest car manufacturers in the world."[44]

The international business community took notice. American machine tool manufacturers who had been doing business with Fiat sensed a windfall. As *Forbes* put it, "the story behind the story" was that as much as three-quarters of the machinery to be installed for the USSR would come from the United States, either directly or indirectly through European subsidiaries and licensees of U.S. firms. Irving W. Peachey of Rochester, New York's Gleason Works affirmed that "this is just a pure business deal as far as we're concerned. We have competitors overseas. If we don't supply the Russians, they will."[45] The opportunities struck some as almost limitless. *Forbes* suggested the potential when it asked, "If U.S. machine tool manufacturers can export to Russia through Fiat, why couldn't General Electric, for example, do the same with its computer technology, using Olivetti as its middleman?" The prospect of "throw[ing] wide open the gates to East-West trade" may have had U.S. businessmen salivating, but at least some members of Congress were worried that the Russians might convert machinery obtained via the Fiat deal (or future deals for that matter) to military use—a scenario exactly the opposite to the one that Valletta had sketched to Secretary of State Rusk.[46] A congressional subcommittee on international trade undertook its own investigation, traveling to Italy, Yugoslavia, Czechoslovakia, and the Soviet Union. The report, while noting that "specific congressional authority is not required" for approving export licenses, stated that "there are ample legislative avenues available to those in Congress who might prefer to have Eximbank credits...denied." In the event, the bank extended credits not to the Soviet government but to Italy's IMI.[47] It was an arrangement that all three parties could live with.

For the Soviet Union the Fiat deal was a big deal not only in terms of the cost and what was being bought. It marked a reversion to an older policy of compensating for the lack of technological innovativeness by purchasing new technology from the West. Khrushchev had begun to move in this direction by seeking Western credits to finance his program for the "chemicalization" of Soviet agriculture, but not since the Ford deal of 1929 had a single contract with a Western company made quite as much of a splash. The deal also signified a return to an earlier, more "internationalist," mode of doing business that had been terminated during the Great Purge, was forced on the USSR to some extent during World War II, but then curbed again with the outbreak of the cold war. The greater intercourse with Western business was thus analogous to academic exchanges and cultural events that denoted a greater openness and confidence among Soviet leaders and belonged very much to the Soviet '60s.

No explanation of the adoption of a new car in the Soviet Union, however, is complete without a (probably apocryphal) story of a Soviet leader giving the model a test drive. In this case it was not the dour Kosygin but his more flamboyant party counterpart, the fervent automobilist Leonid Il'ich Brezhnev, who allegedly took a spin around the Kremlin in a prototype of the Fiat-124 that had been flown to the USSR in a special cargo plane.[48]

Building VAZ, Building Avtograd

On August 22, 1966, TASS reported that Luigi Longo, general secretary of the Italian Communist Party, and Mario Alicata, a member of the party's Politburo, were warmly greeted by the toilers of Togliatti. Banners proclaiming "Let us strengthen the friendship of the peoples of Italy and the USSR!" and "A flaming greeting to the fraternal PCI!" decorated the main thoroughfares of the city. Longo told a mass rally at the synthetic rubber factory that he was very glad that the automobile factory at the center of the agreement between the Soviet Ministry of Foreign Trade and Fiat would be built in a city named after Togliatti. "Togliatti's first political activities occurred in Turin," he said. "The fact that workers and technicians from Turin are coming here, to the city bearing his name, is highly significant. Among them may be the sons and grandsons of comrades who fought alongside Togliatti. Perhaps in a few months Togliatti will be the most Italian, the most Turin-like city in the Soviet Union."[49]

Nearly forty years later, as I rumbled along Togliatti's Southern Avenue (Iuzhnoe chaussée) in a bus past thousands of new Ladas parked in AvtoVAZ's lot, I asked my host, "So, are there any Italian restaurants in Togliatti?" He seemed somewhat nonplused by the question. "No, I don't think so," he eventually replied, adding that his meager stipend as a graduate student at Togliatti State University and the fees he earned as an instructor in the university's extension program didn't permit him to dine out much. I didn't get to dine in restaurants either; my hosts were too hospitable. One evening when I was left on my own, I ventured forth from the university dormitory to stock up on a few items from a nearby food store. It was all so Soviet—the groceries lined up out of reach behind the counter, the badly lit store divided into different sections, the necessity of getting separate chits from the cashier for each department. Was there nothing in Togliatti to remind one of the Italian connection, I wondered. Turin, it turns out, has a Corso Unione Sovietica, but there is no Soviet-Italian Friendship Street or Prospekt Fiat in Togliatti. It is as if Soviet authorities earlier and OAO AvtoVAZ more recently had decided to turn their backs on the Italian origins of the automobile plant, whose founding had so transformed the city. "I completely understand your feelings," a retired Fiat employee who had worked in Togliatti told an interviewer who noted the absence of Italian street names. "Personally, I would dream of seeing a Vittorio Valletta Street in your city."[50]

How did the factory come to be built in Togliatti? The competition began some time before the agreement had been signed. The original 112 entries were quickly whittled down to thirty-nine, and then six. One of the members of the working group that devised Togliatti's bid recalled some twenty-five years later that it was "in the winter, either at the end of 1965 or the very beginning of 1966 that the leading specialists of a number of institutions arrived in Togliatti, and it became clear that we were entering the critical stage." What had helped Togliatti get to that stage was the lobbying conducted in Moscow by the working group, otherwise known as "pushers" (*tolkachi*). They included V. F. Vetlitskii, the regional (*obkom*) party secretary; N. F. Semizorov, the director of Kuibyshevgidrostroi (about which more below); and K. P. Iakovlev, the chief architect of the region. One assumes that at least some of the other contenders dispatched their own *tolkachi,* which raises the question why Togliatti ultimately won out.

Of the six finalists, the Vologda-Iaroslavl' region was allegedly favored by Kosygin. Brovari in central Ukraine and Minsk, the Belorussian capital city, also had their supporters among central party and state officials.[51] But among the four sites in the RSFSR (Belgorod, Gor'kii, Iaroslavl', and Togliatti) Togliatti recommended itself to the republic's Council of Ministers. The council cited three "basic" criteria: proximity to existing supplies of construction materials, machine-building factories, and transportation; the presence of reliable construction organizations; and the possibility of attracting workers form the immediate vicinity who were not already occupied in social production.[52] The first almost went without saying, although Henry Ford once called off a groundbreaking ceremony in the Netherlands because the site for the new plant was half a kilometer removed from water-borne transportation. The third factor was important too, as the middle Volga was one of few regions within the Russian republic where labor reserves were not already exhausted.[53] But the second factor may well have been crucial. Kuibyshevgidrostroi, formed in 1950 to build the hydroelectric station across the Volga, remained the region's primary construction outfit. It built not only dams but factories and, as of 1966, nearly 1.5 million square meters of housing.

Yet another—and probably decisive—factor in Togliatti's favor were the results of a computer-based study conducted by N. P. Fedorenko, director of the Central Economics and Mathematics Institute (TsEMI). The study considered the six proposed sites in terms of projected costs over the period 1967 to 1980 for building the complex of factories, producing the cars, and delivering them to customers. Criteria included levels of capital investment in production facilities; capital investment in housing and service facilities; expenditures on creating a necessary construction base; ongoing expenses on fuel, energy, and materials; and delivery costs. The results showed Togliatti as the least expensive at R 1.278 billion, some R 21 million less than the Belgorod site.[54] On July 20 the party's Central Committee and the Council of Ministers of the USSR issued a joint resolution announcing Togliatti as the victorious candidate for the construction of the automobile factory.[55] Subsequent resolutions laid out in detail ministerial responsibility for the project. The fact that the Ministry of Energy and Electrification was given the main role only made sense in light of Kuibyshevgidrostroi's subordination to it.

The project had high priority. Viktor Nikolaevich Poliakov, assistant minister for automobile production, assumed the position of general director of the "auto factory on the Volga" (the name VAZ—Volga Automobile Factory—did not become official until mid-1967) in September 1966. He immediately began recruiting engineers and administrators from existing automobile, tractor, and other machine-building factories; involved himself in the acquisition of materials for the project; and kept in frequent correspondence with the Soviet "delegation" of engineers working in Turin. That delegation, headed by Evgenii Bashindzhagian, spent six months in Turin hammering out details of how to adapt the Fiat-124 and the Italians' general plan for the factory to Soviet conditions. Bashindzhagian recalled that negotiations were often tense and filled with misunderstandings, linguistic and otherwise.[56] Even so, the length of the stay, the size of the working group, and many aspects of its encounters with Fiat's managers and engineers were far removed from what previous Soviet delegations encountered and how they behaved, for example, in their dealings with Ford during the early 1930s.

The plan for the factory worked out by both sides in Turin called for a facility that by 1971 would accommodate a workforce of forty-three thousand, including five thousand engineering-technical personnel and white collar employees. The entire workforce and members of their families, estimated to be 130,000 people, would be housed in what for all intents and purposes was a new city. Informally known as Avtograd (Auto City), its official name was the Auto Factory District (Avtozavodskii Raion), just as in the case of Gor'kii. Housing construction was to occur simultaneously with the building of the factory. Unlike so many earlier construction projects, including the

Building Avtograd, Togliatti. From *AVTOVAZ: Istoriia millionov, 1966–2006* (Togliatti: OAO AvtoVaz, 2007), 66. Courtesy of AvtoVAZ.

Kuibyshev GES, no tent cities or barracks would offend the eyes, at least in the new city.[57] No POWs or Gulag inmates would be employed. In these respects, Avtograd represented something of a departure from past practices.

It was absolutely clear from the outset that the new town would be a "satellite" for the factory, its sole purpose being to accommodate VAZ employees and members of their families. Anyone released from the enterprise for whatever reason would have to vacate his or her "living space" in Avtograd. This, in other words, was a company town, Soviet-style. Its chief architect was Boris Rafailovich Rubanenko, director of the Central Scientific Research Institute of Experimental and Standard Residential Planning (TsNIIEP), a Moscow-based institute within the State Committee for Construction and Design (Gosstroi SSSR). Rubanenko, who had participated in the Novye Cheremushki housing project in Moscow during the 1950s, and earlier had designed buildings in Gor'kii and Leningrad, assembled a team of architects and engineers to draw up two general plans, one for Avtograd for the period 1968–71, and a second for all of Togliatti over the next twenty-five to thirty years.[58]

The plans envisioned Avtograd rising between the factory and the Zhiguli seashore. It would be separated from the "old" Central District by a five-kilometer-wide swath of forest (a "protected sanitary zone"). Three major buildings would dominate the skyline: a twenty-three-story hotel to accommodate foreign delegations and visiting Soviet dignitaries, a corpus of municipal administrative buildings, and the twenty-six-story tower containing the enterprise's administrative offices. These structures in time would become the center of the entire city of Togliatti, which the architects expected to move westward. That is, with the building of Avtograd, the poorly planned and relatively polluted Central and Komsomol'sk districts (the "old city") would lose population, declining from 187,000 in 1968 to 110,000 by the mid-1990s.[59]

One of the main challenges for Rubanenko's team, and another indication of the centrality of VAZ in the project, was the necessity of organizing the layout of dwellings, streets, and transport so as to convey thirty-five thousand workers to the factory gates in no more than thirty minutes.[60] Postulating a population increase of about forty thousand during each of the first four years, and working with a figure of eight to nine square meters of living space per person, the team calculated the need for an additional three hundred thousand square meters of housing each year. Blocks of apartments would be built around courtyards, thereby significantly reducing the impact of the winds whistling off the water. Recapitulating the previous twenty years of Soviet domestic architectural standards, the architects designed buildings of five, nine to twelve, and sixteen stories. Each apartment would contain from one to three rooms capable of accommodating families of two to five people. They chose large prefabricated concrete panels as the predominant exterior building material.[61]

Rubanenko and his colleagues cleaved to the dominant thinking among Soviet urban planners of the late 1950s and early '60s concerning the provision of services.[62] They worked within the "graduated [*stupenchataia*] system," which consisted of the recursive subdivision of the city correlated to different levels of service as follows:

1. city—specialized shops, restaurants with exotic cuisine, theater, philharmonic, train station, market, city council, sports stadium, hospital;
2. residential district—episodic services within radius of one to 1.5 kilometers for 20–25,000 people (cinema, club, restaurant, café, cosmetics store, dress shop, post office, savings bank, large food store);
3. microdistrict—periodic services within radius of 400–500 meters for 10–12,000 people (school, food and household goods stores, housing office, club, cafeteria, hairdresser);
4. residential group—everyday services within radius of 150 meters for 3,000–5,000 people (service bureau, child care, kindergarten, food shop).[63]

Such ideas heavily influenced the allocation of resources within urban areas throughout the Brezhnev era.[64] Avtograd afforded the opportunity to put them into practice in a brand-new city. As the future capital of the Soviet automobile, the city also merited and received special attention with respect to car ownership and parking. At a time when not even twenty of every thousand Soviet residents owned a car, the architects projected a rate of two hundred per thousand (or one in five) residents for Avtograd. Their automobiles would be accommodated in open-air parking lots, underground garages, and multistory garages located outside the inhabited areas of microdistricts.[65] At least as noteworthy in this self-described "expression of the most progressive ideas of Soviet urban planning" was what the plan did not mention. The absence of any houses of worship should not be surprising for a Soviet city created ex nihilo. In fact, none was built until AvtoVAZ paid for the construction of the spacious, sixty-two-meter-high Spaso-Preobrazhenskii Cathedral that opened in August 2002. Provisions for pedestrians and more generally the encouragement of street life accessible to residents on foot are also conspicuous by their absence. The result is a city best characterized as "sterile." The gender composition of the architectural team—ten of its eleven members were men—may account for the scant attention paid to interior design and, except for references to their "comfortableness" and built-in furniture, silence about kitchens.

Looking back from the perspective of the early 1990s, VAZ's former assistant director S. P. Polikarpov described the enterprise as "a child of the administrative system with all its advantages and shortcomings." More recently, a local historian characterized the city that was created to serve VAZ as "reflecting the spirit of the industrial epoch," with all of its "virtues and deficiencies."[66] It is hard to quarrel with either judgment. Once the government had decided that automobiles would be mass produced and that Togliatti was where this would happen, getting the factory built and housing the tens of thousands of attendant auto workers and their families put a premium on speed. The key advantages of the administrative-command system lay in its capacity to issue instructions downward through ministries, institutes, and other central and regional bodies, and in the absence of institutionalized resistance from local authorities or private interests. Hyperstandardization of materials and design might be identified as the somewhat dubious "virtue" of the industrial epoch. The shortcomings and deficiencies have become too well known to repeat here. Many of them were nicely captured by the sardonic observation made in the 1977 Soviet film *An Irony of Fate* that "one of the great achievements of recent Soviet construction has been to make folks feel at ease when traveling to an unknown city."[67]

But we need to return to the beginning, to the period of their construction, to appreciate what both factory and city represented at that time. Throwing themselves into construction projects was something Soviet citizens did rather often. Digging large holes in the ground and installing large structures in them seemed to be a nearly permanent state of existence during the era of industrialization, which is why Andrei Platonov's use of the foundation pit as a metaphor for the grandiosity and barbarity of Soviet utopianism seems so apt. Beginning with the ground breaking about ten kilometers northwest of the old city in the fall of 1967, the building of Avtograd had many of the ingredients of a Soviet construction novel. Once again (as had been the case with the building of the Central District earlier in the decade, only on a more massive scale), a "whole forest of cranes" appeared on land where previously only "thick weeds" had grown. Earth removal and the race against time were the twin themes that dominated accounts of the enormous project. S. Bogatko and E. Man'ko, the *Pravda* correspondents who filed periodic progress reports, structured their articles around both of them. So many tens of thousands of cubic meters of earth moved, so many tons of cement laid, "Five Hundred Hectares under Roof" (the title of an article from March 1969)—such was the spatial score keeping. As for the element of time, the correspondents reminded readers that planners had allotted "Only a Thousand Days"—the title of a two-part article from September 1968—for the factory to be built; that "the schedules have been tightened," this in an article called "Time Demands"; and that "to lose one minute means losing 2,361 rubles." Ultimately, the moment would come when the switch on the assembly line would be thrown, and, in the words of Kuibyshevgidrostroi's director, Semizorov, "the schedule coordinating the actions of dozens of subcontracted organizations will play its vital role." At that point, if all went well, a car would come rolling off the assembly line every 22 seconds (about as long, the *Pravda* correspondents pointed out, as it takes to wind one's watch, sharpen a pencil, or drink a glass of water), which meant 160 in an hour, 1,100 in a shift, and 660,000 in a year.[68]

Ultimately, which is to say about six months after initially projected but still before the completion of the factory, the two-kilometer-long assembly line did get switched on. On April 19, 1970 (three days shy of the centenary

Schoolchildren dance around a Zhiguli (VAZ 2101 or "Kopeika") that advertises the fiftieth anniversary of the Soviet Union relay race, 1972. From *AVTOVAZ. Istoriia millionov, 1966–2006* (Togliatti: OAO AvtoVaz, 2007), 83. Courtesy of AvtoVAZ.

of Lenin's birth), six cars made their way to the end of the conveyor belt. The VAZ-2101, the Soviet version of the Fiat-124 according to the official nomenclature, was given the name of Zhiguli after the hills on the opposite bank of the Volga. It would be exported as Lada, the Slavic goddess of spring and love.[69] Thus began the life of the "Kopeika" (or kopeck, from the last two digits of the car's numerical designation—2101), the model that would be produced in updated versions (2103, 2105, 2106, 2107) to the present time, some 12.5 million units and counting. Chosen as "Russian automobile of the twentieth century" by readers of the country's most venerable car magazine, it was unquestionably the Soviet "people's car," whether by choice or for lack thereof.[70] Its relatively low price and ease of repair explain its continued appeal, though early twenty-first century Russian hipsters also evince an element of reverse snobbism.[71]

It took awhile for VAZ to achieve full capacity. Daily output rose from 500 in March 1971 to 735 in November. The projections of 2,200 cars a day and 660,000 a year were reached in 1974. By then things had started to assume a fairly routine cast. Iurii Stepanov, a local boy who rose to become secretary of the party committee at the plant and first vice president of the company, recalled nostalgically that when he began working as a machine-construction engineer in 1971 "we lived the factory and its problems, were gladdened by it as if we were related to it.... Yes, work was our life, and we were incapable of being diverted from it even around the table. Our wives would say 'enough about work,' but then we would start up again."[72] In 1975 Poliakov, "one of the last of the Mohicans of those 'red generals' and 'red directors'...who managed to surmount incredible difficulties," left Togliatti to take up his appointment as minister of automobile production. The subsequent life of the

The five-millionth VAZ 2101 ("Kopeika") rolls off the assembly line, October 26, 1979. From *AVTOVAZ: Istoriia millionov, 1966–2006* (Togliatti: OAO AvtoVaz, 2007), 129. Courtesy of AvtoVAZ.

factory was punctuated by celebrations—replete with speeches, flowers, and photographs—in honor of every millionth car produced, new versions of the Zhiguli, and the introduction of new brands such as the off-road Niva in 1977 and the front-wheel drive Samara hatchback in 1984.[73]

The feeling is inescapable that somehow things got less exciting after the factory was up and running and the kinks in the production process had been smoothed out. Valerii Romaniuk, a correspondent for *Izvestiia,* expressed just this feeling when he wrote in 1979:

> Hasn't something been lost today compared with those romantic times? The turbulence, the youthful energy that was endemic to those who were present at the source of VAZ, steadfastly braving the cold, the discomfort, and the separation from loved ones. For the sake of what? The future!

But as he pointed out, we now inhabit the future:

> Is it appropriate to speak about this now, when the handsome factory buildings colored in blue are surrounded by green lawns, and poplars shedding their down? Why not? We remember Magnitogorsk and Dneproges. And today, the history of our country is being written in steel and concrete at KamAZ and BAM. The Volga auto plant is a link in the chain [*v estafete*] of our industry.[74]

The analogies and links were what it was all about, for they were supposed to root and connect a population that had been uprooted, in many cases more than once, and may have been feeling increasingly disconnected from the country's past. When Stepanov cited dinner-table conversation about building the factory as indicative of the organic relationship he and others felt toward it, he was echoing those "fanatics of carburetors and ignitions, champions of shock absorbers" at GAZ, whom Boris Agapov observed endlessly discussing automotive details to the point where "their unfortunate wives and mothers begged them, 'Petya, not another word about the factory! Moisei, you'll kill me with your crank shaft!'" And in truth, among some who had played a leading role in the building of VAZ, this way of thinking and expressing oneself seems to have stuck. Recalling many years later the welders who connected pipes in the freezing cold so that heat could be delivered to VAZ's iron foundry, Semizorov, a two-time Order of Lenin winner, commented that "it was like Magnitogorsk, like Stalingrad Tractor, like ZIL. In all my time, I honestly have never seen such enthusiasm."[75]

Semizorov was not old enough to have been present at these earlier construction projects, but he had heard or read about them sufficiently to know that the "passion" displayed by their participants was replicated in the building of VAZ and Avtograd. Avtograd, the socialist city of the Brezhnev era, would in turn provide inspiration for those building Naberezhnye Chelny and BAM. Already in 1973 one could write about the giant truck factory going up on the banks of the Kama River in the following terms:

> The word KamAZ is worthy of being considered alongside those of Dneproges, Turksib, Magnitka, and Bratsk Hydroelectric. A whole generation of shockworkers' names—the miner Aleksei Stakhanov, the blacksmith Aleksandr Busygin, the weaver Maria Vinogradova, the milling-machinist Ivan Gudov, the locomotive engine driver Petr Krivonos—is applied to the builders of KamAZ. The torch of labor passed from one generation to another, and the consciousness of the debt incurred inspires the young builders of the auto giant.[76]

And so it went...or didn't, because by the time Semizorov died in 1999, many young people probably regarded this "Honored Citizen of the City of Togliatti" as a "*sovok*," someone incapable of breaking out of a Soviet mentality. At some point, it seems, the link was broken, the torch stopped getting passed, and "no credible secular projects remained" in the Communist repertoire. Identifying precisely when this happened should be on the scholarly agenda. Most likely it did not happen all at once but, rather, sectionally, among some people—young urban intellectuals, for example—sooner than others. Also, the secular project that no longer captured people's imagination and enthusiasm was not identical to its original version. It evolved, though evidently not to the same extent or fast enough to satisfy an increasingly demanding urbanized, educated population. Let us take the example of the welders to whom Semizorov referred. He identified three sources of their enthusiasm: first, "just the very act of participating in such a large undertaking inspired people"; second, "to begin a new life here"; and third, "simply...to see these precious [*zavetnye*] Togliatti cars and...to become owners of them." If the first two would not have been out of place at Socialist City, Magnitogorsk, or other heroic construction projects of the Stalin era, the third source reflected the post-Stalin shift toward accommodating consumers' desires, or at least acknowledging their legitimacy.[77]

Abroad, Ladas did well at least until the end of Communism in Eastern Europe, although the popular saying in the German Democratic Republic from the mid-1970s—"Bewahte uns vor lösen Frauen und Autos, die lie Russen bauen" (Beware of aggressive women and cars built by Russians)—suggests a preference for domestic models. Elsewhere in Europe, their appeal varied. In Finland the Lada's heyday was in the 1970s when its price, compared with imports from elsewhere in Europe, was unbeatable and the postwar generation was experiencing unprecedented opportunities of automobility. "By the early eighties at the latest," writes Jukka Gronow, "Lada was not any more to be recommended." The reason was not a decline in quality but rather that by this time Lada's Western and Japanese competitors, "the unspoken points of comparison in [technical] reports, had run far ahead." In Britain, by contrast, the mid- to late-1980s seems to have been the peak period of the Lada's appeal, coinciding with the Thatcherite boom, when "the newly consumerized ex-working classes, heady with the equity that came from council-house sales and the promise of the ready credit that property ownership could guarantee," bought them "in embarrassingly large numbers." High running-and-repair costs and, eventually, emission-control regulations did them in.[78]

The one country where Ladas did not travel was the United States, though it was a close thing. In May 1975, American newspapers reported under the headline "Russia May Sell Car Here" that if a deal then in the works came to fruition, as many as ten thousand Ladas could be sold annually. Alarmed by the prospect, John Ashbrook, a Republican congressman from Ohio, had a statement entered into the *Congressional Record* that read in part: "About the last thing the U.S. needs right now is a Soviet manufactured car....Auto sales of American-made cars are already far below normal. Thousands of auto workers have been thrown out of work....We cannot afford to have U.S. markets flooded with cheap, state-produced products."[79] Ashbrook, who died in 1982 after serving in Congress for twenty-two years, lived just long enough to witness the "invasion" of cheap, non–state-produced Japanese cars. It would be another three years before Malcolm Bricklin succeeded in importing the Yugo, Lada's distant cousin from Yugoslavia.

A Youthful City/A City Full of Youths

Mitya was a twenty-year-old finance major at TGU, Togliatti State University, when I met him in 2004. From his detached demeanor and laconic way of speaking, it was hard to read him, but I liked him instantly. "Why did you choose finance," I asked him at one point. "Simply because where I grew up [on a farm about twenty-five kilometers from Togliatti] the only thing I saw was shit," he replied. The rest of the explanation, presumably, was self-evident. One studied finance to become wealthy enough to avoid spending the rest of one's life in shit. In the second volume of AvtoVAZ's limited-edition collection of interviews, Iurii Sapsai, a much-lauded engineer, is asked what had brought him to Togliatti in the late 1960s. "Our pig-raising sovkhoz sent all its products to Moscow, and we were left with only dung and destitution. Things were particularly bad in the winter. So, what was there to do? Go thieving [*idi voroi*] or for moonshine. But I wasn't able to do that."[80] Both Iurii and Mitya had wanted the same thing: to escape rural boredom and "begin a new life" in Togliatti, the city that had started over and would do so again. Separated by more than thirty years, only one got to start his second life at the same time that Togliatti was about to begin its new life as an automobile city. Let's see what we can learn about Sapsai's contemporaries, those who built Avtograd and worked at VAZ, and about what kind of a city Togliatti became after its rebirth.

They came from all across the Soviet Union (and from Italy too). Ten battalions from the army, demobilized soldiers, graduates of technical schools. By September 1968, they numbered forty thousand; at the peak of construction, sixty-five thousand were on the site. "One could meet dark-complexioned southerners and fair-haired inhabitants from the north," *Pravda*'s correspondents wrote. "One could hear Russian, Tajik, Ukrainian and Buriat, Georgian, Moldavan, Belorussian, Uzbek, and Latvian." The list replays an earlier theme. Addressing another "Mitya" at Avtostroi in 1931, Boris Agapov wrote that "simultaneously with you came hundreds of people the same age from Kursk and Cheboksary, from Ukraine and the north Caucasus." In all, forty-two nationalities were represented at Avtograd in the late 1960s. They included veterans of other construction projects—concrete workers and welders who had labored on Siberian hydroelectric stations, bulldozer operators who had built roads and carved out mines in the extreme north and the Far East. Most, though, had had little if any experience, and were only just entering their twenties. The average age of the city's population was twenty-six.[81]

Many left after the completion of construction, but some stayed to work in the factory, as their employers encouraged them to do and as was typical of previous Soviet heroic construction projects. According to an agreement between Poliakov and Semizorov, those who worked for a minimum of six months in construction and had a good work record were eligible for the factory "reserves"; after eighteen months, they had earned the right to a regular factory job.[82] Such was VAZ's need for workers that the quality of their work probably did not get checked too carefully. Aside from—or even more important than—the job itself, the promise of a decent apartment attracted people to VAZ. But apartment construction lagged behind. Thus in October 1969 several hundred such "*garantiishchiki*," tired of living in dormitories or renting "corners" in apartments in the old city or even in outlying villages, decided "to seek justice" from the chair of the auxiliary shop's trade union committee. His efforts to persuade them to disperse succeeded only after he had arranged a meeting with Poliakov. At the meeting, the director invited the workers to help build the apartments themselves, which they did over a period of six months, thereby reviving the "people's construction" approach to mass housing that originated in the mid-1950s at GAZ.[83]

Willy-nilly, a factory workforce took shape. A snapshot of its demographic structure, obtained from the local archives, shows that in March 1970, one month before the first Zhiguli rolled off the assembly line, VAZ employed 42,668 people of whom 34,494 were workers and 6,407 were engineering-technical personnel. Men made up just under two-thirds of the workforce, but their distribution was uneven. They were 83 and 84 percent of the workers in the two main production shops of the enterprise, but only 26 percent in the less prestigious and lower-paid housing and cultural affairs department. Nearly 60 percent of all workers were thirty years old or younger. More than four of every five were ethnic Russians, which suggests that all those other languages heard among the construction workers were spoken by a relative few, that non-Russians left Togliatti in disproportionate numbers after completing their construction stint, or that *Pravda*'s correspondents had been engaging in the hype characteristic of Soviet construction sagas.[84]

As for engineering-technical personnel, data from January 1969 reveal that in comparison with workers a far greater proportion had some form of higher education (64% compared with 0.6%), were party members (60% compared with 14%), and had reached at least their thirty-first year (65% compared with 42%). Correspondingly, a smaller proportion of engineering personnel belonged to the Komsomol (9.2% compared with 19.8%), which limited membership to those between the ages of fourteen and twenty-eight. All this is as one might expect and is consistent with national trends. As far as gender was concerned, women made up 26 percent of engineering-technical personnel, a figure that was virtually the same at the beginning of 1976. Of 585 people in managerial positions in 1972, only 36 (6.15%) were women; by 1980, the number had climbed to 62, but that still represented less than 9 percent of all managers. Most were employed in the nonindustrial sections that included housing, medical, food, cleaning, and pension administration.[85] According to Ol'ga Kapitonova Vologina, who was hired as chief communications engineer in 1967 (and incidentally was the sole woman among the twenty-nine administrators and engineers interviewed in the first volume of AvtoVAZ's multi-volume collection of memoirs and interviews), "Poliakov traditionally did not permit women in leadership positions."[86] Poliakov, it seems, was not all that unusual. Elsewhere in the Soviet Union, although women were better represented among technical specialists than among skilled workers in industry, they remained largely absent from positions of managerial authority.[87]

On January 1, 1976, the total workforce (not only wage workers but also office staff and engineering-technical personnel) at VAZ was 92,163 of whom just over 38,000 (41.3%) were women. Five years later women numbered 52,000 (45.6%) of a total workforce of 112,231. The increase in the proportion of women was across the board, testifying on the one hand to VAZ's seemingly inexhaustible need for both assembly-line workers and those working in the nonindustrial parts of the enterprise and, on the other, to the relative lack of comparable job opportunities in the vicinity.[88] With some ten thousand babies born every year, the need for children's day care was "colossal." The city did not come close to satisfying the need, and so VAZ stepped into the breach. In May 1968, it set up a children's sector within its housing and cultural affairs department (ZhKU—*zhilishchno-kommunal'noe upravlenie*) to administer preschool and kindergarten programs. From 1975 onward the majority of children in day care attended VAZ-run programs. Overcrowding seems to have been the norm.[89]

The population of the city rose inexorably. In April 1972 the 100,000 residents in the newly created Auto Factory District represented a little less than a third of the 360,000 in the entire city. When the sixth all-Union census was taken in 1979, the city's population was just over 500,000; a year later, it was 521,000 with the Auto Factory District containing slightly more people than the Central and Komsomol'sk districts combined.[90] At this point, the perceptive reader may ask: Wasn't the population of the latter two districts projected to decline? The answer is yes, but if everything in the Soviet Union went according to plan, at the very least there would still be a Soviet Union. As furiously as the pace of housing construction proceeded in Avtograd it could not keep up with the increase in population. In the interest of expanding accommodation, municipal authorities thrust aside concerns expressed by Rubanenko's architectural team about poor air quality and effluence from factories in the Central District. Of paramount importance was to produce cars, and VAZ needed more workers to do that.

Togliatti was a city that offered Soviet authorities a great opportunity to practice both civil and social engineering, the planning of production and of consumption. Though not exactly a tabula rasa before the arrival of the planners and builders in 1966, its prior existence seemed an irrelevance. Recruited from near and far, provided with newly built apartments, the overwhelmingly youthful population that swelled the city had the opportunity to work and live in as close to ideal conditions as the USSR was capable of mustering for its industrial working class. Half a world away, in the Mahoning Valley of eastern Ohio, General Motors claimed it was doing the same thing. When the Lordstown plant opened in 1966 it represented the last word in high-tech automated production, and its future, brokered by GM's recognition of the United Automobile Workers Union as the workers' bargaining agent, seemed bright. But the plant, which employed over ten thousand workers to produce Chevy Impalas and then the subcompact Vega, was soon plagued with wildcat strikes and other forms of labor militancy. Far from emblematic of enlightened industrial relations, Lordstown became a favorite subject of U.S. labor historians and sociologists looking for action.[91]

Wildcat strikes also occurred, albeit rarely, at VAZ. As elsewhere in the Soviet Union, they were short-term affairs settled on the spot. In 1972 workers in the body-assembly shop downed tools for four hours in protest against what they considered an unfair rate system of wages. Foundry workers stopped work for nearly an entire day in 1974 to register their unhappiness with a bonus system that struck them as arbitrary. Their action, which was supported by the union, led to the revision of the system. The only other pre-1989 job action I have been able to document had to do not with VAZ but with the shortage of food in the city's stores. Workers in the paint shop—evidently all women—stopped work for two hours demanding to speak with responsible municipal administrators, and when promised more supplies, returned to work.[92]

The parallel with Lordstown speaks not so much to labor disputes as to the limitations of social engineering. Lordstown was situated in a rural location in part so that it would attract workers who, having to commute to the factory over relatively long distances, were thought unlikely to form strong

"Avtograd was equipped with the full range of institutions to minister to the needs of workers and their families": the headquarters of VAZ's Service Department. From *AVTOVAZ: Istoriia millionov, 1966–2006* (Togliatti: OAO AvtoVaz, 2007), 75. Courtesy of AvtoVAZ.

and lasting bonds. Avtograd was equipped with the full range of institutions to minister to the needs of workers and their families: housing offices, clubs, sports facilities, car repair services, libraries, schools, and so forth. These services were not all that the general plan had promised, and, as one resident noted, "the lack of decorative forms and cozy corners deprived the city of an atmosphere of warmth and humanity." Nevertheless, few would have judged Avtograd a bad place to live, or thought VAZ a bad place to work.[93]

Still, VAZ's workers hardly exuded much "factory patriotism." A survey from the late 1970s found that only 24 percent expressed "pride" in the factory, while 17 percent said that they had "lost" such pride, and 59 percent were "indifferent."[94] Workers' actions also suggested a degree of alienation from the industrial-utopian dreams of Soviet planners and propagandists. Between January and August 1973, guards at the factory gates caught 796 people attempting to leave work with goods valued at R 35,406, and found an additional 606 to have small items such as scraps of leather, pieces of wood, and self-fashioned objects, the value of which was not determined. Thus, within nine months, 3 percent of the workforce had been caught in the act of pilfering. How many passed undetected through the factory gates with tools, parts, and other materials, of course, will never be known. A report to the Auto Factory District's soviet executive committee by the commission on socialist legality and the preservation of public order noted that these figures represented a "significant decline" compared with 1972. Indeed, in that year, guards had stopped 2,548 would-be "plunderers" (raskhiteli) with goods valued at over R 80,000. Some had tried to hide materials in their clothing by stuffing tire tubes into the top of boots or tying car upholstery around the waist. Others used the cars coming off the assembly line to put items behind the paneling of doors or under the hood. Many acted alone, but the report also noted an increasing tendency to form groups "whose methods are becoming more artful."[95]

It would be nice to know what these workers intended to do with the items they pilfered. Sell them on the black market? Set up repair shops on the side? Use them to customize or repair their own cars? Petty theft by workers and employees is at least as old as the Industrial Revolution.[96] The scale is difficult to measure, but generally, the larger the plant, the more opportunities there are for pilfering. In Soviet Russia the endemic shortages of goods of all kinds made pilfering an ever-present temptation. Harsh penalties existed, but management's inexhaustible thirst for labor often led to a lot of looking the other way. Along with absenteeism and alcohol abuse, theft of state property was the scourge of Soviet industry. Of course workers were far from being the only ones who stole from the state. Later in the decade, an American correspondent referred to thefts ("whole rail carloads of raw materials or parts") as "a serious nuisance," and after emigrating, a former international law expert described the entire country as a "kleptocratic state."[97]

As for alcohol, the city's commission reported on "raids" conducted by the police and the people's public-order detachments (druzhina) on stores selling intoxicating beverages, as well as parks, squares, and other outdoor gathering places. According to the report, during a four-and-a-half month period of 1972, 2,690 people received fines on the spot for consuming intoxicating beverages or appearing in an inebriated state in public places, and 2,073 were arrested for acts of petty hooliganism while under the influence of alcohol. The *druzhina* conducted additional raids at selected institutions such as the Kuibyshevgidrostroi Polytechnic, a four-year school located in the Komsomol'sk District that enrolled 642 fifteen to seventeen year olds. As a result of the raid, 87 (of whom 16 were female) of the 360 in their first year of study were arrested for theft, auto theft, hooliganism, or alcohol-related crimes.[98] Within the Auto Factory District raids resulted in 1,195 people being picked up in a state of intoxication during the first six months of 1973, but 1,593 during the corresponding period of the following year.[99]

This is not to suggest these forms of behavior were any more pronounced in Togliatti than elsewhere in the Soviet Union. The organization of the raids, after all, was in response to a decree of the RSFSR's Supreme Soviet "On Strengthening the Struggle against Drunkenness and Alcoholism" throughout the republic. Rather, somewhat surprising is Togliatti's very ordinariness in this respect. Its unusually youthful population, after all, supposedly embodied "mature socialism." Then again, one should not assume that Soviet authorities were any more successful in limiting access to Togliatti than, say, to Moscow where the phenomenon of *limitchiki* (residents without permits) was beginning to assume major proportions. Surely among the 429 people whom the police arrested in the first eight months of 1971 for vagrancy, begging, or parasitism were some whose papers were not in order.[100]

Many of those charged with pilfering or hooliganism were brought before comrades' courts where, if found guilty, they received fines or reprimands. Comrades' courts, institutions with a checkered history that went back to the Soviet Union's earliest years, existed both in the workplace and in residential districts. At VAZ each section or shop had one. In the Auto Factory District comrades' courts were attached to each housing office [ZhEK—*zhilishchno-ekspluatatsionnaia kontora*]. The residential-based courts heard cases involving "violations of socialist communal life [*obshchezhitie*]." For example, the court attached to ZhEK-4 heard forty-one of them during the first nine months of 1975. They involved such infractions as blocking up the refuse chute, incorrectly using the elevator, using the housing fund for inappropriate purposes, failing to pay rent, and behaving in an unacceptable manner in one's own apartment. The latter category covered everything from causing water damage to the building to disruptive domestic disputes to playing music at an excessive volume or at an inappropriate time.[101]

Such matters, though petty, were the stuff of everyday life in Togliatti, and if we want to know what it was like to live in the Soviet auto capital during its first decade, we should pay attention to them. Left at the level of statistically laden, bureaucratic reports, however, they do not distinguish the city from others, whether young or old, large or small. Just as Togliatti had people's public-order detachments, ZhEKs, and comrades' courts, so other

Brezhnev-era cities had these quasi-state institutions staffed by upstanding guardians of proper behavior and public order. Only by getting beyond the laconic compilations to the individual cases themselves can we experience something of the peculiarities of the city that, in the words of its architects, would "develop in accordance with the laws of socialist urban construction to become one of the best and most admired cities of the country."[102]

A Togliatti Marriage

Determining an appropriate mix of apartment sizes was one of the more momentous decisions that Avtograd's architects had to make. They planned, as already noted, for apartments of one to three rooms on the basis of families of no more than five and no fewer than two people. Average living space, a crucial index of Soviet domestic well-being, was to be in the range of seven to nine square meters per person.[103] An obvious question is how families of more than five would be accommodated. Another is what would happen in the case of divorce or other life-changing (or, for that matter, life-ending) events. The parameters of the problem were endemic to Soviet urban life. The devil—and the uniqueness of each city—is in the details. As early as September 1968 *Pravda* was reporting that a "complicated situation" had arisen in Togliatti in connection with apartment construction because of a shortage of highly skilled cadres. Young workers, many of them unmarried, were being housed in dormitories, but more senior workers with families were balking at signing up for the project because their residential needs were not being met and could not be guaranteed in the near future. The solution—to build more apartments to accommodate workers with families—presupposed the availability of such workers.[104]

It would appear that over the next few years the problem was solved; in fact, the authorities may have overcompensated. For when sometime in 1972 Gennadi Efremovich Ukhov, a worker in the assembly plant at VAZ, applied for an apartment for himself and his mother, the authorities turned him down, apparently because the only available apartments were for married people. Ukhov was evidently so desperate to get an apartment that he got himself married. His bride was Zoia Vasil'evna Kuznetsova, who worked as a tutor (*vospitatel'*) at one of the enterprise's dormitory complexes. Kuznetsova, who had a ten-year-old daughter from a previous marriage, was either incredibly naive or pretty desperate herself. No sooner had the three of them moved into their two-room, twenty-nine-square-meter apartment on the western edge of the Auto Factory District than Ukhov brought from the countryside his mother, aged eighty-one, and his sixty-two-year-old sister, announcing to the startled Zoia that the apartment was for his family alone. Shortly thereafter, in January 1973, the miserable Kuznetsova and her daughter fled back to the dormitory.[105]

Next, Ukhov sought to obtain legal sanction from the People's Court for Kuznetsova's permanent removal on grounds of connubial incompatibility. This, he discovered, was possible if he obtained a favorable judgment from the residential comrades' court pertaining to domestic disputes. And so it came to pass that the court attached to ZhEK-5 of VAZ's housing and cultural affairs department received a complaint from Marfa Mikhailovna Ukhova, Gennadi's mother, alleging maltreatment (*oskorblenie lichnosti*) and threats of reprisal by her "former daughter-in-law," Z. V. Kuznetsova. In the meantime, however, Kuznetsova's plight had been taken up by the trade union committee at VAZ, which appointed a commission of five to investigate. The commission made some rather startling discoveries:

1. Before proposing marriage to Kuznetsova, Ukhov had entered into marriage with a woman who had four children, but this woman had second thoughts and refused to help him obtain an apartment. He never did annul the marriage, however.
2. When the five members of the commission entered Ukhov's apartment at 100 Moscow Prospect and identified themselves, they were met with a "torrent of bad language" and "hysterics" from Marfa Mikhailovna. "Good people, help me. They're beating me with sticks," she cried out, evidently referring to the umbrellas that the commission's members were carrying. The neighbors were accustomed to such outbursts, for whenever Kuznetsova visited the apartment to fetch personal items, Marfa Mikhailovna would start shouting.
3. On further investigation, the commission discovered that contrary to the document that Ukhov had presented to the housing authorities claiming his mother was homeless, Marfa Mikhailovna had her own house in the countryside.

Unfortunately for Kuznetsova, the comrades' court that heard Marfa Mikhailovna's complaint did not get to take into account this testimony. On each of three occasions that the court was scheduled to meet, Kuznetsova and her witnesses were absent, either because they were unable to attend or (the record is unclear about this) had not been informed. Thus, on September 2, 1973, the comrades' court resolved to fine Kuznetsova ten rubles and to have her "unacceptable behavior" discussed at her place of work. Her only compensation was that the court asked the factory's residential and cultural affairs office that had granted Ukhov the apartment to partition it, with Ukhov residing in one room and Kuznetsova and her daughter inhabiting the other. Ukhov, however, rejected this Solomon-like solution, presumably because the prospect of living with his mother and sister in one room was intolerable.[106]

There matters stood until Kuznetsova filed an appeal with the executive committee of the Auto Factory District soviet, which turned the matter over to its commission on socialist legality and the maintenance of public order. The appeal was brief, the emotional note it struck being confined to the end:

Ukhov, his mother and sister remain in the apartment while my child and I have been thrown out onto the street. Why has this person who has been mocking me and my child for a whole year remained unpunished, while I am being punished because Ukhov and his relatives have deprived me of a place to live?

In addition to the appeal, the commission heard testimony from N. G. Fishman. A member of the trade union commission that investigated Kuznetsova's situation, Fishman also happened to be her workmate. She began her testimony by extolling Kuznetsova's character:

> This is an honest, conscientious worker. Unfailing in labor. Such workers as Zoia Mikhailovna [sic] stand out in one's memory for a lifetime. Respected in the collective, she has not wronged a single person in three years of work, has not been rude to anyone, has not raised her voice to anyone, is always reserved and composed.

Fishman then recounted her visit to Ukhov's apartment accompanied by other members of the trade union commission and its subsequent investigations.

The record of this sordid tale ends with I. G. Popova, the chairwoman of the soviet's commission, seeking and obtaining unanimous approval from the commission:

1. to ask the comrades' court to hear the case again, this time with Kuznetsova and her witnesses present;
2. to request information from the procurator of the district of Ukhov's former place of residence about the registration of his first marriage;
3. to inquire of the procurator what the appropriate punishment would be for the employee of the agricultural soviet who confirmed that Ukhov's mother was without shelter.

Let's see if we can sort out the issues embedded in this story. Some already have been addressed on a more generalized level; others only this more detailed examination of a single case could reveal. First, it is clear that the shortage of apartments is the catalyst driving the events. The shortage was partly planned—in the sense that all desirable goods were "deficit" (*defitsitnye*)—and partly the result of an adjustment made to the general plan for Togliatti to accommodate more senior workers with families. Second, people were willing to go to extraordinary lengths to obtain permission to reside in Avtograd, breaking the law, breaking hearts, and probably a few other things too. The other side of the coin was the possibility of escape from the deprivations of the countryside. Iurii Sapsai could escape because he was young and had skills (or at least showed the capacity of learning them quickly), but neither Marfa nor her daughter could leave except through Gennadi's scam. Living in the city brought status and comforts unknown in the village, and in the case of Togliatti the association with VAZ and the automobile promised more of both than could be found in any other city that was neither a Union republic capital nor Leningrad.

VAZ intrudes in another way. It provided the institutional nexus between work and home. The ZhEK, although by definition residentially based, actually was an extension of VAZ's housing and cultural affairs department. When Kuznetsova looked for assistance, she found it in her trade union committee even though her strife was, strictly speaking, domestic. And when the comrades' court found her domestic behavior unacceptable, her workmates rather than her fellow apartment dwellers were assigned the task of discussing it with her. Always hard to define in the Soviet context, the line between public and private seems particularly fuzzy in this instance. Perhaps this was because VAZ, the provider of jobs, housing, recreational facilities, and much else, served to intensify the intrusiveness of the paternalistic state.

Finally, this unfortunate dispute and how it was handled illustrates that much remained constant about the state's bureaucratic machine across the decades. Students of the Stalin era know very well that con artists and forged documents were rife, and that taking advantage of gaps in the flow of information between one bureaucratic institution and another occurred frequently.[107] Also striking and by no means peculiar to the Brezhnev era is the dependence of the system on personal testimony, on character witnesses. At the same time, what sets this story—and by implication, the period in which it occurred—apart from earlier times is the absence of political signifiers. For all his shenanigans, Ukhov did not provoke a charge of "anti-soviet behavior" from the court. In fact, the closest anyone came to generalizing about what he had done was when Fishman asserted that "it is not possible to gain satisfaction from Ukhov because there is no law that can bring to order a person who has lost his conscience." Kuznetsova's exemplary behavior as described by Fishman also lacked any political coloring. Evident then is the exhaustion of Soviet rhetorical categories and all they had implied.

From VAZ to AvtoVAZ

From the executive suites and dining halls that occupy the top floors of VAZ's twenty-six-story administrative headquarters, one has a panoramic view not only of the vast factory grounds comprising smelting plants, proving grounds, assembly lines, and other facilities, but of the entire Auto Factory residential district and beyond it the Zhiguli Sea. Like feudal barons gazing out from the top of a donjon over their domains, VAZ's executives could survey the territory below with the feeling that all who worked and lived there depended on them. However, as students of Michel de Certeau, we know that such "totalizing" vertical views are illusory. They invariably fail to take into account the labyrinthine messiness, the ordinary and extraordinary encounters both purposive and accidental, the scheming of a Gennadi Ukhov and the offended outrage of a Zoia Kuznetsova. But they are illusory for another, particularly Soviet, reason. Although Avtograd was a company town from the get-go, the company, VAZ, was itself dependent on higher authorities in Moscow. Like every other Soviet enterprise, VAZ did not control

AvtoVAZ Headquarters, Togliatti. From *VAZ stranitsy istorii, 1991–1996*, ed. A. Shavrin (Togliatti: OAO Avtovaz, 2005), 5:41. Courtesy of AvtoVAZ.

decisions about its products or what to do with the proceeds from their sale; it operated not on the basis of profit and loss but rather on the fulfillment of the plan. And its input into the making of that plan was at best indirect if not supplicatory.

During its first decade or so of operations, VAZ, as a new enterprise, had no difficulty receiving priority in resource allocation. Its assembly lines, while not exactly state of the art by world standards, were the best in the country. But in the 1980s the entire Soviet automobile industry stalled. The most obvious explanation is the inadequacy of investment to replace increasingly worn equipment. Investments instead poured into the oil and gas sector because of their growing importance as foreign-currency earners (15% of the total value of exports in 1970 but 53% by 1985). For central authorities, the car factories were cows to be milked. "Every month we notified the ministry that the numbers had to be corrected for the wage fund, for costs, for profits, for something else," P. M. Kotsura, VAZ's chief economist, recalled, "and each time a little bit more was *pinched* from us."[108] Growth in labor productivity at VAZ, which had averaged 4.1 percent per annum from 1976 to 1980, dropped to 1.6 percent between 1981 and 1985. Figures for the corresponding periods for what Soviet economists called profits were 9.7 percent and 1.6 percent.[109]

The economic choices that increasingly involved "zero-sum" alternatives were symptomatic of a more fundamental problem—the exhaustion of factors of production on which the entire planned economy had rested since its inception in the late 1920s. These were primarily inputs of labor, material goods, and natural resources. For all the talk about automation, intensification, integration of mechanisms, and a scientific-technological revolution, the wastefulness involved in the application of these factors remained undiminished. The demographic data—declining birthrates, and rising rates of infant mortality, alcoholism, divorce, and suicide—was compelling evidence of something seriously amiss.

At first, VAZ seemed immune from the crisis, but soon signs of it were everywhere: in the indices of productivity and profits cited above, in the ever-longer periods between the introduction of new models, the multiplication of complaints about poor quality, complications with suppliers in both Eastern Europe and the Soviet Union, the persistent shortages of spare parts, and the failure to consummate deals with potential partners abroad.[110] The rising tide of theft was another dimension. Between 1976 and 1980, 7,667 instances of theft were reported at VAZ, with the value of goods stolen placed at R 644,000. But in 1981 alone the value of stolen goods reached R 238,400. Whereas in 1979 guards had detained 1,421 individuals, in 1980 the number jumped by 921 to 2,342, and in 1981 by another 770 to 3,112. The temptation to steal parts was well-nigh overwhelming given the enormous differences between official and black market prices. Local sources cite the official price of camshafts as 23 rubles, but "among speculators" they went for 200–250 rubles; Cardan shafts that officially cost 6.50 rubles could be had on the black market for 50–60 rubles. "Like flies to the honey," note the authors of a recent history of VAZ, "people lived off the shortage of automobiles and spare parts."[111]

Criminal activities were becoming more organized and penetrating more deeply into the administration. Audits conducted in 1985 of VAZ's technical service division and its network of parts stores found that 973 individuals had violated "the regimen for the protection of socialist property." The vast majority consisted of division heads and other managerial personnel who had been on the take. The mildness of their punishment—only thirty-three were fired—itself indicated that such activities had become a necessity, or at least a way of life.[112]

As for labor, a comparison with VAZ's earlier years shows the following: a higher percentage of workers employed in secondary and tertiary capacities, a rise in the average level of education and the age of workers, and an inexorable growth in the number of workers employed despite periodic attempts to reduce the payroll. Combined with the leveling of wages and a decline in the quality of work, these trends were all characteristic of Soviet industry in the early 1980s. So too were the increasing difficulties VAZ experienced in recruiting sufficient numbers of new workers. Inadequate and poor quality of housing, day care, and transportation hampered recruitment efforts. In 1982 VAZ began to tap another source of labor: Vietnamese workers.[113]

In the spring of 1985, VAZ's administration embarked on an experiment in self-financing (*khozraschet*). In seeking to free the enterprise from its abject dependence on central ministries, the experiment harkened back to the New Economic Policy of the 1920s, even as it anticipated a key aspect of "perestroika." It was, among other things, the enterprise's way of creating incentives for cost savings and, therefore, it was assumed, greater profit. Everyone at VAZ was to benefit, for, as one Western economist noted, "fixed shares of the profit would be distributed to three unified funds within the enterprise (for investment in production, for material stimulation, and a social and cultural fund)." The administration drew up five-year plans—it was still a Soviet enterprise after all—for anticipated cost savings: 1.9 percent for 1986, 3.7 percent for 1987, and so forth. Unfortunately, the ministries (primarily of Finance and Automobile Production) were unwilling to give up their prerogatives. But perhaps to blame the center is to let VAZ's management off the hook. "An analysis of the further activity of AvtoVAZ," assert the authors of the company's history, "says that declarations to the contrary, the leadership did not pin its hopes very strongly on the results of the experiment and continued to count on centralized capital investment." Little wonder then that "in 1987 the enterprises engaged in 'self-financing' did not display better result [*sic*] than other enterprises."[114]

General Secretary Gorbachev visited Togliatti in April 1986. He called on leading party and managerial personnel to be more ambitious—to dream, as it were. Instead of contenting themselves with trying to meet the world's standards for automobile excellence, he urged them to be trendsetters, "to be, in your own way, legislators of automotive fashion."[115] The VAZ 1111 Oka, a microcar with a 750 cc two-cylinder engine, probably was not what Gorbachev had in mind, but it was the next and, as it turned out, the last Soviet car produced from scratch by VAZ. It began life in December 1987 at KamAZ (and originally was called Kama), although the tiny vehicle that resembled the Fiat Panda had been designed and engineered at VAZ. For several years assembly lines at KamAZ and VAZ cranked them out, but in 1991 production was transferred to the Serpukhov Automobile Factory (SeAZ), which VAZ had absorbed two years earlier. Like the Zaporozhets with which it shared a diminutive size and lack of safety features but not sluggishness, it quickly became the subject of horrifying stories and mordant humor. Perhaps the best thing that can be said for it, other than its relatively affordable price, was that it made the VAZ 2108 and 2109 seem luxurious by contrast.

Looking back at the last years of the Soviet Union, it is a wonder anything was getting produced. Despite the installation of closed-circuit television monitors, magnetic-coded passes, and other security devices, theft of auto parts continued, becoming "a malignant tumor that enveloped production and nonproduction sectors."[116] Workers, emboldened by events elsewhere in the Soviet Union as well as in Eastern Europe, infused the enterprise's Council of Labor Collectives (STK) with new life, turning it temporarily into an organ of protest and even to a degree of workers' control.[117] By contrast, the trade union apparatus and the Communist Party Committee—two of the three institutions that made up the enterprise "triangle"—simply went through the motions. Deprived of one prerogative after another, the party began to lose members. By early 1990, the exodus took on mass proportions. In the meantime, inflation continued to mount, shortages intensified, and labor discipline suffered. Work time lost through absenteeism rose by 20 percent in 1990 compared with 1989; dismissals of workers who came to work drunk or were caught drinking on the job rose by nearly 50 percent; and cases of theft were up 54 percent.[118]

Management, the third corner of the triangle, worked furiously to stave off collapse. It agreed to raise wages and purchased and arranged for closed distribution of huge quantities of consumer goods, ranging from perfume and cigarettes to washing powder. It launched a veritable propaganda blitz through the enterprise's newspaper and radio: "These are tough times, but if we hang together we will see them through." "Stealing from the factory is like stealing from yourself." When Vladimir Kadannikov, who had been elected general director in November 1988, stood as a candidate for the USSR Supreme Soviet, he told the voters, "I live in the same kind of building as you do in the Avtograd District. I walk into the same foul and dilapidated entrances with elevators that don't work and hall lights that are broken. So, I'm familiar with the problems of Togliatti's residents."[119]

But the VAZ administration could also wield the stick. On April 19, 1991, it issued new rules on violations of labor discipline that empowered shop directors unilaterally to determine penalties; only the most severe violations would now require trade union approval. The rules addressed behavior not only at work but also in public and at home, and in this sense they were consistent with VAZ's practice of treating domestic disputes as work related. At the same time, they were indicative of its adaptation to the near collapse of supervening state authority and institutions that compelled VAZ to behave increasingly like a company running a company town. Judging by trade union data, the new rules had absolutely no effect. They show unexcused absences rising by 35 percent and loss of work time up 24 percent, while productivity declining by 12 percent in 1991. Worse was still to come. By the summer of 1992, Kadannikov was lamenting the two hundred distributor belts and four hundred halogen lamps that disappeared every day from cars that had just rolled off the assembly line.[120]

Even as it confronted these quotidian concerns, VAZ was engaged in two struggles that would determine the company's—and Togliatti's—future. One was with central authorities over the tethering of the enterprise to state orders (*goszakazy*). The other involved the conditions of privatizing VAZ. State orders, a hallmark of the Soviet planned economy, required VAZ to deliver to the state a predetermined number of cars at low fixed prices in return for which the state financed operations—also at low, below-cost prices. Notwithstanding experimentation with self-financing, VAZ remained tied to the system of state orders while the entire economy lurched toward market transactions. By the early 1990s the enterprise had become a net debtor, trapped between the modest increase in the price the state paid for its Zhigulis and Samaras and its exploding costs for parts, energy, and other resources. Only in the spring of 1992, by which time the Soviet Union had disappeared, did VAZ break free of this system, setting up its own distributorships. At this point all sorts of hucksters descended on Togliatti to get a piece of the action, turning the city into the crime capital of the country.

The larger context in which the other struggle occurred was the first wave or round of enterprise privatizations undertaken by management and, in some cases, ministries. Most enterprises converted themselves into joint-stock companies with management becoming the majority (or at least key) shareholder. KamAZ privatized in this manner in June 1990. At VAZ two privatization proposals emerged: the STKs advanced one, and the administration proposed the other. The STK version envisioned the state turning over the enterprise at no cost to the entire collective, which would hire new management, presumably under the auspices of the council itself. The administration's version called for limiting workers' shares to 20 percent and reserving a large bloc (40 percent, it was rumored) for a "strong foreign strategic partner." That partner, it soon became clear, was Fiat. The STK leadership appeared ready to compromise, but a more militant group of workers would have nothing of the administration's plan, claimed that managerial personnel were overrepresented at a meeting to decide which version to adopt, and on February 22, 1991, they organized an effective one-hour work stoppage. With the enterprise embroiled in dispute and the political situation in the entire country about to explode, neither Fiat nor any other "foreign strategic partner" was willing to come to the rescue.[121]

Round two of the battle over privatization commenced in 1992 when Anatolii Chubais, chairman of the State Property Management Committee (Goskomimushchestvo), came up with a plan that managed to antagonize both VAZ administrators and the STK leadership. Together with the STK chairman, Ivan Baryshnikov, Kadannikov persuaded Russian Federation President Yeltsin to intervene. On October 12, 1992, he signed a decree stipulating that half of the statutory capital of the firm would become the property of the whole collective. The decree provided the basis for the compromise version worked out by the State Commission on the Privatization of AvtoVAZ. On January 5, 1993, OAO AvtoVAZ was registered as a private company. This marked only the beginning of the complicated process of determining the actual nature and value of the company's property and the procedures by which shares would be sold. But for VAZ, it was the end.

Unity for Some

The overwhelming majority of workers and employees at AvtoVAZ, numbering some 130,000 people, came to be represented in the post-Soviet period by the Automobile and Farm Machinery Workers Union of Russia (ASMR), a lineal descendant of the all-Union organization of Soviet times. The dominant union in the Russian automobile industry, it developed relations with management typical of post-Soviet unions. The union, in fact, represents both management and workers and faithfully pursues a policy of "social partnership in the sphere of labor" much as its Soviet predecessor had. At AvtoVAZ, though, ASMR is not the sole union. Roughly thirty-five hundred workers belong to Edinstvo (Unity), an alternative union formed in September 1990.

Edinstvo grew out of a September 1989 strike. Two months earlier, hundreds of thousands of Soviet coal miners had struck, forming strike committees that laid the groundwork for the Independent Miners' Union (NPG). The strike at VAZ was far less spectacular, a two-hour stoppage organized by the STK. General-director Kadannikov initially rejected demands for higher wages and future indexation of wages for inflation, but after some twenty thousand workers assembled on the square outside the blue skyscraper headquarters, he relented. The STK's subsequent failure to maintain pressure on management appears to have persuaded several activists who took part in this brief stoppage to form their own union a year later.[122]

Edinstvo is that rare post-Soviet union that has maintained a combative position toward management. Twenty percent of members' dues are paid into a strike fund. It is this as much as anything else that, in the view of one sympathetic observer, "sets them apart from the mass of ASMR members, who belong to their union out of a combination of inertia, lingering faith in the paternalistic benevolence of management, and most of all, lack of confidence in their own collective capacity to change things for the better."[123] Its small numbers are therefore somewhat deceiving. The bar of membership being higher, so too is the members' level of activism. In its fifteen years of existence, Edinstvo has waged a number of campaigns pitting it against not only management but also the larger and better-funded ASMR. It has persistently demanded full indexation of wages, no small matter considering the volatility of price increases in the 1990s. As nonpayment of wages threatened to become the default policy of management, it mounted a six-day strike in the final-assembly shop in the fall of 1994. At the instigation of shop-floor activists, it organized a warning strike in October 2000 for higher wages and against mandatory overtime work. In September 2002, it encouraged workers on the assembly line that makes the new model, Kalina, to oppose the addition of a ninth hour by knocking off after eight. It sponsored rallies in support of these demands, took up the grievances of individual workers claiming persecution by management, and in other ways acted to curb management's abuse of power. In undertaking these actions, the union was practicing what its activists had learned from Transnationals Information

Exchange (TIE) and the School for Worker Democracy, two international labor education organizations.

The union's leadership has been nothing if not controversial. Its founding president, Anatolii Ivanov, worked as an electrical engineer at VAZ and in the Tiumen oil fields before becoming a union activist. Physically assaulted twice in 1996 (the second time sustaining two bullet wounds), he was elected in 1998 as vice president of the All-Russian Confederation of Labor, an organization representing new, independent unions. In 1999, voters in Togliatti elected him to the Russian State Duma, and did so again four years later. Even while maintaining strong ties to Edinstvo, he gravitated toward President Putin and his "party of power" (Unified Russia), arguing that workers needed the state's support. Ivanov's successor as Edinstvo's leader, Petr Zolotarev, worked for two decades as an adjuster on VAZ's assembly line before becoming a full-time activist. But he also found himself drawn to politics outside the union, running for mayor of Togliatti in 2001. With the AvtoVAZ leadership throwing its weight behind Nikolai Utkin, few gave Zolotarev any chance. Yet he received a plurality in the Auto Factory District and polled a respectable 41.7 percent of the votes citywide.[124]

Still, Edinstvo's struggle has been uphill and it has not had a lot to show for its militancy. Indexation of wages has fluctuated at no higher than 72.5 percent, and even that has been conditional on the "results of economic activity." The 1994 strike against wage arrears led to the temporary sacking of several dozen activists and the docking of pay of all participants. The strike in 2000 also failed, as did the resistance to the nine-hour shift.[125] According to one local historian, "the administration, the union committee, and then the STK succeeded in creating a patriotic spirit among the labor collective" that made AvtoVAZ a "model of a modern social partnership." "Thus, she adds, "not only was a social explosion avoided, but...the Volga Automobile Factory was able to survive the collapse of Soviet power, the Communist Party of the Soviet Union, and the USSR as well as the extremely difficult transformation of the entire economic system." Edinstvo is conspicuous by its absence from this assessment. And yet, as David Mandel noted a few years ago, "management views it as a threat and a limit on its freedom of action and would like to be rid of it." In these circumstances, the fact that the union has survived at all might be deemed a success. Edinstvo is not for everyone, and quite clearly everyone is not for Edinstvo, but as of 2004, membership was growing.[126]

Togliatti Forever

On December 1, 1996, the voters of Samara Oblast went to the polls and overwhelmingly elected as their new governor Konstantin Titov, the candidate of the Russian Party of Social Democracy. Voters in Togliatti had an additional item on their ballots: a referendum to change the name of their city back to Stavropol'-on-Volga. According to ITAR-TASS, 82 percent of those

who cast a vote opted to keep Togliatti. The results were not legally bind-
ing, since, at 48.6 percent, the turnout was below the 50 percent required
minimum, but to date there has not been another attempt to follow in the
footsteps of Leningrad/St. Petersburg and other Russian cities whose names
have reverted to their pre-Soviet origins. One commentator at the time noted
that "in an unusual twist on the politics of names in Russia, the older generation supported the change but younger people opposed it since there is
already a Russian city named Stavropol." Several years later, the mayor of the
city, Nikolai Utkin, told the visiting EU-Russia Parliamentary Cooperation
Working Group that many who voted in the referendum "had no idea who
Mr. Togliatti had been."[127]

Neither statement should be taken seriously as an explanation for the
outcome of the vote. Not only young people were aware of the existence of
another Stavropol', and while it is possible that some of Mayor Utkin's con-
stituents did not know "who Mr. Togliatti had been," one wonders how Utkin
knew that there were "many" among those who voted. More likely, voters'
unwillingness to change the name stemmed from their association of Togliatti not with a long-dead Italian Communist (or even recently deceased Soviet Communism) but rather with automobiles, and specifically, VAZ. Some
older folks, even those who had arrived in the city after its name had been
changed, may have yearned for a time when there was no car factory and no
Togliatti, but they were a minority. Most people, it seems, could not imagine
life getting any better without VAZ or Togliatti.

Until recently, post-Soviet Togliatti was best known for illegal activity associated with AvtoVAZ. The unraveling of the Soviet state's institutional
infrastructure in the late 1980s left VAZ vulnerable to deals on the side between its executives and a variety of what might euphemistically be called
start-up businesses. Such deals filled the void that opened up between the
collapsing distribution system and the much ballyhooed "market economy,"
then still in the offing. VAZ was no different in this sense from many other
firms producing other goods, but few things attracted as much demand as
cars. "The car wars" of the late-Soviet and early post-Soviet years were not
pretty. Managers bought cars cheaply off the assembly line or while they lay
idle on rail cars and resold them for big profits. The markups that histori-
cally had been absorbed by the state for redistribution were now fueling the
"kleptocracy."[128] Competition was keen, and it was not uncommon for local
Afghan war veterans and underemployed youths to be recruited as enforcers
in the territorial disputes of those years. Not for nothing does a recently published history of the company describe it as having been " 'in the sights' of
the central press," contending that "no other industrial enterprise in Russia
has stimulated such a stream of publications."[129]

Certainly the best-known deal concluded by VAZ's executives was the one
involving its general director, Vladimir Kadannikov, and Boris Berezovsky,
the recipient of a doctorate in applied mathematics and specialist in management theory then just beginning his ascendancy to oligarchic heights. The

arrangement involved the setting up of a dealership, LogoVAZ, that combined the names of the Togliatti car plant and the Turin-based company Logosystems SpA. The Italian connection made it possible—and apparently legal—for Berezovsky to reimport Ladas that had been sent abroad and export the profits from their sale back in Russia. The main source of profits was not so much the markup, although that was considerable, as the arrangement whereby LogoVAZ paid VAZ for its cars as much as two years after acquiring and selling them. This was during the runaway inflation years of 1992–94, when the ruble was losing about 20 percent of its value on average each month. VAZ gained absolutely nothing from this arrangement, but its executives gained a lot because they were major shareholders in LogoVAZ. In subsequent years, LogoVAZ would branch out, becoming the sole dealer of Mercedes and other "*inomarky*" (imported cars) as well as a participant in other ventures unrelated to automobiles.[130]

In late 1993, Berezovsky and Kadannikov launched another project, the All-Russian Automobile Alliance (AVVA), ostensibly to raise capital for a joint venture with GM to produce three hundred thousand units per year of a new "people's car" to be called Kalina. The capital was raised by trading in securities that in turn supposedly could be exchanged for real shares of AVVA stock. Not so much illegal as outside the then existing laws relating to the selling of shares, the AVVA scheme brought in about $15 million, which with interest and reinvestment profits amounted to as much as $50 million. But other than a short-lived venture with a Finnish company that turned out about thirty thousand Opel Astras in Finland, the money was not used for producing cars at all. It was ploughed into buying up about a third of the recently privatized AvtoVAZ and strengthening the ties of the interlocking network of companies in which Berezovsky and AvtoVAZ's executives were the major shareholders.[131] By 1996, Berezovsky was at the peak of his influence, having bankrolled the reelection of Boris Yeltsin as president and getting himself appointed deputy chairman of the National Security Council. AvtoVAZ, however, had "gained the reputation as the most gangster-ridden of any large Russian company."[132] It also was in terrible financial shape with debts amounting to an incredible ten trillion rubles. The government initiated bankruptcy proceedings, but Kadannikov, who had returned to the company as chief executive officer after serving briefly as deputy prime minister, saved the day by reaching an agreement with the just-elected governor of Samara Oblast, Konstantin Titov, to postpone debt repayments.

The tables eventually were turned on Berezovsky, not by AvtoVAZ, which had cut its ties to LogoVAZ years earlier, but by Yeltsin's successor, Vladimir Putin. Within months of his election in March 2000 Putin launched a series of civil and criminal suits against Berezovsky and Vladimir Guzinskii, Berezovsky's erstwhile rival. Before the end of 2000, Berezovsky was in self-imposed exile in Britain. He was eventually charged by Russian prosecutors with having launched a complicated scheme in 1994 to defraud AvtoVAZ out of more than two thousand cars worth $13 million. The case could only have been mounted with the cooperation of AvtoVAZ itself, Kadannikov apparently having turned state's evidence against his former partner after the tax police descended on dozens of the automaker's offices throughout the country.[133]

The connection between the city and AvtoVAZ got stronger in the post-Soviet era. Despite periodic hiring freezes, occasional layoffs, and other maneuvers to trim its labor costs, AvtoVAZ continued to employ upward of one hundred thousand people in the late 1990s and the first years of the present century. Not all its employees work or reside in the city, but there is little that happens in Togliatti that is not run or sponsored by the company, and little that could happen without its approval. Housing and cars, hockey and soccer teams, hospitals and clinics, theater and (as already mentioned) religious worship all rely on AvtoVAZ's largesse. Production, which declined by nearly 30 percent in the mid-1990s compared with 1990, rebounded toward the end of the decade. In 1998, AvtoVAZ added new facilities across the water in Syzran to produce Zhigulis (the VAZ 2106, by this time called Ladas even when sold in Russia). In September 2002 it began production of the four-wheel-drive Chevrolet Niva, a joint venture with General Motors that created twelve hundred new jobs in Togliatti. And in November 2004, its long-awaited Lada Kalina, a compact with a 1.6-liter engine, began rolling off a brand-new dedicated assembly line capable of turning out 220,000 per year. Twenty-seven other enterprises in the area produce components for Lada cars, with AvtoVAZ holding a controlling share in most of them. One is hard-pressed to think of another city its size—the population of Togliatti was 740,100 in 2002—that is so completely dominated by one company. In the United States, company towns flourished until the arrival of the automobile age; in the case of Togliatti, the arrival of the automobile and the departure of the Soviet socialist state were responsible for it becoming a full-fledged company town.[134]

That is not the whole story, though. One of the things that always distinguished the Auto Factory District was its residential social equality. When Kadannikov talked about living "in the same kind of building as you do in the Avtograd District," he was not lying. All VAZ managerial personnel from top management on down lived in more or less the same type of dwellings with not much difference in living space. This became less the case in the 1990s when managers who had accumulated sufficient means and connections started to encroach on the forest zone separating the new from the old part of the city by having separate family homes built there.[135] Other kinds of social distinctions emerged. In 1995, Tatishchev University, a private institution, opened its doors, siphoning off from Togliatti State University those whose family could afford to pay the relatively high tuition for nontechnical higher education.

One of the vacuums created by the collapse of the Soviet Union and its ruling Communist Party was the organization of youth, something that the Komsomol had long monopolized. Not necessarily a popular organization, even in its heyday, the Komsomol was an important dispenser of resources including social connections throughout the country. Its disappearance compounded the cultural bouleversement and economic and social dislocation that many young people experienced, particularly in provincial towns. Left largely to their own devices, young people organized themselves. One Togliatti newspaper claimed that as many as six hundred informal youth groups existed in the Auto Factory District alone in 1997. Among them were neo-Nazi skinheads, religious "sectarians," and local branches of fringe political parties.[136] Togliatti was not exceptional; one could find analogous groups in many if not most of post-Soviet Russia's cities.

Togliatti's youth may have been exceptionally vulnerable to other burgeoning phenomena of the post-Soviet era. The combination of its strategic location along a key drug-smuggling route between Central Asia and Europe and disposable income among the city's second-generation auto workers meant that Togliatti was soon awash with drugs, mostly heroin but also ephedrine, locally known as "vint." The authorities ignored the problem for years, but by the turn of the century the number of registered HIV cases began to soar, reaching 8,300 by April 2003 and 9,114 in February 2004. Experts estimated that the actual number of infected individuals was "as much as five times higher." Intravenous drug use was reported to be at the heart of the epidemic, but heterosexual transmission via prostitution was "rapidly increasing."[137]

What of the other shady characters who muscled their way into the car business in Togliatti—Igor (the Orphan) Sirotenko; the Neverov gang; the director of *Invest-kapital,* Mikhail Kashin; and the others? Compared with Berezovsky and his fellow "oligarchs" who pranced on the national stage, these guys were provincial hayseeds. The wars they fought were largely confined to Samara Oblast and, within it, Togliatti. One could read about their exploits in the investigative articles that the *Togliatti Observer* published under the editorship of Valery Ivanov and his successor, Aleksei Sidorov. But one needed to be careful. Both these journalists (and they are not the only ones) were murdered in gangland fashion, and as far as I know, the cases are still open.

Finally, there is the company itself, which, despite the turmoil of the post-Soviet era, remains intact. In the context of an increasingly globalized car industry, this is no mean achievement. With GAZ having announced its intention to cease its Volga operations, and IzhAvto discontinuing its Oda model, AvtoVAZ became the country's only carmaker. But while it stood to increase market share, the profitability of several of its operations—including the joint venture with crisis-plagued GM—sagged. In December 2005, two months after Kadannikov announced his resignation as general director, the state stepped in, getting six representatives of state-owned companies elected to the new twelve-seat board of directors. Analysts were unsure whether this portended renationalization. A plan to sink five billion dollars into the industry, which was debated at the highest levels of government, met with some skepticism among economists, one of whom was quoted as saying that "carmaking is just not our niche."[138] Meanwhile, foreign companies such as

Ford, Volkswagen, and Toyota have opened or are soon to open assembly plants using domestic suppliers in many cases, thereby circumventing the 25 percent import duties imposed on foreign autos. The fate of what may be the biggest surviving Soviet dinosaur hangs in the balance.

What is truly remarkable for anyone undertaking research on this part of Russia is the extraordinary attention the company has devoted to documenting its past, particularly its Soviet past. Five volumes of reminiscences by and about leading personnel, proceedings of two "scientific" conferences sponsored by the company and held in Togliatti, books by former designers and engineers, a full-blown history of the enterprise by some of Moscow's leading historians, glossy photo albums, bibliographies, museums, libraries—what does this signify? In October 2005, when I traveled to Togliatti to participate in the second "all-Russian scientific conference" on the history of the company, Kadannikov's retirement already seemed imminent. All this reminiscing, it occurred to me, was a way of commemorating his own career. I have since come to believe that this was too cynical (and reductionist) an explanation. Consciously or otherwise, AvtoVAZ was doing what the Ford Motor Company had done at Greenfield Village, the Henry Ford Museum, and the Benson Ford Research Center. It was trying to connect itself to the history of the country from which it sprang, trying to tell its current employees and their dependants in Togliatti stories about a previous generation's trials and tribulations that would make them feel good about working at the plant, make them feel that they were part of a family.

There may be an additional reason. Founded in 1966, VAZ distinguished itself from the more venerable Soviet auto enterprises by its youthfulness, by its lack of a revolutionary or Stalinist past. It was, rather, the factory that was associated in people's minds with mass production for ordinary Soviet citizens—not the military, not the truckers, and not the bosses. It represented the realization of popular pressure for a more consumer-oriented society, a Soviet version of Fordism here understood as mass production for mass consumption. With the advent of perestroika and then the collapse of the USSR, the kind of society to which VAZ catered was destroyed. Petr Abramovich Nakhmanovich, a top manager at the company until his retirement in 2002, recently equated the situation in the early 1990s with 1945 in Germany and Japan.[139] For the twenty-year-old Mityas of the country impatient with their parents' stories of sudden, wrenching adjustments, this may not mean much. They already own fully accessorized Ladas and look forward to obtaining a higher-priced, classier foreign model. But for the millions who were ordinary citizens during the 1960s, '70s, and '80s, and who now are thickening at the waist as they enter their senior years, it is not a bad thing to be reminded of those decades of relative stability and literally to take comfort in them. In this sense, and not this sense alone, AvtoVAZ is still a Soviet Detroit.

chapter 4

Roads

Дорогá дорога, а бездорожье—дороже.

Roads are expensive, but roadlessness is more expensive.
Russian popular saying

Road-building has never been a purely technical task, but...in
all times it has been of the greatest importance for the culture of
peoples and nations.
Fritz Todt, addressing the Seventh International Road
Congress in Munich, September 1934

Unpaved roads are a sign of a country that is still building, advertisements of one that has finished building.
Allan Sillitoe, Road to Volgograd

One of the most often-cited aphorisms in the Russian language, usually expressed with vaguely fatalistic overtones, is the observation, apocryphal though usually attributed to Gogol, that Russia has two misfortunes—fools and roads. These days it is often cited either in connection with a particularly stupid remark by a member of the State Duma, or to lament the condition of...Russia's roads. After all these years? The same complaint? Evidently so.

Whether Russia has suffered from fools to a greater degree than other countries—proportionate to its population, let's say—would be hard to demonstrate, for cross-cultural, transhistorical unanimity on what constitutes a fool would be unlikely. As for roads, there appears less room for disagreement, although the complaint is not free of ambiguity. To associate roads with misfortune is to suggest either that bad things usually happened on Russian roads or that the reasons for being on them were bad, or both. Or maybe misfortune awaited travelers on reaching their destination. Insofar as it had to do with the roads themselves, was it their absence or the condition of those that did exist? The very ambiguity of the aphorism may account for the broad possibilities of its application and, thus, its survival across different generations, political regimes, and technologies.

Roads—where they go and who constructs, maintains, and uses them—can tell us much about a country's economic resources, social organization, and political priorities. They are at once indicative of prevailing attitudes about the natural landscape and its transformation based on the needs of commerce, industry, recreation, and national defense. In the twentieth century, they assumed symbolic significance, no less so than automobiles themselves, as juggernauts of development, progress, and other things as well. In the United States, the road construction boom dates from the late 1910s and 1920s, the era of the Model T and Model A Fords and workers getting five dollars a day for building them. The expansion of roads especially in the United States was synergistic: taxes from gasoline consumption and state-budget allocations financed their construction; private industry provided the automobiles and fuel; businesses large and small took advantage of new opportunities to advertise their services and set up outlets that attracted newly mobile customers; and individual travelers, (ironically) associating highways with freedom and their own independence, turned themselves into consumers.[1]

No such synergies existed—or could exist—in the Soviet Union. The harshness of climatic conditions, the huge distances between populated areas, the paucity of cars, the marginality and then virtual nonexistence of business combined to make road building dependant on a very different dynamic, namely, military and more broadly strategic considerations. Such considerations played a major role in the second bout of long-distance road construction in the United States, the interstate highway system that the federal government inaugurated in 1956. The USSR never did develop its equivalent, although one could say it partially inspired the U.S. system. The Dwight D. Eisenhower National System of Interstate and Defense Highways, to cite its current official name, was made possible by cheap oil and much lobbying from the auto companies, but also by hysteria about a Soviet invasion or nuclear attack and the need for rapid deployment of missiles and troops. It too had its synergies. It both resulted from and perpetuated U.S. dependence on automotive transportation, and especially on the semitrailers and other "rigs" carrying the freight that railroads typically carry in other countries. It also accommodated an immense number of passenger cars that took individuals, friends, and families to places they wanted or needed to go, in many cases because the highway system allowed them to live so far apart in the first place. It soon became part of what made citizens of the United States feel American, what distinguished "us" from other nations: the open road, the vast vistas, the high speeds, the truckers' lingo and gear, the country and Western songs about truckers' loneliness, and the knickknacks sold in the gift shoppes at rest stops.[2]

Eventually, the defense rationale for the system was forgotten—at least by the public. Meanwhile, Soviet highways had come under the scrutiny of American researchers. In 1966 the CIA concluded that the Soviet Union's highway network was "rudimentary," automotive service facilities "woefully inadequate," and dramatic changes decades away.[3] That same year, Holland

Hunter, an American economic historian, published a book on Soviet transport experience and "its lessons for other countries." Citing the reason for the nineteenth-century Russian decision to use broad-gauge rails for its railroads as "partially...a defensive effort to deter a Western invader," Hunter speculated that "perhaps a similar rationale in the 1930s underlay the observed failure to develop a system of paved roads in western European Russia." He also observed that the "the Russian problem of 'roadlessness'...has not yet been fundamentally changed in rural areas of the USSR," that "the total length of all roads under local, regional, or national administration has not increased at all during the Soviet era, since construction of new roads has been more than offset by administrative abandonment of responsibility for maintenance of minor local roads," and that the approximately eighty-two thousand miles of concrete and asphalt highway in the USSR as of 1965 were roughly comparable to the U.S. highway system in 1920. Things evidently didn't improve much thereafter, for in 1984 an American business school research project devoted to Soviet transportation described its road network as "underdeveloped and neglected."[4]

The Soviet Union's road system was indeed rudimentary, but that is only the beginning of the story. Essentially a social history of road construction, this chapter focuses on campaigns to overcome "roadlessness," a condition associated with economic and cultural backwardness. Combating roadlessness included the popularization of roads via automobile expeditions and rallies (*avtoprobegy*) to remote parts of the country, the organization of a system of corvée labor among rural residents, and the mobilization of the army to build and defend roads during World War II. The Soviet approach to road building and maintenance also was characterized by the transference of administrative authority from transportation-related agencies to the state security apparatus, heavy reliance on convict and prisoner-of-war labor, massive projects to build highways analogous to (and inspired by) the autostradas of Fascist Italy and the autobahns of Nazi Germany, as well as less spectacular projects of the postwar decades.

Cars Improve Roads

Were there too few roads in the USSR? What does "too few" mean? Correlating the total length of a country's roads with the number of motor vehicles and comparing the ratio with that of another country might give some indication. For example, in 1970 the Soviet Union was covered by 220,000 kilometers of paved roads and contained about 10 million motor vehicles of all kinds (principally trucks, passenger cars, and motorcycles), producing a ratio of 45 vehicles for every kilometer of paved road. In the same year the United States boasted about 3.2 million kilometers of paved roads and contained about 120 million registered motor vehicles, giving a ratio of 37.5 vehicles for each kilometer of paved road.[5] These are not precise figures, but they do suggest that on a gross national level the Soviet Union's paved road system was bearing an amount of traffic not wildly different from the United States, and in this sense there would not seem to have been a tremendous shortage of paved roads.[6] But a gross national level is a rather gross index. It does not take account of differences between urban and rural roads. Soviet data unfortunately do not reveal such differences, but they do indicate that the 220,000 kilometers of paved roads represented only 43 percent of roads with hard surfaces (a category that includes gravel roads and in other countries is known as all-weather roads), and only 16 percent of all roads in the country. In other words, most roads were unimproved and in the case of improved roads most were unpaved.

Such roads, especially in the western part of the country, were subject to *rasputitsa.* The term refers both to the condition of impassability of roads and the times of the year—the spring thaw and autumn rains—when that condition is prevalent. Rasputitsa has had an enormous impact on the social, economic, and political life of Russia and the Soviet Union. It has affected everything from the timing of the promulgation of the emancipation of the serfs in 1861 to contingency plans for troop mobilization during World War I, and even the outcome of major battles. "Enemy at the Gates (EatG)," a 1994 Operational Combat Series game simulation exercise covering the campaign in southern Russia from November 1942 to March 1943, incorporated "Mud" into its rules. "The spring version of Rasputitsa...will put a halt to all operations," rule 1.3d notes. "In game terms, the mud's advent ends play." In actuality, rasputitsa's advent in the spring of 1943 did halt General Erich von Manstein's "backhand blow" against the overstretched Soviet forces, allowing the latter to regroup in preparation for the summer offensive. This was not the first time a German advance had been thwarted by the combination of unimproved roads and weather. The autumn rains of 1941, "so unexpected and prosaic," contributed to slowing the Wehrmacht offensive after its Panzer Group Four had reached Borodino, scarcely ninety kilometers from Moscow's Kremlin. It is difficult to know what tense to use when referring to rasputitsa, for the problem is not restricted to the past and not limited to roads lacking hard surfaces. As recently as the spring of 2005, a website run by the Belarus Association of International Truckers warned its members about "limitations of movement on several auto routes of general use" within the Russian Federation. "Spring rasputitsa" was the reason it gave for restrictions on vehicle weight limits as well as road closures in Smolensk, Perm, Novgorod, Novosibirsk, and Kirov oblasts.[7]

Rasputitsa is a function of what the political scientist Allen C. Lynch calls Russia's "illiberal geography."[8] Russia's roads buckle and heave, split apart and wash away because of the sudden thawing of masses of snow and ice in the spring and torrential rains in the autumn. Road surfaces and their bedding do not absorb water very well because of the predominance in much of the Eurasian plain of clay-laden soils. But then, we cannot lay the blame for the impassableness of Soviet roads entirely at the door of climate and geography. In 1946—to be sure, a difficult year for road maintenance—the Soviet satirical magazine *Krokodil* published a cartoon entitled "Nowhere to Go Farther," an updated version of Vasilii Vasnetsov's painting of 1882, "Warrior at the Crossroads." Instead of the legendary Il'ia Muromets on horseback, it had a district official leaning out of a convertible pondering an inscription in stone that reads "Drive to the left—a collapsed bridge. Drive to the right—get stuck in pot holes. Drive straight and fall into a ditch."[9] July, the month in which the cartoon appeared, is hardly the season of rasputitsa. Nor can rasputitsa be blamed for the statistic cited by Lynch, namely that "some 40 percent of Russia's villages cannot be reached on tarmac roads."[10] The reference is not to 1946 but to the first years of the twenty-first century.

One of Imperial Russia's legacies to the Soviet state was the network of highways (*chaussées*) connecting the major cities. Serving primarily military and postal functions, they tended to be straight, lined with trees, and occasionally hard surfaced. Zemstvos, the provincial and local governmental institutions created during the Great Reforms of the 1860s, administered local road construction, maintenance, and repair. According to one source, by 1913—a standard benchmark for comparisons between tsarist and early Soviet accomplishments—the zemstvos spent an average of 6–7 percent of their budgets on local road construction, with some devoting as much as 12–14 percent. Rural road maintenance and repair suffered during World War I and the subsequent years of revolution and civil war. To the extent that Soviet authorities concerned themselves with transportation, they gave priority to the railways, partly because trains were vital links between the fuel-supplying regions of the Donbass and Urals and the major cities to the north and west and partly because of the strategic importance of railway workers.

As for roads, Glavkomtrud (Main Committee on Work Duty), one of the many extemporaneously created administrative bodies that operated on an emergency basis, did press into service hundreds of thousands of people to clear them of snow and other debris, repair bridges, and do limited maintenance so that food and fuel could be delivered.[11] Evasion, of course, was a major problem. Hunkering down in their villages in hopes of riding out the tempest of civil war, peasants generally had little incentive to engage in major road work; on the contrary, not for the first time they realized that limiting mobility between town and country had its advantages.

Looking at a map of the RSFSR in 1921, Lenin referred to "vast spaces ... where dozens of versts [1.067 kilometers] of by-roads or, more accurately, roadlessness separate villages from railroads ... meaning that in these places patriarchalism, Oblomovism, and semi-wildness prevail."[12] With the reestablishment of commerce between town and country in the early 1920s, the incentive to improve roads increased, but the means of doing so were severely limited. Average expenditure on roads by rural soviets in the years 1924–27 amounted to less than 1 percent of their budgets, which were generally smaller than the budgets of the zemstvos before the revolution. Nor did the roads of "state significance" fare much better. Whereas in 1913 the tsarist Ministry of Transportation assigned R 557 per kilometer for repair and maintenance, the amount allocated by its Soviet equivalent in the 1925–26 fiscal year was R 350. In Siberia, R 1,450 were spent for every kilometer of highway and R 375 were spent on each kilometer of other roads in 1913; the corresponding figures for 1925 were R 515 and R 105.[13]

In 1922 the Soviet government combined the Administration of Main Roads and the Central Automobile Section of the Supreme Council of the National Economy into a Central Administration of Local Transport (TsUMT), placing the new institution under the authority of the Commissariat of Transportation (Narkomput). As one recent history of Russian roads archly notes, "This was the first 'marriage' of two offices—road management and automobile transport. Such 'marriage-divorces' would be a part of every generation of road and traffic administrators." Indeed, by August of the same year, the "marriage" got complicated: the government vested the Commissariat of Internal Affairs' Main Administration of the Municipal Economy (GUKKh) with responsibility for roads of local significance, that is, all roads except those designated as having general state significance. In the meantime, to handle control of traffic and roads within its purview, TsUMT created regional offices of local transport (OMESy). Messy indeed was this institutional structure. The awkwardness of the acronyms perfectly mirrored that of their hierarchical organization and relationships with other commissariats. By November 1928, it was time for a divorce. A resolution of the Central Executive Committee and the Council of People's Commissars replaced TsUMT with the Central Administration of Highways and Unpaved Roads (Tsudortrans) under Narkomput. Management of roads at the republic level was turned over to Road Transportation Boards (Glavdortrans), while the construction, maintenance, and repair of roads of both state and local significance was to reside in road-transportation organs known (of course) by their acronym as "Dortrans."[14]

Despite the elaborate administrative structure, road construction and maintenance lagged badly in the Soviet Union in the 1920s. Paving streets, either with asphalt or cement, was a major undertaking of municipal governments in many countries during this decade. The pace of such activity assumed particular intensity in the United States where the burgeoning of automobile traffic created an urgent need for paving and where the tax on gasoline made it economically as well as politically possible. Between 1909 and 1927, annual expenditure on roads in the United States rose from $80 million to $1.5 billion.[15] The paving of thoroughfares and central districts was also a major enterprise in major cities of Western Europe, but not in Moscow. When Walter Benjamin arrived there in December 1926 he was struck by "the gleam of snow and mud" on Tverskaia, Moscow's main commercial street, by the relative absence of "the principal instrument in the orchestra of the streets, the automobile horn," and by the "fact" that "nowhere does Moscow really look like the city it is, rather it more resembles the outskirts of itself."[16] Actually, a few of Moscow's streets (including part of Tverskaia where it intersects Okhotnyi Riad) were paved with asphalt by the mid-1920s, but Moscow was exceptional in the extent to which it depended on automotive (truck) rather than wagon transport.[17] Later in the decade, the seaside resort of Yalta experimented with concrete, but generally speaking the small amount of automobile traffic did not warrant expenditure on such materials.[18] In Moscow as well as in other major Soviet cities, when funds became available for improving roads, the materials of choice were cobblestones (*bulyzhnye*), wood pavement (*tortsovye mostovye*), and gravel. Outside the cities hard-surfaced roads of any kind were few and far between, and in vast stretches of Siberia, the far east, and the extreme north—analogous to what one would find in the Northwest Territories, Yukon, and parts of Alaska—they did not exist at all.[19]

We have seen that road conditions were a significant factor in the debate over what kind of an automobile the Soviet Union needed, and in what quantities. The question boiled down to whether the mass production of automobiles should be expanded before roads were improved or be put off until such time as the road system could accommodate increased traffic. Valerian Osinskii believed the answer lay in what he observed in the United States. He noted that while cement and asphalt highways were becoming the norm in the northern parts of the country, in Texas "you will see roads that are even worse than Russian roads," and in Alabama "the picture was absolutely Russian and even Russian squared, worse than in remote parts of Tambov Province." Such conditions did not prevent nearly all six million farmers from owning a car, not to mention their wives, whom Osinskii judged to be "excellent drivers."[20]

In "The American Automobile or the Russian Cart," he categorically rejected the notion that before the USSR could have more automobiles it needed better roads. In 1921, he pointed out, paved roads accounted for only 12 percent of the total length of roads in the United States. That did not stop Ford from producing millions of cars a year. Sure enough, by 1925 the proportion of paved roads had risen to 18 percent. The trend was irrefutable: cars improved roads because "when the rural dweller receives a motor vehicle, he receives the possibility and desire to spend his money and labor on improving roads." "He" receives this possibility because as commerce expanded over roads so did the desire to cheapen its costs, which meant reducing the time to transport goods, which meant improving roads.[21]

This argument surfaced again at the two "debates" sparked by Osinskii's articles. "Either give us solid roads," asserted Ia. Luibovich, one of the participants in the first debate, "or give us a middling vehicle [*seredniatskii avtomobil'*] that can go on a whole range of already existing surfaces." This was backward thinking, responded Namimov, another participant. "Roads and autos are like a human being and its shadow. The automobile leads the road, and not the road the automobile. The appearance of a car will produce a good road." This remark was greeted with applause.[22] Skepticism about cars improving roads was more evident at the second debate. B. E. Shprink, an engineer and member of the Moscow Automobile Club, acknowledged that heavier trucks would cheapen freight rates, but "the trouble is that the bridges in rural areas will not support them." We shouldn't jump from nothing to producing many thousands of automobiles per day, he continued, because we will not have prepared all the bases and raw materials. A representative from the army's procurement department named Fedotov agreed, pointing out that three-ton trucks were unable to reach the industrial town of Briansk because the bridges couldn't hold them and that for this reason authorities in Tula had banned them. Another participant, Tikhonov, was even more adamant about the need to improve roads before massively investing in automobile production. Of the four million kilometers of roads mentioned by a previous speaker, Tikhonov asserted that three million were in such a condition that not only an automobile but even a cart was incapable of traveling on them. Besides, the experience of tractors suggested that in the hands of "our peasants" autos would break down too easily. Several speakers, however, countered such skepticism. "I belong to the group that believes that autos call forth roads," announced a Professor Gribov. "There's no point in being intimidated by a lack of roads," added someone named Smirnov. "Automobiles will create the demand for roads and good roads will create the demand for automobiles, as they have in the United States." He was immediately followed by another speaker who pointed out that when someone brings up the need for roads, peasants respond that so long as they don't have cars, there will be no roads. "Give us automobiles and we'll make you roads."

Perhaps it will help to clarify the stakes involved and the shape of things to come to point out that when the participants in these debates spoke of automobiles, they meant primarily trucks rather than passenger cars. In Russian, a passenger car was always either a "light" (*legkovoi*) or "small-engine capacity" (*malolitrazhnyi*) automobile. Osinskii argued that the USSR needed both cars and trucks, and plumbed for the small or "semi-truck" (the three-quarter-ton Ford model in particular). None of the debaters even mentioned passenger cars until just before Osinskii's final summation. A man named Lebedinov, otherwise unidentified, upbraided the other speakers for having "completely ignored the question of passenger transport. If we think of building an automobile industry only on the basis of the state's means," he continued, "we will be proceeding at a snail's pace. Counting on foreign concessions is also dubious, and the devil knows if they will agree to our conditions." What was necessary, he asserted, was to interest "broad public circles," which, unfortunately, he refrained from identifying any further.[23]

The debates were to some degree a microcosmic version of the industrialization debate that had been raging for years within the state planning agencies and the upper echelons of the Communist Party. Although nobody advocated reliance on peasant carts, those suggesting a moderate rate of automobile production proceeded from the same assumptions as Nikolai Bukharin and others who argued in favor of continuing to rely on market transactions between state-owned industry and peasant agriculture. To them it was no more conceivable that the Soviet Union could industrialize in five years than that every worker and peasant would be seated in an automobile in ten to fifteen. By contrast, Osinskii and other proponents of rapid "automobilization" shared the same urgency as the industrializers who by 1927–28 had gained the upper hand (and Stalin's crucial support) in the debate. So, the USSR would get automobiles just like it would get other industries, but did that mean it would get roads?

Roadlessness and the Path to Socialism

Among the most persuasive arguments in favor of "automobilization" was the one made by Professor Evgenii Chudakov in Avtodor's journal, *Behind the Wheel* (*Za rulëm*). Appearing in the journal's inaugural issue in April 1928, Chudakov's article pointed out that relative to the minuscule number of motor vehicles in the country, the USSR had no shortage of roads. On the contrary, its roads were among the emptiest. The statistics he marshaled were quite graphic (see table 4.1).

Of course, measured by population, the USSR lagged considerably in roads. For every 10,000 people there were 1.7 kilometers of roads as opposed to 450 in the United States, 150 in France, and 39.5 in Germany.[24] Moreover, the argument Chudakov advanced could have been used to delay building new roads or improving the ones that already existed. If the roads were so empty, what was the hurry after all? It thus took a different kind of argument to raise consciousness about the need for road improvement. It also took funding and the recruitment and organization of professionally trained personnel and skilled workers. In 1930, the Central Administration of Highways and Unpaved Roads estimated the need for road engineers and technicians at twenty-nine thousand and "skilled construction workers" at no less than half a million. As for funding, an official from the RSFSR's Road Transport Board reported that central (all-Union) government expenditures on roads within the Russian republic had grown from a meager R 8 million in 1924–25 to three times that amount in 1927–28, and more than twice as much again (55 million) in 1929–30. The latter figure actually represented less than half of the total expenditures on roads when money from local and republic governments, industry, and a special road fund were included.[25] Yet even the total amount of R 141 million was dwarfed by what Narkomput spent on railroads.

Table 4.1. 1928 Chudakov article's statistics in favor of "automobilization"

	UK	France	Germany	US	USSR
Vehicles in use (000)	1023.7	891	319.6	22137	20.6
People/vehicle	34	46	196	5	7000
Vehicles/km²	4.16	1.64	0.67	2.85	0.00097
Vehicles/1 km of road	3.58	3.84	1.51	4.65	0.006
Vehicles/1 km main road	16.43	17	1.7	35.5	0.35

Source: E. Chudakov, "Budushchee avtomobil'noi promyshlennosti v SSSR," *Za rulëm*, no. 1 (1928): 3.

No single road construction project came close to attracting the amount of attention that the party devoted to the Turksib railroad, which absorbed R 161 million during its construction between 1927 and 1931.[26] As far as capital investments are concerned, the state earmarked five times as much for the railroads as for "rail-less" transport in the Second Five-Year Plan (1933–37).[27]

Still, as a book published in 1931 for juveniles pointed out:

> We cannot extend a railroad to every kolkhoz, to every village, to every cooperative. A railroad is a large river, but a large river cannot exist unless hundreds of little rivers, streams, and brooks flow into it....Into the Siberian taiga, the Kirgiz steppe, everywhere, the automobile will penetrate. But for this roads are needed. An automobile without a road is like a train without a track.[28]

The preeminence of railroads—probably inevitable in a country so large and so lacking in motor vehicles—thus not only did not preclude expanding road transportation but on the contrary required it. As Gosplan chairman Valerian Kuibyshev remarked at the Seventeenth Party Conference in 1932, "Given our large agricultural sector, without improved roads it will be absolutely impossible to master the process of production and achieve needed economic results from the harvest." *Pravda* reminded its readers that good roads also had implications for defense and the "growth of socialist culture on the collective farm (kolkhoz)." The estimated losses due to poor roads were staggeringly high: the trade unions' newspaper, *Trud,* put them at no less than two billion rubles a year.[29]

Such arguments in favor of improved roads were not new. In a book on hard-earthen roads published in 1915, two civil engineers had pointed out that "losses to the economy from roadlessness [*bezdorozh'e*] are incalculable." Citing "special scientific investigations," they claimed that "the delivery of grain from a village to a railroad station in Klin District [Moscow Oblast] costs on average the same as its conveyance from Odessa to America."[30] Years of war, revolution, and civil war had only made this situation worse. The crux of the problem was that while the success of the industrialization and collectivization drives of the late 1920s and early '30s may have depended in part on good roads connecting town to country (and country to railroads), the building of such roads depended on the mobilization of human and economic resources already fully engaged in those vast undertakings.

Roadlessness lay at the intersection of the material and the metaphorical. Materially, it had two components: a paucity of roads and the poor condition of the roads that did exist. Represented in statistical terms, the USSR had 22,430 kilometers of highways in October 1929, which amounted to less than half the length of such roads in Sweden, about a quarter of Italy's main roads, and less than a tenth of Germany's and Britain's. As far as maintenance was concerned, a retrospective survey by Gosplan claimed that in 1928–29 nearly three-quarters (73%) of such roads were in "unsatisfactory condition."[31] To visitors from abroad, driving between cities was quite an adventure. George

S. Counts, who drove a Ford across Soviet Russia from Leningrad to Tuapse (on the Black Sea) in the summer and autumn of 1929, described the roads he encountered as those "of a simple rural civilization... [that] had little need for an elaborate system of roads." At least north of Moscow, even the "big roads" were "fashioned by the hand of nature and carved by the wheels of the wagons of peasants."[32]

Others could not remember seeing any roads at all. When David Kempler, an engineer who worked on the Nizhni Novgorod project for the Austin Company, was interviewed in 1976, he recalled that there "were no roads once you get to the city limit of Moscow. I drove it three times, so I know that there are no roads from there on. You just go across the prairie." More exasperating to the Austin engineers was the condition of the road that was supposed to connect the construction site to the Oka River. Having already written twice to Avtostroi about its inadequacies, an engineer named Palmer sent a third letter in November 1929 expressing his "fear... that this road is not going to be in usable shape in the early spring," something that, he bluntly stated, "can not be allowed to happen." Three weeks later, he wrote for a fourth time, noting that the road was "a long way from being finished" and contained "numerous wide and deep gaps."[33]

But as if to demonstrate that cars build roads, the factory's construction was also the occasion for the laying of the first concrete road in the USSR located outside a city. Essentially an extension of the half-kilometer-long assembly shop, it inspired the following poetical reverie from Boris Agapov: "It is smooth like the enamel of an automobile and straight like the ray of a searchlight. One hundred and forty thousand machines are moving along it, four in a row." With such roads, the land of socialism would no longer have to "proceed aimlessly" ("Po Bezdorozh'iu," the title of Agapov's article).[34] Indeed, metaphorically, roadlessness conveyed the sense of being lost or in a swamp, of aimlessness, of not knowing which way to go. Roadlessness, in other words, was the polar opposite of the "path to socialism."

During the 1920s and '30s, this road metaphor did heavy duty in Communist discourse along with others evoking conquest ("storming"), construction ("building"), and organic growth ("developing," "maturing"). Lenin employed it from time to time, such as at the Eleventh Party Congress (1922) when he wondered if his New Economic Policy—imagined as a car (*mashina*)—"is not going quite in the direction the man at the wheel imagines, and often it goes in an altogether different direction."[35] Nikolai Bukharin's "Path to Socialism and the Worker-Peasant Alliance" (1925) used it more elaborately. His assertion of an "evolutionary path," of a "road to socialism [that] runs... *precisely through* market relations" achieved canonical status until the combination of crisis and impatience got the better of the party leadership. At that point, Stalin dusted off one of Lenin's formulations from 1917, namely, the necessity for the proletarian dictatorship to "catch up to and overtake" (*dognat' i peregnat'*) the most advanced countries in economic terms.[36] The fact that both "road" (*doroga*) and "path" (*put'*) could refer to either railroads or roads without rails was not the only reason why translating the metaphorical into the material remained tricky.

"In Russia there are no roads, only directions." This aphorism was not quite as venerable as the one attributed to Gogol but sufficiently well known to be the subject of an August 1931 article in *Komsomol'skaia pravda*. Rejecting the fatalistic implications of the saying, the article asserted that "the *general direction* the party has given our country is *demand roads*!" It is worth pausing over, for it invokes both the material and metaphorical meanings of roadlessness. It opens with passages from Russian classics, each of which describes a form of conveyance stuck in mud. After noting the absence of any reference to the "humble peasant cart" (re: Osinskii), it proclaims that the "revolution rises in arms against the cart. It announces a vigorous campaign to convert Russia from the cart to the automobile," envisioning the day when roads would be "conveyors between agricultural and industrial factories of the socialist economy, ribbons flowing uninterruptedly, effacing the boundaries between town and countryside."[37] Reminiscent of Stalin's speech to business leaders about old Russia suffering defeat after defeat because of its backwardness, the article simultaneously distinguished the new proletarian Soviet Russia from its imperial predecessor and played on Russians' wounded pride.

Ribbons of goods flowing uninterruptedly between town and country were in the future. In the present, roadlessness was ubiquitous. In Stalingrad, one of the fastest growing cities in the country and the site of its own "socialist city" project,

> only 5 percent of the sidewalks are paved. And the 95 percent? They simply don't exist. This is not any bear-hunting corner of the Union, but a city with a large industry, where many tons of goods have to be transported by automobile from one plant to another, from the railway station to the wharves, and from the wharves to the center of the town. This roadlessness, or to be more correct, lack of pavement, is felt most by the automobiles.[38]

If cars improved roads, where was the improvement in Stalingrad?

Roadlessness proved to be a moving target. By the beginning of the Second Five-Year Plan in 1933, the central thoroughfares (now increasingly known as "prospects") and even some of the highways leading out of Leningrad and the capital cities of Moscow, Minsk, and Khar'kov had been "dressed" with asphalt or macadam. "Moscow's roads have been extraordinarily improved in the last two years," Karl Krüger reported to the Seventh International Road Congress in Munich in September 1934.[39] Among those improvements was the installation of stoplights, the first of which hung at the corner of Petrovka and Kuznetskii Most streets. Still, as the number of automobiles—trucks for the most part—steadily increased, the less acceptable it was for any urban road to remain undressed.[40]

It was not, however, automobiles that Lazar Kaganovich had in mind when he told the party's central committee in 1931 that "we must provide for the widening and straightening of streets." In Moscow, whose general plan for reconstruction was devised under Kaganovich's supervision and announced with great fanfare in 1935, Tverskaia and other central thoroughfares were straightened and widened not so they could accommodate great numbers of future motor vehicles but to facilitate massed gatherings of celebrants during Soviet holidays on Red Square, which also was widened.[41] Although a cardinal principle of Soviet urban planning was that no other city should resemble Moscow, the great prospects and squares of Moscow's center prefigured those built on a somewhat smaller scale in Minsk, Stalingrad (Volgograd), and other cities after their devastation in World War II.

Outside the cities, Tsudortrans, the highway administration, had overseen the construction of over one hundred thousand kilometers of new roads, overwhelmingly rural and unpaved. Although this represented only 28 percent of the First Five-Year Plan target of 360,000 kilometers, it was an achievement of sorts to get any roads built at all in the chaotic and often violent circumstances of the Soviet countryside then in the throes of collectivization.[42] Let us not, though, exaggerate the achievements. Travel outside the cities by automobile, especially passenger car, was still something of a rarity. One therefore marvels at the intrepidness of Miss Alva Christensen and Miss Mary L. de Give, both of Atlanta, Georgia. In August 1932 the two women departed in a Ford from Warsaw with "a large supply of tinned foods, a full supply of extra equipment for their car, sensible clothing, a pistol...and $2,500...in travelers checks" to travel to Tbilisi over roads that "were practically impassable." In the course of their trip, according to the U.S. diplomat stationed at the embassy in Poland who met them on their return, they had grown "disillusioned regarding communism" and "may be counted as no longer having any sympathy with the Soviet administration or communism as a solution or a panacea for world political and social conditions."[43]

One wonders how much those "impassable" roads had to do with their disillusionment. Still, there was hope for the future. "We Russians are very far behind and very, very stupid," a party propagandist admitted to a Danish visitor as they traveled by train from Moscow to Voronezh in 1933. But, she added, "when the second five-year plan has been carried through, everything in Russia will be good.... Then we shall drive in motor-cars along splendid roads, and we shall have plenty to eat and good clothes to wear."[44]

Overcoming Roadlessness "from Below"

Soviet authorities classified roads, as already noted, according to whether they were of general "state" or "local" significance. They subdivided roads of state significance into three classes: federal or "Union" roads, highways that were off limits to animal-drawn vehicles and on which a minimum speed limit existed; second class (republic-level) roads; and third class (oblast or *krai*, an equivalent administrative unit generally located in outlying areas) roads. The second- and third-class roads included those linking republic, krai, and oblast centers with the most important industrial sites, railroad stations, and harbors as well as with one another. Local roads also consisted of three classes: district (*raion*), village or rural (*sel'skie*), and those of economic (*khoziaistvennyi*) importance. According to inventories taken between 1931 and 1933, of 1.4 million kilometers of roads in the USSR, fewer than 250,000 were of state significance, while 1.1 million were designated of local significance. Among the latter, rural roads amounted to slightly more than half of the total distance. Roads in the Russian republic (RSFSR) made up 76 percent of all local roads, but only 70 percent of roads of state significance. More than 90 percent of roads of local significance were classified as "unimproved," 38.6 percent were "inappropriate" for automobiles, and a mere 1.5 percent were hard surfaced.[45]

Money allocated for roads in the federal budget went exclusively toward roads of state significance. They ranged from the principal interurban highways to the through road—popularly known as the *Amerikanka* ("American way") for its smooth blacktop—that connected Stalin's dacha at Kuntsevo to the high road to Mozhaisk and which was, of course, off-limits to nonofficial vehicles. Probably because Stalin frequented it, the Mozhaisk highway was kept in super condition. Moscow's Gor'kii Street and Great Kaluga Street received the same treatment.[46] At republic and oblast levels funds also tended to be lavished on the roads about which local officials cared most.

The vast majority of roads, therefore, serving the vast majority of the population, depended on local resources. These being negligible, it is not surprising that sooner or later the local population would be called on to contribute what it did have—its labor, or at least its capacity to work. Such a system of road maintenance and construction, which remained in force for decades, was formalized in a decree issued by the Central Executive Committee of the Soviets and Council of People's Commissars in November 1928. Superseding an earlier resolution of August 1925 that had asserted the need for organizing maintenance but did not mandate the mechanism, it required up to six days a year of labor on the roads. All able-bodied adults residing in the countryside, excluding industrial workers, state employees, and students, were liable for service. The decree authorized district and county (*uezd*) executive committees to determine the amount of service required from each rural settlement. When assessing an individual's burden, the committees were to be guided by whether the individual provided working animals and—characteristic of the class animus of the time—the "category of the population (traders, kulaks, middle-peasants, poor peasants, etc.)" to which the individual belonged. The law also stipulated that on petition a monetary payment not to exceed 20 percent of the annual agricultural or income tax could be substituted for the labor service.[47]

Although couched in terms of "labor participation" (*trudovoe uchastie*) and full of caveats and provisions for opting out, this rudimentary system amounted to conscription or compulsory labor service (*trudovaia povinnost'*), "reminiscent of the *corvée,* or labor obligation, that landowners, the church, and state required of their serfs prior to 1861."[48] One need not go back to serf times for origins, or the French ancien régime for analogies. As already noted, compulsory labor service was used extensively during the Russian Civil War, and in various parts of the country local road maintenance may very well have continued uninterruptedly on this basis throughout the 1920s. The practice was not unique to the USSR, having been used in other places and times when monetary payment was less convenient than the appeal to the common good and/or the threat of punitive state action. In the United States, local road maintenance obligations were quite common and efficacious throughout the nineteenth century and into the twentieth, a point that Avtodor did not omit in promoting the system.[49]

The problem with relying on compulsory labor service was compliance. While roadwork financed by the state's budget reached 70 percent of the planned target in 1929–30, the fulfillment of tasks through compulsory labor service was variously estimated to have been between 15 and 30 percent, and much of the work completed was judged to be of unacceptable quality.[50] The variation suggests the difficulty of arriving at any degree of statistical accuracy about this matter—or even the nature of the matter itself. What was being counted? Was it the number of days of labor performed by all those eligible for conscription? The number of kilometers of road that had been maintained and repaired? The kind of improvements that were made—gravel as opposed to dirt? pebble as opposed to gravel? The monetary equivalent of the work performed or anticipated to be saved by the state as a result of the provision of "free" (besplatnyi) labor? All, indeed, were cited at one time or another, and as late as the First All-Union Road Conference held in May 1932, representatives of state, party, and "public" organizations talked past one another by invoking these different measures.[51]

Compared with what else was happening and about to happen in the Soviet countryside, the donation of six days of labor (less if one brought one's horse) per year to fix roads did not constitute an overwhelming burden. But in reality, such a comparison is beside the point. We must understand compulsory labor as one of many burdens associated with collectivization. These included confiscations of property and livestock, incarcerations, and other impositions that were part and parcel of that process. In some parts of the country, roadwork was only one of several forms of labor service. Others included timber felling, rafting, and cartage (trudguzhpovinnost'). Then there was the propensity of raion and rural soviet officials to "lend" kolkhoz labor and animals to industrial or other enterprises, or to extort such "loans" from individual households in the form of bribes. It thus becomes understandable why the director of Novosibirsk's road construction administration (okrdorotdel) needed to remind district executive committees not to assign village officials responsible for organizing roadwork to other tasks; why peasants performing roadwork resorted to substituting earth, stumps, and large rocks for stones in order to more quickly fulfill their assigned tasks; why, desperate to accomplish some roadwork, the presidium of the Western Siberian Krai executive committee issued a statement that food shortages would not justify failure to perform road obligations, and the Novosibirsk okrug secretary called into session a people's tribunal (*narsud*) to punish those who failed to fulfill their obligations—all this in the singularly chaotic year of 1930.[52]

Rates of participation increased thereafter, albeit slowly. Compliance was still quite spotty in 1931: nearly 100 percent in Nizhni Novgorod and Leningrad oblasts and the Chuvash Autonomous Republic (ASSR); no more than 30 percent in the North Caucasus and Lower Volga; and still negligible in Crimea, Kazakhstan, Turkmeniia, and Tajikistan.[53] Authorities claimed that eight million collective farmers and homesteaders built fourteen thousand kilometers of (unpaved) roads. A year later, it was said, twelve million people built thirty-four thousand kilometers. A statistical collection published by Tsudortrans indicates that by 1934, rural residents contributed 91.5 million labor days to roadwork compared with 49.1 million in 1931. Their livestock worked a total of 36 million days and monetary contributions amounted to R 297 million. Things appeared to be looking up.[54]

Part of the reason may have been a tightening of the law to take into account the radically altered conditions in the countryside. According to a new decree of August 1931, "all available able-bodied laboring peasants, collectivized and noncollectivized, in the ages of 18 to 45" were obliged to "participate without pay [*besplatno*] in new road construction and repair of roads and installations six days per year." Villagers who happened to be engaged elsewhere in seasonal work (*na otkhozhnikh promyslakh*) had to make a monetary contribution equal to not six but twelve days of analogous work.[55] This was not the last emendation of the law. A measure from 1932 required local governments to devote "not less than 10 percent" of their budgets to assisting peasants in the performance of their obligation. The money was to be used to hire "technically skilled cadres" and obtain the necessary equipment and materials. Finally, a law of March 3, 1936, specified the times of the year (spring and fall when free from agricultural tasks), the age range for women (18 to 40), and the radii within which collective and independent farmers could be assigned (fifteen kilometers, instead of the ten mentioned in the 1931 law) and working animals and trucks could be used (thirty and sixty kilometers respectively). It also suggested (point 5) "that it would be more advantageous to both the kolkhoz and the state if, rather than requiring all members of the kolkhoz to perform roadwork, the kolkhoz instead constituted standing brigades whose work would be calculated in the general plan of labor participation established for the kolkhoz's overall membership."[56]

Point 5 may have derived from existing practice. If this were the case, it probably was not the first and certainly would not be the last time the state codified informal arrangements. As one historian recently noted with respect to the last years of the Great Patriotic War and the immediate postwar period:

> Lawmakers and publicists represented nearly all economic activity as if it were part of a highly coordinated premeditated state campaign for victory and

reconstruction. In order to maintain the image of centralized state rule in the context of wartime disintegration, propagandists thus placed the "stamp of the state" on everyday practice even when practice preceded codification and representation.

Roadwork may not have been an "everyday practice," but it did resemble the objects of "countless decrees" issued by "various legislative bodies from the highest...down to the lowest level district soviets...[each] formally instructing local officials and individual citizens to engage in myriad activities for state ends" that already were being pursued for other purposes.[57]

Party and Komsomol activists were yet another group of actors in the drama surrounding conscription for road maintenance and construction. Although not thick on the ground in the countryside, they were capable of kicking up quite a storm, at least in the press. "A Hundred Times!" screamed a headline referring to the stupendous achievement of the Chuvash ASSR, where in just over eighteen months the number of kilometers of improved roads increased, by gosh, by one hundred times. True, there were only thirty kilometers of such roads to begin with, but the rate was accelerating. By January 1, 1931, the comrades had overseen the improvement of twelve hundred kilometers of road, and by August of the same year, the figure was nearly thirty-five hundred. How did they do it? For one thing, by personal example. Each Komsomol member assumed responsibility for repairing ten meters of road. That was about two hundred kilometers right there. Then, they organized sponsorship (*shefstvo*), monthly campaigns (*mesiachniki*), and inspection contests (*konkurssmotry*)—techniques associated with those characteristically First Five-Year Plan forms of labor inducement, socialist competition, and shockwork.[58]

As for the party, one source indicates that the oblast committee (*obkom*) "put the tasks of road maintenance and construction above all others." What that might have meant in practice was explained by an obkom member who admitted in October 1930 that earlier there had been cases of desertion, but the party had set things right by organizing "show trials" of malingering "kulaks," purged district staff for incompetence, and removed at least one district executive committee chairperson for underestimating the importance of the roadwork campaign. The result was a transformation not only in roads but in people's lives. Workers, students, and Pioneers now come to take a look at the fine roads in their free time, he reported. They play the accordion and sing as they stroll along.[59]

The Komsomol's and party's efforts were reinforced by Avtodor, the voluntary society that brought together drivers, automobile enthusiasts, and, more generally, those who believed that "automobilism" could contribute to the Soviet Union's technological progress and economic prosperity. Automobilism in this sense was the equivalent of "air-mindedness," the enthusiasm for machine-powered flight channeled and otherwise promoted by the Society for Cooperation in Defense, Aviation, and Chemical Development (Osoaviakhim). Like Osoaviakhim and other public organizations, Avtodor took its cues from the party. Its main activities were the organization of driver education and training, the dissemination of information about automobiles and their maintenance, and the popularization of road building. Aside from administering a nationwide lottery to raise funds, its principal effort with respect to road building was mobilizing and calculating the results of compulsory roadwork.[60]

The road department of Avtodor's central council served as both taskmaster and clearinghouse for the campaign. The archives are full of stenographic reports from its "central headquarters" about leading the "shock month" against roadlessness, organizing socialist competition, and otherwise fulfilling the "labor participation" obligations of the rural population. Sessions of the department's presidium read like reports from a battlefront. "We will liquidate roadlessness in the First Five-Year Plan," the head of Avtodor's Chuvash branch tells his Moscow comrades. The Central Black Earth Oblast gave more than seven million labor days in 1931, another Avtodor member reported. This was more than the 4.19 million that Leningrad Oblast "gave," but then the latter also recorded two million horse days.[61]

All this was absolutely characteristic of the time. Whether it meant that more roadwork actually was getting done is another matter. Data on participation, meeting attendance, votes in favor of resolutions, and other quantitative indices were the lifeblood of the public organizations, but the relationship between these data and the ostensible reasons for the existence of such organizations could be quite remote.[62] Indeed, the same was true for the trade unions and even the Communist Party. Padding of numbers, and phony ("Izhe-") shockwork were endemic to the process of reporting successes. The Chuvash Republic is a case in point. Its Avtodor was a model, "the yardstick by which all other rural efforts at socialist competition were measured," because of its success in organizing local branches and building and repairing roads.[63] In 1931, it reported that the republic had fulfilled its roadwork plan by 113 percent. For its outstanding work in organizing labor participation in 1932, Avtodor's central council rewarded it with two tractors and R 15,000 to train cadres in road building.[64] Yet, for all of this favorable publicity, the real accomplishments were modest indeed. According to the 1933 inventory of roads conducted by Tsudortrans, the Chuvash ASSR contained a mere 1,440 kilometers of roads with any improvement at all, as compared with 8,560 kilometers of unimproved roads. Proportional to the total length of roads in the republic, this was better than average, though not as good as Leningrad and Sverdlovsk oblasts, Gor'kii Krai, and, especially, the Georgian Soviet Socialist Republic, where over half the total length consisted of improved roads.[65]

Occasionally, Avtodor activists exhibited frustration with the need to rely on the compulsory labor of peasants. "Many consider that it is simpler to have roadwork done on the basis of labor obligations than for pay...but the reverse is the case," its journal complained. Among other difficulties, one could not count on adequate skilled labor but instead had to contend with the presence of women(!). Evidently frustrated by the degree of noncompliance among peasants, the central council in late 1930 urged the government to put more teeth into the law by requiring not six but twelve days of labor from kulaks and by "as a rule" forbidding the substitution of monetary contributions for labor participation.[66] Judging from activists' complaints at a conference with representatives from Tsudortrans, matters did not seem to have changed appreciably by 1935. The fault was not so much with the peasants themselves as with local officials. One activist summed up the attitude of "some leaders of raion executive committees and chairmen of kolkhozes" as being "'comrades, your roads can wait. I have my own roads in the district, and besides, I need to prepare for the harvest, haying, and so forth. I must do my own work.'"[67] Another activist from Ivanovo described how "peasants arrive at the prescribed hour but your foreman [desiatnik] and technician who are supposed to organize the tasks are sometimes three or four hours late. Then, instead of norms that could absorb peasants the whole day, they prescribe less. All this disorganizes the peasants and creates the impression of an unserious attitude toward road construction."[68]

Serious or not, the system was here to stay, whereas Avtodor's days were numbered. After its liquidation in 1935 (about which see below), there was no organization outside the party and the Komsomol to sponsor contests and mesiachniki to publicize good or bad road maintenance. The system was regularized by the issuance of forms distributed to district soviet executive committees and thence to their road departments (raidorotdely). These were fairly elaborate, and to assist their completion, "Gushosdor," the successor to Tsudortrans, also distributed instructions covering the form's nine sections.[69] Did peasants continue to drag their feet over fulfilling their road service obligations as they did with so many other tasks imposed on them as collective farmers, or did they eventually come to regard roadwork as leading to tangible benefits as a direct result of their efforts? The evidence is slight and contradictory, but the proliferation of trucks on collective farms in the late 1930s—largely the result of the state's initiation of retail sales to farms that had fulfilled their procurement plans, it seems—quite possibly changed the equation for many peasants. In 1937 alone cotton kolkhozes in Central Asia obtained two thousand such vehicles, those in the Tatar Autonomous Republic bought nearly a thousand, and the kolkhozes of the Azov–Black Sea Krai acquired 1,460 trucks (and twenty-three thousand bicycles). Pravda reported that Ukrainian kolkhozes possessed 2,651 vehicles on October 1, 1936 but 9,356 on August 1, 1937. Several were demanding passenger cars. Especially as horses "remained a deficit good throughout the 1930s," the availability of these vehicles for collective if not personal business may have provided a hitherto lacking incentive to repair roads.[70] In this sense as well, cars may be said to have been responsible for improving the roads.

Roadlessness and Road Rallies

One of the more inventive ways of campaigning against roadlessness was to organize automobile endurance trials or rallies, known in Russian as *avtoprobegy.* Essentially Soviet variations on a practice that had developed in Western European countries and their overseas colonies, these rallies were generally of two kinds: "agitational" and "expeditionary." The main objective of agitational rallies was to publicize the condition of roads in the expectation that the publicity would raise consciousness of the urgent need for road improvement. Expeditionary rallies were mounted to locate or create roads in previously uncharted territory.

One early morning in July 1929, Valerian Osinskii set out from Red Square in a small caravan of cars on a several thousand kilometer journey. In the account he wrote for Avtodor, the organization whose journal he had been editing since its founding two years earlier, he described his trip as "not a 'real' rally from the automotive-technological and sporting points of view." Rather than the advance of technology or the pure pursuit of sport, it aimed to test four foreign models (Ford, Chevrolet, Willys Overland, and Durant) to determine which was best adapted to Soviet roads.[71] The roads over which the five cars were driven presented them with a severe test indeed. "It is simply amazing," Osinskii noted, "how people can live and work inasmuch as movement on these 'roads' is simply impossible." So poorly maintained were Voronezh's provincial roads that they provoked "wonder whether someone fearing the invasion of an enemy intentionally spoiled [them] to make movement more difficult....In truth," Osinskii wrote, "our attitude toward roads is one of the clearest manifestations of the survival of barbarism, Asiaticness, indolence, and idleness."[72]

A report sent to Avtodor's central council about an agitational rally through Viatka Province, also in the summer of 1929, made the same point (but without the irritated tone). Riding in a prewar Packard and a half-ton Peugeot truck, Bronnikov, the author of the report, and his fellow automobile enthusiasts traveled from village to village lecturing on "automobilization," distributing copies of pamphlets and books produced by Avtodor, giving "demonstration rides" to peasants, showing a film called *Buinaia doroga* (The Wild Road), and selling lottery tickets. But between villages one or the other and sometimes both of the vehicles frequently got stuck in the mud. As a result of delays, crowds that had been gathered to greet the rally sometimes waited in vain and eventually dispersed. "I must say," noted Bronnikov, "that the abominable roads, the mud on our cars, the dirt on our faces and clothes, and the film...were the best agitators for improving the roads and constructing new ones."[73]

A year earlier, in July 1928, an "agitational vehicle" traveled fifty-two hundred kilometers from Moscow to the Volga German Republic and back along a route that took it through nine provinces. One of the purposes of the journey was to organize Avtodor cells in the cities and villages through which the vehicle, an AMO truck, passed. Another was represented by a small sign on the car's body. It read "Build Roads."[74] Popular literature, too, joined the campaign for better roads, albeit in jest. Il'ia Ilf and Evgenii Petrov's novel of 1931, *The Little Golden Calf,* targeted Avtodor and its slogans for satirical

treatment. "Improve the roads! Merci for the reception!" With this insouci-
ant remark and the banner he affixed to his automobile that read "Auto rally
against roadlessness and slovenliness!" Ostap Bender endeared himself to
millions of readers. Pretending to be in the lead car of a rally, Bender and
his fellow imposters milk the town of Udoev (Milking) of its automotive fuel
and parts—a not too subtle jab at the local costs of Avtodor's agitational efforts. Arguably, though, the novel did more to raise the public's awareness
of the need to improve roads than the real rallies it appropriated for satirical
purposes.[75]

When five passenger cars, two small trucks, and a motorcycle left Moscow for Arkhangel'sk on August 10, 1929, the main objective was not so
much to improve roads as to have them built. Avtodor sponsored the "Great
Northern Rally," a three-thousand-kilometer journey, essentially "to define
the future highway (*magistral'*)" to Arkhangel'sk.[76] Such expeditionary rallies were quite popular in the late 1920s and early 1930s in no small part
because of the coverage they received in the press and in newsreels. They
inspired considerable courage but also foolishness. The spirit infusing these
undertakings is well illustrated by the 9,500-kilometer, three-month, Vladivostok to Moscow "reconnaissance rally" of 1930. This was the brainchild of
N. M. Zaborovskii, an engineer who confidently told Avtodor's central council that "our task is to give the country a road, and this road we will find."
Doing this as soon as possible was important because, among other reasons,
tourists were clamoring for "the shortest route in the tour around the world"
and it would be better if "we showed the road to tourists rather than waiting
for them to show it to us." Zaborovskii also cited the "wave of resettlement
directed toward the far east" from the European part of the country (that is,
the banishment of kulaks and other class enemies) as justification for including Ukraine and Belorussia in the rally's program. This, in his view, would
have agitational value.[77]

The rally was cursed from the beginning. Getting all the participants, cars,
and supplies to Vladivostok proved a complicated business that several
times delayed the start. In his postmortem report, S. A. Zaikin, the rally's
commander, used the verb "to swim" rather than "ride" or "drive" to emphasize the appalling conditions and their painfully slow progress. Apparently,
nobody had set up fuel or food bases despite "a whole stack of telegrams."
At one point, a policeman took the rally's participants into custody for five
days because he had received a telegram from regional authorities informing
him not to allow the rally to proceed due to lack of preparations. The coup de
grâce came not far from Khabarovsk (north of Vladivostok) when two of the
three automobiles veered into a swamp to avoid hitting a wayward railroad
locomotive—an incident bursting with symbolic significance. For his part,
Zaborovskii tried to contest much of Zaikin's account. "To speak of roadlessness...is an exaggeration," he told Avtodor's council. With the exception of
the swampy places, the roads were "more or less decent." If you eliminate the
five days we "senselessly" spent in police custody, we averaged one hundred

Moscow–Kara-Kum–Moscow Auto Rally, Tashkent, 1933. Courtesy of Rossiiskii Gosudarstvennyi Arkhiv Kino-Foto Dokumentov (RGAKFD).

kilometers a day, he said. Only Zaikin was against recommencing the rally. Zaborovskii's audience wasn't buying it, though.[78]

If this was the low point for expeditionary rallies, the high was the Moscow–Kara-Kum–Moscow rally of summer 1933. It brilliantly succeeded in promoting the need to improve roads, depending on their poor condition (or complete absence) to produce heroes behind the wheel. In this respect and others it represented the culmination of years of effort by Avtodor and its promotion of Soviet automobilism. The key to the rally's success lay in the decision to make different sections serve different objectives. Within the RSFSR the condition of roads was held to a relatively high standard: Avtodor praised and materially rewarded provincial branches that had prepared the route by installing clear markings, upgrading road surfaces, repairing bridges, and providing adequate service facilities; those that neglected these tasks were subjected to withering criticism. The most striking contrast was between the contiguous Chuvash and Tatar autonomous republics. In the case of the former, "a good road literally became a matter of honor for each kolkhoz," according to *Pravda*'s correspondent, who did not exactly explain how this came to be the case.[79] Its roads earned high praise from the rally's drivers, who, along with newspaper correspondents and other journalists, served as the state's eyes on wheels. "This republic could compete in its roads with the roads of Germany," A. M. Miretskii, the commander of the rally, commented. "With roads like this, I guarantee 80 [kilometers per hour]," declared the driver, Lunde. More to the point was the "guarantee" (or expectation) of "on-time and regular delivery of grain from the depths" of the republic "to the main roads...maximal connections with other regions, [and] the continuation of the republic's cultural construction."[80] Crossing into the Tatar Autonomous Republic, however, the columns of vehicles had to reduce their speed to ten to fifteen kilometers an hour because of "deep ditches, unexpected pits and bumps, loose planks, and ruts and potholes."[81]

Of the more than nine thousand kilometers traversed, however, only some sixteen hundred were on designated main roads (*shosseinye dorogi*); more than six thousand were on dirt roads or paths; and about one thousand were on no roads at all. Most if not all of the main roads were in the Russian republic; most of the dirt roads and all of the "blank spots" were in Central Asia. The essential purpose of the Central Asian portion of the rally—and especially the crossing of the Kara-Kum (Black Sandy) desert—was to demonstrate not so much the need for (better) roads as the durability of the new GAZ Model-A and Model-AA vehicles. In other words, Central Asia was to serve as the Soviet Union's Sahara: the rougher the conditions, the better.

In the more extended accounts of the rally and particularly the collective "diary" that the *Pravda* and *Izvestiia* correspondents stitched together from their daily reports, the Kara-Kum's roadlessness stood for the timeless nomadic ways of Central Asians. ("This is our rally, comrades!" a special plenipotentiary from the Turkmen Council of People's Commissars tells the correspondents: "The introduction of automobiles into the desert carries with it the death of backward nomadism.")[82] The correspondents' account also makes graphically clear the metaphorical path from roadlessness to socialism/communism. As they traverse the desert, the motorists travel through not only space but time, moving seamlessly from the well-preserved past to harbingers of the radiant future. They encounter both camel caravans and airplanes, the ruins of "ancient" cities and newly unveiled—"emancipated"—women, the treacherousness of a landscape seemingly devoid of water and an underground river that held the potential for irrigation canal projects. Such a path was also depicted by the illustrated journal, *USSR in Construction*. "In places where lay the lifeless sands of Kara-Kum," it confidently predicted that "cotton fields will bloom, and in places where for thousands of years sand has drifted over dead mud-brick cities, new cities, socialist cities, will arise....Even now, the stones and sands of Kara-Kum contain sufficient vegetation to feed twenty-five million sheep."[83]

No expeditionary rally ever again matched the prominence achieved by the Moscow–Kara-Kum–Moscow rally. Indeed, few were held thereafter. And yet, Avtodor's files contain some elaborate proposals accompanied by high-flung rhetoric. The dream of blazing a path across Siberia persisted. At a January 1935 meeting to organize a Far East–Siberia rally, the head of Avtodor's automobile department had "no doubt that in the near future we will

"No expeditionary rally ever again matched the prominence achieved by the Moscow–Kara-Kum rally." Postcard photograph of the rally, Azerbaijan, 1933. In author's possession.

see such a route that will give us the possibility of traveling from the Black Sea to the Great Ocean in the most cultured conditions, in the most stylish car that the Stalin factory [ZIS] will soon be producing." "We know that the eastern krais are expanding economically," responded the president of the organization, Andrei M. Lezhava. "[They] are becoming the foundations of socialism.... We must create a path to connect these regions to each other, to organize all-round movement within them." And then, Lezhava's rhetoric really took flight:

> We must strive so that John Morgan, the American consultant to the [Moscow] metro project, could write the same kind of feuilleton that he has written for *Izvestiia* in which he says that we have built the best metro in the world.... Let this foreigner view our work in marking the gigantic foundation of the future auto route uniting one-sixth of the earth's surface and having colossal significance from the point of view of its expanse.

Fifty cars and trucks would make the journey, he went on to say. They would be filmed not to be screened as newsreels, as previous rallies were, but "constructed as a story" (*postroena fabula*). Perhaps Dziga Vertov, the famous "man with a movie camera," could be persuaded to make such a film.[84]

In 1937, a Professor Vetchinkin revived an earlier proposal for an expedition to chart a "main road" (*magistral'*) from Iakutsk in eastern Siberia to

Anadyr, recently designated as the capital of the Chukhotka Autonomous Okrug at the far northeastern corner of Eurasia. Taking note of recent transpolar flights by Soviet pilots, Vetchinkin foresaw increased commercial activity between the USSR and the United States, and suggested that the road "could serve the landing strips and aerodromes in summer and winter and also be used for postal delivery from the airports." Besides, "in the future there might be a stream of American tourists and hunters driving their cars through Alaska and then conveying them by steamship from Nome to Anadyr."[85] This rally, too, seems not to have occurred. It was as if, with the official assertion at the Seventeenth Party Congress in February 1934 that socialism had been achieved in its essentials, there were no more roads—real or metaphorical—to discover.

The rallies that did take place after the Moscow–Kara-Kum–Moscow served other purposes. The agendas of the diesel engine rally of 1934, the "gas generator" (hard-fuel) rally of 1938, and the 1939 rally of cars operating on a mixture of butane and propane gases were essentially scientific-technical.[86] Two 1936 rallies were just as obviously exhibitionary. One, sponsored by the Dinamo Sporting Society, took seven GAZ vehicles over a route of some twelve thousand kilometers. The main purpose of the rally was to "show off new cars in remote regions." The other—the "Great Women's Rally"—"proved that women can fulfill responsible auto-transport tasks no worse than men."[87] Finally, by the late 1930s rallies as sporting events—with explicit defense implications—had made a comeback. This was to be expected, for with the disbandment of Avtodor in 1935 the All-Union Committee of Physical Culture and Sport and Osoaviakhim inherited the responsibility for promoting automobilism. Neither organization was particularly concerned with overcoming roadlessness.

In the meantime, Ilf and Petrov had published an account of their extensive automobile trip through the United States during the winter of 1935–36. Although written in their inimitably jaunty style and containing some very funny passages, *Odnoetazhnaia Amerika* (*One-Story America*) was not a work of satire. Rather, it treated the United States as an exotic land full of wonders. "In the Russia of those years," remarks Aleksandra Ilf, the writer's daughter, "there were no skyscrapers, cafeterias, burlesque (that is, striptease), grapefruits and grapefruit juice, a mighty automobile industry, neon-lit billboards, hot dogs, toilet paper . . . and many, many other things." Among those other things were hundreds of thousands of miles of highways to which the authors devoted a chapter. Roads were, in their view, "one of the most remarkable phenomena of American life. That's life and not only technology."

America lies on a great automobile road. And when you close your eyes and try to recover the memory of the country in which you spent four months, you imagine yourself not in Washington with its gardens, columns, and collection of monuments, nor New York with its skyscrapers, poverty and wealth, nor San Francisco with its steep streets and suspension bridges, nor the mountains, factories, and canyons, but the intersection of two roads and the gasoline station with pumps and advertisements in the background.[88]

Building Highways—Imagined and Real

During the late 1920s Avtodor's journal published several articles praising foreign roads. One, based on letters sent back to the USSR by a group of oil workers from Baku, reported that the surfaces of roads in the United States were so smooth that one could read and write on the buses. More typical was an account by I. Feld'man, chairman of Avtodor's road department, of his trip out west where he counted 250 cars in an hour on a highway between Seattle and Portland, and in California rode along a four-lane, concrete highway. Every ten to fifteen miles he observed a garage equipped to carry out repairs, serve gas, and provide water.[89] But it was not only in the United States—where it seemed to Feld'man "the entire country is behind the wheel"—that one encountered such wonders. In Europe, limited-access tollways first made their appearance in September 1924 with the opening of the Milan–Varese–Como autostrada. That same year saw the founding of Germany's Studiengesellschaft für den Automobilstraßenbau (Stufa), which in 1926 came up with a plan for an extensive superhighway network. Here in essence was the basis for the autobahn system, whose first segment (from Cologne to Bonn) opened in August 1932—six months before the Nazis came to power.[90]

In Soviet discourse, the term *autostrada* referred to modern paved highways for motor vehicles, whether tolls were charged or not. There was a time in the not-so-distant past when the French word "chaussée" would have been used for such roads, but times had changed and the chaussées inherited from Imperial Russia were in various states of disrepair, especially in the provinces. Thus, when Osinskii and several companions drove out to inspect harvest preparations in the summer of 1934, they discovered that the highway between Elets and Voronezh—though still listed on a map—no longer existed. It was, in the words of one of the travelers, "a mere indicator of the direction of movement, to get one's bearings." The phrasing is reminiscent of the above-cited Russian aphorism about roads and directions. The region itself must have been depressingly familiar to Osinskii, for five years earlier he had excoriated its roads as indicative of "the survival of barbarism."[91]

On May 10, 1933, *Pravda* ran an article datelined Gor'kii and headlined "Autostrada Moscow–Gor'kii." It announced approval of plans for the 414-kilometer highway that would be included among the year's priority ("shock") construction projects. Preparatory work on storage facilities for bitumen and for gravel and asphalt bases had already begun. The road, commissioned (though not funded) by Avtodor's central committee, would be a "colossal enterprise" like no other in the country. What made it so was neither its length nor the natural obstacles it would have to surmount, but rather its width. In order to accommodate sixteen lanes segregated for use by fast-moving passenger cars, trolley buses, freight-carrying motor vehicles, motorcycles, horse-drawn vehicles, bicycles, and pedestrians, it would be 150 meters wide. The center lanes would carry vehicles traveling at speeds up to 120 kilometers an hour, while "permanent greenery" (*vechnozelenaia rastitel'nost'*) would border the outer more bucolic pedestrian lanes. The entire "strada" would be equipped with night lights, repair, filling, and recharging (for batteries) stations, as well as small hotels and cafeterias.[92]

Someone must have sounded the alarm bell, for two days later *Pravda* carried a brief notice describing the project as a "complete fantasy." It chastised Avtodor first for having commissioned the Leningrad Auto Road Institute (LADI) to design the autostrada rather than concerning itself with making the existing roadway navigable, and then for trying to force its construction through various state agencies. But Avtodor was not alone. Tsudortrans, too, had gotten caught up in the dizziness and only as an afterthought had undertaken an economic assessment of the project—which showed it to be unnecessary. The incident must have caused Avtodor considerable embarrassment, but it is unlikely to have played a role in the disbanding of the organization two years later. This is more easily explained by the absorption of automobilism within the ever-expanding orbit of domestic security concerns and military preparations in the increasingly threatening international environment.[93] Voluntary organizations such as Avtodor, once thought to be vital in mobilizing individuals and their private desires for public/state purposes, had become so much froufrou, like "permanent greenery" bordering highways.

The reasons for the liquidation of Tsudortrans and its leading personnel are a little more complicated, involving the same dynamics of the purges encountered in the auto factories. On October 28, 1935, Tsudortrans and its lower-level organs (Glavdortrans and Dortrans) were transferred from the Council of People's Commissars to the People's Commissariat of Internal Affairs. The move suggested an upgrading of attention to road building and maintenance, since the NKVD was the most powerful and feared institution in the country. The change facilitated the use of Gulag prisoners in highway work, something previously practiced on an occasional basis.[94] It also meant that Tsudortrans had become superfluous. On March 3, 1936, another resolution of the government "reorganized" Tsudortrans and its organs into the Main Administration of Highways (Gushosdor) and corresponding offices (Ushosdory, Oshosdory) at the Union republic, krai, and oblast levels of the NKVD. Responsibility for the construction and maintenance of local roads was given to district executive committees and village soviets.[95]

Two months before the transfer of Tsudortrans to the NKVD, its director, Leonid Petrovich Serebriakov, an old Bolshevik with a checkered history of opposition to the Stalin faction, was relieved of his duties. A year later he was taken into custody and appeared as one of the defendants in the January 1937 show trial of the "anti-Soviet bloc of Trotskyists." Neither in his testimony nor in his final plea for mercy did he distinguish himself. He readily admitted to having conspired with Georgii Piatakov and others to organize wrecking on the railroads and to have "become in sum an enemy of the people" after "two dozen years as a loyal and devoted member of the party."[96] What he did not admit to—and was not accused of—was sabotaging road construction and maintenance as head of Tsudortrans. Soon enough, however, an elaborate chain was constructed to link him to "Industrial Party wreckers" who had been in charge of road administration as long ago as 1924; to unnamed "antimechanizers"; and to a group of soil scientists whose textbooks "propagandized" the utility of ground soil (*grunt*) as a basic road surfacing material. This undoubtedly was a case of the accuser—engineer A. S. Kudriavtsev—trying to keep his head above water in the torrent of denunciations that contributed to the Great Purge.[97] Serebriakov was eliminated not for his failings as a road transport administrator (great though they may have been) but because his past as an associate of Trotsky and other erstwhile Left Oppositionists had caught up with him.

But there were other victims. Despite a shortage of civil engineers—or maybe because their skills were in such great demand that they needed to be reminded they were just cogs—the rule that nobody was irreplaceable did not make an exception of leading road personnel. Perversely, the more strategically important the institution, the more devastatingly thorough were the purges. Three-quarters of the leading personnel in Narkomput were replaced during 1937–38, the overwhelming majority of them victims of the Great Purge.[98] The number of those working in road administration who suffered the same fate is not known, but it certainly was high. In April 1937 the road engineer Isaak Solomonovich Gokhfel'd, working at the time as assistant director of Gushosdor's planning division, was arrested in connection with the "Minsk Glavdortrans affair" (aka "Trotskyist wrecking organization"). Gokhfel'd served ten years in Siberian camps while, according to Memorial's investigators, "many of his acquaintances were shot."[99] The logic—so to speak—behind the execution in September 1937 of Tsudortrans's deputy director, Stepan Stepanovich Perepëlkin, was likely to have been guilt by association. This perhaps was equally true for others who had worked under Serebriakov and suffered similar fates.[100] Meanwhile, the net kept on widening. By 1939 it had enveloped the secretary of the party committee at the Moscow Automobile Road Institute (MADI), the premier institution for the training of civil engineers. He was accused of having been recruited in 1935 to a "terrorist group" that intended to carry out a "terrorist act" against Lazar Kaganovich, Narkomput commissar and one of Stalin's inner circle.[101] By then, former NKVD officials who had worked in Gushosdor were being arrested and shot.

Even as it was destroying so many lives and careers, the regime was also engaged in an orgy of building. Far from being diametrically opposed, the two processes were as close in the minds of Communist ideologues as purification and transformation. The primary purpose of putting the entire country "under construction" (*na stroike*) may have been to overcome backwardness, but the sheer immensity of many of the projects was bound to inspire awe, and undoubtedly was intended to have that effect. Among all the construction projects, Boris Iofan's enormous Palace of Soviets, designed to be built in the center of Moscow, outdid others in its awesomeness. Too large and weighty for its foundations, it was never erected. But it is significant as the epitome of the three tropes of Stalin-era architecture: verticality, hierarchy, and immobility.[102] Though it embodied the opposite principles of horizontality, levelness, and movement, the plan for road construction that NKVD boss Genrikh Iagoda and Georgii Ivanovich Blagonravov (Serebriakov's replacement as director of Tsudortrans) sent to Stalin in November 1935 also partook of grandiosity. The plan called for earmarking R 846 million from the Union budget for 1936 alone to build three kinds of roads: broad twenty-meter-wide highways or main lines (*avtomagistrali*) analogous to the straight-as-an-arrow railroads favored by the regime; strategic roads near the western and eastern borders of the country; and other roads of Union significance.[103]

The seven main lines, projected to cost R 475 million in 1936 and a total of R 823 million at completion, were clearly the main focus of the plan. Totaling roughly thirty-seven hundred kilometers, they were: Moscow–Leningrad, Moscow–Minsk, Moscow–Khar'kov, Khar'kov–Rostov, Orel–Kiev (part of Moscow–Kiev), Moscow–Gor'kii, and Moscow–Iaroslavl'. The Moscow-centeredness of the schema was no less characteristic of its time than the prime justification for the enormous expenditure of state funds: the prospect, even likeliness, of a pan-European war, and therefore the necessity of strengthening the defense of the country via the rapid deployment of troops and equipment. The example given was the Moscow–Minsk highway, which, so the report claimed, could support the movement of two entire infantry divisions in a single day.[104] The government approved two of the seven for immediate construction—the Moscow–Minsk and Moscow–Kiev highways—and assigned the task to the NKVD. The two roads, the government's directive stated, would have "immense significance for the economy and defense."[105]

Undoubtedly, they would, no less so than the autobahns were having for Nazi Germany. The German program—which employed forty thousand workers in the winter of 1933 but 124,000 by June 1936—represented a threat but also an inspiration to Soviet authorities.[106] "Autostradas are the favorite offspring of fascist regimes," *Behind the Wheel* noted derisively. But, after arguing that the "German autostradas" were intended primarily for military use, the article admitted that "it would be a mistake to ignore the huge potential that the autostradas have for auto transport" and waxed eloquent about their "exemplary maintenance, road signs, and safety features"—all of which held "great interest for our road construction."[107]

Autobahns had many goals, some carried over from their original conceptualization in the 1920s, some specific to Nazi policy, and some that were shared by schemers and dreamers elsewhere. It would be wrong, therefore, to assume some sort of totalitarian penchant for road building in the pre–World War II era. Successive international road congresses (Milan, 1926; Washington, D. C., 1930; Munich, 1934; The Hague, 1938), each attended by thousands of delegates from upward of eighty countries, testify to the near universal popularity of highway construction. Of course, resources and accomplishments varied. With the arguable exception of the United States, Germany stood at one end of the spectrum, engaging in what Detlev Peukert referred to as "razzamatazz about the Autobahn and the Volkswagen." The Soviet Union was at the opposite end. It had no governmental representation on the permanent international commission and did not send delegates to the International Road Congress in Washington or in Munich.[108] It kept its plans for road building under wraps until construction started, and even then the routes remained a secret. Nazi German and Soviet methods of mobilizing labor also differed. The Nazis' *Motorisierungspolitik* was, among other things, also an *Arbeiterpolitik* designed by general inspector for German roads Fritz Todt to soak up as much of the hard-core unemployed population as possible and "to incorporate the worker...into the German national community by engaging him in labour beneficial to the common good."[109] By contrast, the Soviet highways relied on labor supplied by the Gulag, a point that Todt himself emphasized.[110]

In the Soviet case, the NKVD established two camps, one near the city of Kaluga and the other in Viaz'ma (Smolensk Oblast) for the express purpose of providing the labor needed to build, respectively, the Moscow–Kiev and Moscow–Minsk highways. The director of each camp was to do double duty as the director of construction. An NKVD order of February 5, 1936, placed Blagonravov in charge of logistical planning and budgeting for both projects. The two roads, selected from among the seven proposed by Iagoda and Blagonravov, were to be built, in the words of another directive of March 31, 1936, "quickly, solidly (*prochno*), beautifully, and cheaply" with bridges and other structures that "must serve for hundreds of years."[111]

In a recent overview of "the scale, structure, and trends of development" within the labor-camp economy, Oleg Khlevnyuk discerns three phases prior to the Nazi invasion in June 1941: "relatively successful development" interrupted by the Great Purge, during which the camps were overwhelmed by the massive influx of prisoners and "political motives...took absolute priority over economic ones," and then, as the purges abated, "economic growth...achieved through the 'utilization of internal reserves.'"[112] Many gaps remain in our knowledge of the two major highway construction projects administered by the NKVD, but it appears that they both conform to the general trend outlined by Khlevnyuk and exhibit their own peculiarities.

Articles about the two main roads—exuding confidence and full of overheated metaphors—started appearing in the newspapers in the summer of 1936. The Moscow to Minsk highway, *Pravda* announced, would have "no turnpike barriers, no pedestrian or train crossings, and no ravines to hinder the smooth flow of cars." Poklonnaia gora, the hill to the west of the capital from which Napoleon first gazed on the Kremlin in flames, "will be moved a little to the side," the report cheerfully continued, "because the builders don't want to have to deal with hills." Mechanized excavators, shovels, and tractors were being used to build not only the road but hotels, restaurants, and garages. The first cars would travel along the highway by the anniversary of the Great Proletarian Revolution, in three and a half months. The pièce de résistance, however, was what the roads would do for those who participated in building them:

> The men of the NKVD will apply not only their flaming tirelessness but their high degree of discipline, accuracy, and faith in the task. They will raise man from the muck and put him on his feet again, awakening in him the best human feelings, teaching him to labor. Thus, leveling or raising hills, the leaders of construction will not only "straighten out" nature, but man too.[113]

It was just this sort of language—invoking the Soviet ideal of physical labor's transformational effects on individuals and thereby reminiscent of the propaganda surrounding the White Sea–Baltic Canal project's reliance on convict labor—that enhanced among a credulous public the reputation of the NKVD as a paragon of probity.[114]

The Moscow to Kiev highway, the subject of another article, would not be finished before the end of 1937, but one could expect the first two hundred kilometers to Kaluga (site of the labor camp) to be ready in the fall of 1936. Covering a total of 830 kilometers, the road would resemble "the best autostradas of Europe." This was because the project would be "carried out with mathematical exactitude and iron precision characteristic of all the work of the NKVD, that authoritative 'firm.'" Here too shops, restaurants, and hotels would line the highway. And in the future the road would connect Leningrad, Tashkent, Tiflis, even... Vladivostok.[115]

But the projects already were in trouble by the time the articles appeared. On June 3, 1936, the NKVD ordered the transfer of the Moscow–Minsk highway project from Gushosdor to the Gulag with the Gulag's director, Matvei D. Berman, personally responsible for organizing a road-construction department. On July 26, 1936, the deputy director of the Gulag was placed in charge of the Moscow–Kiev highway project and the Kaluga camp.[116] But the switch proved "ineffective." In March 1937 the Moscow–Minsk highway project was returned to Gushosdor. The Viaz'ma camp, however, remained under Gulag jurisdiction.[117] The game of administrative musical chairs reflected problems on the ground. First, Gushosdor's engineers altered the Moscow–Minsk route so that it did not cross so many populated areas; then, they decided to build a parallel track to accommodate tractors, whose spiked wheels would have chewed up the highway's paving. They also came up with a solution to the problem of livestock crossings—arched-stone paths under the highway every five kilometers—but this proved intolerably expensive and was abandoned. Eventually, in June 1938 the plans for the 695-kilometer road were approved.[118]

Meanwhile, on May 20, 1937, Blagonravov, Gushosdor's director, received an order from the commissariat's headquarters to remove all prisoners working on both highways within a radius of thirty-five kilometers from Moscow and replace them with hired labor. The prisoners may have been needed to supplement those already working on the Moscow–Volga Canal, the high-priority NKVD project then reaching its final stages. It is unlikely that this order was carried out, however, or if it was, Blagonravov did not oversee its execution, for five days later, he was arrested. On September 27, 1937, it was the turn of P. A. Petrovich-Shteinpres, director of the Moscow–Minsk construction project and thus of the Viaz'ma camp as well. On March 11, 1938, three months after Blagonravov's death sentence was carried out, Veniamin P. Kniazev, assistant chief engineer of the Moscow–Minsk project, was arrested on charges of participating in a counterrevolutionary terrorist organization. He was executed on September 1 along with several other former Gushosdor officials. The execution of Petrovich-Shteinpres came on March 2, 1939.[119]

Construction nonetheless continued. Occasionally, a notice—somewhat less cheerful than those cited above—would appear in the press. For example, in February 1937, Gushosdor's journal attributed hitches in construction on the Moscow–Kiev road to "lack of care about people," as evidenced by the lack of provision of housing and food. "Instead of educating and raising up people, the leadership resorted to the completely incorrect path (*put'*) of mass repression." A year later, in reviewing progress on highway construction throughout the country, two engineers, Kornienko and Gaiduk, referred to a party control commission report that found "tolerance of scandalous defects and abuses" by "enemies of the people" who "in the course of a long time had inserted themselves into road organizations and did everything they could to impede construction."[120] By this time, Gushosdor had its own labor camp, Shosdorlag (aka Ushosdorlag, Ushosstroilag). Located in Khabarovsk, it contained as many as forty thousand prisoners and supplied labor for road construction throughout the extreme eastern portion of the RSFSR known as the Russian Far East. But it wasn't until several months later, in June 1938, that its director and chief engineer suffered the same fate as other Gushosdor officials—arrest on charges of having been members of a counterrevolutionary terrorist organization.[121] Thus, it is likely that the "enemies" cited by Korneinko and Gaiduk were associated with the Moscow highway projects.

How should we understand these accusations of "defects and abuses"? The annals of the Great Purge are filled with all sorts of fantastical testimony extracted from those under arrest by investigators who themselves could not afford to err on the side of caution. The cases of the hapless Gushosdor officers undoubtedly involved their share of this sort of thing. This is not to deny, however, that abuses had occurred. Rare is the construction project anywhere that does not cut corners, skirt or violate safety rules, and engage in other questionable practices. A labor force consisting of largely unmotivated prisoners compounded the temptation to commit such abuses. What distinguished the two highway projects, therefore, was not that defects and abuses occurred but rather that they occurred in the midst of general, state terror.

With the completion of the Moscow–Volga Canal in 1937, the government raised the priority status of the Moscow–Minsk highway project, which meant advancing its completion date from 1942 to the last quarter of 1940. The size of the Viaz'ma camp population, the main source of labor on the project, fluctuated from a low of twenty-four thousand on January 1, 1938, to a high of nearly fifty thousand six months later. The project's administration divided the workforce into nine sections. Including workers and peasants hired from among the inhabitants of towns and villages on either side of the projected road, the total number of people working at the site reached 105,000. They had use of about twelve thousand horses, some seventy trucks, and thirty tractors. The twenty million cubic meters of earth removed to make way for the road's eighteen-meter-wide trench approximated what was dug out to build the White Sea–Baltic Canal. In addition, 115 bridges, totaling a little over three kilometers in length, were erected. The government mentioned nothing more about the Moscow–Kiev project. The disbandment of the Kaluga camp in February 1938 and the distribution its 16,300 inmates elsewhere suggests either its completion or abandonment.[122]

The quality of construction on both projects left a lot to be desired, but evidently not all the fault lay with the labor force: engineers from Soiuzdorproekt who designed the Moscow–Minsk road had failed to take into account that the sand on which the paving blocks rested would subside more in some places than others; that the firmness of the crushed stone used for paving would vary depending on whether granite or limestone was used; and that building the road across the swampland at the intersection of the Berezina and Skha rivers near the town of Borisov (Belorussia) would require the removal of massive amounts of peat. Still, by the end of August 1938 workers had laid the entire roadbed and during the following year had poured millions of tons of asphalt and concrete into it. Gas stations, repair shops, and hotels were to follow along with extensive landscaping. How close the project was to completion by the time the Nazis invaded is not clear. The NKVD suspended work in March 1941 so that workers could be reassigned to build air bases for military use.[123] Thus, the Soviet Union was spared the ultimate irony of having built a route to its capital city that facilitated its conquest by an invading army. The autobahns, in contrast, unquestionably *did* aid the advance of troops—Allied troops that is, striking from the Rhineland to the Elbe in 1945.

War: Roads of Life, Roads of Death

Soviet roads, the vast majority of which were unimproved at the outbreak of the Great Patriotic War, did not discriminate between invader and defender. The Wehrmacht's trucks did no better in supplying its panzer divisions than the Red Army's motorized regiments did in carrying troops and matériel to and from the front. Both sides relied mainly on rear-axle vehicles that frequently got stuck during the rasputitsa. In this respect the American four-wheel-drive vehicles made a significant difference in that they could travel through rough terrain carrying motorized infantry and artillery. For example, during the offensive in Belorussia in the summer of 1944 (Operation Bagration), such vehicles enabled Soviet forces to travel on marginal dirt roads and through swamps and forests, bypassing German roadblocks and enveloping road-bound German units. Later, the increased mobility obviated the problem of rail conversion once the Red Army advanced into Poland and Germany.[124]

Throughout much of the war, however, and especially during its initial phases, the scarcity of good roads was experienced by the Red Army and the population at large as an unmitigated curse. Almost every account of the invader's early successes cites huge bottlenecks of Soviet artillery, motor vehicles, field kitchens, wagons, and retreating troops that gave "the Nazi planes...the time of their life." Bottlenecks reproduced themselves during the evacuation of Moscow in October 1941. By the end of the year, according to Soviet official sources, over half of the prewar length of all-weather roads (estimated at 136,300 km) was either destroyed or in enemy hands. Truck losses were put at roughly the same proportion, which made the mobilization of horses a critical activity during the winter of 1941–42.[125] With the import of American Lend-Lease trucks, the organization of new truck regiments and battalions, each nominally containing one hundred trucks, and the setting up of a network of fuel and supply depots in the rear, the situation "improved dramatically."[126] Road-building battalions—both military and civilian—helped as well.

Soviet Russia's most remarkable road was not a road at all in the conventional sense. It was an ice road, actually many such, built across Lake Ladoga in the winters of 1941–42 and 1942–43 to transport food and other materials into and evacuate people out of the besieged city of Leningrad. To Leningraders it was the "road of life" (*doroga zhizni*), a literal lifeline to the rest of the country that defied the invader's attempt to starve the city into surrender or obliteration. "In all cultures the road is a metaphor of life," says the catalog to a State Russian Museum exhibit called "Roads in Russian Art," but in actuality there was only one road of life, at least in Soviet times.[127]

The Wehrmacht's seizure on September 8, 1941, of Schlüsselburg (Shlisselburg) at the southwest corner of Lake Ladoga completely severed Leningrad and the land immediately to its east from the rest of Soviet-held territory. Roads across the ice, officially known as military auto roads (VAD) 101 and 102, served as the winter equivalent to the shipping routes across the lake, Europe's largest inland body of water. Their construction, undertaken by road- and bridge-building battalions, began in mid-November immediately after the freezing of Shlisselburg Bay. The first column of GAZ-AA trucks, loaded with flour, began rolling on November 22. The distance across the ice varied from twenty-five to thirty kilometers depending on the route. The approximately seventeen thousand military personnel who surveyed, built, maintained, guarded, and drove across the road of life faced danger from enemy artillery and air attacks, blinding snowstorms, frostbite, and the breaking up of ice. On a single day—December 6—the army lost 126 vehicles, presumably from bombardment, accidents, and submersions.[128]

The amount of supplies transported across the ice did not increase appreciably until late December, too late for tens of thousands of Leningraders who simply died from starvation. On December 25, the Military Council raised the bread ration in the city in expectation of supplies flowing more regularly and plentifully, mandating further increases in January and February. Drivers exerted themselves to achieve at least two trips per day. Some racked up three and even five, spending eighteen to twenty hours in the cabins of their GAZ-AA and ZIS-5 trucks. During the last few weeks the road was in operation it bore over four times as many supplies as it had in November and December. In all, 361,000 tons of cargo, of which 262,000 consisted of food, was transported across it. Historians have characterized the ice road's contribution to Leningrad's defense and the survival of the city's population as "outstanding" and "difficult to overestimate." Part of that contribution consisted in evacuating people to Ladoga's eastern shore. By the end of April, over half a million people (an average daily rate of five to six thousand) had escaped the siege in this way. During the summer of 1942 electric cable and gas lines were laid on the lake bed, but in the winter the ice roads returned, this time accompanied by railroad spurs.[129]

Throughout the war and beyond, the Soviet media hailed the road of life as indicative of the bravery and ingenuity of the Red Army, the wisdom of the country's political leaders, and the fortitude of its loyal, patriotic citizens. In many cases, the celebration was accompanied by invoking the near-sacred, and certainly inspirational, example of the *podvig* or self-sacrificial heroic deed. The writer Vera Inber, whose siege diary describes the Ladoga truck drivers as "sacred," partook of this tradition, as did Aleksandr Fadeev and others.[130] The same unalloyed patriotic sentiment is embodied in the Road of Life Museum located in the village of Osinovets (Vsevolozhskii Raion), the former western terminus of the ice road. The museum, which opened in September 1972, is rather diminutive, certainly nothing like the "super-shrines" also erected in the Brezhnev era at Volgograd, Kiev, and Brest.[131] It contains rooms of relics dedicated to the memory of the "immeasurable courage, fortitude, and heroism of the defenders of Leningrad." Stripped of references to the friendship of peoples or the leadership of Comrade Stalin or the Communist Party, it still proclaims—at least on its website—that "behind each exhibit, behind each battle relic lies the destiny of man, the podvig." It is just the sort of place to attract aged veterans with time on their hands and schoolchildren brought there on excursions.[132]

But like much else once held sacred in Soviet times, the blockade and the road of life are no longer sacrosanct. Since the fall of the Soviet Union, foreign novelists have used the setting to play up the melodramatic possibilities of young love cruelly snuffed out.[133] Scholars have taken advantage of access to previously closed archives and other sources to revise the story. The new versions tend to eschew former emphases in favor of second-guessing decisions by the Supreme Command in Moscow and the Military Council of the Leningrad Front. For example, one Western historian notes that "no large-scale air evacuation of civilians seems ever to have been considered," implying that in addition to those evacuated over the road of life during the winter of 1941–42 other Leningraders could have been saved.[134] Another, though ultimately abandoning this line of thinking, gives voice to it by writing:

> Undoubtedly more could have been done. With greater foresight many more children and dependents could have been evacuated in the first weeks of the war. Larger food reserves could and should have been accumulated, and stored securely. Rations could have been reduced earlier.... *The ice road across Lake Ladoga could have been brought into full operation sooner.* Higher priority could, theoretically have been given to the transport of food supplies and evacuees, less to that of industrial goods and materials.[135]

The ice road now figures more often as part of the seamy side of surviving the blockade. References to special teams of police turning back thousands of Leningraders desperate to cross it during the winter of 1941–42 and army officers taking advantage of their official position to steal goods stored in warehouses at either end of the lake share space with more positive evocations. The road, it seems, was as much the source of "fantastic rumors" of enormous quantities of food as a means of delivering the food itself.[136] Even the name of the road is now contested, with memoirists such as the scholar Dmitrii S. Likhachev contending that it was known as "the road of death (and not at all the road of life, as it has been white-washed subsequently by our writers)."[137]

If memory of the ice road has changed since Soviet times, other roads built during the 1940s as part of the war and postwar reconstruction efforts were not commemorated or publicly remembered at all during the Soviet period. The difference surely has to do with the extraordinariness of the ice road and its role in the survival of millions of people. It also may be due to the different sources of labor involved. In the case of VAD 101 and VAD 102, battalions of Red Army soldiers, Leningraders conscripted into labor brigades, and kolkhozniki from the vicinity of Lake Ladoga provided the muscle power; in the case of building, repairing, and maintaining auto routes elsewhere in unoccupied, recently liberated, and annexed territory, prisoners and POWs from camps under the supervision of Gushosdor supplemented the individual military road administrations (VDU—*voenno-dorozhnye upravleniia*) under the Red Army's own Main Road Administration. It turns out that these roads too were sites of contributions and sacrifices.

During the war, Gushosdor operated four corrective-labor camps (ITL—*ispravitel'no-trudovye lageria*), three of which it inherited from the Gulag and one of which had been a prisoner-of-war camp dating from 1939 (see table 4.2). Data for 1944 show that of a total of 16,619 prisoners in all four

Table 4.2. Corrective-labor camps administered by Gushosdor during World War II

Name	Dates	Location of camp	Roadwork	# prisoners
No. 1	07/42–11/45	Riazan' Obl., Penza Obl.	Riazan'–Penza–Kuibyshev	6,738
No. 2	1/44–11/45	Golitsyno Station, Moscow Obl.	Moscow–Minsk	4,225
No. 3	11/43–11/45	Orel city	Moscow–Khar'kov	2,769
No. 4	7/43–1/44	Chuvash ASSR	Gor'kii–Cheboksary–Kazan'	2,887

Source: M. B. Smirnov, ed., Sistema ispravitel'no-trudovykh lagerei v SSSR (Moscow: Zven'ia, 1998), 402–7.

camps at the beginning of the year, 1,456 (8.76%) died before the year was out. The death rate was highest at the No. 3 camp in Orel (13.9%) and lowest at the camp in Moscow Oblast (8.40%). We have a gender breakdown for only one of the camps, No. 1, where of 5,848 prisoners on April 1, 1942, 435 were women, of whom 294 had been convicted of counterrevolutionary crimes.[138] This camp was originally established as Viazemlag (Viazma, Smolensk Oblast) to provide labor for the Moscow–Minsk highway. It was evacuated to Penza in 1941 and transferred to Gushosdor in February 1942. A resolution of the Council of People's Commissars dated July 15, 1942, called on Gushosdor to participate in the building of the Riazan'–Penza–Kuibyshev road, and for this purpose it sent "several thousand" prisoners from the camp to the roadbed and mobilized the local population and its draft animals.[139]

Otherwise, the contribution of prisoners to road building during the war seems to have been modest compared with that of both army battalions organized under the military road administrations and civilians conscripted for roadwork. The latter rarely are mentioned in histories of the war but occasionally turn up in commemorative histories of road building produced by oblast road administrations. Thus, we learn in one devoted to Ivanovo's roads that as late as the spring of 1941 authorities recruited thousands of people from all over the oblast for a major highway construction project linking the towns of Kovrov and Kineshma via Shuia. Suspended at the outbreak of the German invasion, work resumed in 1942, but this time with wooden planks rather than stone or asphalt as the hard surface. "It would be desirable," the authors write, "to mention by name all those who in the difficult conditions of war led the road-building organizations of the cities and raions." They do manage to mention a few of the recipients of the "honored roadworker" (pochetnyi dorozhnik) medal, while noting that the government passed a resolution on July 24, 1942, awarding it to "many engineering-technical personnel, workers, and kolkhozniki."[140]

Prisoners of war were a major source of labor for road building as they would be for most other forms of construction and reconstruction after World War II. On September 25, 1939, within days of the Soviet occupation of eastern Poland, NKVD commissar Lavrenty Beria signed an order (No. 0315) to build a highway ("in the shortest time") running between Novograd, Volyn-skii (Nowogródek), Rovno (Równe), Dubno, and L'vov (Lviv/Lwów). Dubbed Western Ukrainian Road No. 1, it would connect L'vov, the major city in the newly annexed territory, with Kiev and be built by up to twenty-five thousand Polish POWs. The entire operation was run by Gushosdor from Rovno. Prisoners were distributed along six sectors of the road and provided with food, sanitary conditions, and work clothing "according to Gulag standards." In January 1941, the entire camp was moved to construction sites along an east-west road running from Proskurov through Tarnopol, L'vov, and Iavorov (Jaworow) to the new western border facing the Nazi-occupied Generalgouvernement.[141] What happened to the prisoners after the Nazi invasion of the Soviet Union is not clear, though judging from what we do know about the fate of many other Polish prisoners—for example, the several thousand officers and soldiers whose bodies were uncovered by the Germans in Katyn Forest near Smolensk in April 1943—they were unlikely to have been treated well.[142]

Transit Route (Durchgangstrasse) IV, a project under the control of the SS, seems to have been an extension of Western Ukrainian Road No. 1. It was to traverse Ukraine from L'vov in the west through Stalino and all the way to Rostov-on-Don, a distance of some twelve hundred kilometers. The project also may be considered an extension of the autobahn program in that technical supervision was provided by Organization Todt, formed by Fritz himself in 1938 to do just this sort of thing. Part of the "annihilation through work" (*Vernichtung durch Arbeit*) policy adopted by the SS Einsatzgruppen in the fall of 1941, the construction project was one of many to combine the two aims of extracting labor from and disposing of the large pool of Jews confined in concentration camps. At first, it drew on Ukrainian Jews and Soviet POWs, but with prospects for these sources diminishing, the SS turned to Romanian authorities to supply additional workers. According to a report of an international commission on the Holocaust in Romania, the prefect of Tulchin (Vinnytsa Oblast) turned over three thousand Jews, most of whom were from Chernovtsy, to the SS on August 18, 1942, for work on the Nemirov–Bratslav–Seminki–Gaysin segment of the highway. Those considered not fit for work were executed; the remainder were sent to work at breaking rocks and building the highway under the supervision of Ukrainian and Lithuanian guards. During 1943 Organization Todt also constructed a bridge across the Dnepr-Bug estuary at Ochakov. It is estimated that "several thousand workers" perished on each of these projects.[143]

A Captive Labor Force

The Nazis supervised the building of some roads, but many more were damaged and suffered from neglect in the course of the war.[144] Although the destruction of railroad lines was more systematic and severe, repairing roads was also a postwar priority. Soviet authorities would exact reparations from

Eastern European countries to give the USSR access to capital equipment and entire "trophy" plants, but they had little difficulty justifying the use of POWs in rebuilding roads, railroads, bridges, mines, factories, apartment buildings, and other structures. The entire "empire" or "archipelago" of POW camps—some 267 at their peak of operation—was run by the NKVD/MVD's Main Administration of Prisoners of War and Interned Personnel (GUPVI). It paralleled and—especially after Stalin's amnesty of July 5, 1945, released about 40 percent of the penal labor force—rivaled in scope and claims on resources the better-known Gulag system.[145] Since the opening of Soviet archives we have learned a great deal more about these camps and the experiences of the more than three million POWs who passed through them, though there is still considerable room for disagreement about the completeness of the picture that emerges from the documents.[146]

The roadwork projects itemized in MVD's Order No. 0118 of April 29, 1946 relied heavily on prisoners of war. To meet the order's targeted completion date of 1950, GUPVI set up seventeen new camps that simultaneously served as construction sites administered by Gushosdor.[147] The regimen in the camps resembled that of the Gulag—which is to say harsh, especially during the famine year, 1947. As in the Gulag, a monetary incentive system encouraged fulfillment of work norms, although instead of "socialist" emulation, POWs were supposed to engage in "labor" emulation. Occasionally, higher officials intervened to curb abuses. For example, a written complaint from an anonymous prisoner about overcrowding and lack of proper heating, water, and food at a camp in the Bashkir ASSR provoked an investigation that confirmed the allegations. The deputy minister of Internal Affairs thereupon threatened to hold the camp authorities criminally responsible unless they took immediate action to rectify the "intolerable" situation. By contrast, an investigation of Gushosdor's Camp No. 3 found that "engineering-technical personnel...and camp division employees had weakened their insistence on prisoners' fulfillment of output norms," had become too familiar with them, and had allowed them to associate with the local population. Finding this also intolerable, the authorities removed several camp officers and enjoined those who remained in charge to improve work discipline by applying a system of differentiated food distribution based on fulfillment of norms as well as punitive measures (namely, additional hours of work) to those "systematically failing to fulfill output norms."[148]

The situation along the Riazan'–Penza–Kuibyshev road, administered by Gushosdor as Camp No. 1, must have been unique. In 1945, more than three hundred officers and sergeants who had been prisoners of war in Nazi Germany and who had successfully passed through the filtration process to which all returning Soviet citizens were subjected, worked as section heads, foremen, and brigade leaders on the project. Not long after their arrival at the camp, "by the irony of fate," so too did contingents of German POWs. It is hard to imagine many of the guards coddling their new charges, though perhaps some were able to identify with them. The Germans, in any case, not only built the road itself but also erected housing and administrative buildings, including the headquarters of the Moscow–Kuibyshev highway administration in Penza.[149]

In addition to prisoners of war, Gushosdor also used convicts, deportees (*pereselentsy*), and freely hired workers in varying combinations. For example, Site No. 4 depended mostly on POWs plus a small contingent of hired workers, at least in the year 1948. During July, a month of peak activity, POWs numbered 7,040 of a total of 7,340 "workers." Hired workers from local kolkhozes and other institutions also supplemented POWs on the Moscow–Khar'kov road construction project. But as Major Tabachnikov, director of the Belorussian Ushosdor, reported, the "experience of 1947 showed that the attempt to organize the hiring of labor in Belorussia did not have practical results." This was because, in his view, the basic labor force in the western oblasts consisted of independent farmers (*edinolichniki*) who "do not want to work on production," while "the eastern oblasts are suffering severely from the effects of German occupation." He therefore requested that the Gulag provide an additional twelve hundred convicts. In contrast, the Karelo-Finnish SSR Ushosdor anticipated that slightly more than half of the 1,416 workers it needed for 1948 would be hired, while the remainder would be split between convicts and deportees. Overall, Gushosdor reported possessing a work force of 57,945 people on November 1, 1947.[150]

Like directors of any enterprise, the heads of Ushosdor offices furnished budgets that included labor costs. They calculated the anticipated number of workdays, the monetary value of output, and wages for each worker. Much of their data were fictitious, but the wage figures are interesting for comparative purposes. The range of daily wages in 1947 for five locations was R 10.01 to 15.30 with a median of R 13.40. Monthly equivalents can be obtained by multiplying by twenty-four, the standard number of workdays per month. This produces a range of R 240 to 367 and a median of R 322.[151] It is not clear on what basis these wage rates were calculated (that is, whether an MVD-wide rate or some other standard was used), but data for average monthly wages in major branches of Soviet industry show that these are very low figures indeed. For all of industry, the figure was R 626 in December 1946 and R 687 in September 1950. For construction (the nearest equivalent branch of industry), the figure for the latter date was R 565.[152]

Among the projects of these years that relied heavily on prisoners of war was a major section of the Moscow–Khar'kov–Simferopol' highway some 930 kilometers in length. Portions of the highway had been constructed before and during the war, but its modernization and completion during 1948–50 may have had something to do with a rainstorm in the summer of 1948. The story goes that during one of his very infrequent postwar automobile excursions outside the Kremlin, Stalin's car got stuck in the mud near the Shchekin chemical plant in Tula Oblast after a heavy downpour. On his return to Moscow, he immediately called a meeting of (Ministry of Internal Affairs?) officials and gave them two years to turn the pitted route into an up-to-date surfaced road.[153] The story lacks authentication but could explain the urgency of the messages conveyed to those in charge of the project at a special meeting on February 15, 1949. The director of Gushosdor, Lieutenant General Ivan Liubyi, asserted the importance of combating "seasonality." "Road workers must work from January to January," he announced. Deputy Minister Vasilii S. Riasnoi was even more demanding. "We must provide the best automobile highway that our country is capable of," he said. "Work on this road must be at a higher level; we simply cannot afford to put up with ignoring the quality of construction work." To those in charge of quarries, the message was equally blunt: "Give the quantity of rocks assigned for each site [stroika]. Mobilize everything to get it done."[154] For their troubles, Liubyi and several other MVD officers received the Stalin Prize, second degree, in 1951.

There were other possible reasons for the high priority attached to this road's construction. The road, after all, was the main north-south thoroughfare, important both for trucked transportation of goods and people. Defense considerations also cannot be ruled out. But then, neither can the predilection of Soviet leaders—Stalin included—for Crimean vacation spots. Overall, enough work was extracted to enable a GUPVI officer to report that from 1941 to the end of 1949 prisoners of war had built or restored some 2,100 kilometers of paved roads. Aside from the Moscow–Khar'kov–Simferopol' highway, these included the Penza–Kuznetsk road (135 km); Piatigorsk–Mineral'nye vody–Nal'chik (104 km); part of the Leningrad–Tallinn highway (50 km); and the Moscow–Minsk "autostrada" (700 km).[155] As for quality, Patrick Sergeant, one of the few Western motorists to travel "along the broad motor road to Kharkov"—the Moscow–Khar'kov highway—found it in 1955 "like the relatively small number of Soviet main roads...broad, straight, usually empty and well made, except for the occasional two-inch gaps between the concrete sections."[156] When, three years later, two former prisoners of war from Germany traveled farther south in their diesel-powered Mercedes, the inhabitants of the little villages along the way praised it as this "fine road" built by the travelers' compatriots![157]

By January 1950, when the GUPVI officer's report was filed, the pool of POWs had just about dried up. Though the Special Road Construction Corps (ODSK), formed in December 1945 from Soviet army units left without assignment at the end of the war, was still at Gushosdor's disposal, it could not meet the nearly inexhaustible need for labor.[158] Gushosdor already had begun to increase its dependence on convicts in 1948, and by October 1949 it had completed the conversion of prisoner-of-war camps to corrective-labor camps (see table 4.3). This arrangement, in effect a reversion to the status quo ante of the war years, would persist until the reorganization of the MVD and the transference of Gushosdor to the newly created Ministry of Automobile Transport and Highways in 1953.

Gushosdor's camps were not alone in providing laborers for roadwork. At least thirteen other camps did so as well, often ancillary to other functions. Convicts at Sakhalinlag, for example, built a road from Traptun to Okha to link up the Ministry of Oil Production's Dal'neft facilities; convicts from

Table 4.3. Corrective-labor camps administered by Gushosdor, October 1949–April 1953

Name	Location of camp	Roadwork	# prisoners
			(max.–min.)
No. 1	Kursk Obl. (1949–50)	Kursk–Khar'kov	4,334–904
	Voroshilovgrad (1950–52)	Debal'tsovo–Novoshakhtinsk	
	Moscow (1953)	Moscow Obl.	
No. 2	Khar'kov	Khar'kov–Belgorod;	2,303–183
		Khar'kov–Simferopol'	
No. 3	Orel (1949–50)	Moscow–Kursk	5,210–3,903
	Stalinsk Obl. (1950–52)	Zakomel'skaia–Debal'tsevo	
	Moscow Obl. (1953)	Moscow Obl.	
No. 4	Kuibyshev	Kuibyshev–Stavropol'	2,068–836
No. 5	Nebitdag (Turkmen SSR)	Turkmen SSR for oil ministry	3,170–2,541
No. 6	Baku	Azerbaijan SSR for oil ministry	2,634–2,607
No. 7	Zaporozh'e Obl. (1949–50)	Khar'kov–Simferopol'	4,226–2,444
	Poltava (1950)	Kiev–Rostov on Don	
	Stavropol' Krai (1950–53)	Armavir–Mineral'nye vody	
No. 8	Zaporozh'e Obl.	Khar'kov–Simferopol'	7,555– 485
	Kiev	Kiev–Lubnyi	
No. 17	Leningrad	Leningrad Obl.	4,128–1,205
	Leningrad–Moscow;		
	Leningrad–Kingisepp		
No. 19	Moscow	Riazan', Iaroslavl', Dmitrovsk,	1,068*
		Gor'kii, and Volokolamsk	
		highways	

Source: M. B. Smirnov, ed., *Sistema ispravitel'no-trudovykh lagerei v SSSR* (Moscow: Zven'ia, 1998), 460–68.

* Represents number of prisoners on January 1, 1950.

Leningrad's Construction Camp No. 496 were sent to the Belomor Canal to build roads and railroads in 1947; Construction Camp No. 994 convicts built roads in addition to a railroad spur in Krasnoiarsk Krai, while those from Nizhniaia Tura (Sverdlovsk Oblast) built roads when they weren't engaged in wood processing or agricultural work.[159] Inmates at several other camps produced materials used in road construction such as crushed stone, sand, cement, and asphalt. It is to all of those engaged in such labor that Nikolai Zabolotskii, an inmate in the Gulag camps of the far east from 1938 to 1945, dedicated his poem "Builders of Highways" (Tvortsy dorog), which ends:

> Here, in the temple of primeval nature,
> Through thickets, woods resisting night and day,

Collapsing in the swamps, in waters sinking,
And losing hold of cliffs, we carved our way...

The waves of Okhotsk Sea welled out to meet us.
The frightened birds took wing from cool green blades.
At highways edge we stood erect, triumphant,
All pointing to the sky our blazing spades.[160]

Reliance on convict labor was far from unique to the Soviet system. Convict road gangs were a common means of building roads in the United States throughout much of the twentieth century, especially in the rural South where they "met distinct social and economic needs" and "provided the state with a means of racial control." Not until the 1970s were they phased out, only to reappear as a crime-deterrence publicity stunt in the late 1990s in Alabama, Florida, and a few other states. Convicts also "met distinct social and economic needs" in the USSR, although racial control was not part of the equation. Why did they cease to be an important resource for the Soviets even as, at least in the case of Alabama, "the number of convicts and road camps increased steadily throughout the 1950s and reached a height...in 1960"?[161] Some insight into the process of their disbandment can be gleaned from the archival documents in Gushosdor's files. They detail serious and repetitive complaints in the early 1950s of low productivity, poor-quality work, and, especially, escapes by prisoners.[162] One such report from Deputy Director Ivan Pavlov to heads of individual Gushosdor camps in March 1952 refers to the case of a certain Kostin who, as part of a brigade breaking rocks at a rail junction, "slipped away, changed clothes and in the guise of a freely hired worker, got past the control point, sat in a car for awhile, and then escaped." Another escapee, Liapin, described as a former accountant for a pool of cars (*avtokolonna*), fled while being transported to a production brigade. In both these and other cases cited, the prisoners were without supervision (*raskonvoirovannye*), a condition described by one historian as "widespread" owing to "economic expediency."[163]

Cost was indeed an important factor. It is hard to know whether and if so why running camps became more expensive, but things evidently got so bad by August 1951 that Lieutenant General Ivan Dolgikh, head of the Gulag, justified his proposal for the closing of Gushosdor's camps almost solely in these terms. The proposal prompted an objection from Gushosdor's director, Colonel Nikita Litvin, who had taken over from Liubyi in 1950. In a letter to the MVD's minister, Sergei Kruglov, Litvin pointed out that where contingents from camps had been already withdrawn, road construction had been curtailed. Even roadwork on the high priority Volga–Don canal project was being jeopardized. It simply wasn't possible, he continued, to replace prisoners with a freely hired labor force because Gushosdor didn't have the right to recruit workers; even if it gained the right, few could be persuaded to go to the far north or other places with "difficult climates."[164]

Litvin seems to have won this particular round, but with the death of Stalin in March 1953 a far more radical measure for reducing the incarcerated population was adopted. This was the amnesty decree submitted by Beria and adopted by the Supreme Soviet's Presidium on March 27, 1953. The decree resulted in the release over the next three months of approximately 1.5 million prisoners, or some 60 percent of the entire labor camp population.[165] No single factor but rather a concatenation of fiscal, administrative, and political considerations was responsible for the decision to abandon reliance on convict labor for road building and other construction work. Among these considerations were the advances in roadwork technology that made it possible to replace shovel-wielding gangs with machines. The mechanization of earth-moving operations at Gushosdor projects, for example, increased from a reported 46.5 percent in 1946 to 80.4 percent in 1950, for rock crushing from 37 to 66 percent, while cement-laying was almost entirely mechanized by the latter date.[166]

"I Refuse to Invest the People's Money in Roads"

The loss of a captive labor force eliminated the rationale for keeping Gushosdor, the principal administrative unit responsible for the construction and repair of roads of state significance, within the Ministry of Internal Affairs. But just where it would go evidently was not thought out very well, for once it had been detached from MVD it began an odyssey with many stops. First it resided within the Ministry of Transportation. Then, before the year 1953 was out, it was stripped of its responsibilities for construction and placed within the newly formed Ministry of Automobile Transport and Highways. Construction was henceforth the responsibility of another major unit within the ministry, Glavdorstroi. Meanwhile ministerial name—and function—changing proceeded apace at the republic level. In the RSFSR, for example, the Main Road Administration (Glavdorupr), which answered to the republic's Council of People's Commissars/Council of Ministers, survived until 1953, when its functions were transferred first to the Ministry of Road and Transport Machinery, then to the Ministry of Automobile Transport, then to the Ministry of Automobile Transport and Highways (Minavtoshosdor RSFSR).[167]

These peregrinations reflected the same old bureaucratic struggle between road management and automobile transport that had begun in 1922 and had already resulted in several marriages and divorces. The two sides fought over the distribution of funds and other resources, not because they were oblivious to their shared interests but because funds were always inadequate to the tasks at hand. Yet, the road builders did get their machines, or at least some of them, and utilized them to the extent that the proportion of all-weather roads ("with hard surfaces") increased inexorably, and among surfaced roads, the proportion of those that were paved also rose (see table 4.4). The utilization of road construction machinery was greatly facilitated by machine road stations (MDC). The first of these date from the late 1930s, but it wasn't until the 1950s that they got bureaucratic traction, increasing from forty in 1948 to 240 by the end of 1955.[168] Operating essentially on a contractual basis, they

Table 4.4. Improved roads in the USSR, 1940–1960 (in thousands of kilometers)

Year	All-weather roads	Paved roads (cement, asphalt)	Percentage paved (%)
1940	143.4	7.1	0.5
1950	177.3	19.2	10.8
1953	194.2	30.3	15.6
1955	206.8	41.1	19.8
1956	214.5	47.1	21.9
1957	225.7	52.0	23.0
1958	235.9	58.5	24.8
1959	251.0	66.6	26.5
1960	271.0	77.0	28.4

Sources: *Narodnoe khoziaistvo SSSR v 1957 g.* (Moscow: Gos. statisticheskoe izd-vo, 1958), 573; *Narodnoe khoziaistvo SSSR v 1962 g.* (Moscow: Gos. statisticheskoe izd-vo, 1963), 421.

had their own crews of surveyors, engineers, drivers, and mechanics, thereby substantially contributing to the professionalization of road building. Their "high-speed production line" (*potochno-skorostnyi*) approach to both road and bridge building and their use of graders, scrapers, bulldozers, stump removers, rotary snow cleaners, and other mechanized equipment represented the last word in "the industrialization of construction."[169]

Despite evidence of greater mechanization and road improvement during the 1950s, the old complaints about the condition of roads—and in some parts of the country their scarcity—continued to echo. "What colossal losses!" a history of Russian roads exclaims in connection with the idle time—estimated at forty to sixty days per years—that each vehicle in good working order and with freight on hand spent because of the impassableness of roads. It also claims that "up to 60 percent" of tractors were occupied in "the unproductive work of towing cars and making deliveries over long distances," that "as a result of roadlessness... 10 to 15 percent of hayfields and 5 percent of grain perished under the wheels of motor vehicles," and that grain harvests along country roads were 15 to 35 percent less than elsewhere because of the "permanent cloud of dust hanging over the roads."[170] It was not that roads and bridges were in worse shape in the 1950s than they had been before, although the absence of comparative data makes it impossible to be certain on this score. Rather, collective and state farms had become more truck dependant, and bad (or no) roads consequently less tolerable.

Perhaps this accounts for the withering criticism of Nikita Khrushchev for rejecting agronomists' and raion party secretaries' suggestions to finance the construction of roads in the Virgin Lands, his much publicized project for recruiting young farmers in overcrowded areas of Russia and Ukraine to expand grain cultivation in the marginally arable lands of northern Kazakhstan and western Siberia. "What kind of roads?!" he is supposed to have shouted at a meeting of party officials in Akmolinsk after touring the fields in a Volga sedan. "They're not needed in the steppe where you can drive anywhere you like. I repeat they're not needed. I refuse to invest the people's money in roads." If only Nikita Sergeevich had realized the value of roads, historians argue, capital investments in agriculture could have been reduced, yields would have increased, and the Soviet Union could have taken its place among the "civilized" countries of the world. They even fling "Gogol's" inimitable phrase at him, suggesting that the biggest fool is the one who had the power to overcome Russia's other misfortune—roadlessness—but did not use it.[171]

"Who is to blame" is an old Russian pursuit that became especially popular—with often deadly results—under Stalin. Its application to Khrushchev is unfortunate because it is misguided. It is reminiscent of some of the bumptious generalizations that occasional travelers from the West made about the roads during the cold war. Noting, for example, that the route he took between Minsk and Vitebsk was paved, the French lawyer Pierre Pruvost wrote that such a road was a luxury because "since the overthrow of the tsars, not one kopeck has been spent on road repair." Other than the Moscow–Brest-Litovsk and Leningrad–Yalta via Moscow routes, "tarred roads don't seem to exist in the USSR."[172] The Soviet network of improved roads may have been "rudimentary," as Holland Hunter called it, but it wasn't as rudimentary as the ill-disposed Frenchman claimed.

Khrushchev was no more or less antiroad than his predecessors. During his tenure in office Soviet construction crews completed such major projects as the Voronezh–Saratov, Vladimir–Ivanovo, and Sverdlovsk–Cheliabinsk roads, as well as the 109-kilometer MKAD (Moscow Ring Road). They also began building the Moscow–Volgograd highway. But more to the point, it was under Khrushchev that a threshold was crossed in the financing and provisioning of labor for road construction and maintenance. On April 26, 1958, the Council of Ministers issued a decree establishing a 2 percent tax on automotive transport intended to generate 30 percent of the revenue for the maintenance of general state- and republic-level roads. A year later, on April 7, 1959, the Presidium of the RSFSR's Supreme Soviet decreed that all kolkhozes, sovkhozes, industrial, transportation, and other enterprises should contribute to the upkeep of roads either monetarily or in kind. The decree thus transferred the responsibility from individual peasants to institutions that were free to hire, appoint, or otherwise supply the requisite work force, striking a blow against the legal inequalities between rural and urban residents. Most paid fees toward the staffing and equipping of raion road departments (DEU), though in some of the more remote regions sovkhozes, kolkhozes, and timber mills assumed direct responsibility.[173] In places such as Stavropol' Krai, where during the Seven-Year Plan (1959–65) some 1,458 kilometers of roads were improved, the decree's impact was immediate. Throughout the USSR, there were 379,000 kilometers of all-weather roads in 1965 and 489,000 kilometers by 1970. Corresponding figures for roads covered with cement or asphalt were 132,300 (35%) and 205,000 (41%).[174] The gains, in other words, were fairly steady.

Where local resources proved inadequate, the Soviet Army was apt to fill the gap. Crews of recent recruits, stretched out along trenches with shovels in hand, were a common sight throughout the country in the last decades of the Soviet Union's existence. By 1990 some 329,000 soldiers were serving in 501 construction units that had been farmed out to civilian agencies, including the republic-level ministries of automobile transport and highways. Positive incentives, so elusive among road gangs in previous decades, appear to have been lacking as well in these units, which one historian has described as "dumping grounds for...undesirable conscripts" with "a reputation for having the worst discipline in the army."[175]

But the heart and soul of road construction and maintenance were the staffs of district and regional offices, people like Valentina Nalimova, who started working in 1962 in Siberia and who came to know "every meter of asphalt laid with our hands" between Krasnoiarsk and Irkutsk, and Tulun and Bratsk, and was awarded orders of Lenin, Honored Road-Worker, and the highest of all honors, Hero of Socialist Labor; or like I. A. Tepliakov, who worked from 1936 to 1969 as a road foreman on the Velikii Ustiug (Vologda Oblast) roads where he "literally knew every stretch of road, every pothole, and the freight-carrying capacity of every bridge however small"; and like A. M. Geleranskii, another Honored Road-Worker, who began clearing snow from the roads of Belozersk (Vologda Oblast) with a shovel in 1947, and served in a variety of capacities over the next forty-five years before winding up as chairman of the veterans' council.[176] What motivated them? Perhaps they came to identify with "their" roads as a bit of Soviet territory over which they had some degree of control, or maybe the uniforms they wore gave them some esprit de corps.

Judging from available statistics (see table 4.5), their efforts were not in vain. But if it was true that cars built roads, even the significant increase in the number of cars in the 1970s and '80s left a lot of roads unbuilt or at least unimproved. As late as 1990, eighty-three cities and 155 district centers without the status of cities had no direct connections to Moscow by all-weather roads, and as many as seventeen hundred collective and state farms lacked such connections to oblast and republic capitals.[177] Moreover, the more roads that were built and surfaced, the more challenging it became to maintain the entire network.

Table 4.5. Length of roads in RSFSR according to surface (in thousands of kilometers)

Year	1970	1975	1980	1985	1990
Cement and asphalt	69.1	98.6	148.4	195.2	254.2
Gravel/crushed stone	129.1	152.3	173.6	168.6	145.8
Dirt	343.0	267.0	175.8	102.0	55.5
Total	541.1	518.0	497.8	465.8	455.5
of which all-weather	198.2	250.9	322.0	363.8	400.0
percentage all-weather (%)	36.6	48.4	64.6	78.1	87.8

Sources: Z. M. Gal'perina, *Bezdorozh'e ili platnye dorogi v Rossii?* (Novosibirsk: EKOR, 1995), 32.

Russian motorists could be excused for thinking that the condition of Russia's roads was deteriorating, an observation that conformed to what most citizens were experiencing during the years of perestroika. Whether the objective situation was actually improving, travel by automobile over long distances remained an (often unwelcome) adventure, and even within the limits of Moscow and other major cities it could be unpredictable. Alan Sillitoe, the British novelist who undertook a road trip through Soviet Russia in the mid-1960s, ultimately may have been right. The decline in both the amount and proportion of unpaved roads paralleled the gradual but inexorable abandonment of the quest to build something called socialism. The appearance in the late 1980s of billboards advertising cars and other consumer durables coincided with the terminal point of that process.

The undeveloped condition of much of Russia represented an affront to the Bolsheviks' assumptions about building socialism on the basis of an already developed capitalism. Aside from egregiously offending such assumptions, roadlessness kept vast stretches of the countryside outside of the Bolsheviks' political orbit, stymieing their efforts to bring peasants along the metaphorical road to socialism. In more remote parts of the country such as Central Asia, roadlessness could be rationalized as a feature of the region's timelessness and thereby paradoxically its proximity to socialism. But, elsewhere, the absence of improved roads spurred efforts that involved a great deal of coercion, much of it against the very same peasants who were supposed to benefit from improving them. Sillitoe's comment only makes sense if one distinguishes unpaved but improved from unimproved roads. Unpaved roads included graded and graveled surfaces that were characteristic of much of the Soviet road network into the 1960s. Thereafter, as the number of automobiles proliferated and roads became increasingly accessible to not only truck drivers and others on official business but individual car owners and their families (as well as Sillitoe and other foreigners), both expectations and needs rose. At this point, the USSR was still engaged in building, but what was being built was not so clear any more. Both literally and metaphorically the road to socialism began to look increasingly chimerical.

chapter 5

One of the Most "Deficit" of Commodities

> The automobile is not a luxury, but a means of transportation.
> Ostap Bender in Il'ia Il'f and Evgenii Petrov,
> *The Little Golden Calf*

> Socialism is the goal. The automobile is the means.
> Slogan on a banner from a parade in Leningrad,
> August 1928

In September 1915, the Kadet (Constitutional Democratic Party) politician Vasily Maklakov published a fable in the liberal newspaper *Russkie vedomosti* about a "mad chauffeur." "Imagine," he wrote, "you are driving in an automobile on a steep and narrow road" when "suddenly you realize that your chauffeur is unable to drive either because he is incapable of controlling the car on steep gradients, or he is overtired and no longer understands what he is doing." Seated in the automobile are several competent drivers, but they dare not try to take the wheel for fear of causing a fatal accident. The chauffeur not only does not listen to reason but "mocks your anxiety and helplessness: 'You will not dare to touch me!' He is right, for while you might be willing to risk your own life, you are traveling with your mother and will not dare to endanger hers. On the contrary, leaving the wheel in his hands, you try to help him with advice."[1] Coming in the midst of Russia's disastrous war effort and the political crisis provoked by Nicholas II's dismissal of the Duma, it did not take a political genius to figure out that the mad chauffeur was none other than the tsar, the competent but helpless drivers were the liberals, and the mother was Russia.

Maklakov was hardly the first to place Russia in a swiftly moving vehicle. Nikolai Gogol famously ended part 1 of *Dead Souls* (1841) with the image of Russia "speeding like a troika which nought can overtake.... Whither, then, are you speeding," the author asks, "O Russia of mine? Whither?" Gogol did not predict doom for Russia, however. On the contrary, he believed that one day it would "force all nations, all empires to stand aside, to give you way!" Alas, at least one émigré writer, devastated by the outcome of the revolution and civil war, converted Gogol's troika into an automobile with a 100-horsepower engine. Behind the wheel he placed not a mad chauffeur but the devil himself: "a doctrinaire ignoramus and violator, swaggering with self-confidence, the devil of Bolshevism, laughing at the world, and driving the dear car to hell."[2]

Literary Allusions

Yuri Leving, a specialist on the life and works of Vladimir Nabokov, observes in his study of the great stylist's penchant for "the poetics of Russian urbanism" that "from the beginning an aura of the catastrophic surrounded the automobile outing. The auto, as a rule, was associated with unrestrained, spontaneous power....It brought on death, which immediately became the public property of the street (and the writer)."[3] Such writers notoriously included the Italian Futurist Filippo Tommaso Marinetti but also his Russian contemporaries Valerii Briusov and Vladislav Khodasevich. Each expressed an attraction to the automobile's death defying—but also death dealing—capabilities.

To young Volodia Nabokov, growing up in the privileged world of St. Petersburg society, autos were anything but symbols of death. His family owned several cars. While most of his classmates relied on the tram to get to the Tenishev School, Volodia arrived in a Wolseley driven by a chauffeur in livery. For trips to the family's estate at Vyra, the chauffeur preferred a red Opel NAG with red leather seats that could get up to one hundred kilometers an hour on the open road.[4] Nabokov also fondly recalled the yellow and blue limousine in which "Collette," his first sweetheart, arrived from Paris to Biarritz in 1909. Leving thinks that the automobiles of Nabokov's childhood are the "connecting link between his autobiographical and fictional prose," and that in contrast to the pain of exile, the comfort and excitement of the auto trips he took as a child were inextricably associated with the Russian motherland. In this sense, 1915, when Nabokov was sixteen years old, was a watershed year. That was when their chauffeur, Pirogov, who had left the tsar's service ("because he didn't want to be responsible for any kind of motor he didn't like"), was called up and replaced by "the crude, bow-legged, black-haired Tsyganov, a former racing car driver with a wild expression in his yellow eyes." It happened to be as well the year when the young Nabokov made his first and last solo car trip by jumping behind the wheel of a car that Tsyganov had left idling and driving it into a ditch.[5]

Two years later, over the protestations of Vladimir's father, Tsyganov decided to save the Wolseley he loved so much from seizure by the army by disassembling it and hiding its parts in places only he knew. Nabokov recalls that his father, Vladimir Dmitrievich, might have taken him to court "if other more important events had not interfered." Another of the Nabokovs' cars participated—or almost participated—in those events. This was the Benz that Aleksandr Kerensky, seeking to flee from the Winter Palace during the

October Revolution, requested from Vladimir Dmitrievich. Evidently, the previous night the Bolsheviks had disabled all the cars at the disposal of the Provisional Government. A prominent Kadet politician who occupied a number of important positions in the short-lived government, Nabokov's father sympathized with Kerensky's plight. He refused the request, however, claiming, according to his own account, that "the car was weak and battered and hardly appropriate for the proposed purpose."[6]

Evidently, that was when the Provisional Government's prime minister obtained one of the cars belonging to the American embassy staff, for Kerensky made his escape on November 7 in "an American official car, under cover of the American flag."[7] Later that day, John Reed and Louise Bryant arrived at the Winter Palace seeking an audience with Kerensky but were told by an attendant that he had left for the front, adding, "and do you know, there wasn't enough gasoline for his automobile. We had to send to the English Hospital and borrow some." Reed has Kerensky arriving that night at Gatchina. The next day the intrepid automobile reached Luga, 149 kilometers southwest of the capital, where "he was well-received by the Death Battalions stationed there." Picking up the story at this point, Bryant reports that the car transporting "Antonoff" (Vladimir Antonov-Ovseenko, commissar of military affairs who led the storming of the Winter Palace) broke down on its way to Pulkovo, "where the Red Guards were digging trenches to hold a front against the advancing Cossacks." He and his fellow passengers tried to commandeer a car that came by with a soldier at the wheel, but "the soldier had no respect for authority. 'You can't take my car,' he announced with great finality. 'I'm going back to get supplies for the First Machine Gun Regiment. They don't need any more men, they need bullets."[8] In this case, too, it could be said that cars and death—of the Provisional Government—were associated.

Writers continued to make the association—albeit without the obvious political connotations—after the Bolsheviks came to power. Semen Iushkevich, an Odessa writer who emigrated after the revolution, called his story about two lovers who meet by chance on a city street "Automobile," not because it facilitates their romance but because it ends it. Parting, she glances backward and smiles like an angel while he does exactly the same from gratitude. But at that very moment, a truck "impetuously flew around the corner... and, like a scythe, sliced up Maria Pavlovna," leaving Malinin to ponder the succession of seemingly unrelated gestures that conspired to bring about the tragic accident.[9]

Of course, many writers in the 1920s used autos for this purpose. American high school students know that it was Jay Gatsby's big yellow car that ran over Tom Buchanan's mistress, Myrtle Wilson, whose husband just happened to run a garage.[10] In Hermann Hesse's *Steppenwolf* (1927) automobiles seem to have minds of their own as they "hunt for pedestrians," flattening them against the walls of buildings "while airplanes circle above the senseless chaos."[11] But it is in Ilya Ehrenburg's *The Life of the Automobile,* which the author described as "not a novel" but "a chronicle of our time," that the automobile reached its apotheosis as an agent of death and destruction. The time was the late 1920s: Ehrenburg who at this time was neither a Soviet writer nor an émigré but perhaps a little of both, wrote the book in Paris between February and June 1929 and published it that same year in Berlin. It opens and closes with fatal car accidents. In between are chapters on the assembly line, tires, gasoline, and the stock exchange, each placing the automobile at the center of capitalism's creative destructiveness. By the last chapter, on roads, it becomes apparent that the automobile is a synecdoche for capitalism itself:

> Sentimental neighbors wipe their noses, of course, and philosophically minded people argue about the "new peril." Commissions discuss protective laws. But the automobile keeps right on doing its job. Sir Henry Deterding was destined to create an oil empire. Monsieur André Citroën was destined to turn out cheap cars. Karl Lang the cabby was destined to cross intersections. The automobile works honestly. Long before its birth, when it is still just layers of metal and piles of drawings, it diligently murders Malayan coolies and Mexican laborers.... The automobile runs down pedestrians.... It can't be blamed for anything. Its conscience is as clear as Monsieur Citroën's conscience. It only fulfills its destiny: It is destined to wipe out the world.[12]

In case one mistakenly assumed that the Soviet Union could exempt itself from the car's destructive logic, the last incident in the book is about Boris Ignatevich K., an Oil Trust executive in Moscow with a "venerable but well-preserved Ford at his disposal." Comrade K. also has at his disposal Musya G., a clerk at the AMO car factory, who "even before meeting K.... knew that automobiles were now a lot more important than Lermontov." One evening, as K. speeds toward Musya's apartment along Bogorodsky Boulevard ("as though he were in America and not Sokolniki"), the car strikes Musya, killing her instantly. "They put the corpse in the automobile. The engine breathed loudly. The Ford was a fine fellow, it hadn't suffered."[13]

Automobiles had other auras besides death. Marinetti famously associated them with sex and beauty, beauty that outdid that of the Winged Victory of Samothrace. Surely another association was freedom—from schedules and set routes—"a genuine auto-mobile, a self-propelling craft" that offered "the attraction of travel guided by nothing but individual pleasure and mood." And then there was that "unrestrained power" that produced the intensification or compression of time through the attainment of "straight-as-an arrow speed." This is what Marinetti meant by beauty, "the beauty of speed. A race car, its body adorned by great pipes like serpents with explosive breath." The history of the automobile, notes Wolfgang Sachs, conformed to that of other inventions in that it, too, was "full of deviations, of paths not taken and then forgotten." In this case, what would prove to be the main path was determined by "a special class of expectations...to ever higher speeds and performance capabilities." Those ever higher speeds quickly came to symbolize or inspire visions of sweeping away the detritus of tradition, "pensive immobility, ecstasy and slumber...museums and libraries...morality, feminism and all opportunist and utilitarian cowardice," as Marinetti put it.[14]

There is no need to continue to cite the Italian futurist because Russia had its own home-grown futurist poets. Among them, Vladimir Mayakovsky is considered to have been the urbanist par excellence. Though not profuse, references to autos in his poems from before the October Revolution do exist. For example, in "The Huge Hell of the City" (1913), described by Edward Brown as "a series of metaphors in four stanzas," automobiles are "ruddy devils" with "explosive yells." "In an Auto" is a poem that attempts to create through broken rhymes the effect of "passing snatches of conversation heard from a moving automobile," an effect "not unlike that of Natalya Goncharova's 'The Cyclist,' painted early in 1913."[15]

After 1917, cars were no longer devils but invariably appeared on the side of the revolution (or the poet, which amounted to the same thing). In *Mystery-Bouffe,* a play from 1918 that Mayakovsky revised in 1921, they were present along with trains and streetcars in the Communist paradise, "wrapped in rainbows." Among other Things (a hammer, a sickle, machines, fabrics, etc.), they put themselves at the disposal of the Unclean, who have emancipated them from the "parasites." In "The Fifth Internationale" (1922), the automobile serves as a metaphor of revolutionary transformation: "With headlights by Marx and Company / The automobile of dialectics tore into the years, / as the future dispersed their darkness." Since movement, preferably rapid movement, was so important to Mayakovsky, automobiles as well as trains and airplanes were bound to be mobilized to accelerate the "March of Time" and its destruction of *byt,* the tediousness of everyday life. Automobilists or drivers figure in the same way. In "Heroes and Victims of the Revolution" (1918), a poem with clear affinities to *Mystery-Bouffe,* the automobilist who drives an armored car that causes the White Guardist to tremble like a leaf keeps company with a Red Army man, poor peasant, sailor, seamstress, laundress, telegraphist, railroad worker, and other "heroes." In *Mystery-Bouffe,* the Truck Driver is one of the Unclean who travel through Hell (where they drop off the Clean), to Paradise, the Land of Chaos, and eventually the promised land of the Communist paradise. Finally, in a less cosmic manner, the poet in "Conversation with a Tax Collector about Poetry" (1926) identifies himself with "proletarians" who are "drivers of the pen."[16]

Automobiles were thus valuable to Mayakovsky for their allusive qualities. They were important to him in more conventional ways as well. Between October 1915 and the Bolshevik Revolution, Mayakovsky did his military service at the Petrograd Military Automobile School where he was employed as a "skillful and experienced draftsman." Judging from the substantial body of poetry he composed during these two years, and the fact that the assignment kept him away from the front, it was a truly fortunate assignment. A second noteworthy encounter with cars occurred in the summer and fall of 1925 when he traveled to the land of the automobile, the United States, and visited its capital city, Detroit. In his travelogue, *My Discovery of America,* he notes that he toured the Ford factory "in a state of great excitement," but then he mocks Henry Ford's aphorisms and the imposition of military-like discipline on the tourists. Yet, he confesses that despite the familiarity of the assembly line from newsreels, "you come out from it completely stunned." Stunned too, or rather completely exhausted, are the workers he observes at the end of their shift as they "staggered onto the trams." "In Detroit," he writes perhaps with tongue in cheek, "you find the highest divorce rate. The Ford system gives its workers impotence."[17]

Mayakovsky eventually purchased a car, not in the United States but in France, after much prodding from "his ultimate and always love," Lily Brik. In May 1927 Lily wrote to him in Paris that she wanted "a little car" (*avtomobil'chik*), preferably a "little Ford" (*Fordik*), and only "the latest model." Her notebook for 1928 lists what her "Volodia" should buy in Paris. The car with all the accessories including two spare wheels and a baggage compartment in the rear was by a wide margin the most expensive item. In her letter of November 2, 1928, she instructs him to send $450 to Amtorg for a "Fordik." Mayakovsky in the meantime had been trying to sell a film script to René Clair to obtain the money for the car. He failed in that effort, but nevertheless amassed enough to make the purchase. It was neither a Ford nor the latest model but a 1924 Renault NN, about which he wired Lily on November 10. Two days later he wrote a lengthy letter that included a drawing of the car with a cat (her name for herself in her letters to him) sitting on the hood. He was hard at work on a play (*The Bedbug*) and a scenario that would pay for the first gas guzzled by the four-cylinder 6-horsepower "Renoshka," thenceforth the name of the car. Lily, confessing that she was "dying of impatience," asked him to send details about its dimensions, color, and decorations. Mayakovsky returned to Moscow in December. The Renoshka arrived the following month. It undoubtedly helped to smooth relations with Lily after her Volodia divulged that while in Paris he had fallen madly in love with Tatiana Iakovleva, daughter of Russian émigrés.[18] Brown writes that "Tatiana did not command all his affection during his visits to Paris, but was obliged to share him with an object of bourgeois comfort." Mayakovsky could not but commit both objects to poetry. The former was immortalized in "Letter from Paris to Comrade Kostrov on the Nature of Love" (1928, in which he writes of love "humming, / that the heart's / stalled motor / has begun working again," and that "Cars / dash / along the street / but they can't knock me down. / They understand, / the smart ones: the man is / in ecstasy."), and in "Letter to Tatiana Iakovleva" (1928, which he read to Lily Brik on his return to Moscow).[19] The "Renoshka" was the subject of a poem published, appropriately enough, in Avtodor's journal. Called "Answer to Future Gossip" (*Otvet na budushchie spletni,* 1928), it clearly was intended to preempt criticism at home about his purchase of "six horses / gassed up / in my four cylinders." The poet is confronted by voices that whisper: "Tell me, / is it true / that in Paris / you bought / an auto / for you?" He answers in the affirmative ("Of course / I did / and stop talking rubbish"), boasting "The whole street / falls on its face / When my six beauties / neigh." But as a true Soviet patriot, he promises that should the state need his car in the event of war, he would have no problem bridling it and turning it over. "So / please pardon me / for bringing / from Paris / a Renault / and not perfume / and not a necktie."[20] Mayakovsky probably did bring perfume (if not neckties), for Lily requested several kinds. But let us grant him poetic license. The problem was not with the perfume; it was with the car. Basically, the Renoshka betrayed Mayakovsky. In a period when almost nobody had a private car, Mayakovsky not only had one, but because he couldn't drive, hired a cabbie to serve as chauffeur.[21] Otherwise, Lily, who did have a license, drove it, gladly accepting a request from Aleksandr Rodchenko to photograph her dressed in several different outfits and filling up the tank. Having made his reputation skewering Messieurs the Clean (*Mystery-Bouffe*), the philistines of neobourgeois contentment ("About Some Trash," 1921; Prisypkin in *The Bedbug*), and other targets of proper proletarian wrath, Mayakovsky appeared to have succumbed to the very weaknesses for which he castigated others. The "proletarian" poet Dem'ian Bedny allegedly taunted him for having "a private car."[22] And at the worst possible time—1929, the year of Stalin's "Great Turn" ("*velikii perelom*") that launched the Socialist Offensive. Agriculture was being collectivized; town planners were dreaming of collectivizing child-rearing and a lot else. The car was not the only thing Mayakovsky owned that attracted criticism, but it was the most difficult to reconcile with the puritanical principles of cultural revolution.

The parallels with another avant-garde poet and playwright of the Left—Bertolt Brecht—who was two years Mayakovsky's senior, are almost uncanny. Elias Canetti, the Bulgarian-born German writer who met Brecht in Berlin in 1928, recounted that he was "repulsed by him" because Brecht "cared only about matter." Canetti continues:

> I railed against the advertisements contaminating Berlin. They did not bother him; on the contrary, he said, advertisements had their good points: he had written a poem about Steyr Automobiles and been given a car for it. For me, these were words from the devil's own mouth. His boastful confession floored me.... Ibby said: "He likes riding in his car," as though it were nothing.... "He talks about it as if it were his girlfriend. Why shouldn't he flatter it *beforehand* in order to get it?"[23]

Mayakovsky's little car sits in a museum in Moscow along with other Renaults, a testament to the unhappy relationship in the 1920s between Soviet citizens and the private automobile.[24] It was one thing to use the automobile as a metaphor of technological promise, of revolutionary transformation, and even of the throbbing of a heart in love, but quite another to keep one for oneself, especially at a time when confiscations were proceeding again on a mass scale. Mayakovsky could proclaim his willingness to sacrifice his car in the interests of state security, but that wasn't good enough for many who previously had lionized him. His purchase of a car had made him an apostate of the collectivist faith. It had led him on the path to danger. Lily evidently kept the car after her Volodia committed suicide in April 1930.

Cars Take Sides

In January 1913, when Nabokov was being driven to school and Maya-kovsky was poetically imagining himself riding in a car, the entire empire contained some 8,856 motor vehicles (7,308 cars and 1,508 trucks). Moscow, which had registered 826 vehicles in 1911—up from 518 the previous year—saw an increase to 1,303 private cars alone by 1913. Of the 2,200 vehicles registered in 1914, 1,700 were private cars, 200 were trucks, and the remaining 300 were "hired" vehicles. The number, though not great, was sufficient to support two voluntary organizations—the First Russian Automobile Club (PRAK) and the Moscow Automobile Society (MAO)—and a journal for automobile enthusiasts, appropriately if unimaginatively called *Automobilist*. Businesses catering to automobiles (as well as motorcycles and airplanes) included the Triangle (Treugol'nik) and Conductor (Provodnik) tire companies, and the Nobel and Gargoyle oil and gas firms. Autos themselves could be purchased from dealers on Bol'shaia Dmitrovka (Lorraine-Dietrich) and on Georgiev Lane (Fiat, NAG, Gregoire). Aside from privately owned cars, Moscow's streets and garages accommodated a fleet of taxis (from 1909), buses (from 1907), trucks, an ambulance or two, and three police wagons.[25]

Automobile societies promoted interest in "automobilism" by sponsoring exhibitions, races, and rallies. The Russian (later Imperial) Automobile Society organized four international exhibitions before the war, three in St. Petersburg (1907, 1910, and 1913) and one in Moscow (1908). The first and second of these were accompanied by races between St. Petersburg and Moscow. Automobile enthusiasts held rallies along other routes and organized races covering distances from one to one hundred kilometers. As elsewhere in Europe, auto sport in Russia was an overwhelmingly male pastime that, like automobile ownership itself, was largely confined to scions of well-to-do bourgeois and noble families.[26]

This changed rather suddenly with the outbreak of the Great War. The tsarist armed forces, according to a Soviet source, possessed a mere 711 vehicles when war was declared. Of these, it classified 259 as light automobiles, 418 as trucks, and 34 as specialized vehicles. In the course of the war, the state requisitioned over 4,000 vehicles, nearly a third of the total in the empire, and placed orders for some 30,500 with firms in the United States, France, Italy and Britain. By October 1917, approximately 20,000 had arrived. Among them were Pierce Arrow and White trucks from the United States, Fiat F-15s, luxurious Packards assigned as staff cars, and British-built Austin armor-plated cars.

The balance thus was tipped in favor of state ownership of automobiles, a situation that would persist for the next half century. Some of the most vivid images from the revolutionary year 1917 are of cars and trucks careening through the streets of Petrograd and Moscow with machine guns mounted on turrets and Red Guards and other rifle-bearing passengers spilling out of the sides. Many such vehicles, converted for military use, "changed sides" more than once during the ebb and flow of revolutionary power. Hence, Patrick Wright's reference to one vehicle "of indeterminate loyalty...passing slowly up and down the street" and others "daubed over with huge red letters announcing their conversion to the Revolution."[27]

Lenin speaking from atop an armored car after arriving at the Finland Station on April 3, 1917, had great iconographic significance. Ten years later, in *October,* Sergei Eisenstein memorialized the image, adding fluttering flags and crisscrossing klieg lights. This was not the only occasion on which Lenin used an armored car as a platform. He did so again in January 1918 to, as Wright puts it, "launch the Red Army." But when it came to getting around town, there was no reason not to utilize the more elegant cars the Bolsheviks had appropriated from His Majesty's Personal Garage—forty-six in all, including several Delaunay-Belleville limousines, a few Mercedeses, a Daimler or two, a six-cylinder Renault, a Rolls-Royce Silver Ghost, and a Turcat-Mery— along with its staff of expert mechanics and drivers. The fleet of cars and their drivers accompanied the Soviet government to Moscow in March 1918. They thereafter were at the disposal of the party elite. Lenin's favorite, or at least the one that most often conveyed him to meetings outside the Kremlin

Cars Take Sides: Trotsky haranguing a predominantly military crowd "in American fashion." Courtesy of the New York Public Library.

and on days off to the countryside, was an open Delaunay-Belleville. Later, several Rolls-Royces ordered from Manchester replaced the aging cars "inherited" from the tsar.[28] The auto historian Lev Shugurov has traced what happened to at least one of the Rolls-Royces that had chauffeured Lenin: "The worn-out automobile passed to a trade union of fishermen in Kerch," he writes. Damaged in an accident at the end of the 1930s, it was saved from the scrap heap by an enthusiast, later restored at ZIL, and placed in the Lenin Museum where it remained until Boris Yeltsin ordered the museum closed in 1993.[29]

There is no reliable source for the number of motor vehicles in the country at the time of the Bolshevik Revolution or for some time thereafter. Estimates for 1917 vary from 9,525 (of which only 2,343 were said to be operative) up to nearly 28,000. The wide variance may have had to do with the time of the year the numbers were tallied, but more likely it reflects the impossibility of obtaining accurate data. Besides, one can never be sure what actually was being counted. Were motorcycles included in one set of figures but not the other? Were tractors or armored cars? Regardless of what was being counted, many vehicles soon made their way to the scrap heap, and at least a few must have emigrated with their owners. There is some evidence as well of auto theft and the smuggling of cars across the relatively porous Soviet-Finnish border. Numbers of vehicles in subsequent years were reported as significantly lower: 6,621 for June 1918 and 7,592 for April 1919.[30] "On the streets [of Petrograd], a coffin-like quiet," the symbolist poet and novelist Zinaida Gippius noted to her diary on December 2, 1918. "There are no horses (they've been eaten); automobiles, all in Bolshevik hands, are broken, and rare. Here and there, ragged pedestrians stumble through the deep snow, past bedraggled stores with their signs ripped off."[31]

Automobiles are few and far between in photographs of street scenes from these civil war years, though authorities did make sure to round up what was available for the May Day celebrations and pageants commemorating the October Revolution. Aside from an acute shortage of spare parts, the main problem in keeping motor vehicles running was fuel. Lacking gasoline, vehicles unhappily consumed mixtures of grain alcohol, heating oil, naphtha, and whatever other hydrocarbons happened to be around. The vehicles themselves were often no less eclectic in their composition. Hotchkiss motors powering Laurin-Klement frames with gear boxes from Benz; White and Renault bodies mounted on Berliet chassis, with engines and appurtenances from who knows where; Fowler motors installed in Packard trucks—such were the contraptions that Muscovites called "mixed soup" (sbornaia solianka).[32]

During the summer of 1921 when famine afflicted large parts of the RSFSR, the Commissariat of Transportation organized an expedition of trucks to remove 3.4 million puds (about 120 million pounds) of grain from collection points to railroad stations in Akmolinsk Oblast (then part of southern Siberia, eventually incorporated within the Kazakh SSR). A report on the

Table 5.1. Imports, production, and presence of motor vehicles in USSR

Year	Present in USSR	Produced in USSR	Imported*			
	(on January 1 of each year)		Cars	Trucks	Other**	Total
1913	8,849	200 (est.)	4,444	972	0	5,416
1922	n.a.	0	101	87	n.a.	188
1923	n.a.	0	485	302	n.a.	787
1924	13,667	10	157	151	20	328
1925	14,460	116	418	698	142	1,258
1926	15,304	366	1,008	1,087	323	2,418
1927	16,494	475	302	678	290	1,270
1928	21,551	835	559	799	129	1,487

Sources: Tsudortrans, *Avtodorozhnoe khoziaistvo SSSR v tsifrakh: statisticheskii sbornik* (Moscow, 1935), 154–55; Boris Shpotov, "Ford in Russia, from 1909 to World War II," in *Ford: The European History, 1903–2003,* ed. H. Bonin et al., 2 vols. (Paris: P.L.A.G.E., 2003), 2:528.

*Except for 1913, 1922, and 1923, figures are calculated according to the fiscal year that ran from October 1 to September 30.
**Buses, ambulances, fire trucks.

relief effort filed with the commissariat described it as the "first experience in Russia of the planned use of trucks for transport on a large scale."[33] The lack of any other information on what must have been a truly desperate effort is unfortunate. In any case, the decline in the number of vehicles in service throughout the country bottomed out by the middle of the decade thanks to the ingeniousness of anonymous mechanics and a small but growing contingent of imported vehicles. The upward trend continued over the next four years, owing to the expansion of imports and, to a lesser extent, domestic production (see table 5.1). Still, one should not place too much reliance on the figures. For when the first issue of Avtodor's journal appeared in April 1928 it gave three different estimates of the number of vehicles in the country: (1) 19,000 ("of which approximately 6–7,000 are pathetic invalids that only nominally can be counted as automobiles"); (2) 20,600 ("in use"); (3) 18,032 (or 745 fewer than in Rumania).[34]

A scarce resource even by the end of the decade, motor vehicles belonged overwhelmingly to the state. According to a survey from January 1928, state institutions accounted for 77.9 percent of all vehicles. The distribution among state institutions was quite broad: 44.7 percent had only one vehicle; 35.4 percent had from two to five vehicles; 17.3 percent had between six and twenty; and only 2.6 percent had more than twenty. Among those in the last category, the armed forces and the secret police possessed the largest number, followed by transportation, post and telegraph, and municipal administrations. The priority enjoyed by the military was reinforced by a decree of the Central Executive Committee (TsIK) of the Soviets and the Council of People's Commissars (Sovnarkom) of February 22, 1924, that subjected all vehicles (private and state-owned cars, trucks, motorcycles, and bicycles) to conscription (*povinnost'*) in the event of a military mobilization.[35] Whether for military or civilian purposes, the utilitarian function of motor vehicles was paramount. In contrast to an estimated global ratio of six light automobiles to every truck (7:1 in the United States and 2.8:1 in Europe), a government commission under People's Commissar for Transportation Jan Rudzutak concluded in 1926 that "at least for the time being conditions in the USSR do not present the possibility of such a broad development of light automobiles." At this point, nearly ten years after the October Revolution, there were fewer such vehicles in the country than in 1913, or one car for every 7,000 inhabitants.[36]

Motor vehicles were overwhelmingly concentrated in the cities of the European part of the country. Of some eighteen thousand registered in January 1928 just over half were domiciled in Moscow and Leningrad. One indication of Moscow's preeminence was that it alone came under a Sovnarkom decree (June 10, 1920) laying down rules for the use of automobiles. It was almost as if there were too few elsewhere to worry about. The decree contained provisions one might expect to encounter in any traffic code. It set speed limits for cars and trucks (the former at 25 versts [16.5 miles] and the latter at 15 versts [10 miles] per hour), required that vehicles contain horn signals and be driven on the right-hand side of the street, and authorized the Moscow Soviet's Transport Department to appoint auto inspectors to police the use and condition of vehicles. Other rules were more peculiar to the fledgling Soviet state. They stipulated that any vehicle present in the city for more than twenty-four hours had to be registered with the Transport Department; that vehicles belonging to a fleet had to carry log books listing the time of departure and return and the route taken to be signed by both driver and dispatcher; and that automotive travel was routinely restricted to members of certain central and Moscow city governmental institutions (i.e., the All-Russian Central Executive Committee, people's commissars and members of the commissariats' collegia, the Cheka, the All-Russian Central Council of Trade Unions, and the Moscow City Soviet) "and persons traveling with them." Visas could be granted by the Moscow Cheka to other Soviet officials and persons accompanying them on the request of certified institutions, but under no circumstances could vehicles be used "for travel to theaters, concerts, etc."[37]

These rules probably were never intended to be strictly enforced, and as the number of autos grew, they were quietly shelved. In 1924, Moscow introduced regular bus service. The first buses were a couple of converted Model T trucks, but they soon were outnumbered by more capacious and reliable British Leylands. Taxi service, absent since the October Revolution, was restored in the summer of 1925 when a fleet of fifteen newly imported Renaults appeared. As the demand for professional drivers increased, so did their numbers—from 2,653 in 1923 to 3,985 in 1926. At the same time, the number of draymen and coachmen dropped from 9,161 to 5,798. This meant that whereas in 1923 there were 3.5 horse drivers for every motor vehicle driver, by 1926 the ratio had closed to 1.3:1.[38]

Although the volume of vehicular traffic in Moscow did not approach that of major European or North American cities, it was sufficient to create occasional traffic jams such as the one with which Vassily Aksyonov opens his epic novel *Generations of Winter* ("Just think—in 1925, the eighth year of the Revolution, a traffic jam in Moscow!"). Aksyonov described the event as a "cause for rejoicing," a sign that "life is coming back, along with dreams of prosperity."[39] The proliferation of automobiles also led to an alarming increase in the number of road accidents. From 1,600 in 1926, the number of accidents rose to 2,292 in 1927, and 1,083 in the first half of 1928. Nearly five thousand people sustained injuries s a result of these accidents, 15 percent of which proved fatal. Mikhail Prezent, a member of the editorial staff of Avtodor's journal, despaired at Muscovite drivers' lack of discipline; they adamantly refused to stay on the right-hand side of the street, ignoring signs in trams and buses to do so. Perhaps this was because, so another commentator surmised, they represented an intermediary type between coachmen and aviators, having inherited the former's "coarseness" and displaying the technical daring—but not necessarily competence—of the latter.[40]

There doubtless were other reasons. An official investigation of the physical and mental condition of professional drivers elicited complaints of hunger pangs, leg cramps, stupor, and, "especially among young drivers, frequent hallucinations." Of fifty bus drivers not one was considered in good health and only four of thirty car and truck drivers made the grade.[41] But this would not explain how pleasure drivers such as Lily Brik got into accidents. Lily hit an eight-year-old girl while driving her beloved Renoshka one day in the summer of 1929. The girl, she claimed, was crossing the street with her mother at an "unfavorable spot, took fright, froze as if rooted to the ground, then began to rush about like a chicken...I braked sharply but nevertheless slightly knocked her off her feet." Fortunately, the girl was not injured, although the matter did go to court. Much to her relief, Lily was exonerated.[42]

Further afield, things were quite different, or rather, had remained remarkably unchanged. Passenger cars and even trucks continued to be rare sights in the country's villages. Their growing presence in the major cities thus had the perverse effect of intensifying "the contradiction between the culture of the town and the barbarism of the countryside"—the contradiction Bolsheviks were determined to overcome and for which they had introduced the New Economic Policy.[43] In the long run, the villages would have these vehicles too, but like literacy, electricity, and other attributes of modernity, villagers had to want these things before they could have them. At the very least, they had to overcome the hostility—or fright—with which they greeted them. Familiarizing peasants with motor vehicles therefore was a first step toward overcoming the contradiction inherited from capitalism.

Showing cars, trucks, and motorcycles where none had traveled before constituted one of two objectives of the All-Russian Experimental Auto Rally (*avtoprobeg*) organized by the Commissariat of Transport's Central

Administration of Local Transport. The other was to determine which models were best suited to Russia's legendarily poor roads. TsUMT officials prepared for the event by recruiting representatives from the Scientific Automotive Institute, the fuel administration, Rubber Trust, military authorities, and the just-founded Moscow Automobile Club (MAK). For the car rally that ran from September 16 to 25, 1923, they assembled twenty-four Soviet-owned vehicles and thirty-seven from abroad. The designated route took the cars from Moscow's Red Square out of the city in a southerly direction, then west through Viazma to Smolensk and Vitebsk, turning north to Pskov and Petrograd, and returning via Novgorod and Tver' to Moscow, a distance of sixteen hundred kilometers. The truck and motorcycle events covered shorter distances. *Pravda* reported enthusiastic crowds along the route, including Komsomol youths waving banners and others strewing flowers along the path of the cars. As in international rallies, the organizers issued a booklet of rules and penalties, carefully calculated the amount of fuel each contestant consumed, and awarded prizes in various categories.[44]

The 1923 All-Russian Auto Rally leaves Moscow. Courtesy of Rossiiskii Gosudarstvennyi Arkhiv Kino-Foto Dokumentov (RGAKFD).

Two years later, a more ambitious All-Union Automobile Rally—divided like its predecessor into separate competitions for cars, trucks, and motorcycles—was held under the joint auspices of the Moscow Automobile Club and the Commissariat of Transport's Board of Road Transport (Glavdortrans). This time, eighty-three cars traveled from Leningrad to Moscow and thence to Tiflis before returning to Moscow, a distance of forty-seven hundred kilometers. The event attracted veterans of the European rally circuit including "the famous racer, Scholl," who left Leningrad three days after the start but made up for lost time by averaging "not less than 100 kilometers per hour." It also received extensive coverage in the press. Day after day *Pravda*'s "special correspondent" Al. Perovskii filed reports from along the route—Tula, Orel, and Khar'kov on August 22; Artemovsk and Izium on the 24th; Rostov-on-Don by the 25th, onward to Piatigorsk and Vladikavkaz, and thence along the Georgian Military Highway to Tiflis, the four columns of cars, arranged by body weight and engine capacity, proceeding one after the other in stately fashion. Almost everywhere crowds greeted them with flowers, applauded, shouted encouragement, and otherwise showed keen interest. Even in the high mountains where "the appearance of cars...resembled a miracle" the local inhabitants "know that these are friends and vigorously wave their hats." This was, in the estimation of another correspondent, "the largest demonstration of the force of our Union" since the agricultural exhibition of 1923. And, like the exhibition that had prompted the introduction of tractors in areas that had not seen them before, so this rally would stimulate the use of trucks to bring grain to the railheads and manufactured goods to the villages. Even two thousand—forty to fifty in each province—would make a significant difference, he argued.[45]

Breakdowns and the elimination of a few of the cars from competition were a part of every rally, and this one was no exception. More out of the ordinary was the death of the German driver, Werle, from having consumed tainted (poisoned?) ice cream "on the road" in Artemovsk, an event that almost caused the cancellation of the entire event. And somewhere between Orel and Tula "a peasant woman, welcoming the [motorcycle] drivers, threw apples at them one of which hit an American driver in the head and broke his glasses." Perovskii represented these incidents as accidents, but that was not necessarily so. After all, why would Russian peasants react positively to the dust the vehicles raised, their destruction of crops growing along the roadside, their ungodly noise that frightened the livestock, and their killing of fowl? What other than propaganda such as Perovskii's would have disposed them positively toward drivers demonstrating their prowess behind the wheel? Perhaps that apple was an expression not of greeting but of "motorphobia," a condition well known in rural parts of Europe.[46]

This is no more than a supposition, but the case for such an interpretation is strengthened by the experience of another American, George S. Counts, who drove his Ford across Soviet Russia in the fall of 1929. Counts wrote that "ordinary children in the villages and along the road were a source of constant anxiety" because "they seemed to regard the automobile as an object of sport and would throw missiles as it passed." The missiles were "not pebbles, but good sized stones" and left quite a few "scars" on the car's body. Kids will be kids, but Counts noted that these practices "are not universal among the children of the country.... They rather seem to flourish in those intermediate districts in which the adjustment to this new invention is in process." Perhaps the road between Leningrad and Moscow was one of these intermediate districts, for when the writer Boris Pilnyak drove the Chevrolet he had purchased in the United States along this same route in the mid-1930s its appearance also provoked little boys to throw stones.[47]

Friends in Moscow and Leningrad had warned Counts that peasants might take out their long-standing hostility toward city dwellers and opposition to collectivization on his car. Fearing that he "must have looked like a commissar touring the country," he admits to going "forth among the villages prepared for the worst." The worst did not occur, but because peasants followed no clearly defined rules regarding the right-of-way, badly misjudged the speed of the approaching car, and allowed animals to stray into its path, they did, he concluded, constitute a hazard to automotive excursions. Such behavior might be attributed to unfamiliarity, but there is a long history in Russia (and elsewhere) of peasants playing on and deriving advantage from their image as naïfs, and that may have been what was going on here.[48]

The popular association of cars with both the city and officialdom persisted through the decade of the 1930s and perhaps beyond. Reporters covering the Moscow–Kara-Kum expeditionary rally of 1933 noted—as had Perovskii eight years earlier—that the participating vehicles were the first glimpse many of the rural folk along the route had ever had of such marvels of modern technology. Indeed, to the Kazakh nomad encountered somewhere between Aktiubinsk and Irgiz near the Aral Sea, the presence of cars meant that Stalin himself was present ("It cannot be that there are cars and no Stalin!"). As in the case of the seventy-year-old peasant from the Northern Krai who wrote that if he ever got to Arkhangel'sk he would "take a good look at those cars, which I have never seen," these associations seemed to have positive connotations. The same could not be said, however, for the head of the village soviet near Rybinsk who was roused one evening by the arrival of an M-1 bearing two sojourners on their way to Moscow. The villager, wrote Gennady Andreev-Khomiakov, "seemed to be sizing us up. We came in a car—so it followed that we were officials, but what kind? Did we have business with him, or were we just passing through?"[49]

Distribution

The appearance of a car signified an official on the road, because with very few exceptions—Pilnyak, for example—cars were not available to anyone but officials. But how did officials acquire them? Being "one of the most 'deficit' of commodities," cars became a capital asset of the state and their distribution constituted an important part of the exercise of state power. But the state consisted of thousands of different institutions on various levels (Union, republic, oblast, municipal, and so forth) to say nothing of the parallel party bureaucratic structures. Which ones got the automobiles and how did they do it? Before the Soviet Union started to produce its own cars and trucks in significant numbers, acquiring them involved getting in the queue for an imported model, the numbers of which fluctuated quite radically from year to year (see table 5.1). We do not have a very good idea of the decision-making process for this period, but thanks to the research of Valery Lazarev and Paul Gregory, both economic historians, we now know who made the decisions, the procedures they employed, and at least to some extent the thinking behind the decisions they made in the 1930s.[50]

Lazarev and Gregory identify four institutional players in the official distribution process: (1) "the Dictator"—essentially an unofficial commission within Sovnarkom headed by Sovnarkom's chairman, Viacheslav Molotov; (2) "the Planner"—Gosplan and, from 1931–35, Tsudortrans, a "specialized planning body...which collected, organized, and processed orders from different channels for Gosplan"; (3) "the Supplier"—units of the Commissariat of Heavy Industry in charge of supplying vehicles; and (4) "Consumers"—applicants for orders ranging from Sovnarkom's central garage to commissariats, regional governments, enterprises, and even individuals. These actors engaged in two quite different kinds of distributional processes. Lazarev and Gregory label them "wholesale" and "retail," apparently to denote that, in the case of the former, recipients were not end users but rather served as clearinghouses. Wholesale transactions covered upward of 70 percent of all vehicles distributed in any three-month period (quarter) and were relatively straightforward. Decisions about wholesale distribution in theory were made by Sovnarkom but actually by the Molotov "commission." They were derived from requests submitted to the commission by commissariats and other "corporate consumers." The commission processed these requests with the assistance of the Planner. The Supplier's role was to ensure delivery to the successful claimants based on existing or anticipated supplies. Retail transactions were essentially ad hoc decisions by the Dictator to distribute vehicles from its "reserve fund." The notion that Molotov, Stalin's protégé and chief deputy since the early 1920s, would have had ultimate say over the institutional destination of automobiles seems both faintly ridiculous and absolutely characteristic of the administrative-command system for distributing goods.

The data that Lazarev and Gregory provide for both wholesale and retail allocations for 1933 can tell us which institutions were most successful in obtaining motor vehicles. The data show that 45.4 percent of all vehicles distributed through the wholesale process went to agriculture and the food industries, 17.9 percent went to the Commissariat of Heavy Industry, 13.8 percent to the army, 6.6 percent to "control agencies" (essentially the secret police, known by its initials as the OGPU); 5 percent to civil administration, and smaller percentages to nine other institutions. When it came to retail distribution, civil administration received a fifth of all vehicles, the party got 12.5 percent, agriculture and food industries slightly less, followed by social services, and arts and media. The army does not appear as the recipient of retail distribution because, so the authors surmise, "military allocations were separate and recorded elsewhere."[51]

In reality, the analytical distinction between planned wholesale and ad hoc retail distributions tended to be quite blurred. Virtually all of the quarterly "wholesale" distributions that Gosplan (the "Planners") devised and the Molotov commission initially approved were amended by the latter to include specific allocations as in these instructions from the first quarter of 1933: "From the 550 assigned cars select 525 for first-order delivery to chairmen of interregional commissions for designation of the harvest and second-order delivery to political sections [politotdely] of MTS." Similarly, from the second quarter: "Require NKZem and NKSovkhoz to direct vehicles received by them to districts of early harvest." Moreover, in addition to quarterly distributions there were monthly ones, and in the case of the fourth quarter, a supplemental distribution list. The list combined such large "corporate" consumers as the army (250 cars, 2,000 trucks) and the Commissariat of Heavy Industry (800 cars, 1,500 trucks) with lower-order district party committees (400 cars), political sections of machine-tractor stations (300 cars), shock-workers of the harvest (50 cars), the Lenin Library, Academicians Karpinskii and Marr, and the writer Aleksei Tolstoy.[52]

Circumstances on the ground constrained decisions about who or which institution would receive autos and in what quantities. The famine that swept Ukraine, the North Caucasus, and the lower Volga in 1932–33 trumped other considerations.[53] Hence, deliveries to institutions dealing with the harvest received "first-order" priority, while the agricultural and sovkhoz commissariats were instructed to direct their vehicles to regions "of early harvest." For their part, institutions normally specified whether they wanted cars or trucks (or some of each) because the two types of vehicles performed different functions. Trucks were good for hauling freight and, especially in rural areas, people too; they also could be a source of income for institutions that leased them to others in need of transport. Cars had little economic rationale, but members of the nomenklatura (appointees to positions within the system of appointments that were made by successively higher party organs) increasingly sought them as a matter of personal convenience and prestige. From time to time the Molotov commission also concerned itself with prestige as when it "urgently" instructed the Commissariat of Foreign Trade to purchase three Lincolns from abroad and inquired about the number and ownership of Rolls-Royces throughout the country.[54]

The tremendous desire for autos combined with the fact that their nominal owner—the "Dictator"—lacked the capacity to monitor their whereabouts seemed almost to invite illicit behavior. Lazarev and Gregory cite an investigation by the Moscow Party Control Commission that discovered among the Fords sold for foreign currency one purchased by a fictitious foreigner "who

was later identified as the swindler Kogan, previously an Intourist employee."
More often, swindlers impersonated Soviet officials, a tactic that became "a
familiar part of the Soviet urban landscape in the interwar period." "One
Khalfin, a native of Tiflis," proved particularly adept at the game. As *Izvestiia*
reported, "If Khalfin needs a car, he immediately phones the garage of some
People's Commissariat: 'Hallo! Bring out the Commissar's car.' And in a few
minutes Khalfin is riding in the car."[55]

The state was capable of playing a sort of confidence game, too. Starting on
March 1, 1930, Sovnarkom sold automobile promissory notes (*avtomobil'nye
obiazatel'stva*) "to kolkhozes, other cooperative and public organizations, and
individual toilers in need of automotive transport." These were, according to
Lazarev and Gregory, "the numerically most significant type of 'retail' sales."
The price for the first of four issues, due to mature in 1931, was R 1,850. By
this method, the state expected to swell its coffers by nearly R 32 million.[56]
However, purchasers of such notes were in for a rude shock when it turned
out that there were not enough vehicles to back them. Prompted by Gosplan,
the Molotov commission began releasing cars from its stock to overcome the
difficulty, giving first priority to rural-based cooperatives and public organizations (e.g., the Communist Party).[57]

In the meantime, however, the commission had received disturbing news
from a GAZ employee, who wrote that "more than a thousand machines
have accumulated under the open sky." When pressed for an explanation,
the factory's director, Diakonov, reported that the number was only 490 and
a shortage of rolling stock was preventing him from transporting them to
their prescribed destinations. Such instances—this apparently was not the
first—of failure to deliver what the commission had approved wreaked havoc
with the distribution system, turning it, in effect, into a lottery system.[58]

When it came to ordinary mortals (as opposed to institutions and high-
ranking members of the nomenklatura), practically the only way to obtain
a car in the 1930s was via officially organized national lotteries. Beginning
in 1928 when Avtodor issued three million lottery tickets at fifty kopecks
each, the lottery was a major component of that organization's activity. In that
first year Avtodor advertised 3,391 prizes. Among them were an (unspeci-
fied) automobile plus two years of maintenance (or R 10,000 in cash); twenty
Fords and other foreign models priced at R 1,500 each (or, if one preferred, a
tractor); twenty motorcycles; dozens of auto trips, presumably all expenses
paid, from Moscow to Crimea, Leningrad, Nizhni Novgorod, and Tula; books
on auto maintenance; and annual subscriptions to Avtodor's journal, *Behind
the Wheel*. The 1930 lottery contained over ten thousand prizes, but the top
prize was now a speedboat rather than a car. By 1934, the last year in which
Avtodor sponsored a lottery, the ticket prices had doubled to a ruble but the
total value of the nearly twenty thousand prizes was R 2.3 million. They
included seventy cars and six hundred children's pedal cars.[59]

Avtodor's lottery was not the only one to offer automobiles as prizes. The
Society for Settling Toiling Jews on the Land, an organization founded in

1925, sponsored its fourth lottery in 1932. One of the winners (of a Ford) was a Comrade Tuev, a worker at a wire and nail factory in Artemovsk. The only problem, as Tuev reported to a local official from the Commissariat of Worker-Peasant Inspection, was that the car had not been delivered. Correspondence on the matter eventually reached as high as Molotov commission member Valerian Kuibyshev, though even then it was not clear whether delivery was imminent.[60] The case makes one wonder whether others received what they won and if not what recourse they had. The lotteries continued regardless. After Avtodor's liquidation, Osoaviakhim became the main distributor of cars via lotteries. By 1940 it announced its fourteenth, which included four ZIS-101 limousines and 18 M-1s among its prizes. It also revealed that the previous year's winner of the grand prize—a ZIS-101 priced at R 27,000—was a man named Dzhurunskii, a cashier on a sheep-breeding sovkhoz in Aktiubinsk Oblast, Kazakh SSR. No information was available on what citizen Dzhurunskii did with his prize, assuming that it reached him.[61]

By 1940 Gosplan was still submitting quarterly plans to Sovnarkom for the distribution of cars and trucks. These, as before, were divided into allocations to institutions (primarily commissariats) and administrative-territorial units (Union republics, Moscow and Leningrad, and now Tbilisi and Baku as well). Reflecting the proliferation of models since the early 1930s, Gosplan now expressed its figures in terms not merely of trucks and cars but make as well, as in so many ZIS-5, GAZ AA/AAA, and IaG-6 trucks, and KIM, M-1, and ZIS-101 "light automobiles."[62] The tasks of reviewing these figures and making ad hoc adjustments on the basis of special requests no longer was performed by an unofficial group (the Molotov commission) but rather by Sovnarkom's Economic Council (EKOSO).[63] Judging by data from the third quarter of that year, the tasks had not become any easier. Although the number of vehicles to be distributed had increased to forty thousand, Gosplan calculated institutional demand at 94,800. Moreover, no matter how finely tuned the plan, it could not anticipate every contingency any more than had earlier plans. Thus, EKOSO had to consider drawing on its reserve fund to meet unanticipated requests such as the one it received from the Leningrad City Executive Committee. It seems that nobody had thought to replace the city's ambulances after their mobilization to the Finnish front in the Winter War of 1939–40.[64]

It is clear that cars and trucks were constantly being transferred from one institution to another. Sometimes this involved only a reallocation of administrative control over vehicles—a paper transfer. On other occasions it was likely to mean their physical relocation from one garage to another. The most ambitious redistribution effort was the one undertaken in Moscow during 1937 when the government decided to replace GAZ-A and imported Ford sedans and convertibles with newly minted M-1s. After receiving tune-ups, the older vehicles were to be sent to provincial cities and kolkhozes. This exercise, which included the replacement of the old British Leyland buses by five hundred ZIS-8 models, was part of a broader initiative to enhance the prestige of the capital city of the Land of Socialism. Evidently, though, not everyone cooperated. "A number of Moscow auto firms have violated the government's decree," it was reported, "and continue to use the [GAZ-A and Ford] vehicles for travel around Moscow." According to a directive straight from NKVD chief Ezhov, their drivers faced arrest and from three-to-five days' incarceration, passengers were hit with a fine of one hundred rubles, and those in charge of the garages were subjected to criminal prosecution.[65]

Another objective of the exchange emerged when it turned out that the more than four hundred individuals who lined up to receive their replacement M-1 included those with "doubtful" claims to ownership. Among them were several former Avtodor activists, officials from the also defunct Tsudortrans, the Main Administration of the Auto-tractor Industry (GUTAP), and, in particular, the head of GUTAP's garage, Iakunin. The latter, it seems, was very naughty indeed. Having "turned the GUTAP garage into his private shop," he in one year (1936) sold R 28,000 worth of parts, ten trucks, and eight cars. In other words, he engaged in his own private form of redistribution.[66]

When it came to automobiles there appear to have been no limits to the degree of control the party and central state organs were willing to exercise. It is hard to think of an example that better illustrates the "administrative-command" approach to economic management than does Gosplan's directive that five M-1 cars be confiscated from the TASS news agency. Why? Because they were needed to fulfill the supreme economic planning organ's order that 4,091 M-1s be converted to taxis.[67]

Drivers

The first automobiles required a great deal of time and training to keep them in running order. This and the perils of early automobile travel—inclement weather, unpredictable road surfaces, skittishness of horses and other animals on the road, inadequacy of garage facilities especially in urban areas— persuaded most owners to hire chauffeurs who doubled as mechanics. In the United States the heyday of the chauffeur was the first decade of the twentieth century when their skills were at a premium and their status was more likely to be compared to that of railroad engineers than to that of coachmen. But improvements to the designs of tire mountings, drive shafts, and ignition and lubrication systems "undercut the chauffeurs' mechanical authority" and meant that "the wealthy motorist no longer needed to have his mechanic on board at all times." At the same time, mass production put cars within the reach of a broader range of Americans who neither desired nor could afford the services of a chauffeur. The strategic advantage that chauffeurs briefly enjoyed as workers thereupon shifted to garage-based mechanics, although the "mythic power" derived from their mechanical knowledge was typically more limited—essentially to the time it took to repair the car.[68]

The chauffeur-mechanic on whose services well-to-do car owners had depended at the dawn of the automobile age survived far longer as a significant social category in the Soviet Union than it did in the United States. Driving motor vehicles continued to be a job rather than a personal convenience in the USSR, because most vehicles were trucks and because operating, maintaining, and garaging a car required more time than someone in another job had to spend. As the American correspondent Eugene Lyons wrote, referring to the chauffeur of his recently acquired Ford:

> The care of an automobile under Moscow conditions required the full time and attention of at least one person. Gasoline rations must be obtained at specified distributing points. Garage space (at a cost twice as big as the average Soviet worker's total wages) must be located, if found at all, at a point ten miles from one's home. The slightest repair job necessitated days or weeks of routine grief.

That was to say nothing of navigating Moscow's streets, "thick-packed with the humanity...and slow-moving peasant carts."[69] Neposedov, the director of the factory that employed Andreev-Khomiakov, was an exception that proved the rule. He lavished so much time on the M-1 the People's Commissariat of Forestry had granted him for his personal use that he had none left for his job. People consequently "became indignant because...he was referring visitors with all manner of business to the technical director" instead of dealing with it himself. Indeed, the purpose of his trip to Moscow as related by his traveling companion was to obtain new tires for the car, which, although new itself, had arrived with old ones.[70]

The different histories of driving in the United States and the USSR can be traced etymologically. In early twentieth-century America the term chauffeur (from the French for fireman or stoker of steam-powered vehicles) apparently applied to anyone who drove an automobile, whether for pleasure or hire, and was used in preference to the English "driver." By the mid-1910s the term's meaning had narrowed and now applied to a driver-mechanic, and eventually a professional or paid driver, of a motor car. In Russia, precisely because professional driver-mechanics remained almost the only kind of driver to be found, the term *shofër* continued to be used more or less generically. *Pravda,* for example, referred to the drivers in the 1925 All-Union Automobile Rally as *shofëry* (as well as "*shoffëry*"), but it also employed the Russian-originated term *voditel'*. So did the already-cited article from Avtodor's journal that described drivers as transitional types between coachmen and aviators. In certain circumstances, such as when referring to bus drivers, *voditel'* was used in preference to *shofër,* but otherwise the terms were (and would remain) interchangeable, as in this 1937 statement: "The Central Committee of the Union of Drivers [*shofërov*] repeatedly has indicated the necessity of improving its political and cultural work among drivers [*voditelei*]."[71]

Like other workers who had not done so previously, drivers unionized on an all-Russian scale shortly after the October Revolution. The All-Russian Union of Drivers and Automotive Technicians emerged from a congress of unions representing drivers of military and civilian vehicles that was held in January 1918. In September 1919 it became the Union of Transport Workers, broadening its representation to include stevedores, carters, garage and repair shop mechanics, and workers in aviation. After eight congresses and a change in name to the Union of Drivers and Aviation Workers, the union split in 1934: Aviation workers received their own union while drivers were henceforth represented by separate territorial unions: Moscow and Leningrad (from 1940, the Center), the South (with a central committee in Khar'kov), and the East (based in Novosibirsk).[72]

Because of the heterogeneity of union membership, it is difficult to get an accurate sense of how many full-time drivers there were. A union survey from 1924 lists "automobile transport workers," a category that included both garage-based mechanics and drivers, as numbering 19,901 in May 1922 but only 13,352 in June 1924. As a proportion of the union's membership, this represented a decline from 16.5 to 9.0 percent, well below the figures for packers and carters.[73] The decline, which reflected the exhaustion of prerevolutionary vehicles, evidently ceased shortly thereafter thanks to the influx of imported cars and trucks. By October 1928 the union counted 17,701 workers in automobile transport, a number that grew to 43,713 by October 1930.[74] But this was only a foretaste of what would happen once AMO/ZIS expanded, thousands of knocked-down Ford A and AA vehicles were assembled in Moscow, and the new Nizhni Novgorod factory started operations. In January 1932, *Krasnyi transportnik,* the organ of the union's central committee, reported with some alarm that there were "vehicles without drivers, auto lots without engineers." By the middle of the year, the need for new drivers to be trained by December was put at 156,000.[75]

Suddenly, driver-training courses seemed to be everywhere. Soiuztrans, the largest auto transport firm, with branches throughout the country, trained the largest number—sixty-eight thousand during 1931–32, according to one account. But other firms, such as Lenkomtrans in Leningrad and Mosavtogruz in Moscow, offered them too, as did individual auto depots, ZIS, the garages of the commissariats of heavy industry and agriculture, and branches of Avtodor. Inevitably, the quality of the courses varied and in some cases was shockingly low. Corruption entered into the picture in the form of automobile inspectors accepting bribes. In the Russian town of Armavir, it was reported, one could obtain a first-class driver's license for R 150, a second-class license for R 100, and a third class for R 75. And among the automobile brigades on state farms and machine tractor stations, it was alleged in 1934, 35 percent of the drivers had no license at all.[76]

In preparation for its founding congress in January 1933 (the only one to encompass delegates from throughout the USSR), the Union of Drivers counted a membership of nearly 220,000. According to the union's census, members represented just over three-quarters of all people employed in auto depots and garages. Drivers in the RSFSR made up 75 percent of the total (and 72% of union members) throughout the country; 12 percent of drivers worked in Ukraine; 5 percent were in Azerbaijan; and smaller percentages lived in the remaining republics. Over a fifth (77,195) of all drivers were employed in Moscow, and together with their counterparts in Leningrad they made up over half of all drivers in the Russian republic and nearly 40 percent of the total in the entire Soviet Union.[77] What little data I could find on the ethnic composition of drivers date from 1929. They point to a preponderance of Russians. In Uzbekistan, for example, Russians outnumbered ethnic Uzbeks 1,705 to 1,302; in the Chuvash Republic, 368 of 515 drivers were ethnic Russians.[78] The apparent lack of effort at the center to increase the proportion of titular nationalities is striking in light of such efforts in other walks of life.

The gender imbalance among drivers, largely a function of the persistence of prejudices about women's incompetence with respect to machines and the vulnerability to sexual advances of unaccompanied female travelers, also provoked little commentary and no discernible action during the late 1920s and early 1930s—a time when few Soviet professions were as male dominated.[79] Even the call by the Seventeenth Party Congress for an additional seven hundred thousand drivers to be trained by the end of the Second Five-Year Plan (1933–37) did not lead to a recruitment drive targeting women. In this respect, the Great Women's Auto Rally, organized by the auto club of the Union of Moscow and Leningrad Drivers in the summer of 1936, marked a dramatic departure. It took forty-four participants—all women—on an "unprecedented journey" in ten cars and four pickup trucks covering nearly ten thousand kilometers in the course of two months. The rally, as an editorial in *Trud* put it the day after the cars crossed the finish line, "proved that women can fulfill responsible auto-transport tasks no worse than men." It was no different from what Pasha Angelina and her all-female tractor-driving brigade had accomplished several years earlier, or what the all-female crew aboard the airplane *Rodina* would "prove" two years hence. At the time of the rally, women made up eighteen thousand (far from all of them employed as drivers) of a total membership of 140,000 in the Moscow and Leningrad drivers' union. Over the next several years, stories and photographs of the rallies and other women drivers appeared frequently in the pages of *Behind the Wheel* and other publications—not only on International Women's Day. The effort to break with stereotypes about women and machines and to recruit female drivers took on serious proportions as the threat of war increased, which may be why photographs sometimes showed both male and female drivers adorned with gas masks.[80]

All the while, the drivers' unions were engaged in a major effort—prodded by the party and assisted, so long as it existed, by Avtodor—to reshape the behavior of drivers. The unacceptably high rate of automobile accidents was surely the impetus, but lurking behind that concern was alarm about "auto hooliganism." Data on accidents pieced together from a variety of sources suggest that at least in Moscow the rate was falling in the mid-1930s (see table 5.2). However, rather than congratulate drivers for the trend, a *Pravda* editorial on the subject accused transport organizations and garages of covering

Table 5.2. Registered motor vehicles in Moscow and rate of accidents

Year	Cars	Taxis	Buses	Trucks	Other	Total	Accidents	Accidents/ 100 vehicles
1927	1,373	120	166	1,544	n.a.	3,203	2,292	72
1932	2,628	394	280	4,310	275	7,887	n.a.	n.a.
1933	2,740	394	389	5,534	358	9,415	11,543	122
1934	3,397	418	458	7,586	751	11,859	10,735	90
1935	5,927	492	536	10,855	686	18,496	7,903	43
1936	n.a.	485	n.a.	n.a.	n.a.	24,616	n.a.	n.a.

Sources: Za rulëm, no. 9 (1928): 24–27; no. 6 (1936): 4; no. 3 (1937): 30; A. G. Tumanian, *Avarii na avtotransporte* (Moscow: Zhur-ob"ed, 1936), 14.

up accidents. A "transport group" from the party's Control Commission was reported to have discovered eighty-five such instances at a single depot. *Pravda* also faulted auto depot heads for failing to make timely repairs to their vehicles and for being fatalistic about the likelihood of accidents. But the editorial could not have been more blunt about where it put the blame. "The absolute majority of accidents," it asserted, "are the fault of drivers."[81]

What was wrong with drivers? For one thing, they drank. Although forbidden by law, drinking on the premises of garages and depots was not uncommon. Nor was it usually a solitary activity. Indeed, "*p'ianki*" (drinking bouts or booze-ups) probably were no less ingrained in the culture of drivers than in other male-dominated professions. The authorities cracked down hard on drivers who caused multiple fatalities while intoxicated. Several received death sentences.[82] But drunken driving remained a scourge of the profession. It was not the only one. The culture of the *shofër* also included propitiating mechanics and supervisory personnel with vodka, never giving an inch to (or at least not allowing one's vehicle to be passed on the highway by) another driver, using one's vehicle to transport people and goods on the side for extra income, intimidating pedestrians, and habitually using foul language.[83] Most of these activities fell under the official rubric of hooliganism.

Whence these practices? Perhaps the profession attracted a certain type of personality or someone with certain proclivities, and other types then took up similar practices under pressure to conform to the expectations of their peers. Cross-cultural and transhistorical comparisons are hazardous, but it is worth citing the explanation that the sociologist Lawrence Ouellet gives of the behavior of truckers in the United States during the 1980s. In his view, "work is more than a battle for more money or better pay rates and against monotony and fatigue. It is a place where the self is forged. Truckers attempt to manipulate the workplace to construct a positive self, a self they can live with, that places them in a satisfactory relation to their social world." The "self" of the individual beginning a career as a driver was not, therefore, fully formed. It developed in constant relation to and in interactions with others, and it was always highly gendered. "Gender," writes Ouellet, "was central to drivers' agendas, strategies, and interpretations of the work experience. So was the pursuit of some sense of freedom" and "feelings and emotions ranging from frustration and boredom to contentment and exhilaration."[84]

The image of a driver in Soviet Russia was that of a somewhat irreverent character willing to take risks. In happier times, the image could be coded in positive terms. In "I am a Chauffeur," a poem from 1928 by the Odessa poet Osip Kolychev (1904–73), the eponymous driver rejects "Avtodor's promises" and "jaunty jingles" and sets out like a hawk flapping its wings for a thousand miles through the "benzene-soaked air." But as times changed so did standards. A decade later, cleanliness had become an important attribute of "culturedness," a quality to which drivers seemed oblivious. They still used gas and oil instead of soap and water to wash their hands, a model driver complained, and when he insisted on putting on overalls before checking underneath his vehicle, he was apt to be mocked by his colleagues as a "dandy."[85]

From the point of view of the guardians of more "cultured" behavior too much of what drivers did on the job amounted to "individualized labor lacking in control."[86] Their penchant for risk taking, physical prowess, and disorderliness smacked of what U.S. labor historian Stephen Meyer has called "rough manhood."[87] Ouellet invokes a different image, that of "the imagined cowboy...roam[ing] about the countryside, sometimes alone, sometimes joining other drivers for companionship" to characterize his American truckers. Although Russia did not know of cowboys, it did have a history of wanderers, Cossacks, and other freebooting elements to whom drivers could be compared and from whom one might imagine they had sprung.[88] When Sasha Pankratov, the hero of Anatolii Rybakov's Arbat trilogy, is asked by a prospective employer whether he wants to work as a mechanic, he replies, "No thanks. I don't want to answer for others. I'd rather drive." Pankratov, incidentally, has just returned from three years of Siberian exile and needs to be careful because, as his mother tells him, "they persecute people like you, picking on the slightest thing."[89] Like miners working in underground darkness, drivers had more freedom than most factory workers, and many took advantage of it.

The driving profession did not attract too many educated people. Data from Ivanovo for 1933 show that 160 of 1,758 drivers had "in the range of nine years" of schooling, 244 had an incomplete secondary education, 1,324 had primary education, and 30 were illiterate.[90] There is no reason to suspect that these proportions were atypical. Driving also seems to have been something of a haven for shady ("class alien") types, or at least that is the impression left by the lurid accounts of fatal accidents. Koshkin, who crashed his bus into a train, killing seven passengers and seriously wounding seven others, was the son of a kulak who passed himself off (more imposters!) as a member of the Komsomol so that he could get into the Mosavtotrans driving school. Vshivkov, who plowed his truck into a group of Red Army soldiers marching along a road, killing several, "had many specialties, lived in many towns and villages, studied various courses, leading a 'wandering' (*gastrolërskii*) kind of life."[91]

Concern about this sort of thing undoubtedly fed into and was heightened by the "exchange" of documents among drivers that Tsudortrans and the drivers' unions organized in 1935. The timing of this exercise closely coincided with the verification of party documents mandated by the party's central committee. As in that case, documents had to be surrendered to the authorities and their bearers undergo new attestation. Similar too was some of the rhetoric associated with the exercise. "Uncovering hidden infiltrations of the party by enemies, rogues, and swindlers" was the main purpose of the verification according to the central committee. As for drivers, *Pravda* reported that the exchange of documents in Leningrad turned up former tsarist officers ("even a major-general"), thieves, and other criminals, and in the countryside, drunkards had fallen under the influence of such elements after they had been driven out of the cities. "The great need for drivers," explained one of *Behind the Wheel*'s correspondents, "has facilitated the infiltration...of former kulaks, the disenfranchised (*lishentsy*), bandits, etc."[92]

There were, to be sure, responsible drivers. The party committees and the unions kept on the lookout for drivers who stayed out of trouble and maintained their vehicles in good working order, rewarding them publicly as an incentive to others. The advent of the Stakhanovite movement spelled ever-greater publicity and rewards for good drivers. Just as Busygin received accolades for turning out a record number of crankshafts at GAZ, so Comrade Shul'pinskii, the best driver at a garage that serviced the gold mining industry in Bashkiria, deserved the country's gratitude for his feat. Having received a brand new ZIS-5 truck in June 1934, he drove it for nineteen months, clocking 101,073 kilometers without it needing any major repairs. And what is your secret, Comrade Shul'pinskii? Simple: "I don't overload the vehicle, I change the oil frequently and the air filter at least three times a month, and I keep the truck clean." For his pains, Shul'pinskii was awarded a trip to the union's sanatorium, a watch, and a bonus of a thousand rubles. Other Stakhanovites impressed the authorities—if not their colleagues—by overfulfilling their delivery norms, economizing on fuel consumption, and remaining accident free over the long haul.[93]

"Driver Ivanov," the subject of a biographical sketch that appeared in *Behind the Wheel,* was one of them. Before the revolution, he had worked as a stonemason, a peddler, and a guard at a garage before becoming a driver serving "private owners." "October gave him his own vehicle"—a statement that would be astonishing if it weren't for its actual meaning, which was that "now automobiles became the property of the people, and so him [Ivanov] too." He continued working in the same garage that had been nationalized to serve the Supreme Council of the National Economy and then the Commissariat of Heavy Industry. The Buick he looked after "is always exemplarily clean and neat." And in twenty-five years, he had not one accident.[94] Hooray for Driver Ivanov!

Phantoms, Fantasies, and the Fortunate Few

On October 17, 1933, fifteen-year-old Nina Lugovskaia went for a walk with a friend in Moscow's Novodevichy Cemetery. "When we were almost there," she wrote in her diary,

> we had to stop at the fork to let a turning car pass. It was an odd sort of car, it looked a bit like an ambulance; it had large windows and a brightly lit interior.…One of the military men sitting by the window closest to us looked at us intently and even turned his head. It can't be, perhaps we made a mistake? Could it really be he? I didn't think so then, and even now I'm not entirely sure.

Although elsewhere in her diary Nina had no qualms about mentioning Stalin's name and excoriating him in the most unequivocal terms, she did not do so after seeing—or thinking she had seen—him up close. Perhaps this was because, as the diary's editor explains, Stalin was rumored to visit his wife's grave in the cemetery. From the context there was no need to state the obvious. If even in Moscow people associated automobiles with officials, then it must have been a special (or "odd sort of") car that transported Stalin.

Or, maybe she really was "not entirely sure" what or whom she had seen. Her account of the whole incident is suffused with the aura of the spectral or gothic. Note how just after the "brightly lit" car had passed, everything was plunged into darkness: "The widely spaced street lamps shone dully," Nina wrote, "blanketing the streets with gloom." "Dark figures" walked across the paved entrance road; a "pitch-black slope" led down to a pond over which "black crooked willows" hung. "The darkness and the emptiness were eerie…it was so dark we couldn't bring ourselves to go any farther.…The city lights did not penetrate here, and everything was drowned in utter blackness.… 'Let's go back!' I said."[95]

Nina's was not the only phantasmagoric encounter with the passenger Stalin. The epigraph to the third volume of Vassily Aksyonov's Moscow Saga is a line from Boris Slutskii's 1955 poem, "God": "And God came driving by in five automobiles." This God, accompanied by a secret police entourage, was not the one who dwelt in the far-off heavens. "Sometimes you saw him, even / Alive—upon the Tomb." The author saw him as a specter passing along the Arbat (one of Moscow's main thoroughfares), some time between night and dawn, peering out of his "all-seeing window / With his all-penetrating gaze."[96] Yet another phantom automobile from this era, the one used by NKVD boss Lavrenty Beria, became something of an urban legend. Nina and her friend pursued the car carrying Stalin (or someone of his likeness); Beria pursued adolescent girls in his car, or had his bodyguard cruise the streets of Moscow to bring them to him. That at least was the gist of stories that circulated at the time, were presented as evidence at Beria's trial in 1953, and ever since then have fed the reading public's desire for salacious stories about the bad old Commies. In the most lurid of these accounts, the car Beria and his aide took for their "escapades" was described as a "huge black Packard limousine" that had "a curtain half covering [its] greenish windows." In others it is simply described as a limousine or a "limousine with...dark tinted windows," or "a great black car with smoked glass windows."[97] Girls on their way home from school were said to be the most vulnerable. Beria the rapist now rivals the ruthless policeman, the nurturer of the Soviet atomic bomb, the would-be liberalizer, and other images.

The most common fear-inducing automobiles—in fact, a refrain in recollections and reconstructions of the Stalin era—were the NKVD's Black Ravens (*chernye voronky*) or Black Marias (*chernye marusi*). The provenance of these terms is uncertain. U.S., British, and Australian police vans and paddy wagons were also called Black Marias (pronounced Mariah) in the nineteenth century, but whether this is the source of the Russian usage is doubtful. "Almost every night the GPU's black raven came to take someone away," recalled a former resident of Rostov-on-Don, echoing many other memoirists' accounts.[98] Probably the best-known reference to the Black Marias of the Stalin era comes in the prologue to Anna Akhmatova's "Requiem" where it serves as a synecdoche for the Great Terror: "Dead stars hung above us, / And blameless Russia writhed. / Under boots stained with blood, / And the Black Maria's tires."

Alexander Solzhenitsyn, who devotes a few pages of *The Gulag Archipelago* to them, states that the "first Black Marias appeared at the same time as the very first trucks on our still cobblestoned streets...in 1927."[99] There is, however, a file in the archives containing correspondence dating back to May 1923 that details the purchase by the Moscow City Soviet of a three-ton Packard truck and its conversion by one of the factories (not AMO) within the Central Administration of State Automobile Factories to enable it to convey up to twenty-five prisoners. The vehicle, according to the contract, was to be painted in "whatever color is desired," which may or may not have been black. Evidently, no sooner had it gone into service, then on its third trip to the Taganka Prison the first two gears "fell out."[100]

Solzhenitsyn adds that "for many years the Black Marias were steel-gray and had, so to speak, prison written all over them." Only later, after the war, were they disguised with bright colors and items of food ("Bread," "Meat," "Drink Soviet Champagne") written on their sides.[101] When it came time for Evgeniia Ginzburg to be transferred in one—this was 1937—the Black Maria was painted navy blue. She had seen it often near her apartment in Kazan and assumed it carried milk or groceries. Ginzburg's account of her arrest is a useful reminder of a more generalized fear associated with cars, at least among those who expected to be arrested at any moment:

> "Paul! A car!"
> "Well, what of it, darling? It's a big town,
>   there are plenty of cars."
> "It's stopped. I'm sure it has."

> My husband, barefooted, would leap across to the window.
> He was pale but spoke with exaggerated calm,
> "There, you see, it's only a truck."
> "Don't they use trucks sometimes?"

When the time came, it was neither the arrival of a car nor a truck that signaled the end of Ginzburg's freedom but a telephoned invitation from an NKVD official who "could not have been more amiable and charming."[102]

One is tempted to see cars and trucks of the 1930s as symbols of the Stalinist state's might and repressiveness, or to assume that everyone regarded them as such. But evidently the association of cars with fearfulness and death was more diffuse, indicative of the persistence—or more likely, reconstitution—of a link that predated the Soviet period, as we have seen. Traces of rumors from February 1931 have been found in the former Leningrad party archive about a "black car" that was kidnapping strangers at night and taking them to "a blood-spattered room where human corpses were being taken apart." Interpretations as summarized by the OGPU (Joint State Political Directorate, successor to the GPU) included the car belonging to a secret Jewish organization involved in some kind of religious ritual, belonging to a secret organization of believers to kill the Jews, representing the coming of the Antichrist and the end of the world, and serving the OGPU in its campaign against people of the former ruling classes (*byvshie liudi*). As Olga Velikanova notes, "these conjectures represent the spectrum of stories typically generated in the mass consciousness."[103] That they were being projected onto an automobile suggests the at best ambivalent feelings toward the mechanical beasts.

At the same time, even at the height of the Terror, "the most richly symbolic artefact of the twentieth century, the automobile" turned out to be polysemic.[104] In addition to inspiring fear and trembling, cars could conjure up a world of impossible luxury and leisure; they were the stuff of escapist fantasies and dreams that, one imagines, were all the more necessary during those apocalyptic times. What Benjamin Braslavsky remembers most about his boyhood visit from Sverdlovsk to Moscow in 1936 were the foreign cars: "I remember in particular a Hispano-Suiza standing next to the Hotel National with its long body decorated with the figure of the flying crane. When in the 1950s, I heard Vertinsky ('the blue Hispano-Suiza sings you lullabies in a gentle swing'), I knew what he was talking about, although the one I saw was black."[105]

These cars were not always available to have their tires kicked, so to speak. They might have appeared in the pages of newspapers, magazines, and journals. They could be found on canvas or celluloid. Mikhail German recalled "some kind of magazine, *Murzilka,* it seems," publishing "images of insignias from Ford, Fiat, Buick, Dodge, Pontiac, Packard, Hispano-Suiza, etc." German's memory is accurate. The seventh issue from 1937—yes, 1937—of that children's magazine contained a two-page supplement with forty-nine emblems, including the exquisite Guynemer stork of the Hispano-Suiza.[106]

By 1937, M. Il'in's *How the Automobile Learned to Run,* which offered a brief history of automotive technology beginning with the steam engine—the "babushka" of automobiles and locomotives—had reached its sixth edition. A seventh followed in 1940. V. Tambi's *Avtomobil',* first published in 1930, contained illustrations of racing cars with names like "Golden Arrow," "Sunbeam," and "Bird."[107] They resembled the ones depicted in Petr Vil'iams's "Auto Rally," a painting from 1930.

"Oh, the cars of the thirties!" German exclaims nostalgically.

> Enormous and loud, driven by serious (and it always seemed, not very young) chauffeurs, the automobiles, of which even the most chic often required painful exertion to start, were dazzling apparitions of the future, longed for by boys who thought not about acquiring them but rather "going for a spin" and, should they be really lucky, holding onto the wheel for some time and honking the horn.[108]

German's reference to boys instead of "boys and girls" or the gender-neutral "young people" is understandable given socialization patterns of the time. Yet, the quintessential representation of car driving from this period actually has

New Moscow, Iurii Pimenov, 1937. Oil on canvas, 140 x 170 cm (55 x 67 in.). Courtesy of the Tret'iakov Gallery, Moscow.

a woman behind the wheel. It is "New Moscow," Iurii Pimenov's oil on canvas from 1937 that manages to celebrate the leisure cars afforded, the emancipation of women, and the reconstruction of the city. The new Moscow is seen from the back seat of a convertible driven by a young woman with bobbed hair who is wearing a fashionable cotton print dress. She is driving down Okhotnyi Riad from Teatral'naia in the direction of the Manezh Square. The just-completed headquarters of the Council of Labor and Defense (soon to be occupied by the State Planning Commission and now the State Duma) looms up ahead on the right and on the left is the new Hotel Moskva. It must be summer, for the convertible is open, and pedestrians strolling along the street are in short sleeves. The sheen on the road, reflected on the windshield, gives the impression it has rained recently. The foregrounded car is the only convertible. The others are M-1 sedans (recent additions to Moscow's streets) and a few buses. If we look more closely at the car we can just barely make out a figure attached to the hood that appears to be a greyhound, the insignia of a Lincoln. And then there are the carnations, one red and one white, sticking out of a vase that is attached to the left side of the windshield.

Oh, the cars of the thirties! How many convertibles sporting carnations were among them? How many were driven by women? The canons of socialist realism to which Pimenov conformed did not encourage such inquiry. The point was not to reproduce reality literally but to portray its "revolutionary" possibilities. In the singularity and anonymity of the woman at the wheel lay the painting's appeal. Her outing in a motor car was something like a dream, a Soviet dream, in which it seemed that those grandiose buildings intended to inspire awe had been located precisely to accentuate the pleasure of driving toward them. Maybe it is this pleasure principle, so commonly evoked in Western advertising, that gives the painting its allure. There is, in any case, a near-contemporary cinematic equivalent to Pimenov's painting. *The Radiant Path* (Svetlyi put'), Grigorii Aleksandrov's musical comedy from 1940, was a Cinderella story set in the present and starring Liubov Orlova as the ex-chambermaid who becomes a record-breaking Stakhanovite textile weaver. Orlova had starred in three earlier musical comedies directed by Aleksandrov, and in each she had risen from the ordinary people (or in the case of *Circus,* from American racism and exploitation by her Nazi manager) to the heights of fame and happiness. In an unforgettable scene from *Radiant Path* she quite literally rises as she is whisked off by her fairy godmother in a convertible that ascends into the sky above the Kremlin and through the clouds as cartoon storks fly by. At first, the fairy godmother is driving, but as the car flies toward the All-Union Agricultural Exhibition grounds (after an excursion that takes them over snow-capped mountains!), she disappears and our heroine takes the wheel. As it descends, the car circles around Vera Mukhina's "Worker and the Collective Farmer," a sculpture that symbolized, among other things, gender equality.[109]

Assuming that Pimenov's young lady had a license, she would have been among an estimated five thousand nonprofessional drivers or "enthusiasts" (*liubiteli*) in Moscow. This term was preferred (at least in print) to "owner" mainly because the cars such people drove were not necessarily their own property. As described in a 1936 profile, nonprofessional drivers fell into two categories. The first were "distinguished people" such as state prize awardees, Stakhanovites, and others on whom the state had bestowed cars as special gifts or had given them special permission to purchase. We already have encountered a few such folks—Lily Brik, the Stakhanovite Aleksandr Busygin, the writer Boris Pilnyak, and Mikhail German's father, Iurii, also a writer. They—and presumably lottery winners as well—legally owned their automobiles in accordance with Article 10 of the Soviet Constitution, which guaranteed citizens' right "to own, as their personal property...articles of personal use and convenience."[110]

The second category of people consisted of "responsible leaders of economic institutions and enterprises."[111] Although not a resident of Moscow, Andreev-Khomiakov's boss, Neposedov, fell into this category. Most "responsible leaders," however, lacked the time or skills to dispense with chauffeurs. Some, it turns out, had quite nice cars at their disposal. The Molotov commission's interest in Rolls-Royces was sparked by a suggestion from Commissar of Defense Klement Voroshilov to replace the most aged ones with Cadillacs and Packards. Voroshilov had a personal interest in the substitution since one of the Rolls-Royces was in his possession; another was used by Pavel Postyshev, party boss in Ukraine.[112] Evgeniia Ginzburg reports that "'ruling class' children" who spent their winter holidays at a former noble's estate not far from Moscow "divided all those around them into categories according to the make of their cars. Lincolns and Buicks rated high, Fords low. Ours was a Ford," she adds, and her son, Alyosha, "was quick to sense the difference this made."[113] Scrupulousness about the use of cars varied. Inna Shikheeva-Gaister recalled that her mother had no problem using the car that had been assigned to her father, a deputy commissar of agriculture, but that her future father-in-law, the editor of ZIS's newspaper and "honest to a fault," never let his wife ride in the car assigned to him.[114]

With the privilege of owning or at least having the use of a car went possibilities previously undreamt of. Among these was automotive tourism. Why, after all, should the likes of George Counts and other foreigners be the only ones to travel the highways and byways of the country? (Actually, by the summer of 1935, when the authorities began to promote auto tourism, foreigners were no longer being permitted to make such trips.) Since the honored citizens in possession of cars obviously deserved them—and they soon would be joined by outstanding Stakhanovites—why shouldn't they be allowed to take to the road with their loved ones? During that first season of Soviet "*avto-mototurizm*" the fortunate few included Stalingrad Tractor Factory engineers and their families who drove in a caravan to Sochi; L. Kalusovskii, a Moscow engineer who traveled with his family to the Crimea; the filmmaker Lev Kuleshov (best known for his 1924 film *The Extraordinary Adventures of Mr. West in the Land of the Bolsheviks*), who made it all the way from Moscow to the Tajik capital of Stalinabad; a group of journalists who traveled in a one-and-a-half-ton truck to Sukhumi; and Commander Reviakin of the Black Sea Fleet, who traveled with his wife twenty-five hundred kilometers by motor-cycle from Sevastopol' through Ukraine.

Unfortunately, very little, if anything, had been done since Counts's journey to accommodate road-weary travelers. "Almost all our auto tourists complain about the lack of maps, guides, service stations, and advice bureaus," *Behind the Wheel* reported. The main difficulty, though, was the absence of gas stations. This made supplying oneself with extra fuel tanks and other supplies an absolute necessity before departure. An engineer named Kurchevskii, by far the best prepared, brought a field kitchen, a first-aid kit, chains, extra batteries, a visor, and, for travel through snowy mountain passes, skis that could be attached to the vehicle instead of front wheels. No wonder "Kurchevskii's tourist automobile attracted a lot of attention." Soon, it was hoped, there would be garage-hotels equipped for technical service and shops selling auto parts, not to mention "coaching inns" run by kolkhozes and sovkhozes where the tourists themselves could lodge.[115]

By 1937 the auto tourists counted among themselves the Stakhanovites Busygin and Faustov and several engineers from GAZ. Engineer Kalusovskii was at it again, this time with Sukhumi as his intended destination. But alas, there still was nobody to help these and other travelers sort out what supplies to bring (or where to get them), the routes they should take, what sort of preventive maintenance they needed to do, and where they could get information about road conditions and the weather. Not a single guidebook or map had been produced to assist them. This was in sharp contrast to the United States where Ilf and Petrov had spent weeks traveling by car and where, they reported, gas station attendants not only fill up the tank and check the oil and the water in the radiator but wash the windows and do minor repairs and adjustments—and all at no extra charge! They also provided maps that listed hotels and tourist sights on the reverse, and these too came free with the purchase of gasoline.[116] Certainly there was more that the responsible organizations (the All-Union Committee for Physical Culture and Sports, Avtodor's successor; automotive clubs; the tourism bureau of the All-Union Central Council of Trade Unions; GUTAP; the Oil Trust; the Auto Repair Trust; road departments) could do to make touring by car less onerous. The question was whether the needs of a rather small—if privileged—clientele outweighed other considerations.

Auto Sport: "Capable at Any Moment"

In the summer of 1936, as the Great Women's Auto Rally was about get under way, another rally was just concluding. Sixteen participants took seven vehicles from GAZ on a fifty-eight-day road trip to the Pamir Mountains and back, a journey of some twelve thousand kilometers. The rally was sponsored by the Dinamo Sports Society, a "voluntary" organization better known for its soccer team, created in 1923 by the NKVD. Aside from the length of the trip and the elevations attained, the rally distinguished itself from others in two respects: the drivers were all nonprofessionals ("amateur sportsmen") and they performed a series of what were referred to as "militarized-sporting" tasks that included bivouacking, spending the night in sleeping bags, driving at speeds up to 50 km/h while wearing gas masks, and high-speed travel in military formation. Both innovations were almost immediately adopted by other rallies—"militarized" rallies from Rostov to Novorossiisk and from Cheliabinsk to Sverdlovsk; a night rally in gas masks from Moscow to Serpukhov; a gas mask rally from Moscow to Kiev; and an eleven-thousand-kilometer rally of wives of Red Army officers from the Siberian town of Chita to Moscow.[117]

That spring and summer, in fact, were filled with all kinds of auto events: automobile crosses, nonstop intercity races (Leningrad–Moscow–Leningrad; Rostov-on-Don–Moscow; Ufa–Orenburg–Ufa; Kiev–Khar'kov–Kiev), "figure" competitions in which cars performed acrobatic maneuvers, and one-kilometer races ("*kilometrovki*") from a standing position and with a moving start. The latter race, held on August 31, 1936, outside Leningrad on the Kiev highway, was won by G. Tsvetkov in a modified GAZ-A with a time of 31.9 seconds. According to one account, the event marked "the beginning of the history of Soviet auto sport records."[118]

Why this sudden eruption of automobile and motorcycle sports? For automotive enthusiasts it offered an opportunity to indulge hitherto repressed desires to demonstrate their own technical and driving skills and achieve increased speeds. It was facilitated by automobile clubs that inherited the mission (and at least to some extent the property) of Avtodor. Like Avtodor, the clubs were "public" organizations. To the extent that they answered to state authority it was the All-Union Committee on Physical Culture and Sports Affairs and its network of republic and local committees, but as the committees were responsible for administering all sports including tourism, attention to the clubs and their needs was not great. Clubs existed at the city as well as at (large) factory levels. ZIS, for example, had one that organized a winter autocross involving the cars of leading Stakhanovites as well as those of engineers. The Leningrad club, the most active, counted among its membership more exalted company including the writer Aleksei Tolstoy, the film directors Georgii and Sergei Vas'ilev, the chess champion Mikhail Botvinnik, and the arctic explorer and Lenin prize-winner Nikolai Urvantsev. It excelled at organizing races—sixteen during the summer of 1936 alone—but also was proud of having trained six hundred nonprofessional car and motorcycle drivers. For the 1937 season, it looked forward to co-organizing with the ZIS club a repeat of the 1936 Moscow–Leningrad–Moscow race.[119]

On March 12, 1937, the team of Boris Udol'skii and N. Makarov crossed the finish line of the Moscow–Leningrad–Moscow race in a time of 20 hours and 23 minutes, a full hour and 32 minutes faster than their record-setting time of the previous year. On May 30, 1937, Tsvetkov's kilometer mark was broken by Aleksandr Lavrent'ev (30.58 seconds or 117.72 km/h). Two weeks later, Lavrent'ev was bested by Anton Gerel' (30.06 seconds or 119.76 km/h) who broke his own record the following month. Then came the turn of two Leningrad taxi drivers who received permission from their boss to modify the engine and body frame of a GAZ-A that had been retired from the fleet. On September 30, 1937, outside Kiev, Georgii Kleshchev's and Sergei Trusillo's "gazik-taxi" beat Gerel's car and other entrants, setting a new Soviet record of 142.07 km/h. This was not close to what Malcolm Campbell's Bluebird had achieved, but as Boris Udol'skii remarked, "some day our 'Red Bird' will measure up to the record-setters from bourgeois countries."[120]

If not exactly household names, these men were heroes to those who followed auto racing. They were professional racing-car drivers in all but name, not unlike the soccer players whose first league season dated from 1936. It is hard to judge the extent of auto racing's popularity—there were no specially built tracks until after the war—but it undoubtedly was growing. It grew thanks to official promotion of the sport and increasing coverage by the press. *Behind the Wheel,* for example, added a regular column in 1937 on "avtomotosport," and no issue has been without sports news since. It is also possible that like fencing, sambo (the Soviet version of martial arts that received the imprimatur of the All-Union Committee on Physical Culture and Sports Affairs in November 1938), alpinism, and other "special interest" activities, auto racing created its own community of rabid participants and fans who could not understand why the rest of the country did not share their passion and for whom nothing was quite as important as the season's schedule of events and preparations for them. Official competitions, record keeping, prizes, medals, and other honors served to validate the community's existence and enhance its sense of importance.[121]

These kinds of activities and the passion with which they could be pursued do not conform to the dominant image we have from this period of a cowed and atomized population. But in pursuing their passion, sports enthusiasts were not exactly bucking official sanctions. Why did auto sport receive official backing? Diane Koenker explains analogous support for "proletarian tourism" in part by the military-related skills (e.g., map reading, use of a compass) it entailed.[122] The potential military application of not only auto rallies but all automobile and motorcycling sports represented the alpha and omega of state support. A heightened sense of the Soviet Union's military vulnerability occasioned by growing international tensions combined with the perceived shortage of automobile drivers to produce this support. "In September 1918," wrote A. Grechanik in one of many articles that began to appear about lessons to be learned from the Great War, "the Americans transported up to one million soldiers from one flank to another by automobile."[123] An army consisting predominantly of farm boys with no prior experience of mechanical engines was an army doomed to defeat. Tractor- and combine-driving were assets, but those who knew how to handle an automobile would, so the thinking went, make the best tank, armored personnel carrier, and truck drivers, "should the time come."

"Youth, to the automobile!" proclaimed a *Pravda* headline. "Thousands of new automobile circles and clubs to be created," it continued. The article itself was by Commander Innokentii Khalepskii, head of the Red Army's Motorization and Mechanization Administration since 1929 and formerly of Avtodor's automobile section. It was one of the more explicit in connecting sport to driving and driving to defense. "It is well known," wrote Khalepskii, "that the attraction to auto sport is huge in our country." This apparently was why "thousands of Komsomolites are striving to obtain the skill of chauffeur, combine operator, [and] tractor driver." Such a desire would benefit socialist construction, but "in case of need, they could transfer [literally, "change their seat"] from the automobile and tractor to a military machine and become fearless tank drivers." In case defense-minded readers needed more persuasion, Khalepskii provided it: "In capitalist countries, and in particular Germany, motorized sport is getting a lot of attention." It was the German national sports administration that was supervising the training of drivers, and on an increasing scale. But "we have every opportunity to make the training of nonprofessional drivers and the development of automobile sport broader and better than in fascist Germany."[124]

Khalepskii's article was part of a "discussion" initiated by a letter to *Pravda* from the legendary pilot and Hero of the Soviet Union Anatolii Liapidevskii.[125] He too managed to link the need for more drivers—five to six hundred thousand within a year—to the "enlivening" of avtomotosport, and the latter with defense. "Our Red Army," the letter asserted, "must systematically receive people who have mastered the art of driving" so that there would be a sufficient number of tank and armored car crews. Others had more specific suggestions. Boris Udol'skii, "expressing the opinion of all auto racers," called for the establishment of Soviet grand prix races. Robert Eideman, chairman of the Central Council of Osoaviakhim (until his arrest two months later), asserted that auto sport deserved the same amount of support as aviation sport had received. All were critical of its neglect by the committees on physical culture and sports affairs. The discussion concluded with an editorial referring to the hundreds of thousands of youths whom the country needed to be "capable at any moment to transfer to armored cars and tanks."[126]

Variations on the theme of "if there is a need" included a testimonial by the wife of a senior lieutenant explaining that she learned to drive so that "when [note, not "if"] it will be necessary, I can sit in a tank with my husband and defend our country." The Piatigorsk auto club got into the act by organizing a militarized rally in which GAZ-AA trucks were camouflaged as they practiced delivering grain to elevators. Then, there were the drivers. Nikolai Kaleniuk, champion of the Kiev–Minsk race, had been behind the wheel since 1930 and in the ranks of the Red Army since 1935. The important thing to know about him was that it was the Red Army that had taught him self-possession, sangfroid, and other admirable traits.[127]

As the threat of war grew ever stronger, so did the connection between auto sport and defense. New forms of rallies and crosses emerged: those in which drivers had to wear gas masks and fire small-caliber weapons while at the wheel; a competition in which truck and motorcycle drivers—in this case, women—drove through an "infected zone" on the Leningrad highway wearing their masks; several rallies in which trucks used hard fuel; rallies testing the new Grachev-designed off-road vehicles. But the "enemies of the people" were doing their best to undermine physical-cultural work, penetrating the leadership of the organizations responsible for mobilizing drivers. This was why the All-Union Committee had to be relieved of its responsibility for promoting automobile driving in favor of an organization devoted to civil defense training (Osoaviakhim).[128]

The wheel had come full circle. Cars, which largely had been the playthings of the aristocracy, were mobilized for war service after 1914. During the 1917 revolution they served both sides, but the more armored and fearsome they became, the more they conformed to the image that the Bolsheviks had of metal in motion and, indeed, of the Bolsheviks themselves. Despite uniquely restrictive rules about who could drive where and for what purpose, cars became increasingly demilitarized in the 1920s. They assumed utilitarian purposes more in keeping with the task of reconstruction and, eventually, socialist construction. They helped to bring in the harvest, get out the word, and convey officials from home to office and back, or on inspection tours. A few even got to perform more leisurely activities. As they grew in number and variety, it became more difficult to keep track of them, to know who really deserved them and how they were to be serviced. Some were given away and some were taken away from their "personal users," who, taken into custody, no longer had any use for them. As war approached, cars, drivers, and driving were discursively remilitarized in preparation for the real thing.

The champion driver Boris Udol'skii experienced much of this history personally. His biography, as a profile published in 1937 put it, was inextricably "connected with the development of our automobile culture." Born in 1903, he was already working as an auto mechanic by the time of the revolution. He thereafter served as a motorcyclist in the Red Army, a student in various military-technical courses, a driver in military campaigns against the Basmachi (the Soviet term for anti-Soviet "bandits") along the Soviet Union's southern flank, and a chauffeur for the GPU and then the Commissariat of Defense. Clearly, though, Udol'skii's love was auto racing. During the 1920s and well into the next decade he participated in some of the most grueling rallies. His yearning for high-speed competition was satisfied when, in 1936, he set one speed record after another, and was handsomely rewarded with a new M-1.[129] When we last encountered Udol'skii, he was dreaming of setting new records in a Soviet version of the Bluebird.

We lose touch with him during the war years, but in the archive of *Autopilot,* an online Russian journal, there exists a photograph of a Soviet officer standing next to a Mercedes 230. The photo was snapped just after the war, not far from the Leipzig airport where the officer and the car apparently were about to embark on a plane bound for the USSR. The officer was Boris Udol'skii. The only other information provided by the journal is that after the war, too old to return to racing, Udol'skii chauffeured high-ranking officers winding up his career in the early 1980s as a chauffeur driving "cargo no. 200," that is, zinc coffins arriving from Afghanistan.[130]

chapter 6

Cars, Cars, and More Cars

The automobile—our friend. But how badly organized
its life is in the city!

Za rulëm, 1966

"Curiously," wrote the Dutch-born novelist and essayist Hans Koningsberger
in 1968, "the Soviet Union is now a highly industrialized country, but in its
private sector is only on the threshold of the gasoline age." Consequently,
"the Westerner in his own car...moves in an odd way back through time."[1]
Curious this was because moving back through time was not what one was
supposed to be doing in the Soviet Union. Stalin himself famously had said
that the Soviet Union had to catch up to and overtake the advanced capitalist
countries or else it would go under. The Soviet Union did do a lot of catching
up over the next several decades, but hardly by riding in passenger cars.

Koningsberger's sense of moving back in time was among his strongest and,
ironically, most positive impressions of the Soviet Union. "Aesthetically," he
remarked, "the rareness of gas stations is a boon.... Roads without billboards
and without gas stations show how our world once looked, how it was supposed to look, one would be tempted to say.... It is marvelous to visit a carless
landscape in your own car." Carlessness in the case of the Soviet Union and
Eastern Europe should not, he insisted, be attributed just to backwardness,
"for there are very much more backward countries nonetheless crowded with
the Western web of roads, gas stations, and cars." In contrast to the cities
of Koningsberger's adopted country, the United States, those in Russia "are
not only still free from smog, they are also, still, less hurried, less eager, less
atomized." In Red Square, on a spring evening, "there was a hushed lumi-
nosity, a silence stemming from the absence of all engines, such as we have
almost forgotten exists." But it was in the countryside, "on those quiet roads"
where one was "still on the far side of that time fence." There, one could
experience the full force of retrotopia, returning "by chance to a childhood
nostalgia of innocence."[2]

"The rareness of gas stations is a boon." One of the few in the center of Moscow. Author's photograph.

What else was curious was Koningsberger's reference to the "private sector." Cars, after all, inherently (and often quite negatively) impinge on the anonymous public; moreover, they typically require massive state expenditures, regulation, and personnel. Yet, even (or especially?) in a society where the ruling ideology was so unreceptive to the ownership of private property, cars became objects valued precisely because they afforded a degree of privacy and personal autonomy. Writing shortly after the end of the Brezhnev era, the journalist David Willis noted that "the Soviet automobile is many things: a status symbol, a problem to operate and maintain, an export item exploited to earn foreign exchange, an instrument of Party control, a staple of the black market, and a symbol of individual independence."[3] What he did not explain was how it got to be all those things and what sort of work, ideological and otherwise, was involved in making it so.

Half a century after automobiles had profoundly transformed American society and its culture they began to insert themselves into the lives of Soviet citizens, thrusting the country willy-nilly into the "gasoline age." The progressive intrusion of passenger cars into everyday life engendered not only a "car-driver" matrix—to cite John Urry's term—but conflicts and adjustments that often blurred the boundaries between private and public (or, in Soviet terms, personal and social) spheres. It had unanticipated consequences for the state and for relations among individuals. In expanding opportunities for car ownership but leaving the provision of infrastructure and services to semilegal or illegal "second economy" activity, the state under Leonid Brezhnev found itself engaged in a Faustian bargain over a notoriously individualistic mode of transportation. For better or for worse, motorists from abroad like Hans Koningsberger would not have the roads to themselves for very much longer.

The Alliance and the Fruits of Victory on Wheels

"Better fewer, but better," Lenin once quipped in reference to what it would take to improve the efficiency of the young Soviet state apparatus. This was not the model to follow, however, when it came to the army's motorized transport. During the undeclared border war between Soviet and Japanese forces in the summer of 1939, the thousands of tanks, trucks, fuel tankers, and armored cars amassed by the Soviet side made an important contribution to the Soviet victory. By contrast, documents from the ensuing Soviet–Finnish Winter War (November 1939–March 1940) suggest that a poorly organized transport system was one of the things that hobbled the Soviet effort. During discussions that Stalin and Commissar of Defense Voroshilov initiated with top army officials in April 1940, several officers pointed to this weakness. One revealed that his division was "under-supplied with horses by 23 per cent and by motor transport by 60 per cent." Another spoke of the lack of support services in general, adding that "the army was motorized, but repairs were poorly organized. And our motor transport stood idle to no purpose, because the vehicles were out of order and could not be used."[4]

If motorized mobility of troops and weapons was an important lesson to be learned, little opportunity remained to apply it before the Nazi invasion. The cessation of passenger car production, the conversion from automobile to tank assembly, the army's requisitioning of vehicles from other state institutions, and the diversion of fuel supplies to the armed forces—all were part of the immediate response to the invasion. The routs suffered by Soviet forces during the first few months of the war largely negated them. Tens of thousands of vehicles were destroyed, captured, or otherwise taken out of action. The remaining machines did heroic service. The novelist Vasily Grossman, who covered the war as a correspondent for the Red Army's newspaper, referred to the one-and-a-half-ton truck that was put at his and other correspondents' disposal as "Noah's Ark" because it had "saved so many dozens of people from the flood that came from the west." Grossman also shared use of an M-1 that barely made it back to Moscow. Dented all over by shell fragments, it conveyed to the editorial staff in Moscow the precariousness of the retreat more graphically than anything the correspondents wrote or said.[5]

Grossman arrived in Stalingrad on the eve of the war's decisive battle. Witnessing the columns of retreating Soviet soldiers, he conveyed their damaged psyches in terms of the wounds inflicted on their vehicles:

> Trucks with grey-faced wounded men, front vehicles with crumpled wings, with holes from bullets and shells, the staff Emkas with star-like cracks on the windscreens, vehicles with shreds of hay and tall weeds hanging from them, vehicles covered with dust and mud, passed through the elegant streets...past shining windows of shops, past kiosks painted light blue and selling fizzy water with syrup, past bookshops and toyshops. And the war's breath entered the city and scorched it.[6]

By this time, Studebaker, Dodge, GMC, and International trucks, Willys and Ford jeeps, and fuel and parts were beginning to arrive in Soviet ports and airfields courtesy of the United States government's Lend-Lease program. These and other supplies were badly needed and much appreciated.[7] Of all vehicles delivered to the Red Army during the course of the war, foreign imports accounted for some two-thirds—roughly 312,000 of 463,000 units. Making up less than a third of the army's motor pool, they nonetheless gave a psychological boost to a besieged country's population, serving as a tangible representation of the wartime alliance.[8] In this respect, the vehicles bore similarities to other wartime imports such as the Douglas DC-3 transport planes, Spam, and Hollywood films ranging from *Sun Valley Serenade* to *The Grapes of Wrath*.[9]

But no matter how many vehicles the Red Army obtained, there never were enough. This was the conclusion reached by the future novelist Anatolii Rybakov, who spent the war serving as staff commander of a variety of auto divisions and depots. Rybakov adds that spare parts, tires, and fuel were also in short supply, and that lacking a sufficient number of drivers his unit recruited them from among the "doomed men" of the punishment battalions. Like many others he praised the imported vehicles as real workhorses that proved more than equal to the rugged terrain, all kinds of inclement weather conditions, and indifferent maintenance. Officers who landed Willys jeeps instead of the less reliable M-1s were those with the greatest pull, and the vehicle's prestige redounded to them.[10] As for trucks, the Studebakers had an unparalleled reputation for excellence, which may be why they entered Soviet popular culture as a byword for all vehicles shipped from the United States.

Soviet civilians, too, had the opportunity to see if not ride in them during the war. The memoirist Benjamin Braslavsky reports that in his native Sverdlovsk the three-axle Studebakers with their "massive tires" were such common sights that the then-fashionable boots with thick soles made of red-colored rubber became known as "Studebakers." Another source indicates that by the end of 1944 the army was transferring Lend-Lease vehicles to organizations located in the rear. Many of these were involved in agriculture, which had been starved of transport as a result of the requisitions earlier in the war and the priority given to the front thereafter. By January 1946 some 485 trucks, half those belonging to the Krasnoiarsk region's grain procurement apparatus, were American.[11] Some of the Willys and Ford jeeps wound up on collective farms where they survived into the 1960s serving chairmen and other local bigwigs.

Still other U.S. autos found their way to the Ministry of Internal Affairs (MVD). A memorandum from August 1944 on the status of motor vehicles in the ministry's Far East branch (Dal'stroi) indicated that its six hundred Studebakers had begun arriving there in 1943. By the beginning of 1946, Dal'stroi's Studebaker fleet had increased to 1,080. Overall, the ministry laid claim to 5,773 Studebaker trucks. A year and a half later, the number of Studebakers was up to 8,500. With 4,400 Ford 6s and 1,100 Dodges, the contribution of U.S.-made trucks to the MVD's fleet amounted to 14,000. This may have been the high point, for the exhaustion of spare parts—some of which could be produced only with U.S.-made machine tools—led to attrition. A census from January 1950 reported that foreign models had declined over the previous year from 24 percent of the motor pool to 17 percent.[12]

The utility of the "Studebakers," like the alliance that was responsible for their presence in the Soviet Union, had its limits. Yet the high reputation they enjoyed during and immediately after the war among drivers, mechanics, and the broader public persisted throughout the subsequent decades of cold war. Through cannibalization, the sum of their parts turned out to be greater than the whole. When installed in the body of a GAZ or IaZ (Iaroslavl Automobile Plant) truck, a Dodge engine or a Studebaker transmission perpetuated the alliance on wheels, in fact, extending it in the form of a Soviet-American hybrid.

The other major external source of motor transport during the war consisted of "trophy cars" (trofeinye mashiny) that the Wehrmacht had abandoned or that the Red Army had captured. Boris Udol'skii, whom we met earlier, was not the only military officer to return from defeated Germany with an automobile in tow. The Soviet victory found many others in possession of such vehicles. Anatolii Rybakov had two cars at his disposal when he lived in Reichenbach (east of Jena) in 1945–46—an Opel Olympia and an Opel Kapitan. He drove the latter all the way back to Moscow after his discharge.[13] Technically the property of the state, the trophy cars were supposed to be distributed by the Council of Ministers via Gosplan. Thousands gained ownership of such vehicles (which incidentally included not only German but also Czechoslovak, Italian, and French cars), although not always by legal means. An anonymous report sent to the party's Control Commission in February 1947 alleged, for example, that Captain Iu. M. Minkin of the Automobile Administration's third section, First Ukrainian Front, bought an Opel for 361 rubles under the guise of purchasing auto parts. He repaired it for 450 rubles and registered it as his own with the State Automobile Inspectorate (GAI), the branch of the police with responsibility for auto and road safety. A month later, he managed to register a second vehicle, a Mercedes-Benz, although he presented no documentation of its purchase or previous ownership. Inspector Maksimov approved the paperwork in return for getting his M-1 repaired by the First Ukrainian Front's auto administration and for use of the Mercedes. In another instance, Lieutenant-Colonel Cherniak registered a Mercedes-Benz in the town of Orekhovo-Zuevo without any proof of purchase simply by bribing a GAI officer. The police, it should be added, helped themselves to cars they had confiscated.[14]

Wherever they appeared, these Mercedeses, Horsches, Opels, and Tatras drew crowds of admiring spectators. Was it the tangible material proof of victory or the widespread assumption of the cars' technical superiority that attracted them? Probably both, but as the novelty wore off, the trophies turned out to be liabilities for many who had brought them into the country. In the absence of a ready supply of replacement parts, the cars, often not in the best shape to begin with, either went up on blocks where they rusted out over time or were sold to people who had the time and interest to fix them. But they were not the only German-made cars that could be seen in the country. Toward the end of 1945 a small trickle of BMW 321 sedans began to appear. These prewar models were assembled at BMW's Eisenach facility, located in the Soviet zone of occupation and operated as a Soviet-owned company, Awtowelo. By the end of 1948 the factory had turned out nearly six thousand. From 1949, the BMW 340, a modified version of the prewar 326, went into production, and by the time of Stalin's death in March 1953 the factory had produced more than twenty thousand. At least a few were exported to Western Europe as well as to the USSR. From 1952, when the Munich-based BMW company won the right to restrict its name to its products, they bore the moniker of EMW (Eisenacher Motorenwerke) and a red/white (rather than blue/white) insignia.[15]

Shugurov estimates that in 1950 about 30 percent of all cars in Moscow were foreign models. The proportion might have been higher had it not been for the gradual accretion of Pobedas and Moskviches. Every year the government made a certain percentage of domestically produced cars available for purchase—R 16,000 for a Pobeda and R 9,000 for a Moskvich—but that did not stop members of the Soviet elite from seeking one via the old-fashioned route of petitioning Molotov. Petitioners included the writers Kornei Chukovskii and Arkadii Perventsev, the wartime radio announcer Yuri Levitan, the pilot and war hero Ivan Kozhedub, and Aleksei Stakhanov, the pride of the Donbass whom various accounts describe as frequently turning to Molotov and Stalin with requests. Some petitioners were successful but many were not. Some individuals were so valuable that they did not have to ask. Igor Kurchatov, the physicist in charge of the Soviet atomic bomb project, may have been one, for otherwise Stalin probably would not have told him in early 1946 that despite the losses incurred by the state during the war, it was "surely possible...that several thousand people can live very well, and several thousand people better than very well, with their own dachas...and with their own cars."[16]

In the early 1950s, according to Braslavsky, membership in the "association of automobilists" conveyed the stamp of official approbation but also inspired snobbism. "Within this society, the owners of Pobedas regarded Moskvich owners condescendingly." Could this have had anything to do with Perventsev's request for a Pobeda? He claimed that he needed it to help gather material for his new book and that a spinal injury made it difficult for him to get around in the Moskvich he already had.[17] Other citizens—"scientists and collective farmers, writers, artists, and worker-Stakhanovites," according to the Ministry of Automotive Transport's journal, were obtaining Pobedas and Moskviches in automobile stores that had opened in many large cities. In Tashkent alone collective farmers had purchased 105 Pobedas and 1,150 Moskviches in 1949. "Demand for these cars is growing continually," it was reported in another article accompanied by a photograph of a Samarkand machine-and-tractor-station brigade leader and Uzbek Supreme Soviet deputy standing in front of her Pobeda. Other issues featured a cover illustration of a parking lot filled with Moskviches belonging to miners in Karaganda, and a story about the Klara Zetkin collective farm in Azerbaijan where as many as twenty collective farmers owned automobiles.[18]

"Car ownership itself is being cheered," wrote Vera Dunham describing the "Big Deal" that the Stalinist state offered the "Soviet middle class" after the war. Miners in Karaganda and Uzbek and Azerbaijani collective farmers hardly qualified for middle-class status, but, in the tradition of the socialist-realist narrative, ownership by a select few among the toiling masses was a harbinger of the radiant future that awaited others if they only worked hard enough.[19] How many people actually did acquire a car in the postwar years? In 1950, Soviet factories produced 64,554 passenger vehicles. With the exception of a few ZIS and ZIM limousines, they were all Pobedas and Moskviches. Of the total, 5,176 (8%) were exported and 36,378 (56%) were assigned to institutions, turned into taxis, or reserved by central authorities for special needs. That left 23,000 (36%) for sale to individuals. Numbers fluctuated considerably over the next few years. In 1952, only 16,000 cars (27% of the total produced) were put up for sale to the public, but three years later a whopping 64,000 (59%) were available for purchase.[20] This unprecedented number inspired quite a few people to put their names down for future purchase. Braslavsky (then still a student in a Sverdlovsk institute) and two of his friends were among them. In 1956 they signed up to buy a Moskvich, an act they celebrated by gorging themselves on stuffed oysters, drinking vodka, and calculating how much time they had before their number threatened to get close enough to require them to come up with the money.[21]

Hard-Driving Men

"We met a number of lorries, but saw few cars," wrote Patrick Sargeant about his trip from Moscow to Khar'kov in the mid-1950s. When Heinz Lathe and Günther Meierling headed south to Tula in their diesel-powered

Mercedes in 1958, they passed long lines of trucks, but the first car they met was "after we have gone 43 kilometers (27 miles)."[22] Wherever else cars were traveling in the USSR it didn't seem to be on the main highways. Truck traffic was not heavy by American or even European standards, but on the major access roads outside Moscow and other major cities those "long lines" were an increasingly common sight.

During the 1950s, the number of trucks produced in the country's factories rose from 294,000 to 362,000. Production continued to outpace that of passenger cars but by a decreasing margin. By 1964, the year of Khrushchev's ouster, the ratio of cars to trucks stood at 1:2.1 as compared with 1:3.5 in 1953 (see table 6.1). Throughout this period, the 2.5 ton GAZ-51 (along with its off-road variant, GAZ-63) was the Soviet Union's leading truck, rivaled only by the slightly heavier and slower ZIS-150 and the UralZIS-355. Also encountered on the highways of that time were three-axle vehicles such as the ZIS-151 and the IaAZ 210 and 214. The total amount of freight transported by these and other vehicles increased nearly fivefold (from 1.8 to 8.4 million tons) during the 1950s.[23]

The expansion of trucking was accompanied by an increase in the number of professional drivers. More than half a million strong at the end of the war, they were again, as they had been before the war, overwhelmingly male. Women who were recruited in large numbers as drivers during the war still made up some 15 percent of the total in 1945. But a year later their

Table 6.1. Production of passenger cars, trucks, and buses, 1946–1964

Year	Cars	Trucks	Cars/Trucks ratio	Buses	Total
1946	6,289	94,572	1:15.0	1,310	102,171
1947	9,622	121,248	1:12.6	2,098	132,968
1948	20,175	173,908	1:8.6	2,973	197,056
1949	45,661	226,854	1:4.9	3,477	275,992
1950	64,554	294,402	1:4.5	3,939	362,895
1951	53,646	229,777	1:4.2	5,260	288,683
1952	59,663	243,465	1:4.0	4,808	307,936
1953	77,380	270,667	1:3.5	6,128	354,175
1954	94,728	300,613	1:3.2	8,532	403,873
1955	107,806	328,047	1:3.0	9,415	445,268
1956	97,792	356,415	1:3.6	10,425	464,632
1957	113,588	369,504	1:3.2	12,316	495,408
1958	122,191	374,900	1:3.1	13,983	511,074
1959	124,519	351,373	1:2.8	19,102	494,994
1960	138,822	363,008	1:2.6	22,761	523,591
1961	148,914	381,617	1:2.5	24,799	555,330
1962	165,945	382,355	1:2.3	29,180	577,480
1963	173,122	382,220	1:2.2	31,670	587,012
1964	185,159	385,006	1:2.1	32,919	603,084

Source: Annual figures cited in Alain Dupouy, *L'automobile en URSS—Chronologie de 1917 à 1990* (Grenoble: Dupouy, 1991).

representation had dropped to a mere 2.4 percent.[24] In subsequent decades, the notion that women could handle big rigs became inconceivable. It was not so much the driving itself, insisted the head of a physiological laboratory for professional drivers in 1979, "but the repair of such machines, [and] the removal of obstacles in the road now and then requires significant physical exertion, which is too much (*protivopokazano*) for women." For reasons that probably had to do with their fixed and relatively short routes within urban spaces as well as low pay scales, tram, bus, and subway driving remained open to women and indeed by 1970 over half of those so employed were female.[25]

Trucks carried not only freight but people too, especially in the countryside where they served as unofficial (in fact, illegal) supplements to bus service. "The Russian lorries do stop," Lathe and Meierling wrote. "We do not meet any empty lorries at all. There are people with suitcases on all of them."[26] Encounters with truck drivers were therefore fairly common, although their very irregularity imparted to them a sense of adventure.

In Rybakov's novel *Drivers* (*Voditeli,* 1950), the director of a provincial town's auto depot, Poliakov, reassigns one of his drivers, Maksimov, from driving a bus to the oldest truck (a model from 1934) in the garage:

> "I don't agree to the truck, Mikhail Grigor'evich. I have a first-class license."
>
> "I'm not talking about the class," Poliakov cut him short. "A first-class driver doesn't put an unwashed vehicle in the garage. I can't leave the best bus on the depot in such slovenly hands. Go take the ZIS 24–26."[27]

Drivers, apparently the first Soviet novel to take as its prime subjects this occupational group, earned its author a Stalin Prize. In his memoirs, Rybakov admits to not being very proud of the novel, but he does defend its "authenticity." "Many authors wrote about factories and plants. I saw my advantage in that they were writing about what they didn't know, while I knew about automotive stuff (*delo*)." It contained, he continued, "no doxology, glorification, eulogies, or false pathos; not once is the name of Stalin mentioned. The characters are all ordinary people, drivers, loaders, and mechanics." The real drivers with whom the author discussed the novel shortly after its serialization liked it well enough. The hero, Poliakov, displayed a "Bolshevik straightforwardness" that they appreciated. They also approved of the portrayal of Demin, the driver for whom "work was his life rather than merely a profession" and who belonged to the elite category of those clocking a minimum of one hundred thousand kilometers between capital repairs. But they also had criticisms. Poliakov, they felt, was too passive in his dealings with the bossy administrator of the Auto Trust. Too much space was devoted to the machinations of the swindler Vertilin, and Demin's decision to spend the night sleeping in his cabin in front of the brickworks so that he would be first in line to load the next morning seemed a distortion (because of its moral dubiousness) of the Stakhanovite movement the character was supposed to represent.[28]

"In the thirties the heroes were pilots, masters of the skies, but now drivers, the masters of the earth, had replaced them. People at that time were interesting, different—without second thoughts, without intrigues, without subterfuge or subtexts. Direct, simple, and reliable." These are the words not of Rybakov but of the young director Aleksandr Kott, speaking a few years ago about his film *Two Drivers (Ekhali dva shofëra)*. The "now" and "that time" to which he referred were the late 1940s, a time that in retrospect seemed happy because victory in the war had given people a feeling of empowerment, or so Kott imagined.[29] Historians and many people who actually lived through those years of famine and political repression may think of them otherwise, but if anyone experienced freedom—at least freedom of movement—it was long-distance truck drivers. Rybakov gave voice to their exuberance:

> A long trip! Only a driver knows the poetry of these words. In them is the noise of wind, intense sun, the evening coolness of endless fields, the smell of the forest, silvery lakes and rivers, cities and villages, chance night lodgings, new people, new places.
>
> Broad and spacious! Neither stoplights nor policemen. Put the pedal to the metal, don't worry—be happy! [*Zhmi na vsiu zhelezku, mchis' tol'ko pesni poi!*].[30]

It was not exactly the myth of the open road so frequently invoked in American country and Western music, advertising, and certain Hollywood films and novels. But it was about as close as anyone in the Soviet Union was likely to get.

Their relative freedom made drivers liminal figures in the Soviet countryside. They tended to come from collective farm villages but were no longer tied to them, either psychologically or legally, for they were contracted to the machine and tractor stations of state farms. Many had acquired their mechanical skills in the army and seen action in the war. Yet their lack of formal education and cultural refinement was bound to keep them at arm's length from urban sophisticates. In Soviet fiction they come into contact with all kinds of people, typically assisting the needy and vulnerable and being taken advantage of by (but eventually gaining the upper hand against) the nefarious. In the 1955 film, *The Case of Rumiantsev (Delo Rumiantseva,* dir. Iosef Heifitz), the simple and honest driver gives a lift to a young woman whose bicycle is broken. From this a romance springs, but before they can marry he is thrown in jail for unknowingly transporting illegal goods.[31] In Vasily Shukshin's stories, the drivers were fond of women, but despite (or maybe because of) their forwardness they did not develop close attachments. They were, like all of Shukshin's heroes, "loners by choice."[32] In "The Classy Driver," twenty-six-year-old Pashka Kholmanskii is "dangerous or handsome, it was hard to say." When they first meet, Pashka tells Nastia Platonova, the village librarian and "a local beauty," that he is from Moscow, only to deny it the next day. In "Grin'ka Maliugin," the eponymous character, a veteran of the tank forces, becomes a local hero when he jumps into a truck that had caught fire and drives it away from a fuel depot. Interviewed in the hospital by a female reporter, he begs her to visit him again only to tell his ward mate that it is not he who is in love with her but rather the reverse. These characters—along with the stuttering hero of "Crankshafts"—are collapsed into one in *There Lives This Guy* (*Zhivet takoi paren'*, 1964), the first film Shukshin directed. The film opens with Pashka Kolokol'nikov driving his GAZ-51 along the Chuiskii road (*trakt*), the same remote Altai Mountain track that figured in the popular song "The Ballad of a Driver." It ends with him recuperating in the hospital, having just dreamt of Nastia and becoming reconciled to his itinerant, independent way of life.[33]

What the drivers in these stories do not do is get paid in kind with the goods they transport; sell goods on the side; abuse the system of "natural loss" to provision themselves, their relatives and neighbors; or "swear like a driver."[34] They would not be allowed to appear on the screen or in print as heroes if they did. Interviewed a few years ago, Gershon (Grisha) Goldshteyn, who worked as a truck driver in his native Kiev from 1948 to 1990, denied engaging in law-breaking himself ("I did not...we only watched those people who did something—stealing, etc.") but described an environment filled with temptations to do so. Grisha was well paid, especially after he started driving bigger trucks all over Ukraine in the early 1960s, but he felt he earned every kopek: "I had much more responsibility than any factory worker.... If you are behind the wheel, you are responsible for the truck, for yourself, for the surrounding people, for the road." It also was "very hard physical work...especially in winter," with a lot of unpaid overtime. Correspondingly, he was glad to have been able to provide "for my life, that of my family, and those around me" but "wouldn't wish [the job] on an enemy."[35] Among truck drivers, pay depended in theory on the category of one's license, the size and nature of the truck(s), the distance combined with the weight of the freight ("ton-kilometers"), the nature of the freight, the frequency of repairs, and a few other factors that seemed to require a degree in higher mathematics to figure out.[36] In practice, as Grisha Goldshteyn's experience demonstrated, directors of auto bases and dispatchers rotated drivers in and out of certain kinds of runs to give everyone an opportunity to stock up on goods to which they were entitled as part of the state's system of writing off a percentage as "spoiled." Such would remain the case for decades to come.

The Management of Desire

Viktor Sukhodrev, English-language interpreter to successive Soviet leaders, recalled in 2005 that when Nikita Khrushchev told Americans in September 1959 that Soviet citizens had no interest in owning a car or a home, he thought to himself (even as he faithfully translated the boss's words), "I want a car! I want a house!"[37] Having the opportunity to travel abroad and observe life among the Western bourgeoisie, Sukhodrev may have felt unusually frustrated by his own government's failure to accommodate such desires. But he was not alone in his awareness of what the United States had to offer in the way of automobility. When in 1956 the U.S. State Department resumed publication of its Russian-language magazine *Amerika,* cars and the lifestyle they supported were featured prominently. Readers could learn about Joe and Margery's "house on wheels" (a trailer home), a "city of stores for the suburbs" (a mall—"attractive, spacious, and comfortable"—in Seven Corners, Virginia), and, of course, the cars themselves ("low-bodied, with comfortable seating, and powerful engines, good for city driving as well as lengthy trips").[38]

Soviet authorities restricted circulation of the magazine to a small number of well-placed and reliable citizens, though even (or especially?) among them this form of "soft power" may have had its intended effect.[39] For its part, the Ministry of Automobile Production made available information—albeit not nearly as flattering—about U.S.-made cars.[40] Direct contact with U.S. and other foreign cars remained quite rare, although in this and so many other respects, Muscovites were relatively privileged. As one automobile enthusiast recalled from his youth in the early 1960s, "parking spaces at embassies, buildings where diplomats lived, and the hotels Metropol' and Natsional'—these were our automobile showrooms."[41] And then there was the U.S. Trade and Cultural Fair. Held in Moscow's Sokolniki Park in the summer of 1959, the exhibition displayed a Cadillac De Ville, Chevy Impala, Ford Thunderbird, and eighteen other Detroit beauties. According to the diplomatic historian Walter Hixson, who has seen reports by Soviet authorities, the automobile display "may have been the single most popular exhibit," especially among men. "Visitors peppered the guides with questions about the cost, availability, and maintenance of the new automobiles," he adds, citing one report of a visitor "who almost begged the guide to sell the exhibited cars."[42]

Such reports can be read in various ways. It might be considered as evidence of political disloyalty. After all, as the "kitchen debate" between Khrushchev and Vice President Richard Nixon had demonstrated, consumer goods had become a battlefield in the cold war. More straightforwardly, visitors' interest in learning about (if not buying) the cars indicated desire, though not necessarily for American cars alone. United Press International's correspondent at this very time, Aline Mosby, described her MGA with some exaggeration as "next to Lenin's tomb, the biggest attraction in Moscow," adding that "Russians are crazy about cars the way Americans are crazy about visiting royalty."[43]

Desire, I would argue, is a more appropriate term than demand, because as an independent variable, demand had little purchase in Soviet political economy. Desire, rather than demand, was what lay beyond the party's "rational" determination of needs. A nonquantifiable category, it had ethical rather than economic foundations.[44] Under Stalin, luxury items such as cars were distributed or otherwise made available as rewards to those who made celebrated contributions to society. Under Khrushchev, the state pursued contradictory policies with respect to the production and provision of durable consumer

Table 6.2. Production of durable goods and destination of cars, 1950–1965 (in thousands of units)

Year	1950	1955	1960	1965
Televisions	n.a.	495	1,726	3,655
Refrigerators	n.a.	151	530	1,675
Washing machines	n.a.	87	895	3,430
Passenger cars	65	108	139	201
of which:				
sold to population	23 (36%)	64 (59%)	62 (45%)	64 (32%)
exported	5 (8%)	13 (12%)	30 (22%)	49 (24%)
distributed	36 (56%)	31 (29%)	47 (33%)	88 (44%)

Sources: TsSU SSSR, *Narodnoe khoziaistvo SSSR v 1967 g.* (Moscow: Gos. stat. izd-vo, 1968), 200–201; V. M. Iamashev, "Volzhskii avtozavod: prervannyi ryvok za mirovoi modernizatsiei," in *Istoriia OAO "Avtovaz": Uroki, problemy, sovremennost'. Materialy I Vserossiiskoi nauchnoi konferentsii, 26–27 noiabria 2003 g.,* ed. A. E. Livshits and P. A. Nakhmanovich (Togliatti: OAO Avtovaz, TGU, 2003), 234.

goods. Durable goods for the home were produced in ever-increasing numbers, significantly narrowing the gap between the Soviet Union and advanced capitalist countries. Car production also increased both absolutely and relative to that of trucks, but the numbers available for purchase by individuals remained virtually unchanged (see table 6.2). The government thus both acknowledged the legitimacy of citizens' desires to own a car and frustrated the fulfillment of that desire. It promoted rentals as an alternative to other forms of car usage, but did very little to make this alternative attractive. And it tried to compensate for the failure of its policies by touting its export of cars, trucks, motorcycles, and mopeds to "more than thirty countries including the United States."[45] These policies, practices, and claims reveal a fundamental ambivalence about private ownership of cars that pervaded Soviet society in the Khrushchev years from the party leader himself to residents of apartment blocks, the traffic police, and the media.

Nikita Khrushchev dropped two bombshells at the Twentieth Party Congress in February 1956. One was his "secret speech" to a closed session in which he detailed the crimes of Stalin and denounced the "cult of personality" that made them possible. The other, contained in his report to the opening session of the congress on February 14, concerned the "wasteful" use of passenger cars assigned to state officials. It would, of course, not do to equate the significance of the two. The secret speech changed the course of Soviet history; it was the first act in the unraveling of Communist ideology and political power throughout the world. But if one had asked congress delegates which posed the more immediate threat to their perquisites and lifestyle, most would have pointed to the first secretary's call for eliminating the practice of assigning cars and drivers to individual officials and replacing it with a system of "official taxi fleets." As a concession to the comrades, Khrushchev allowed that "where required, cars could be distributed to individuals, but they would have to learn how to drive themselves." It is not clear whether Khrushchev considered the assignment of cars or drivers as more wasteful. It is also not clear whether the "applause" registered in the stenographic report of the congress was occasioned by support for the measure or relief that it did not go any further.[46]

The reorganization of automobile distribution began in April 1956 when ministries and other institutions and organizations had to turn 50 percent of their fleets over to auto firms. In Moscow alone this amounted to the transfer of some four thousand cars—at least in principle. Some of the cars were sold to the public, but others found their way back through rental agreements to the institutions that had possessed them previously and thence to individuals within those institutions. In the course of 1959, the government formalized and simplified these arrangements. By the end of that year, *Behind the Wheel* was reporting on a "new form of servicing the population with transportation—the issuing of cars for hire without drivers." True, before receiving a car the subscriber had to pass a driving test and a test of repair skills, but the possibilities after doing so seemed endless. One could hire a car for a few hours or a month, for work, to go fishing, or on a camping trip. Also available for hire, at least in theory, were inflatable dinghies, skis, tents, and other camping equipment. As Khrushchev had boasted to a mass meeting in Vladivostok in October 1959:

> We want to set up a different arrangement from capitalist countries for using passenger cars.... We will use cars more rationally than the Americans. We will give full development to taxi fleets from which people can obtain cars for necessary trips. Why would a person break his neck over where to keep a car, why take the trouble when there is a better way that answers to the interests of society as a whole and to each citizen?[47]

Ivan Petrovich Pastukhov, the main character in the 1958 film comedy *A Driver by Accident* (*Shofër ponevole,* dir. Nadezhda Kosheverova), was the sort of person targeted by Khrushchev's scheme. As the film opens, Pastukhov, director of "Glavuprsnabsbyt" (an acronym for a fictive state bureaucratic agency dealing with sales of supplies) is looking forward to his hard-earned summer vacation. The first day of the vacation arrives along with Ivan Petrovich's Volga and its driver, also named Ivan Petrovich. Driver and passenger head out of Moscow to appropriately peppy music. On the way, they fill up the gas tank out of turn thanks to the driver's acquaintanceship with the (female) service station attendant and then spend a relaxing afternoon fishing. When the chauffeur is suddenly stricken with back spasms, Pastukhov takes the wheel and just manages to get him to the hospital. There, because he has borrowed his boss's jacket, the driver is mistaken for Pastukhov who in the meantime has trouble proving his identity. The case of doubly mistaken identity and Pastukhov's misadventures with a car he is barely capable of keeping on the road provide much of the humor.[48] Thus a highly unstable and ambiguous situation is rendered as harmless fun. Audiences could take away two diametrically opposed messages: do not assume the role/identity of a professional driver, and, because all ends well, look how much fun it is to drive![49]

Meanwhile, the politically safe message that Soviet citizens gave to foreign inquirers was the same one their leader had conveyed to Americans during his visit in 1959. "Poor Americans," Muriel Reed was told during her stay in the Black Sea resort of Sochi, "they can't seem to live without a car, a refrigerator, or a television." "Would you like to have a car?" she asks Sergei, one of her hosts. "He sighed. 'I don't have to want a car. It's enough for there to be better public transportation.'"[50] This was a perfectly reasonable position, one that without doubt had its genuine adherents. And they were not to be disappointed. The Moscow metro, carrying several million passengers a day, was just about to expand further to the southwest, the northwest, the west and south. Leningrad, Kiev, and, in 1967, Baku also were served by subways. Still, it was hard to get to the dacha or visit relatives in the village on the metro. The availability of cars in theory made their desirability in practice inevitable. One did not have to want a car, but many did anyway.

What about renting, the more socially responsible way of using cars? It too had possibilities, but its rationality was difficult to see amid the problems uncovered by journalists who investigated Moscow's rental sites in 1960. They found subscribers (that is, those who had qualified for renting) camping out overnight in front of offices because there were no more cars to rent; cars approved for rental that needed all manner of parts replaced; cars out of service for weeks because of relatively minor repairs, and cars with "reserved" signs on their windshields that stood unused for the whole weekend.[51] Teething problems? Kinks to be worked out? It was hard to say. But two years later, there was little to recommend the system at all. Pobedas and Moskviches were being leased with 150,000–200,000 kilometers on the odometer. Eighty percent of the cars in Moscow were stored under the open sky. Worst of all from the state's point of view, the system was a financial drain. The head of the Moscow taxi administration made some useful suggestions for turning things around such as introducing insurance for drivers (instead of the state covering 80% of the cost in case a car was totaled) and altering rates seasonally. Otherwise, referring to an increase in the number of accidents and breakdowns, he fulminated against the "irresponsibility of some citizens" whose attitude toward state property was "careless and sometimes even criminal" and recommended that trade unions be more careful in issuing attestations to future subscribers.[52]

The problem was at once simpler and more complicated than promoting greater moral probity or tightening up bureaucratic procedures. It had to do with an insufficiency of investment, manifested in the abysmal shortage of cars for rent (one for every forty customers in Moscow), their aging condition, and the near absence of spare parts. Reflecting the system's low priority was the subordination of rental offices to the Taxi Transport Administration, itself a division of Moscow's General Transport Administration. Scarcity, though, was experienced differently by different citizens. Those without connections or favors to trade (*blat*) had to put up with camping overnight, accepting defective cars, and engaging in other makeshift arrangements that perhaps were only marginally better options than relying on public transportation.[53] More privileged customers had no problem qualifying as subscribers, making reservations, and obtaining the better sort of cars with or without drivers. Such starkly different experiences proved endemic to the entire shortage economy, which depended only marginally on monetary resources.

So powerful was the desire for cars that it easily transcended legal restrictions. Although more pervasive under Khrushchev's successors, most of the activities that the state defined as criminal got their start in the 1950s. These included using influence or connections to jump the queues and obtain a new car for which one had registered; registering different members of one's family; circumventing the state's commission (*komissionnye*) stores in purchasing a secondhand car; engaging in "speculation" (that is, the buying and selling of goods with the aim of making a quick profit) in spare parts; transporting agricultural products for resale at higher prices in cities (another form of speculation); and evading restrictions on the purchase of fuel by buying up vouchers.[54] The rental system itself survived Khrushchev's removal from office but was no longer advertised as a solution to the massive and seemingly unquenchable desire for cars.

Tourism, which only increased the desire for cars and better road service, also demonstrated the dynamic in which state management of desire led to wayward if not illegal behavior. "The growing well-being of the Soviet people," proclaimed a *Behind the Wheel* editorial of June 1956, "finds its expression in particular in the development of automobile tourism."[55] The magazine, revived by DOSAAF (the Voluntary Society of Assistance to the Army, the Air Force, and the Navy founded in 1951) after a hiatus of sixteen years, actively promoted auto tourism. In 1956 alone it featured articles on the Moskvich's collapsible table and fold-down seat for sleeping; on the new tourist season; on the best routes to take in the Baltic, Ukraine, the Caucasus, and the Urals; and on preparing a car for a lengthy trip. It published a song ("Behind the Wheel") that celebrated driving with one's girlfriend through "native expanses, valleys and mountains" and, at the end of the tourist season, an evaluation of facilities along the Moscow to Yalta route. In subsequent years it reported on the growing popularity of camping (*kemping*) and campsites in the Russian republic.[56] The songs kept on coming, too:

> Oh, you mountainous roads.
> Who has been will never forget you!
> And not for nothing it is said,
> That the driver who a mistake makes,
> Makes a mistake only once.[57]

Avto-turizm actually encompassed two different kinds of activity. One was the highly organized, purposeful travel that distinguished Soviet-bloc tourism in general. The purpose was to develop the skills of driving and reconnaissance—useful in time of war—and, as one tourist guidebook put it, "to better know the Motherland, its extent and beauty, to develop a sense of national pride and patriotism."[58] Thus, as early as 1956, members of auto clubs sponsored by DOSAAF could earn "Tourist USSR" badges by driving at least one thousand kilometers over five days. By 1965 the minimum distance was increased to three thousand kilometers over six days. To accomplish this feat DOSAAF advised prospective tourists to travel in groups with an appointed leader, "train regularly," consult with experienced tourists, work out routes with control points in advance, and, of course, take plenty of supplies (bottled water, oil, lubricants, brake fluid, insulating tape, soap, etc.) and spare parts. Such preparations were necessary because long-distance travel remained precarious.[59]

The other kind of tourism consisted of spending time at resorts (*kurorty*), rest homes, and sanatoria. This too was to be purposeful, with staff on hand to organize physical exercise, lectures, and excursions. It also theoretically was regulated, with trade unions and other institutions chartering transportation by bus or train and controlling the distribution of accommodation vouchers. Although facilities expanded rapidly during the 1960s, they did not come close to keeping pace with the increase in demand occasioned at least in part by vacationers' acquisition of wheels.

Such were the circumstances in which "wild tourists" (*dikari*) emerged. *Dikari* stereotypically combined the self-reliance of DOSAAF-sponsored tourism with unauthorized use of beaches and other facilities ostensibly restricted to resorts. It recently has been argued that "wild and planned tourism…were more complexly intertwined than official sources admit."[60] That may be so, but the "wildness" of tourists—that is, their ability to travel where and when they wanted, relying on their own supplies of food rather than the resort's often indifferent cuisine—was greatly enhanced by their access to individual motorized transport.

As *Driver by Accident* demonstrated, comedy helped to negotiate the ambiguities of new phenomena. Sergei Mikhalkov's play *Dikari*, first performed in September 1958 and later adapted to the screen (as *Three Plus Two*, dir. Genrikh Oganisian, 1963), has three "wild" male tourists camping on the Black Sea coast alongside a new Moskvich that had brought them "from afar." They are wild in two senses—they do not have reservations at a resort and they forego such niceties of civilization as shaving and wearing long pants. The sudden appearance of two attractive young women, also driving a Moskvich and claiming the same camping site, upsets their Robinson Crusoe–like existence. Each group tries to ignore the presence of the other but with diminishing ardor. Roman and Vladlen decide to make themselves civilized and pair off with the women (Stepan, an up-and-coming physicist and owner of the Moskvich, seems too preoccupied with car maintenance to shave or

otherwise engage in wooing). In the end, wary of "complications and contradictions," Zoia and Sil'va decide to ditch the suitors. The ambiguous ending
leaves us unsure whether the play endorsed or was critical of "wild" tourism. It also seemed to want to it both ways on private ownership of cars. "No
matter what you say," Vladlen at one point tells Stepan in mock seriousness,
"private ownership is reflected in the psychology of humans. You poor slave
of four wheels! How many times must I teach you that machine must serve
man and not the reverse!"[61]

The play, although a fantasy, was made believable by the advent of privately owned cars. The loosening of travel restrictions facilitated the very
"wildness" it exposed (if not celebrated). A cultural history of the Soviet '60s
notes that before that decade road trips had specific destinations and serious purposes that required official sanction. The Komsomolites who headed
for the Virgin Lands in the 1950s, thereby emulating the Twenty-Five Thousanders of the era of collectivization, were hardly idle pleasure seekers. In
the larger, metaphorical sense, their politically inspired travels were part
of the country's journey along the road to socialism. The '60s were different. Here was the decade of "spontaneity of movement," when "nondescript
people traveled along the roads without authorization. Where to and for what
purpose? Wherever and whatever. Such was the novelty that for these nomads there was no definite goal." Accompanied by their guitars (very much
the instrument of the '60s), they sang the songs of Bulat Okudzhava, Iurii
Kukin, and Iurii Vizbo...and they drove.[62]

Cars, though, needed gas, and access to gas was notoriously difficult for
private car owners. Not only were gas stations scarce, but the complex system gave top priority to drivers of commercial vehicles and required all gas
purchases to be recorded by hand in ration books (*zabornye knizhki*). "What
Sisyphean labor it has become to buy gas," *Behind the Wheel* complained as
it listed the rules laid down by no less than the Ministry of Finance and the
State Bank.[63] Evasion seemed inevitable. In the meantime, another comic film
from the Khrushchev era had raised the profile of an occupation that, like
so much else associated with automobiles, was gaining in public visibility.
This was *Queen of the Gas Pump* (*Koroleva benzokolonki,* dir. A. Mishurin,
1963), a film reminiscent of Stalin-era Cinderella stories such as *The Radiant
Path*. Liudmila, the plucky Cinderella character, dreams of a career as an ice
dancer but settles in the meantime for the menial job of gas station attendant
somewhere outside of Kiev. As an American visitor to the Soviet Union noted
in the late 1950s, "attendants are usually women," a clear indication of the
occupation's low pay if not low status.[64] But Liudmila was no ordinary *za-
pravshchitsa*. At first overwhelmed by the crush of waiting customers and
the station manager's inefficient system for recording purchases, she soon
masters the job (on roller skates!) and even organizes emergency bridge repair for which she is rewarded with an invitation to study road construction.
Unlike *Dikari*, the film contains no ambiguity. It is rather a manual for proper
behavior by drivers and a lesson in determination to do well ("to do one's

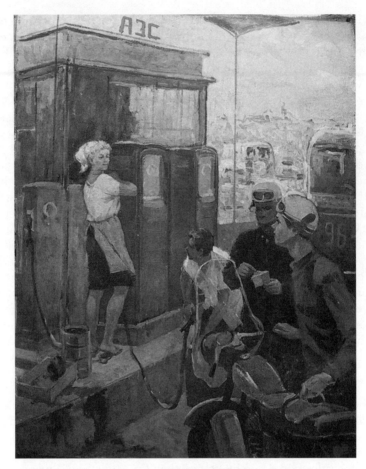

Nadezhda Kompaniets-Kiyanchenko, "Queen of the Gas Pump," 1974. Oil on canvas. 100 × 80 cm. Used with permission of the New Gallery, Moscow.

best at what one does," as Liudmila repeats to a bus driver), a lesson made palatable by the film's lightheartedness.[65]

Especially in cities and during the long cold winters when they weren't being used, cars needed to be garaged. "As brand new blocks of apartments are opened they are almost immediately surrounded by a slum of patchwork garages put together by anxious owners of precious autos." Thus did the *Baltimore Sun*'s correspondent in Moscow, Howard Norton, describe the changing landscape he observed in the early 1960s.[66] And such was the content of a three-panel cartoon that appeared in the satirical magazine *Krokodil* in 1960. The first panel showed "the beginning of construction" with bulldozers demolishing old wooden housing in the foreground and cranes erecting ferroconcrete blocks in the rear; the second panel labeled "Built" showed a pristine apartment block surrounded by newly planted trees; and the final

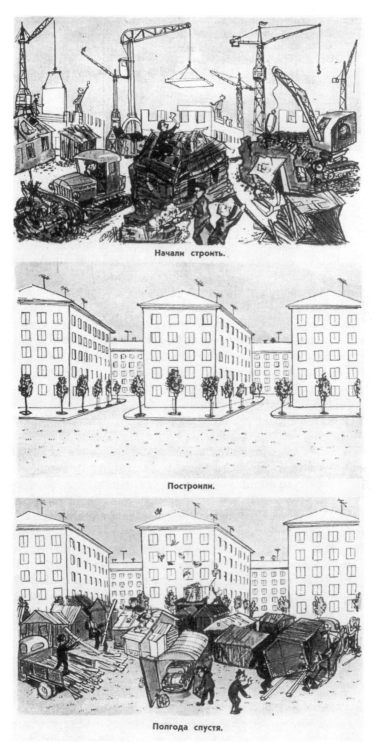

Garages disfiguring new apartment blocs. *Krokodil*, no. 15 (1960).

panel displayed metal and wood garage boxes disfiguring the courtyard of the same apartment block "half a year later."[67] The problem of what to do with privately owned cars was hardly new. Thirteen years earlier, the same magazine had run a cartoon labeled "How Muscovites [*Moskvichy*] Store the Moskvich." Each panel presented alternatives to garages, one more absurd than the other. The final panel showed a Moskvich in a lion's cage. Of course, the car would be inaccessible to its owners, but at least it would be kept intact and never stolen.[68]

During the 1950s, most car owners in Moscow either had to leave their cars in the open air in courtyards and on streets or drive to the outskirts and garage them far from their downtown residences. Both practices had their drawbacks. It was not that there were no parking facilities in the city center but that many were reserved by ministries and cultural institutions such as the Bolshoi Theater and often went unused. To alleviate the situation, the RSFSR's Council of Ministers issued a resolution in December 1958 permitting "the construction of collective garages" for which it instructed local soviets to make land available.[69] Architects proposed a variety of facilities ranging from single- and multistory "garage boxes" to more elaborate underground structures that could accommodate several hundred vehicles as well as repair shops. But throughout the Soviet Union the norm seemed to be single-automobile garages and open-air parking in courtyards.[70] Indeed, in many cases, the structures that housed cars didn't deserve to be called garages. Sheds would be more accurate.

If car owners felt aggrieved by the lack of garages, many among the vast majority of residents without cars resented not only the garages but the drivers themselves. Referring to letters to the Leningrad press and resolutions passed at residents' meetings, Steven Harris writes that "given the opportunity to voice their collective input, residents overwhelmingly rejected garages." Why? For some it was that "car owners, their automobiles, and single-car garages dirtied new housing estates and generally got in the way of people's everyday lives." For others they served as scapegoats for the inadequacy of public transport, presumably on the grounds that if officials were made to rely on buses, trams, and the like rather than their own cars, they would improve public conveyances. Judging from the terms that were used to refer to car owners—"private persons" (*chastnye litsa/chastniki*) and "independent proprietors" (*edinolichniki*)—there also was a moral dimension. To own a car was to set oneself apart from the community.[71]

Finally, car ownership put one at the mercy of the traffic police. Special detachments of police assigned to control traffic (*otriady/otdely regulirovaniia ulichnogo dvizheniia,* usually abbreviated as ORUD) date from the early 1930s in Moscow and other major cities. By the 1950s, they were being merged with the State Automobile Inspectorate (GAI), an institution formed in 1935 under Tsudortrans and, after its dissolution, under the NKVD's Worker-Peasant Militia. It was GAI that initially had responsibility for "the struggle against accidents and injurious use of auto transport; the development of technical standards and measures of auto transport operations; supervision of driver training; [and] publication of rules for maintaining vehicles in good order."[72] In other words, it was GAI that standardized license plates and the classifications of drivers, determined the amount of fuel each kind of vehicle involved in transport work should consume per one hundred kilometers, and carried out inspections of transport and transport facilities. GAI also bore responsibility for enforcing the rules of the road that were standardized on January 1, 1961, with the issuance of the Traffic Regulations for Streets and Roads of the USSR.[73]

It is difficult to be precise about when the traffic police—both *"ORUDtsy"* and *"GAIshniki"*—acquired their reputation for dishonesty. Taking bribes from motorists who violate traffic rules is not necessarily universal among police forces, but it appears to be widespread. The problem in the Soviet Union was that traffic police had unusually wide latitude in assessing code violations. The punching of a hole in a driver's license to indicate an infraction—a practice that was adopted for the entire country in the course of the 1960s—virtually invited bribes, especially by those who were in danger of getting the dreaded third hole that spelled suspension. Konstantin Simis, a former defense lawyer who left the Soviet Union in 1977, noted that "at the slightest infraction—and even for no reason at all—the GAI inspector will flag down a private car with a grandiose gesture of his police baton and will adopt a monumental pose, not moving from his spot, waiting for the driver to come up to him at an obsequious trot." He adds that the standard rate for avoiding a hole in one's license was a mere one ruble if there were no previous violations, three to five if the license already was penalized, and fifty rubles if alcohol could be smelled on one's breath. Other opportunities for a little—or in some cases, more than a little—money on the side included the driving exam (for which driving instructors often served as middlemen, arranging payment in advance), the annual springtime mechanical inspection (for which the going rate was ten rubles in the RSFSR but higher in the Transcaucasian republics), and off-the-books transportation of produce from collective and state farms destined for city markets.[74]

It is all well and good for Lieutenant Ivan Tsar'kov, chief of the GAI in Kirov Oblast from 1952 to 1964, to claim that he "always lived by the principle of 'better poor but honest'" and taught his colleagues the same, but the contrary principles of "let's settle the matter between us" and "thank you very much" seem to have been expected by both motorists and the road police.[75] Yet, despite the rich lore among motorists about the shamelessness of the traffic police, the only qualities one finds in the commemorative literature published under the auspices of the post-Soviet State Inspectorate of Road Traffic Safety (GIBDD—Gosudarstvennaia Inspektsiia Bezopasnosti Dorozhnogo Dvizheniia) are courage, compassion, and in the case of individuals killed in the line of duty, martyrdom.[76]

The GAI's greatest challenge was the "struggle against accidents," for as the number of motor vehicles on the road increased so inevitably did the number

"Drivers! Remember. Alcohol inhibits alertness, leads to accidents and human sacrifices," 1959. Poster reproduction.

of car crashes. Unfortunately, we do not have the data to determine whether the rate (crashes per vehicle-kilometers traveled) was climbing as well. What we do know is that the proportion of vehicles that were passenger cars (both privately owned and distributed) was on the rise (see tables 6.1 and 6.2). Is it possible that an unintended effect of the Khrushchev administration's campaign to reduce reliance on chauffeurs was that the proportion of bad drivers was also increasing? I am referring here not only to a lack of driving skills. Truck drivers' reputation of fondness for alcohol, while probably deserved, should not obscure the very real likelihood that many new car drivers shared this weakness.

The problem was sufficiently serious for the Presidium of the RSFSR's Supreme Soviet to issue a decree on October 5, 1961, "On the Responsibility of Drivers for Driving in an Intoxicated State." The decree stiffened penalties to one year's deprivation of a license for a first infraction and three years for a second offense within a three-year period. Cases that resulted in injury or damage were subject, as they had been in the past, to criminal prosecution.[77] Information from the memoirs of Lieutenant Tsar'kov, the poor but honest cop from Kirov Oblast, suggests that the decree had a limited effect—if any—in curbing drunken driving. Tsar'kov mentions 1963–64, the last two years of his leadership of the Kirov branch, as the most difficult, for "discipline among leading officials in the oblast fell sharply.... Many leaders of enterprises, collective and state farms, and party officials drove means of transport in an intoxicated state and caused accidents resulting in serious consequences." Among those means of transport were many GAZ-69 jeeps, evidently the preferred vehicle of those provincial and local officials who enjoyed getting out on the road. In Fyodor Abramov's novella of January 1963, the district committee "Gazik" was "a new jeep with a canvas top ... usually driven by 'him' in person, that is, by the first secretary, while the rest of the district committee workers used an old, rather battered jalopy." Tsar'kov cites at least two leaders who crashed their GAZ-69 jeeps while intoxicated. One of them was the chairman of the Kirov Oblast Executive Committee, I. F. Ob'edkov, the same Ob'edkov who had appended his signature to the Kirov Oblast's application of the Supreme Soviet's decree.[78]

Cars as Property

Pity the poor automobilist (in Russian, *avtoliubitel'*, a term that combines the notions of amateur and enthusiast). This was the message of an article appearing in *Izvestiia* in January 1965, a few months after Khrushchev's forced retirement. "I'm an engineer, and it took me ten years to come up with the money for this car," the driver of a Zaporozhets complained when he stopped late one evening to give a lift to the reporter. "And here's what I don't understand.... It baffles me why when a person buys a television, a piano, a carpet or other junk it's called the growth of well-being. But deny yourself all these charms, go into debt and obtain the most modest automobile or even win a Moskvich in the lottery, and you immediately become a suspicious private person [*chastnik*]." To be a *chastnik* meant to endure rude treatment by police who dismissed "hooliganism" (randomly inflicted damage) against individually owned cars with the comment that "you must understand that private persons are not liked here" and who were known to stop drivers on Sunday to fine them for driving dirty cars. And where was one to wash one's car? Not in the courtyard—the community (*obshchestvennost'*) wouldn't permit it. The nearest car wash is fifteen kilometers away and you would have to wait at least three hours for your turn. As for parking, at nine rubles a month a parking place in the open air cost more than a two-room apartment with central heating and hot water.[79]

Clearly it was time to change attitudes toward car owners. "Older citizens," wrote V. Stepanov in March 1966, "remember a time not too long ago when wristwatches and bicycles were luxury items, to say nothing of radio receivers, televisions, and vacuum cleaners. But now these things have entered into daily life." So too would automobiles, the article continued, including them along with motorcycles, furniture, and radio receivers as items whose supply was increasing.[80] Five months later, Stepanov returned to the issue of "Your

Personal Property," responding to a letter writer from Rostov-on-Don who had expressed hostility toward individual ownership of cars by assuring him that "especially in connection with the rapid development of technology and the growth of production, the car undoubtedly will become more accessible and cease to be regarded as a luxury item."[81] Later, during the Brezhnev era, the impressive increase in the proportion of households with televisions and refrigerators provided obvious precedents for the expansion of car owner-ship and the identification of the passenger car as simply another item for "personal use."[82]

This Soviet discourse diverged sharply from that of the West, where ad-vertising emphasized "men, motors, markets and women."[83] In the USSR the emphasis was not on interesting consumers in purchasing cars but on in-creasing popular acceptance of those fortunate enough to have done so. The taint associated with possession of a car, though, was not so easily removed. El'dar Riazanov's *Look Out for the Car!* (*Beregis' avtomobilia,* 1966), judged by one critic "the most important intellectual comedy of the '60s," managed both to articulate popular assumptions about the crookedness of car own-ers and to express sympathy for that beleaguered group of people.[84] On one level, it is a film about someone whose childlike sense of justice leads him to commit crimes for which even the police can excuse him. The "someone" is Iurii Detochkin, a mild-mannered insurance agent; his crime is stealing cars. Iurii steals cars from bribe takers and other swindlers, sells the cars on the side, and turns the money over to an orphanage. The chief victim of Iurii's peculiar kleptomania is Dima Semitsvetov, the proud owner of a beige Volga. Dima is a fairly reprehensible character. He is in sales—a very un-Soviet occupation—extracts bribes from customers for Western-made stereo equipment, has dealings with all kinds of speculators, and even says at one point that he doesn't like Soviet power. Indeed, the film implies that if any-one is a victim, it is Iurii who used to work as a chauffeur but suffered a car accident that left him with a severe concussion and, evidently, a heightened moral sensibility.

But like many good comedies, the film wants to have it both ways. As the narrator notes:

> One might think that not everything has been done yet to poison the joy of an owner. But considerable successes have been achieved in this respect. A car owner has no free time. When he isn't fixing or washing it, when he isn't filling it with gas, inflating the tires, wandering about town in search of spare parts, or wearing himself out transporting friends to and from their apartments, he is experiencing fear. It is the most basic animal fear that some-body will steal his car. Each owner is convinced that some thief already has his eye on his movable property.[85]

Moreover, the film does distinguish between "good" and "bad" car owners. Maksim, the investigator assigned to the case, warms to Iurii and is willing to let him go free until Iurii makes the "catastrophic mistake" of stealing a Volga from a doctor of physical and mathematical sciences—that is, from someone above reproach. "You, Detochkin, have sunk to banal larceny," Maksim shouts at him in disappointment.[86] Iurii, we discover at the end, did do time for his crime.

If finding the means to obtain them was one dimension of car ownership, what was done with them was yet another. Unlike most of the household goods to which they were compared, cars could be used to generate "unearned income" (*netrudovoi dokhod*). Let us return to the persecuted, Zaporozhets-driving engineer. Did he just happen to encounter a pedestrian late at night and generously offer him a ride to the Kiev station? Or was he actually cruising for clients, that is (I hasten to add), using his car as a taxi? If it was the latter, he would have crossed the line dividing "personal" from "private" property. As Stepanov explained in his "conversation with readers" about "ours" and "mine," personal property—like refrigerators and cars—was "that which is destined exclusively for the personal needs of the owner or his family." It "cannot be used for profit, enrichment, or earnings."[87]

Not in theory at least. But according to an intrepid American couple who "studied the Soviet automobile industry closely since a visit to Russia in 1961–62,...large numbers of Soviet motorists have...[been] using their cars for various illegal activities, like driving out to the country and stealing cabbages from collective farms [and] hiring one's car out for taxi service or buying up scarce foods."[88] If this was known to American visitors, it was no secret to Muscovites, or for that matter, the police. For his part, Stepanov referred to the practice as being common in "bourgeois countries" where "such an automobile constitutes private, though not capitalist, property," analogous to cottage industry (*kustar*) workshops and peasants' garden plots in the Soviet Union.

The notion that in the Soviet Union cars were not used for "profit, enrichment, or earnings" was, frankly, disingenuous. Unlike journalists' tales, court cases resounded with the ambiguities of car ownership and use: Could a citizen buy a car and then present it to his son as a gift? Did the owner of a car who has been assigned to the far north or a posting abroad, or who was confined to the hospital for an extended period, have the right to transfer ownership and use to an unrelated person? Could one citizen legally swap his Moskvich for a Jupiter motorcycle and Astra tape recorder that belonged to someone else? Should an automobile pass into the common ownership of a collective farm household after the death of its owner? If, in the event of a divorce, the court grants the woman ownership of the car but the man retains ownership of the couple's shares in the cooperative garage, is she justified in demanding that the shares be turned over to her? The difficulty in deciding these and other cases came down to the fact that while "the automobile as an article of property to which is attached the right of personal ownership occupies the most prominent place along with a residence, in law it is not treated as an object of personal property in isolation from other legally sanctioned things."[89] A car, it turned out, was not just like a television or refrigerator.

Cars and Car Owners

However inconsistent Khrushchev's populism and commitment to reinvigorating the collectivist ethos of Soviet Communism may have been, Brezhnev, who took over as general secretary in October 1964 and continued in that position until his death in November 1982, hardly tried.[90] The Brezhnev administration sought a different kind of legitimacy, one rooted in what Western commentators have expressed in terms of "bargains," "contracts," and "deals." In one version, Brezhnev provided the guarantee of stability, secure and undemanding jobs, and a slowly improving standard of living in return for acquiescence to authoritarian oligarchic rule. In another, dubbed "the Little Deal," the state tolerated "a wide range of petty private economic activities, some legal, some in the penumbra of the legal, and some clearly and obviously illegal...in exchange for restraint on managerial discretion, and the repression of overt political dissent."[91] This "acquisitive socialism," dominant in the Brezhnev era, formed the ecosystem of car ownership. But the reverse is also true, that is, that the expansion of car ownership did much to remove the stigma—ideological and popular—from acquisitiveness, making it possible, indeed necessary, to engage in other economic activities, petty and otherwise.

The government's announcement in the spring of 1966 that passenger car production would quadruple from two hundred thousand to eight hundred thousand per year during the Eighth Five-Year Plan (1966–70) signaled an important qualitative shift in state policy.[92] Nineteen-seventy-two was the first year in which more cars than trucks were produced. By 1975 the country was producing 1.2 million cars (667,000 at VAZ alone) or six times as many as in 1965.[93] Two other trends during these years are worthy of note: by 1975 the proportion of new cars "assigned for sale to the population" more than doubled to two-thirds of all cars produced, and, owing largely to the selling off of used state-owned vehicles, the percentage of used cars owned by individuals increased. The combined effect of these trends was that by the mid-1970s there were over of 5.5 million privately owned cars in the USSR, nearly four million of which were in the Russian republic and Ukraine. Whereas in 1970 only 2 percent of Soviet households possessed a car, it was 5 percent in 1975, 10 percent by 1980, and 15 percent in 1985 (see table 6.3).[94]

As rapid as was the increase in car ownership, international comparisons show the USSR consistently had among the lowest car densities within the Communist-bloc countries of Eastern Europe, to say nothing of Western Europe or the United States (where there was one car for every 1.9 people in 1978).[95] Contemporary Soviet sources repeatedly stressed that the car density level in the United States was an inappropriate standard for the USSR because it was the result of the "one-sided," "hypertrophic" development of

Table 6.3. Production of trucks and cars, 1965–1990 (in thousands of units)

Year	Trucks	Cars	of which:		
			for export	*for domestic sale*	*for distribution*
1965	380	201	49	64	88
1970	525	344	84	123	137
1975	696	1,201	296	800	105
1980	787	1,327	329	n.a.	n.a.
1985	823	1,332	266	n.a.	n.a.
1990	780	1,252	n.a.	n.a.	n.a.

Source: TsSU SSSR, *Narodnoe khoziaistvo SSSR v...* [annual series] (Moscow: Gos. stat. izd-vo).

individual, as opposed to mass, transportation, which had led to unenviable levels of traffic congestion in major urban areas and the attendant problem of air pollution.[96] They might have added that by the 1970s many commentators in the United States were blaming America's love affair with the automobile for other social maladies as well: rapacious destruction of wildlife habitats; impoverishment and ghettoization of inner cities associated with white flight to suburbs and suburban mall construction; transformation of towns and their outskirts into service stations for cars; and increasing numbers of accidental deaths and injuries.[97]

What was the desired level of car ownership for a country such as the USSR? One study from the early 1970s expressed it in terms of 230–250 cars per 1,000 people, this at a time when the actual level was closer to 20 and the level in the United States was 426.[98] By 1985 Gosplan had scaled this target down to 93 per 1,000 people, though with the actual level of 45 per 1,000 the goal was still not close to being achieved.[99] Only the Baltic republics had reached or were within striking distance of this figure (see table 6.4). Who were these lucky folks and their counterparts in other Soviet republics? The simple (but somewhat misleading) answer would be those who could afford the price of a car. Expressing the conventional wisdom among Western commentators, John Kramer noted in 1976 that prices were "deliberately set to preclude all but the most affluent from acquiring automobiles."[100] Thus, at R 5,500 a VAZ-2101 (Zhiguli) from 1973 cost the equivalent of 3.5 times the average annual wage of a Soviet worker, while the price of a Moskvich-2140 in 1977 represented "twenty months earnings for an average family with two income earners." There appears to have been little change in these equivalencies at least for the remainder of the Brezhnev years.[101] What made these administratively set prices such an effective mechanism for limiting the purchase of cars was the requirement of a 25 percent down payment at the time of order and the balance paid in cash on delivery. In surveys from 1978 and 1983, car purchasers reported that it took them an average of eight years to save up enough to buy a new car.[102]

Much of this time would have been spent waiting for the car's delivery after the initial down payment. That is, a second limit to the deal that the

Table 6.4. Density of automobile ownership
by Union Republic

Union Republic	cars/1,000 people	
	1977	1985
USSR	26	45
Estonia	61	96
Lithuania	50	93
Latvia	45	81
Georgia	35	71
Armenia	32	56
Turkmenistan	24	46
RSFSR	21	44
Ukraine	21	46
Belorussia	21	39
Kazakhstan	21	39
Azerbaijan	18	30
Kirgizia	17	34
Uzbekistan	16	36
Tajikistan	14	35
Moldavia	14	33

Sources: William Pyle, "Private Car Ownership
and Second Economy Activity," Berkeley-Duke Occasional Papers on the Second Economy in the USSR,
no. 37 (1993), 49, and A. Arrak, "Ispol'zovanie avtomobilei lichnogo pol'zovaniia," Voprosy ekonomiki,
no. 7 (1978): 134 (for 1977); Izvestiia, Aug. 14, 1988:
3 (for 1985).

state offered was the delay that owners often faced before taking possession
of their cars. Waits were legendarily long, sometimes ten years, but usually
in the range of four to six.[103] During that period, the organization or institution through which aspirant owners placed orders might have its priority
in the queue lowered or raised, off-the-books arrangements might be made
concerning the equipment (though rarely the color) of the car, and deliv-
erers could accept bribes for queue jumping. Moreover, it was well known
that "members of 'elite' groups...receive special consideration in the allocation of cars." Aside from high-ranking party officials, these groups included
members of prestigious organizations such as the Academy of Sciences and
the Writers' Union; industrial executives; outstanding artists, actors, professional athletes, and other recipients of honors and medals; and disabled veterans of World War II.[104]

One could buy a used car through state-run commission shops (kommissi-
onye magaziny), but here, too, the system effectively limited their purchase.
The shops set prices and charged a service fee of 7 percent.[105] Prices were
set at high levels, though often not as high as those that sellers informally
established with prospective buyers who agreed to pay the difference "on the
side" (na levo).[106] Consequently, the actual price paid for a used car "was often

higher than the price at which it had originally been sold," notwithstanding depreciation.[107] This situation—which in a sense reflected both desire and demand—appears to have been systemic in Communist Eastern Europe.[108]

In class terms, 58 percent of car owners in a 1983 survey were described as "people with occupations involving primarily mental labor," 35 percent were workers (evidently both industrial and agricultural), and the remaining 7 percent consisted of pensioners, students, the handicapped, and others listed as not employed.[109] The overrepresentation of people in the first category is noteworthy, as "intelligentsia" accounted for only some 15 percent of the total population according to the 1979 census.[110] Class differences loomed large not only with respect to actual ownership but also aspirations, judging from a study carried out in the Azerbaijani city of Lenkoran and reported in the leading Soviet journal of sociological research. The study found that only 4.4 percent of state-farm workers owned a car, compared with 12 percent of industrial and building workers, and 11.5 percent of "intelligentsia and office workers." More significant, 18.3 percent of state-farm workers "want[ed] to acquire" a car, compared with 28.9 percent of industrial and building workers and 41 percent of intelligentsia and office workers. Whereas a car topped the list of items desired by intellectual workers, it ranked second among industrial workers' desires and fourth among state-farm workers.[111]

Consumer choice was not something in which the Soviet "dictatorship over needs" excelled.[112] Nevertheless, researchers at the All-Union Scientific Research Institute for the Study of Consumer Demand did seek to discover preferences for specific models of cars among different occupational groups. It turned out that as of 1974 "engineering-technical and scientific workers" preferred the VAZ-2103, teachers and doctors were inclined toward the Moskvich-427, and pensioners were at opposite ends of the price and prestige spectrum in their preferences for the Zaporozhets-968 and the Volga-24.[113]

Anecdotal evidence suggests a considerable degree of status-consciousness about models. When the writer Vladimir Voinovich announced to a hotel clerk in Minsk that his car was a Zaporozhets, he was met with a scowl, because while "others may not,...a clerk in a good hotel knows that important people never drive anything less than a Zhiguli." Policemen also made distinctions, knowing that they could "always squeeze a ruble out of the driver of a Zaporozhets," had "to be more polite with the driver of a Zhiguli," should leave Volga drivers alone, and were expected to salute Chaika and ZIL limousines.[114] Foreign cars were clear markers of "high *klass.*"[115] And why not, when none other than Leonid Ilych Brezhnev himself was reputed to have a "private stable of more than a dozen fast and expensive cars" including two Rolls-Royces, a Cadillac, a Mercedes-Benz, and a Citroën. "When I am at the wheel," Brezhnev told an interviewer in 1971, "I have the impression that nothing can happen"—surely the ideal situation for the party's general secretary.[116]

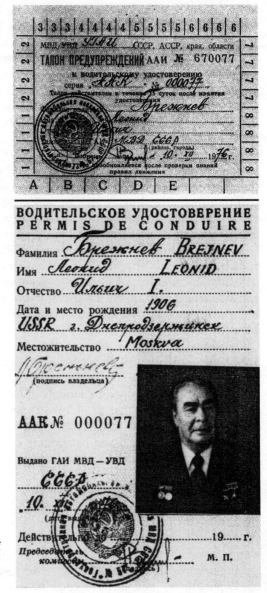

Leonid Ilych Brezhnev himself was reputed to have a "private stable of more than a dozen fast and expensive cars." Photocopy of Brezhnev's license.

Driving a Faustian Bargain

Back from a car trip in the summer of 1966 that took him from Volgograd to Moscow, A. Druzenko, a special correspondent to *Izvestiia,* contrasted railroads "with their signaling systems, stations, restaurants, snack bars, kiosks, medical stations, and so forth" to the "almost empty" highways he encountered. Whereas Hans Koningsberger's experience of these "roads of

Gogol" would provoke him to wax nostalgic, they had the opposite effect on Druzenko. He envisioned a time when "on both sides of the road would gleam comfortable STOs [service stations], gasoline dispensers, cafes, hotels of concrete and glass....Round the clock technical service would be available. Billboards would stand along the roadside brightening the night with their neon glow. At the entrance to the city you would be able to familiarize yourself with its detailed plan and list of sights."[117]

Unfortunately for Druzenko and other motorists who shared his dream, the bargain that the Soviet government struck with them did not include anything more (and usually meant much less) than the most rudimentary of services. Driving and maintaining a car in the Soviet Union thus ironically involved more individual initiative and risk-taking behavior than in the capitalist West. The fear that cars, cars, and more cars would activate individualistic tendencies at odds with "the nature of our society, and the principles and norms of our moral system" turned out to be justified, though not necessarily because individual car owners reveled in the experience of owning a car.[118]

"In Russia," wrote the authors of a book on global "automania," "they say that owning a car brings joy twice in an owner's life—when it is bought and when it is sold. In between there is only torture."[119] It wasn't that the cars were badly built. After all, the Fiat-124 was European Car of the Year when

A gas station on the Moscow River. Author's photograph.

it was introduced in 1966, and even if the Lada's reputation abroad suffered because of its cheapness and no-frills interiors, mechanically it had little to apologize for.[120] The problem was not so much the cars themselves but rather the lack of infrastructure to support them. If the Soviet economy was a shortage economy by design, then the automotive sector was designed very well. In 1963, there were some seventy thousand individually owned cars in Moscow and all of eight STOs; by 1980, the number of service stations had increased to thirteen, but the number of cars had risen to an estimated 250,000.[121] One could buy auto parts at special stores of which in 1968 Moscow boasted thirty-one and Leningrad twenty-one. Still, three quarters of respondents to a national survey of automobile enthusiasts cited the lack of spare parts among the difficulties associated with using their cars.[122] Fourteen years later, in 1982, "more than" 160 car parts were reported to be in short supply (*defitsitnye*).[123] Gas stations were not numerous either: in 1977 about five thousand (of which thirty-five hundred were fixed and fifteen hundred were trucks dispensing fuel in rural areas) served nearly six million privately owned cars. In many parts of the country gas was rationed, limiting travel within a radius of no more than 250 kilometers.[124] Finally, most urban housing projects continued to ignore drivers' need to store a car over the winter or simply park it overnight; in Moscow, for example, only three out of ten private cars were so accommodated in 1973.[125]

Why was the bargain the state offered to car owners so limited? Why were they so ill served? It wasn't for lack of awareness of their needs. From 1973 there existed an All-Union Voluntary Society of Auto Enthusiasts (VDOAM) that registered more than two million members by its second congress in 1978. Institutes devoted to the study of automobiles and related transportation issues abounded. Articles by researchers specializing in such issues appeared regularly in sociological journals. Newspapers carried exposés by special correspondents and letters from irate drivers. The *Literary Gazette,* a weekly closely identified with an intelligentsia readership, organized "auto-club debate sessions" to deal with the "problems of automobilization." And there was *Behind the Wheel,* the popular magazine for automobile enthusiasts whose print run exceeded two million by 1972. Not for lack of articulate lobbying did automobilists suffer.

The problem was "the bureaucratic maze"—Moshe Lewin's term for the Soviet system in which the Communist Party functioned as "one agency among others" (albeit as the administration's "linchpin") and the modus operandi was "bargaining with the ministries." Such a system—or lack of a system—made it virtually impossible to carry through a significant shift of priorities or resources because other units could nullify action that had the potential to adversely affect them. Each employed an army of "pushers" (*tolkachi*) who competed for the attention of officials from "the engine of the economic system," the State Committee for Material and Technical Supplies (Gossnab). And when they did not get their way, as was often the case, they employed "all sorts of devices and practices and an independent supply-cum-marketing system" that "acquired a life of its own."[126] The result was, as Mikhail Gorbachev famously put it, stagnation.

These trends impacted automobiles with particular force because of the disequilibria between the rapidly increasing numbers of privately owned cars and the inadequate provision and poor quality of spare parts. The relevant Union ministries—of automobile transport, construction, industrial construction, automobile production—did not lack for plans to supply parts and service. VAZ developed plans for its own network of centers and stations—modeled on Fiat—to service the Zhiguli.[127] But somehow, securing the land on which such centers would be built, the materials needed to build them, the parts to be produced in the requisite sizes and quantities, the staffing of the centers with adequately trained mechanics—none of these could keep pace with the rapidly increasing numbers of cars on the road or waiting to be fixed. Everything—from brake drums, to seat belts, to cement for more and safer roads, to the bricks, reinforced concrete, and steel for garages, not to mention the service centers themselves—was in short supply.[128]

Did this mean that, although minuscule by U.S. and Western European standards, the density of individually owned cars in the Soviet Union was "hypertrophic" compared with service and repair capacities? It certainly seemed so judging from a 1969 memo sent by the RSFSR's minister of automobile transport to that republic's State Planning Commission (Gosplan). Service stations in many cities, the minister reported, "are little more than primitive [*kustarnye*] workshops. Besides servicing transport some undertake the repair of washing machines, refrigerators, sewing machines, and other household items"—after all, the stations were part of the distribution system controlled by the Ministry of Housing Services.[129]

Things were looking up, though. "If today our stations have only 800 technical service bays, then by 1976 their number will increase to 4,850," the director of the RSFSR's network of service stations promised in 1971. "The supply of parts is increasing every year," car owners were assured by the republic's minister of automobile transport in May 1973. We will double the number of auto service centers and increase by one-and-a-half times the number of technical service stations during the Tenth Five-Year Plan (1976–80), promised VAZ's technical service director in 1976. "By 1983 or 1984 the capacity of auto technical service centers will more or less correspond to demand," a Gosplan official predicted in 1978.[130] Nevertheless, as of 1982 it came closer to "a little more than 30%, and for parts, 35–40%."[131] Little wonder that drivers routinely removed their windshield wipers and often their sideview mirrors when leaving their car overnight or that an English-language guide for foreign motorists recommended doing so "because otherwise there is a chance that someone may fancy them as souvenirs."[132]

So what was a Soviet automobilist to do? Here we come to the heart of the matter and at least one way in which a car was like a refrigerator or television. Owners could either take care of the problem themselves or pay someone working on the side. Admitting that the figures were probably underestimates, one source in 1978 claimed that 30 percent of owners serviced their own cars and another 14 percent relied on the services of a friend or paid someone. One or the other or both of these percentages would have risen thereafter, for reliance on the state's network of service stations was reported to have declined quite markedly between 1977 and 1982.[133] Whether relying on one's own technical skills or those of someone else, the parts used in the process were likely to have fallen off the back of the state's trucks and thence into "private hands."[134]

What was true of spare parts was even more the case with fuel. The paucity of legally obtainable supplies of gasoline and the ease with which truck drivers were able to pad their distance and haulage reports combined to make the coupons distributed to truck drivers readily marketable items. The cooperation of gas-station attendants in this business was often necessary and apparently widespread. The estimated amount of gasoline thereby obtained by car owners was an astonishing 7.5 billion liters, worth R 2.4 billion in official prices in 1984. This second-economy phenomenon was so large as to dwarf its legal first-economy equivalent.[135]

Indeed, in many ways the state accommodated to this illegal activity. "Car owners," averred a participant in a roundtable discussion among sociologists and automotive experts in 1981, "involuntarily are compelled to raise their own technical culture, which can be considered a positive development."[136]

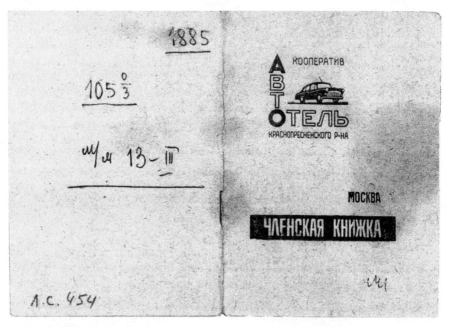

Membership book to Auto Hotel cooperative, Krasnopresensk District, Moscow, 1968. Membership entitled one to space in the cooperative's garage. In author's possession.

But many owners lacked the time or wherewithal to do repair work, as in the stereotypical case of the professor of physics who turned to the likes of "Uncle Vasia," the pensioner who fixed cars in his spare time.[137] The Uncle Vasias may not have been to the liking of upstanding Soviet citizens, but they were absolutely essential, and were among the tradespeople (*kustarno-remeslenniki*) whose trades were listed as legal in a commentary on Article 17 of the 1977 Constitution.[138]

One concession led to another. Whether owners fixed their cars themselves or hired the services of a mechanic, space was needed to make the repairs and store the cars. What had offended apartment bloc residents' aesthetic sensibilities in the 1960s—cars scattered around courtyards, stored in rusting metal sheds, or up on blocks and covered by tarpaulins like bodies awaiting burial—became nearly ubiquitous in subsequent decades. Garage space and the cooperatives that enabled people to obtain it entered into novels, movies, and the courts, demonstrating how cars sucked into their orbit the neighbors, relatives, and workmates of motorists.[139] The worst fears of ideologues from the now bygone era of Khrushchev were realized when it became apparent that people talked of little else but their cars, their cars' troubles, and where they could get them fixed. The protagonist of a short story from the mid-1980s sighs:

> Everything changed. Automobiles began to weigh on the brain. Take the newspaper—they write only about cars. Turn on the television—they show only auto factories....We gather for March 8 [International Women's Day], but do you think we talk about women? The men smack their lips and even before swallowing their food continue a conversation about changes in traffic regulations....At work it's worse. I go out to smoke and socialize. Start a conversation about chess or football. No sir! They talk, gesticulate, and argue about brakes, coasting, the technical inspection....I start to tell Ivan Burov in confidence that Mariia Petrovna from the technical department has put on weight regardless of the lack of a husband, and he says, "Maybe she's got wheels so that she can find a husband."[140]

And so...

Car ownership thus tended to divert time and attention away from social functions and responsibilities. How much time? According to questionnaire data from 1977, owners reportedly averaged 162 hours per year looking after their cars, or about a half hour a day.[141] As the number of car owners increased, approaching eight million by 1985, so did the time they aggregately spent filling up the tank, obtaining and changing oil and spark plugs, performing minor mechanical repairs, and engaging in other unmediated "man-machine" tasks. Those who lived in parts of the country where the winters are severe but who nonetheless drove cars all year round had to put in extra time round the clock. As one informant put it, "I had to warm up the car before going to sleep, get up at 4 a.m. to do it again and once more at 8, just like feeding a baby." Such activities were essentially private in the double sense of being at the discretion of the individual performing the tasks and of a particularistic as opposed to collective nature.[142]

Not all the time that motorists spent with their cars, however, was spent alone. Car maintenance and repair often involved social—or more precisely, homosocial—interaction. Surely one of the unintended, though in retrospect not surprising, consequences of the bargain the state struck with car owners was that it provided an additional opportunity for male bonding. Beginning with after-school automobile circles organized by the Komsomol and continuing into the army, adolescent boys and young men learned the basics of auto mechanics and driving skills, bonding not only with the machines but with their peers in what one ethnographer has called "technical masculine sociability."[143] Those 162 hours a year generally were not spent with one's spouse or sweetheart but rather, if with anyone, with mechanics like "Uncle Vasia," parts suppliers, or fellow car owners—all of whom tended to be men. In a society where public information was plentiful—except for the kind that consumers most wanted—one discovered the location of a given consumer item most readily by word of mouth. If foodstuffs and furnishings were the province of women, then items related to cars tended to be male terrain.

Courtyards, alleys, roadsides, and fields, previously gender-neutral spaces, were appropriated for the predominantly masculine activities of car work and car talk. The interiors of parked cars served as alternative living rooms for men seeking privacy or a place to withdraw after a row with their wives.[144] Garages, furnished with old chairs, and perhaps a heater and a cot, became sites of celebration—places to drink vodka and consume sausage and pickles. As they learned car mechanics, sons were initiated into these rites. Recently, a woman from Murmansk—where the garages are known as "seashells"— told a BBC reporter that "behind all these doors, inside all these garages without windows, there is so much going on, like it's a secret society."[145]

Faust enters into the bargain because in mass-producing cars and allocating most of them to the "population" the Soviet state virtually guaranteed that millions of its citizens would become entangled in webs of essentially private relations that were ideologically alien and often in violation of Soviet laws. Thus, ideological strictures (against promoting personal autonomy and encouraging materialistic values) that had contributed to the lack of infrastructure ironically drove car owners to enter into and expand the private sector, which in turn should have heightened ideologically based concerns. Instead, consistent with what else we know about the last years of the Brezhnev era, the state threw in the towel. Ideological strictures ultimately proved no match for the appeal of a heated underground garage and other accouterments of the automotive age.[146]

But like Osinskii's and Agapov's dreams from another era, this dream would never be realized. For the overwhelming majority of car owners, the stories told to me by two Muscovites with a lot of automotive experience were immediately recognizable. We shall call them by their nicknames, Sasha and

Vadim. Sasha, the younger of the two, was born in 1960. At age twelve he joined an "automobile circle" (*avtokruzhok*) at the local Palace of Culture. These circles, also known as clubs of young automobilists, were among the most popular activities for adolescent boys. They gave kids the opportunity to sit behind the wheel, put a car in gear, and even drive under controlled conditions with adult supervision. Sasha went to a military school where he hoped to become a helicopter pilot but instead learned car mechanics. After turning eighteen, he received a license and began a career as a truck driver attached to the auto depot of the All-Union Central Council of Trade Unions. During the 1980s he owned three cars: a 1976 Zhiguli (VAZ-2103), which he bought for R 7,600 from a commission store in 1983 with help from his parents and in-laws; a brand-new 1986 Moskvich-2141; and a Samara 2108 ("Vosmërka"), also a 1986 model.

His first car needed a lot of repairs, but as Sasha put it, "first car, first love." To obtain parts, he used to travel to a site off the MKAD (the Moscow Ring Road) near the Dmitriev Highway. There, at 1 or 2 a.m., flashlight in hand, he would choose among parts displayed on the ground by illicit suppliers. A less expensive alternative was to drive some twenty-five kilometers out on the Warsaw Highway to a six-story building selling VAZ parts. The problem with this store was that it frequently ran out of parts, a situation its director variously attributed to suppliers incorrectly predicting demand, drivers buying up "everything that their eyes fall upon" out of fear they will not be available when needed, and small-time secondhand dealers "who will stop at nothing."[147] Such stores hardly existed for Moskviches, which was unfortunate because Sasha's was "a nightmare"—the rearview mirror had been mounted upside down, fifth gear occasionally slipped into neutral, grease would pour out from below the dashboard onto the floor, and fuel leaked all over the engine and eventually the body of the car. As for the Samara, Sasha put three hundred thousand kilometers on it.[148]

Vadim, who is some ten years older than Sasha, acquired his first car in 1978. It was a Zhiguli, as were the other three he was to buy, all secondhand. "I had no choice, really," he told me one evening over the phone from his home in California. "A Volga was too expensive, the Moskvich was of low quality, and a Zaporozhets, well, that was no car at all."

"Why so many cars in just a few years?" I asked.

"The reliability of a car went down after three or four years. You find yourself going to the repair shop every other week, and that often meant taking the car to the other side of the city. And you never knew what kind of crap they would install."

Vadim bought his first car from someone who was planning to emigrate and needed dollars. Vadim's mother, who by this time lived in the United States, paid a relative of the guy $800. The car was about three years old and already had a "rough bottom," meaning it was rusted. Vadim kept it for two years. His second car was a hatchback for which the official price in the commission store was R 7,700, but he paid the owner R 9,000. Sure enough, after two or three years, that car wasn't worth maintaining either. The third car was bought from the widow of a veteran who lived in the building. After her husband died, she had little use for the car, never having learned to drive. Vadim helped her get theater tickets from time to time.

> Several years later I decided to sell it, but first it needed a paint job. I had to go to Iaroslavl' [a distance of over 200 km] to get it painted. I spent the whole day there at the shop and was totally ignored. The system was humiliating. If you don't know anybody, nobody will give you service. You had to make some- one's acquaintance, which I eventually did. I found a guy in Moscow who worked in Iaroslavl' who agreed to paint the fucking car. Two whole months went by. On the day I was supposed to pick it up, I went by train very early in the morning. When I arrived I discovered the car had not been reassembled. "No worries" (*nichego strashnogo*). Just wait, I was told. I waited the whole day. When the technical station was about to close, I nearly cried.
>
> "Why are you doing this to me? I've been here the whole day," I said.
>
> The guy took pity on me and stayed after closing time to assemble the car. I paid him, got in, and turned the ignition. The battery was dead. [Vadim then scrounged around Iaroslavl' to find and install a battery.] I got home at one in the morning. It was one of the worst days of my life. I had to keep one hand on the wheel and the other holding my eyes open as I drove. I'll never forget it. It was more than twenty years ago, but I'll never forget it.[149]

Why put up with such misery? If owning a car was such "torture," why tor- ture oneself? I already have referred to male bonding, but there was more to it than that. Judging from Muscovite drivers' well-earned reputation for aggres- siveness and disregard for seat belts, one might think it was to assert oneself and defy authority (and death too).[150] For Sasha it had to do with "mobility," feeding the family from the garden surrounding the dacha that was difficult to get to without a car. For Vadim it was a combination of "convenience" and "prestige," and also "a chance to earn some extra cash in the evening" when he turned the car into a taxi. That stratagem was no certain thing, as occa- sionally he would give rides to drunks who threw up on the upholstery and "students" who, after being taken to their destination, claimed they didn't have the money to pay the agreed upon fare. But there also were more pleas- ant encounters.

Sasha's and Vadim's accounts encompassed the years of perestroika, al- though neither mentioned any change—for better or for worse—associated with Gorbachev's reforms. What *did* change was a result of Gorbachev's other guiding principle—glasnost. Published accounts by hapless motorists of treatment at the hands of STOs now became more graphic. A. Krasiukov wrote from Saratov, for example, that after waiting several weeks for body- work to be done on his car, he was informed that the needed color for the paint job was not in stock and the car would have to be sent to another shop. After the car was returned, assembly and reupholstering took another three weeks. "It would seem that finally I would be happy," he wrote, "but that was not so. I discovered a mass of defects and things not done [*nedodelok*]. On top of that, the switch to the emergency light, the weather-stripping in the trunk, and the fuel cap had been stolen." After repeated entreaties to the STO, "some things were replaced, some things were fixed, and some things still have not been done. I don't have sufficient words to describe the frayed nerves, time, and additional means all this cost me. The STO must be held accountable before the client for the period of the work and its quality."[151]

Then, there was twenty-seven-year old Andrei Aksenov, a photographer from Arkhangel'sk who decided to go on a hunger strike in protest against the arbitrariness and red tape of that city's STO. Having waited for three months for bodywork to his Zhiguli, he declared, "Until my car is repaired I will not go home or eat any food." In this case at least, things ended well. The director announced that Aksenov's car would be ready by Friday. But, as *Izvestiia*'s correspondent noted, there was no guarantee such a tactic would work again.[152]

Car owners were far from unique in resorting to other means because they needed services that the Soviet state was not providing. The list of second-economy activities and favors exchanged is a long one: residents of apartments and dachas requiring materials for or repairs to refrigerators and washing machines, parents seeking to enhance their children's educational credentials, patients needing medicine. Many of these transactions predated the advent of mass car ownership and probably involved larger numbers of people. All eroded the state's dictatorship over needs and mitigated the inadequacies and inconveniences associated with the planned economy. Perhaps, though, it is because the ownership and use of automobiles impinged on so many others in so many ways that cars, cars, and more cars seem to have played a particularly large and invidious role in popular disillusionment with Soviet socialism.

conclusion

Only in a car can one experience Moscow's recent post-modernity.
RICHARD LEAMAN, *Autopia*

In 1990, with the Soviet Union on the brink of collapse, its auto factories turned out just under two million vehicles—1.2 million cars and 780,000 trucks. These figures were below levels ten years earlier although they still made the USSR the world's eighth largest car producer and fourth largest producer of trucks. In that same year R. M. Gasanov, a Soviet journalist whose previous work had taken him into the realm of industrial espionage, published a book on the "favorite child of the century"—the automobile. Gasanov's book ranged far and wide over the globe to present a lot of data on automobile companies, and included attractive illustrations of all manner of cars—conventional, luxury, racing, experimental, prototypical. It also contained the following assessment of Soviet automobiles in comparison with those from the rest of the world:

> While over there they made automobiles and flexible production systems, we put the emphasis on organizing ministries and departments. They created work, while we tried to cultivate "the new man." They paid for good work and we roused the enthusiasm of the people. They bought raw materials and produced cars, we sold raw material and bought auto factories. They attracted talent and we obstinately rejected it, seeing it as heterodox. Over there, experts congregated; over here, members of party committees congregated. There, people were chosen according to the task and their capabilities; over here, by questionnaire.

Gasanov then described the inevitable consequences:

> Over there, the automobile became a mode of transportation; over here, a symbol of knowing how to live, namely, by working as little as possible and consuming as much as possible. Our raptures about our social order led us to the

point where we lagged behind the level of development of the auto industry in the rest of the world, and now can only dream of catching up. The fantasy of how smartly, quickly, and in such a revolutionary manner we would bypass them has led to nothing but still greater backwardness.[1]

Recalling Petr Chadaaev's indictment from 1829 of a Russia that did "not seem to be an integral part of the human race," the contrasts Gasanov drew between "over here" and "over there" have a certain brutal simplicity. They reflected the disillusionment and even despair of the Soviet Union's last years, speaking in particular to the frustrations of actual and would-be motorists who had become acutely aware—thanks to glasnost—of the limitations of Soviet automobility. It mattered little that in reality things were not quite so great "over there" either. In their desire to liberate themselves, Soviet citizens scarcely noticed that the vaunted "flexible production systems" of the West were inspiring books that included "roadblock," "decline," "death," and "fatal" in their titles.[2] Nor did the global environmental costs of ever-greater automobile dependence seem to impinge on them.[3]

Not for the first time, the determination to catch up to and overtake created a dynamic that proved as seductive as it was destructive. Cars became ubiquitous in post-Soviet Russia but nowhere so much as in Moscow where sidewalks were transformed into instant parking lots and traffic into and out

Outbound traffic on Prospekt Vernadskogo, Moscow, 2005. Author's photograph.

of the city center soon acquired legendary proportions. And no wonder when the number of registered automobiles—estimated to have been about six hundred thousand at the time of the Soviet Union's collapse in 1991—reached 3.5 million in 2006 without the slightest indication that the upward trajectory would tail off.[4] Ads for cars appeared everywhere. An enormous Mercedes logo was erected on top of the House on the Embankment, the former residence of the Soviet elite located across the Moscow River from the Kremlin. Huge banners with giant images of BMWs and Daewoos extended across building sites. Automobile magazines in both print and online versions advertise, evaluate, and offer advice on every imaginable auto-related product and service. Autos have changed what people buy, where they shop, what they see, and where they live. Large warehouse stores—of which IKEA was one of the first—have sprung up on the outskirts, requiring all but the most intrepid to use a car to shop at them. Streetscapes have been transformed by neon-lit signs large enough for a motorist to read in the seconds it takes to pass them on the way out to his or her "kottedzh."

Outside Moscow the changes have been somewhat less dramatic, although the extent of highway construction has been impressive. By 2002, the total

Mercedes-Benz logo on the House on the Embankment opposite the Kremlin with a beat-up Lada in the foreground, Moscow, 2003. Author's photograph.

BMW advertisement draped across the venerable Hotel Moskva while it was being torn down, 2003. Author's photograph.

length of paved roads in the Russian Federation reached 759,000 kilometers, nearly three times the amount reported in 1990. Thanks in part to funding from the European Bank for Reconstruction and Development, the Chita–Khabarovsk highway, a project begun way back in 1978, was opened in February 2004. It is intended to be a section of the Moscow–Vladivostok highway, which—when completed in 2008—will be the largest continuous hard-surfaced road in the world.[5] If in Soviet times the nostrum was that cars built roads, one could say that at the start of the twenty-first century oil and gas are the primary engines of road building. The same natural resource boom has also produced enough wealth to fuel an ever-expanding market for cars.

Car ownership in Russia, which stood at 75 per thousand inhabitants in 1993, reached 150 ten years later. The total number of cars was approximately 11 million in 1992, surpassed 20 million by 2000, and reached 25 million in 2003. Forecasts in 2002 put new car sales rising from 1.5 million in 2003 to more than 1.75 million by 2007. Already in 2005, car sales exceeded 1.8 million. Lada (the classic Zhiguli, Samara, and 110–112 models) remained the largest-selling brand throughout the 1990s and into the first decade of the twenty-first century with a market share hovering around 40 percent. The number of imported cars—many of them circumventing import duties—grew from a few thousand in 1992 to over half a million in 2002. While German models poured in across the western borders and at ports, Japanese second-hand cars reigned supreme east of the Urals. At the same

Moscow parking, 2005. Author's photograph.

time, foreign companies began setting up operations in Russia. In 2003, about fifty thousand Russian-produced or assembled foreign cars were sold in the country.[6] Among assembly facilities, the Avtotor operation in Kaliningrad (the Russian enclave on the Baltic between Poland and Lithuania) has been particularly successful in attracting kits from foreign manufacturers. KIA was first, followed by BMW, but more recently General Motors has supplied Cadillacs, four different Chevrolet models, and the H2 and H3 Hummers that sell well in Moscow. Ford has a production facility outside St. Petersburg that turns out its Focus and Mondeo models, but in June 2005 Toyota broke ground for a factory in the vicinity, Volkswagen found a site for an assembly plant in the Kaluga region, and Daimler-Benz indicated its intention of building one soon.[7]

The explosion in the number of cars has led to a significant increase in the number of road fatalities. The 29,468 road deaths recorded in 1996 translated into 20 fatalities per 100,000 people. The only country in the former Soviet bloc with a higher rate was Latvia at 22.1. By comparison, the United States's rate was 15.8, Italy's was 10.8, and the UK's was 6.1. According to another measure—road deaths per 10,000 motor vehicles—the most dangerous country in the former Soviet bloc was Kyrgyzstan where the rate was 41.4. Russia with a rate of 14.3 was below Azerbaijan and Kazakhstan and just above Latvia. More recent data from 2003 show that not only did the number of road deaths increase to 35,600 but so did the per capita fatality rate, which reached 24.77. Explanations vary from the poor condition of all those Ladas and "old cars imported from western Europe" to poor road infrastructure, the police's lack of equipment to enforce speeding controls, and "aggressive driver behavior."[8] Ehrenburg if not Maklakov would have understood.

Through it all, the Soviet automobile survived and lives still. Beaten-up Zhigulis and Moskviches clog courtyards, especially in outer, less posh districts of Moscow and other major cities. They course around the major thoroughfares trying to avoid being run off the road by bigger, more powerful vehicles and appear as wrecks on TV news segments reporting on "accidents." Occasionally, it is possible to spot a Chaika, and not only in auto museums. One year President Putin takes the U.S. president for a spin in his 1956 Volga; the next, he shows off a '72 Zaporozhets, the first car he ever owned. The Soviet automobile survives metaphorically too. When the right-wing Liberal Democratic Party gained seats in the 2003 Duma elections at the expense of other more moderate parties, its leader, Vladimir Zhirinovsky, chortled that "parties like SPS [Union of Right Forces] and Yabloko could work in small countries, like the Baltic countries or the Czech Republic. But Russia is a KamAZ truck, and SPS and Yabloko want it to be a Mercedes. A Mercedes does not drive on our roads." Zhirinovsky was tapping into a vein of popular humor that pits the Mercedes against the Zaporozhets. In every encounter, the Zapor (the quintessence of Soviet consumer [dis]comfort) bests the haughty representative of Western capitalism.

As for KamAZ trucks, on August 19, 2003 (twelve years to the day after the abortive coup against the Gorbachev government), a bomb exploded outside the UN headquarters in Baghdad claiming among its twenty casualties the UN's top official in Iraq. According to the FBI agent on the scene, the bomb had been placed in a vehicle that was a "Soviet-made military flatbed truck known as a Kamaz." How did he know the truck was "Soviet-made," that is, more than twelve years old? Never mind. Thanks to the Internet, the entire world learned that the truck was Soviet, for agent Fuentes's diagnosis was picked up and reported without commentary or correction by virtually every online news service, including Russian ones.[9] For how much longer, though, will Soviet vehicles—real and imagined—survive?

notes

Introduction

1. Victoria de Grazia, *Irresistible Empire: America's Advance through Twentieth-Century Europe* (Cambridge: Harvard University Press, 2005), 78–81. On Ford's European operations, see Mira Wilkins and Frank Ernest Hill, *American Business Abroad: Ford on Six Continents* (Detroit: Wayne State University Press, 1964), and Hubert Bonin, Yannick Lung, and Steven Tolliday, eds., *Ford: The European History, 1903–2003,* 2 vols. (Paris: Editions P.L.A.G.E., 2003).

2. de Grazia, *Irresistible,* 91.

3. *Ekonomicheskaia Zhizn',* Nov. 1, 1931, 3; *Pravda,* Oct. 1, 1931, 1; *Cleveland Press,* Apr. 25, 1931, 16; *New York Evening Post,* Nov. 19, 1930, 1–2; *Detroit News,* June 25, 2001. For other references to "Detroit on the Volga," see Bruno Abescat, "Les ouvriers de la Volga," *L'Express,* Mar. 23, 2000; and the interview from July 27, 2001, with Konstantin Titov, governor of Samara Oblast, on his website, www.titov.samara.ru/en/interview/ (accessed 10.16.05).

4. Joe Kerr, "Trouble in Motor City," in *Autopia, Cars and Culture,* ed. Peter Wollen and Joe Kerr (London: Reaktion Books, 2002), 126. "Implacable assembly lines" is from de Grazia, *Irresistible,* 233. See also Terry Smith, *Making the Modern: Industry, Art, and Design in America* (Chicago: University of Chicago Press, 1993), 15–55.

5. For citations, see Alan M. Ball, *Imagining America: Influence and Images in Twentieth-Century Russia* (Lanham, Md.: Rowman and Littlefield, 2003), 51. See also Boris Shpotov, "Ford in Russia, from 1909 to World War II," in *Ford: The European History,* 2:505–29.

6. For an analysis of the popular science literature, see James T. Andrews, *Science for the Masses: The Bolshevik State, Public Science, and the Popular Imagination in Soviet Russia, 1917–1934* (College Station: Texas A & M University Press, 2003), 39–118.

7. Mary Nolan, *Visions of Modernity: American Business and the Modernization of Germany* (Oxford: Oxford University Press, 1994), 39–42, 91–92. See also Charles Maier, "Between Taylorism and Technocracy: European Ideologies and the Vision of Industrial Productivity in the 1920's," *Journal of Contemporary History* 5, no. 2 (1970): 47–57.

8. Vladislav Todorov, *Red Square, Black Square: Organon for Revolutionary Imagination* (Albany: State University of New York Press, 1994), 10.

9. Socialist City was the original name of the residential district intended to accommodate workers employed at the Gor'kii Automobile Factory and their families. It also was used for other, analogous projects especially during the First Five-Year Plan (1928–32).

10. L. M. Sabsovich, *Goroda budushchego i organizatsiia sotsialisticheskogo byta* (Moscow: Gostekhizd., 1929), 42. Sabsovich estimated that it would take fifteen years to achieve socialism in the USSR. His *SSSR cherez 15 let* went through three editions in 1929. In *SSSR cherez*

10 let (Moscow: Moskovskii rabochii, 1930) he considered ten years sufficient. He also claimed that "within a very short time, cars will become a still more necessary element of work and life for us than in America" (94).

11. Cited in S. Frederick Starr, "Visionary Town Planning during the Cultural Revolution," in *Cultural Revolution in Russia, 1928–1931*, ed. Sheila Fitzpatrick (Bloomington: Indiana University Press, 1978), 214–16.

12. N. Osinskii, "Pis'mo, napisannoe 6 noiabria 1937 goda," *Prozhektor*, no. 45 (1928): 10–11. Reprinted in N. Osinskii, *Avtomobilizatsiia SSSR 1930: Stat'i, ocherki, rechi, 1927–1929* (Moscow: Gosizdat, 1930), 236–43.

13. V. Osinskii, *Itogi i perspektivy avtomobilizatsii (Rech' na I Vseukrainskom s"ezde Ukravtodor)* (Khar'kov: USSR Ukravtodor, 1929), 4, 19, 25. Osinskii usually used "N," a convention dating back to the nineteenth century, instead of a first name, but here retained the "V" (for Valerian).

14. Lewis H. Siegelbaum, "Introduction: Mapping Private Spheres in the Soviet Context," in *Borders of Socialism: Private Spheres of Soviet Russia*, ed. Lewis H. Siegelbaum (New York: Palgrave Macmillan, 2006), 4–5.

15. This was the obverse of the phenomenon discussed in Katherine Verdery, "The 'Etatization' of Time in Ceausescu's Romania," in her *What Was Socialism and What Comes Next?* (Princeton: Princeton University Press, 1996), 39–57.

16. See Steffen Böhm et al., "Part One: Conceptualizing Automobility," *Sociological Review* 54, no. 1 (2006): 1. See also the special issue on "Automobilities" of *Theory, Culture & Society* 21, nos. 4–5 (2004) with contributions by Urry and others.

17. Tim Edensor, "Automobility and National Identity: Representation, Geography, and Driving Practice," *Theory, Culture & Society* 21, nos. 4–5 (2004): 101–20 (quotation at 108).

18. *Bol'shaia sovetskaia entsiklopediia*, O. Iu. Shmidt, ed. (Moscow: Sovetskaia entsiklopediia, 1926), vol. 1:331. The third edition of the encyclopedia (1970) defines automobile as "a means of road transport with its own engine" (1:410).

Chapter 1. AMO–ZIS–ZIL–AMO-ZIL: Detroit in Moscow

1. S. V. Voronkova, "Stroitel'stvo avtomobilnykh zavodov v Rossii v gody pervoi mirovoi voiny (1914–1917 gg.)," *Istoricheskie zapiski*, no. 75 (1965): 159. The other four firms were Russian Renault, Russo-Baltic, V. A. Lebedev, and Aksai. There also were plans to build a state-owned factory in Mytishchi, near Moscow, to be supplied primarily by the British Engineering Company of Siberia (Bekos). On the war-industries committees, see Lewis H. Siegelbaum, *The Politics of Industrial Mobilization in Russia, 1915–1917: A Study of the War-Industries Committees* (New York: St. Martin's, 1983). For more on the Riabushinskiis' businesses, see V. Ia. Laverychev, *Monopolisticheskii kapital v tekstil'noi promyshlennosti, 1900–1917 gg.* (Moscow: MGU, 1963). It was Stepan Riabushinskii for whom Fedor Shekhtel designed the magnificent modernist house (1900–1902) at Malaia Nikitskaia, 6. Maxim Gor'kii resided in the house from 1932 until his death in 1936.

2. *Istoriia Moskovskogo avtozavoda imeni I. A. Likhacheva* (Moscow: Mysl', 1966), 20.

3. Tim Colton, *Moscow, Governing the Socialist Metropolis* (Cambridge: Harvard University Press, 1995), 21.

4. Colton, *Moscow*, 23, 77, 232–33; Kenneth M. Straus, *Factory and Community in Stalin's Russia: The Making of an Industrial Working Class* (Pittsburgh: University of Pittsburgh Press, 1997), 33–44; Sergei Kanunnikov, "85 let nazad v Simonovskoi slobode zalozhen zavod AMO," *Za rulëm*, no. 8 (2001): 154–55.

5. Voronkova, "Stroitel'stvo," 160–61.

6. See Major-General G. G. Krivoshein's report of July 13, 1917, to the Preparatory Commission of the Special Council on Defense in *Ekonomicheskoe polozhenie Rossii nakanune Velikoi Okt'iabrskoi sotsialisticheskoi revoliutsii, Dokumenty i materialy*, 3 vols. (Moscow: Izd. Akademii nauk SSSR, 1957), 1:387–91. See also Voronkova, "Stroitel'stvo," 162; Kanunnikov, "85 let," 155.

7. *Istoriia Moskovskogo avtozavoda*, 23–63; Tsentral'nyi Arkhiv Goroda Moskvy (TsAGM), f. 415, op. 16, d. 465 (Materials on the "events" at the AMO factory from May 3, 1917), ll. 1–9. Bondarev subsequently served under the anti-Bolshevik ataman Kaledin during the civil war. Later, he worked at the agricultural machinery giant Rostelmash and in the Main Administration of the Auto and Tractor Industry. In 1935 he returned to AMO (then, ZIS) to work in the

bureau for the reconstruction of the factory. Two years later he was arrested and soon thereafter executed. Makarovskii appears to have joined the administration at Russo-Balt before being promoted to assistant director of the Central Administration of Auto Factories. He was much decorated by the Soviet government despite his opposition to Bolshevism in 1917.

8. L. M. Shugurov, *Avtomobili Rossii i SSSR*, 3 vols. (Moscow: Prostreks, 1993–98), 1:52–54. The trucks sent to Russia are described and illustrated in *The White Service Record, a Portrayal of the Military Performance of White Trucks in the Service of the United States and Allied Nations* (Cleveland: White Co., 1919) available in the Western Reserve Historical Society Library.

9. TsAGM, f. 415, op. 16, d. 516 (Reminiscences of comrade A. V. Kuznetsov), l. 29; d. 247 (I. E. Fetkevich reminiscences from Oct. 18, 1927, and Dec. 25, 1932), l. 23. Both Kuznetsov and Fetkevich refer to lighters, but the former also mentions ploughshares. See also M. Simkhovich, *AMO v 1921–1924 gg.* (Moscow: Izd. Avtozavoda im. Stalina, 1933), 15–18; *Istoriia Moskovskogo avtozavoda*, 75–89.

10. For accounts of Moscow workers' disenchantment with the Bolsheviks as manifested in strikes, antigovernment demonstrations, and election results, see William J. Chase, *Workers, Society, and the Soviet State: Labor and Life in Moscow, 1918–1929* (Urbana: University of Illinois Press, 1987), 48–52; Richard Sakwa, *Soviet Communists in Power: A Study of Moscow during the Civil War, 1918–21* (London: Macmillan, 1988), 240–47; Jonathan Aves, *Workers against Lenin* (London: I. B. Tauris, 1996), 111–57; Simon Pirani, "The Moscow Workers' Movement in 1921 and the Role of Non-Partyism," *Europe-Asia Studies* 56, no. 1 (2004): 143–60; and Simon Pirani, "Mass Mobilization versus Mass Participation: The Bolsheviks and the Moscow Workers, 1921–22," paper presented at the convention of the American Association for the Advancement of Slavic Studies, Boston, December 2004.

11. According to Ford Motor Company records, 2,016 Russians (16% of the entire workforce) were employed at Highland Park in November 1914. Stephen Meyer, *The Five Dollar Day: Labor Management and Social Control in the Ford Motor Company, 1908–1921* (Albany: State University of New York Press, 1981), 77.

12. Information in this and the subsequent paragraph comes from the following sources: TsAGM, f. 415, op. 16, d. 516, ll. 25–28; d. 1 (Memoirs of former director of AMO, A. A. Adams), ll. 1–45; d. 477 (Protocols—letters, telegrams, 1919–24), ll. 29–31, 45; d. 593 (Materials on party organization at AMO, 1922), ll. 34–36; Simkhovich, *AMO v 1921–1924*, 5–57; *Istoriia Moskovskogo avtozavoda*, 96–100, 103–7; Vladimir Lota, "Kto Vy, polkovnik Adams?" *Sovershenno sekretno*, no. 11 (2001): 15–16.

13. See also N. Andreev, "Lenin na nashem avtozavode, iz vospominaniia rabochikh im. Stalina b. AMO," *Za rulëm*, no. 2 (1934): 8–10: "The Americans sincerely wanted to demonstrate how to work properly. But they were accustomed to conditions of mass automated processes that were worked out exactly to the finest detail." Cf. the fate of another group of Russian-American reemigrants (dubbed "all righters") who ran the Moscow Tool Factory from 1919 to late 1921 in B. Ratner, *Istoriia Moskovskogo Instrumental'nogo Zavoda* (Moscow: OGIZ, 1934), 57–82. Adams later would enjoy considerably more success in another line of work. Under the guise of running Technological Laboratories, a New York-based company, he spent a decade working for the GRU (Main Intelligence Administration) gathering information about U.S. weapons research including the atomic bomb project. He died in 1969 and was made a Hero of Russia in 1999 by a presidential order.

14. *Istoriia Moskovskogo avtozavoda*, 106–7.

15. J. V. Stalin, *Problems of Leninism* (Peking: Foreign Languages Press, 1976), 117. On Sverdlov Communist University, the "Party's flagship institution" founded in 1920, see Michael David—Fox, *Revolution of the Mind: Higher Learning among the Bolsheviks, 1918–1929* (Ithaca: Cornell University Press, 1997), 86–90, 125–27.

16. "Quite often, technological capability is emphasised as a precondition for technological progress in latecomers. . . . And it is sometimes argued that technological capability is partly an output of technological progress." Jang-Sup Shin, *The Economics of the Latecomers: Catching-up, Technology Transfer and Institutions in Germany, Japan and South Korea* (Routledge: London, 1996), 30.

17. Rossiiskii Gosudarstvennyi Arkhiv Ekonomiki (RGAE), f. 1884, op. 5, ed. kh. 43 (Correspondence with STO, industrial section of Gosplan, Sovnarkom, and other institutions on distribution to AMO of order for eight hundred three-ton White trucks and the possibility of producing 1.5 ton Fiat-type truck), ll. 12, 34, 50, 62.

18. *Istoriia Moskovskogo avtozavoda,* 114–27. Judging by the absence of storerooms in the shops and the backup at the main storeroom where "the entire job of issuing tools is put onto one person," the application of Taylorism could not have been too extensive. See *Ekonomicheskaia zhizn',* Oct. 2, 1924, quoted in Donald Filtzer, *Soviet Workers and Stalinist Industrialization: The Formation of Modern Soviet Production Relations, 1928–1941* (Armonk, N.Y.: M. E. Sharpe, 1986), 158.

19. I have borrowed "compensatory symbolism" from Scott Palmer, *Dictatorship of the Air: Aviation Culture and the Fate of Modern Russia* (New York: Cambridge University Press, 2006), 35–36.

20. On the Prombron, a modified version of the 1915 Russo-Balt S24–40, see Shugurov, *Avtomobili Rossii,* 1:53–57.

21. Ibid., 1:56–61, 74; *Motor,* no. 17–18 (1925): 316. See also *Motor,* no. 1 (1925): 5–7.

22. The underfunded Trust was absorbed by the Moscow City Soviet in 1927. For details, see RGAE, f. 2352, op. 1, d. 440 (Materials on the transfer of the Auto Trust to the Moscow Council of the National Economy), ll. 4–8.

23. *Istoriia Moskovskogo avtozavoda,* 129–37.

24. Ibid., 156.

25. For two such reports, see the memorandum cosigned by Valerii Mezhlauk and Evgenii Chudakov in RGAE, f. 2352, op. 1, ed. kh. 440, ll. 48–61, and Sorokin's "prospective plan" from Oct. 3–14, 1927, in TsAGM, f. 415, op. 16, d. 502 (Correspondence of Auto Trust with Moscow Soviet), ll. 4–38. See also the resolution of the Council of Labor and Defense from July 13, 1928 in d. 502, l. 100.

26. TsAGM, f. 415, op. 6, d. 7 (Correspondence of Auto Trust with Brandt, 1928), ll. 1–40; Tamara Leont'eva, *Likhachev* (Moscow: Molodaia gvardiia, 1979), 37, 57–58; *Istoriia Moskovskogo avtozavoda,* 142–44, 149–50. The Autocar Company was founded in 1897. After 1911 it produced only trucks. In 1932 it was bought by the White Motor Co. Its papers are deposited at the Benson Ford Research Center in Dearborn.

27. *Istoriia Moskovskogo avtozavoda,* 149–51. For an English-language draft of the contract with the Auto Trust, see RGAE, f. 7620, op. 1, d. 707 (Agreement on technical assistance), ll. 146–58.

28. TsAGM, f. 415, op. 6, d. 26 (Correspondence with American engineer Brandt, 1929), ll. 73–78, 105; d. 27, ll. 17, 21–22; d. 43 (Inquiries into pace of reconstruction and correspondence with Central Committee and Commissar of Worker-Peasant Inspection, 1930), l. 1–8; RGAE, f. 7620, op. 1, d. 707, ll. 25, 37; *Istoriia Moskovskogo avtozavoda,* 153–54.

29. *Istoriia Moskovskogo avtozavoda,* 153–54. Cf. the account in Straus, *Factory and Community,* 54–58.

30. Antony Sutton, a chief critic of Western technological assistance to the USSR (on grounds of military security), repeatedly described the enterprise as "Brandt-built" in his *Western Technology and Soviet Economic Development, 1930 to 1945* (Stanford: Hoover Institution Press, 1971), 177–79. See also Sutton, *National Suicide: Military Aid to the Soviet Union* (Melbourne: Australian League of Rights, 1973), appendix B, 258: "Who Built the ZIL Plant? The Arthur J. Brandt Company of Detroit, Michigan."

31. S. S. Khromov, ed., *Industrializatsiia sovetskogo soiuza: Novye dokumenty, novye fakty, novye podkhody,* 2 vols. (Moscow: Institut rossiiskoi istorii RAN, 1997–99), 2:252–53, 256–57.

32. On the turbulent politics of the Moscow party organization, see Catherine Merridale, *Moscow Politics and the Rise of Stalin: The Communist Party in the Capital, 1925–32* (London: Macmillan, 1990), 50–51, 55–64, 68–78, and Colton, *Moscow,* 201–9. On Ordzhonikidze as Likhachev's patron, Leont'eva, *Likhachev,* 57–58, 91–94.

33. *Rasstrel'nye spiski, Moskva 1937–1941, "Kommunarka," Bytovo: kniga pamiati zhertv politicheskikh repressii,* ed. L. S. Eremina and A. B. Roginskii (Moscow: Zven'ia, 2000), 392. Sorokin's disguise of his Jewish ethnicity was not unusual among Soviet Communists of his generation. See Yuri Slezkine, *The Jewish Century* (Princeton: Princeton University Press, 2004), 220–22, 244–45.

34. Leont'eva, *Likhachev,* 38.

35. *Pravda,* Oct. 2, 1931, 1; *Istoriia Moskovskogo avtozavoda,* 182.

36. *Pravda,* Dec. 19, 1932, 2; Oct. 2, 1931, 1 (cartoon); Oct. 18, 1932, 1 (cartoon).

37. *Pravda,* Dec. 19, 1932, 2.

38. This was a rhetorical construct that Stalin used in January 1933 with respect to the aviation industry as well. See Palmer, *Dictatorship of the Air,* 197–98.

39. Soviet factories never did catch up to Detroit's, but eventually the USSR could claim victory with respect to constituent materials and related items. By the mid-1980s it produced 80% more steel, twice as much pig iron, and five times as many tractors as the United States. The victory proved hollow, though. Economic success in the United States and other "advanced capitalist countries" had long since ceased to be measured in these terms, while the USSR simply "had failed to adapt to an economy that depended on silicone and software." Eric Hobsbawm, *The Age of Extremes: A History of the World, 1914–1991* (New York: Vintage, 1994), 247.

40. Cited in Kendall E. Bailes, *Technology and Society under Lenin and Stalin* (Princeton: Princeton University Press), 49.

41. Shugurov, *Avtomobili Rossii,* 1:79–82. *Istoriia Moskovskogo avtozavoda,* 249. Vazhinskii was shot on Mar. 6, 1938.

42. G. Z. Shmaglit, "Na stroitel'stve AMO-ZIS," in A. V. Kuznetsov et al., *Direktor: I. A. Likhachev v vospominaniiakh sovremennikov* (Moscow: Molodaia gvardiia, 1979), 116–29; Directive No. 245 from People's Commissariat of Heavy Industry, Feb. 16, 1935, in ibid., 239–40. With Likhachev entirely in charge of the project, it went more smoothly than the first reconstruction. Still, the budget he submitted to the Commissariat of Heavy Industry was judged by the commissariat's accountants to be inflated by nearly 90%, earning the director a reprimand from his patron and friend, Ordzhonikidze.

43. *Istoriia Moskovskogo avtozavoda,* 219–20.

44. TsAGM, f. 415, op. 16, d. 579 (Reminiscences of cadre workers of ZhKO, 1916–60), ll. 57–59, 73. The party's Central Committee issued a decree on May 8, 1932, to expand rabbit breeding in Moscow, Leningrad, and Ivanovo-Voznesensk oblasts, precipitating a rather "shrill" press campaign during the summer. For details, see Filtzer, *Soviet Workers and Stalinist Industrialization,* 94.

45. TsAGM, f. 415, op. 6, d. 43, l. 9; op. 16, d. 579, l. 74.

46. TsAGM, f. 415, op. 16, d. 579, ll. 82–84 (Bumbul'), 104 (V. G. Korchagin), 128–29 (Ia. E. Kaplun).

47. Shugurov, *Avtomobili Rossii,* 1:92–93. The ZIS-101 also was referred to as a Buick. See *Trud,* Oct. 30, 1933, 2. For an article on the L-1 that forecasts twenty thousand a year, see *Pravda,* May 9, 1933, 3.

48. Shugurov, *Avtomobili Rossii,* 1:93–96; Inzh. Vazhinskii, "Legkovoi avtomobil' ZIS-101," *Za rulëm,* no. 19 (1934): 14–15; Sutton, *Western Technology,* 178.

49. For an account of Stalin's visit to ZIS in July 1935 to inspect the car's motor, see Achmed Amba, *I Was Stalin's Bodyguard* (London: Frederick Muller, 1952), 188–89.

50. Shugurov, *Avtomobili Rossii,* 1:94–96; Vazhinskii, "Legkovoi avtomobil'," 14.

51. Mikhail German, *Slozhnoe proshedshee* (St. Petersburg: Iskusstvo SPb, 2000), 32–33. I thank Susan E. Reid for referring me to this source.

52. *Za rulëm,* no. 19 (1937): 3–4. The defects eventually prompted the formation of a governmental commission in June 1940 under the automobile expert and member of the Academy of Sciences, Evgenii Chudakov. It made a number of modifications. Shugurov, *Avtomobili Rossii,* 1:96.

53. Kristin Ross, *Fast Cars, Clean Bodies: Decolonization and the Reordering of French Culture* (Cambridge: MIT Press, 1996), 19.

54. *Istoriia Moskovskogo avtozavoda,* 298–320. On the installation and operations of these factories, see ibid., 335–59.

55. See Mikhail M. Gorinov, "Muscovites' Moods, 22 June 1941 to May 1942," in *The People's War: Responses to World War II in the Soviet Union,* ed. Robert Thurston and Bernd Bonwetsch (Urbana: University of Illinois Press, 2000), 108–33; "Iz vospominanii khudozhestvennogo redaktora G. V. Reshetina," in *Moskva voennaia, 1941–1945: Memuary i arkhivnye dokumenty* (Moscow: Izd-vo ob'edineniia Mosgoarkhiv, 1995), 111–12; and Gennady Andreev-Khomiakov, *Bitter Waters: Life and Work in Stalin's Russia,* trans. Ann E. Healy (Boulder: Westview, 1997), 166–84.

56. Shugurov, *Avtomobili Rossii,* 1:161–68. On UAZ and UralAZ, see respectively, "Otkrytoe Aktsionernoe Obshchestvo 'Ul'ianovskii avtomobil'nyi zavod," at http://www.uaz.ru, and "URALAZ JSC" at http://www.uralaz.ru.

57. D. Zaslavskii, "Pervenets," *Pravda,* Apr. 6, 1946, 3.

58. Ibid.; I. Likhachev, "ZIS-110 i ZIS-150," *Pravda,* Apr. 6, 1946, 3. Likhachev claimed that fuel expenditure was a full 25% less than in the ZIS-101, which would mean that the 101

was using well over thirty-two liters per one hundred kilometers. The engine required fuel with the then relatively high-octane level of seventy-four. For this and other technical details, see L. Shugurov, "Poslevoennyi pervenets," at http://www.mkmagazin.almanacehf.ru/vehicle/zis_110.htm (accessed 7.21.05).

59. *Istoriia Moskovskogo avtozavoda,* 403–10; "U sovetskikh-sobstvennaia gordost' ZIS-110," at http://www.molotovgarage.ru/histori.htm (accessed 1.13.07).

60. Michael Sedgwick, *Passenger Cars, 1924–1942* (New York: Macmillan, 1975), 165; Shugurov, *Avtomobili Rossii,* 1:185–87.

61. Not for nothing did a Podolsk-based company devoted to restoring Soviet antique automobiles entitle its capsule history of the car "The Soviet People Were Proud of Their Own ZIS-110." See note 58.

62. TsAGM, f. 415, op. 2, d. 659 (Reports from the director and inquiries on preparation and output of the ZIS-110 for 1945), ll. 35, 70–71. The memo distinguished between Moscow and "the periphery."

63. Lev Shugurov, "Zagadka sovetskogo 'Pakkarda' (Istoriia marki ZIS)," at http://www.automir.biz/articles/?art=170 (accessed 7.21.05). On Stalin's fleet, see Hedrick Smith, *The Russians* (London: Sphere Books, 1976), 48. The convertible had a more ceremonial function: from 1955 it replaced the horse in leading military parades on Red Square.

64. Slezkine, *Jewish Century,* 275. See 301–8 for data on the representation of Jews in both the "economic base" and the "ideological superstructure."

65. G. V. Kostyrchenko, *Tainaia politika Stalina: Vlast' i antisemitizm* (Moscow: Mezhdunarodnye otnosheniia, 2001), 619–26. See also Kostyrchenko, *Out of the Red Shadows: Anti-Semitism in Stalin's Russia* (Amherst, N.Y.: Prometheus Books, 1995), 226–33. For Smith's account of his visit and his characterization of its director as "a first-class production engineer," see William Bedell Smith, *My Three Years in Moscow* (Philadelphia: Lippincott, 1950), 141. It could not have helped Eidinov—or Likhachev—that Smith was appointed director of the Central Intelligence Agency in October 1950. Fitterman "sat" in Vorkuta until released in the general amnesty that followed Stalin's death in March 1953.

66. Kostyrchenko, *Tainaia politika,* 620; N. S. Khrushchev, *Vremia, Liudi, Vlast',* 4 vols. (Moscow: Moskovskie novosti, 1999) 2:30–31; Marcus Wheeler, *The Oxford Russian-English Dictionary,* ed. B. O. Unbegaun (Oxford: Clarendon Press, 1972), 324.

67. *Istoriia Moskovskogo avtozavoda,* 432, 440–42. ZIS evidently was the first Soviet factory to produce refrigerators for domestic use. Likhachev was part of a state commission that decided to proceed with refrigerator production in 1949. ZIS began production in April 1950.

68. Ibid., 441, 627. Shugurov (*Avtomobili Rossii,* 1:232) is emphatic that the ZIS-151 was "not the Soviet version of the Studebaker, International or GMC." ZIL continued to overfulfill its targets for refrigerators at least into the 1960s. It transferred bicycle production in 1959 to a separate facility in Zhukovskii, Moscow Oblast (See *Istoriia Moskovskogo avtozavoda,* 576, 499–500, and RGAE, f. 398, op. 1, d. 56, l. 74).

69. *Istoriia Moskovskogo avtozavoda,* 453–61; "Internat'l Auto Fair Closes, Changchun Dreams of Becoming China's Detroit," *People's Daily,* Aug. 30, 2001, at http://english.peopledaily.com.cn/english/200108/30/eng20010830_78811.html (accessed 1.15.07).

70. Shugurov, *Avtomobili Rossii,* 1:187 and 2:49.

71. "Autosoviet: ZIL" at http://digilander.libero.it/cuoccimix?ENGLISH-automotorusse9-G(Zil).htm (accessed 08.05.05).

72. Dave Brownell, "1955 Packard Caribbean Convertible," *Sports Car Market* (Feb. 2000): 17. On Teague, see Michael Lamm and Dave Holls, *A Century of Automotive Style: 100 Years of American Car Design* (Stockton, Calif.: Lamm-Morada, 1996), 96–99.

73. Shugurov, *Avtomobili Rossii,* 2:10–11. According to one source, 40% of the vehicles in the Russian army consist of ZIL-131 trucks. See Leonid Sinserov, "The Post-Soviet Automobile Industry: First Signs of Revival," *Actes du GERPISA,* no. 28 (2000): 112.

74. Straus, *Factory and Community,* 187–98, 212–44. On Ford's near-legendary Sociological Department, see Clarence Hooker, "Ford's Sociology Department and the Americanization Campaign and the Manufacturing of Popular Culture among Assembly Line Workers, c. 1910–1917," *Journal of American Culture* 20, no. 1 (1997): 47–53; Georgios Paris Loizides, "Deconstructing Fordism: Legacies of the Ford Sociological Department," PhD diss., Department of Sociology, Western Michigan University (2004); and Steven Watts, *The People's Tycoon: Henry Ford and the American Century* (New York: Knopf, 2005).

75. TsAGM, f. 415, op. 16, d. 579, l. 104.

76. *Istoriia Moskovskogo avtozavoda,* 270–73; Straus, *Factory and Community,* 229–33. The Palace of Culture, designed by the Vesenin brothers and built in 1931–37, was the last constructivist building to be erected in the Soviet Union at least until the revival of the aesthetic in the 1960s.

77. TsAGM, f. 415, op. 16, d. 579, ll. 135 (S. A. Okutin), 113–14 (Korchagin).

78. *Istoriia Moskovskogo avtozavoda,* 553; Colton, *Moscow,* 526. For a brief history of ZIL's hospital, see http://www.zilhospital.ru/history.htm (accessed 11.27.05).

79. On the plant in Sverdlovsk-44, see http://www.novouralsk.ru/prom-zil.html. Authorities created the city in 1945 as part of the Soviet atomic bomb project.

80. Re the statement by a social scientist in *Moskovskaia Pravda* (July 4, 1988, 3) cited in Colton, *Moscow,* 517: "The bigger the enterprise and its profits, the more resources it can allocate to fortifying its 'social home front,' and vice-versa."

81. Carine Clément, "Russia in Transition: Lost Pride of the Working Class," *Le Monde diplomatique* (Jan. 2000), at http://mondediplo.com/2000/01 (accessed 08.15.05); notes from conversation with Boris Shpotov who was a student at Moscow State University at the time (May 22, 2006).

82. Smith, *The Russians,* 74–75.

83. Colton, *Moscow,* 516, 551–52.

84. N. B. Barbash, "Physical Development of Infants as an Indicator of the Condition of the Urban Environment," *Soviet Geography,* vol. 24 (1983): 204–13.

85. Interview with Aleksandr Blinov, Sept. 13 and 18, 2004, in Moscow. Donald Filtzer, *Soviet Workers and the Collapse of Perestroika: The Soviet Labour Process and Gorbachev's Reforms, 1985–1991* (Cambridge: Cambridge University Press, 1994), 28–29.

86. Iurii Nechetov, "Korona Rossiiskoi avtoimperii," *Za rulëm,* no. 4 (2000): 66–67.

87. Colton, *Moscow,* 709–10; Helen Fawkes, "Russian Limos Near End of Road," BBC News World Edition (Mar. 12, 2003), at http://news.bbc.co.uk/2/hi/europe/2841135.stm (accessed 8.5.05).

88. "Otkrytoe aktsionernoe moskovskoe obshchestvo 'Zavod imeni I. A. Likhacheva,'" at http://www.avtomash.ru/pred/zil/zil_istori.htm (accessed 8.7.05); *Financial Times,* July 25, 1994, 8.

89. *Moscow Times,* Aug. 15, 1996, 18; BBC News World Edition (Feb. 6, 1998), at http://news.bbc.co.uk/1/hi/world/monitoring/54265.stm (accessed 8.17.05); Gregory Feifer, "Privatisation and Elite Prerogatives," *Russia Journal,* in Johnson's List #3101 (Mar. 21, 1999) at http://www.cdi.org/russia/johnson/3101.html (accessed 8.17.05).

90. See http://www.ukcar.com/history/ZIL/ (accessed 8.5.05); T. Lysov, "'Bychok' v khoziastve—veshch' poleznaia," *Osnovnye sredstva,* no. 3 (2004) at http://www.os1.ru/ (accessed 8.18.05); Viktor Dmitriev, "'Bychok' nabiraet skorost'," *Literaturnaia gazeta,* no. 29 (2004) at http://www.lgz.ru/996 (accessed 8.18.05).

91. Quotations from Clément, "Russia in Transition." See also David Mandel, *Labour after Communism: Auto Workers and Their Unions in Russia, Ukraine and Belarus* (Montreal: Black Rose Press, 2004), 64, 78.

92. *Pravda,* Feb. 5, 2005, at http://www.english.pravda.ru/printed.html?news_id=15396; Johnson's List #7085 (Mar. 2, 2003); Fawkes, "Russian Limos Near End;" Richard Owen, "Putin Takes Glory Road in Khrushchev Zil," *Times* (UK), July 20, 2001, in Johnson's List #5357.

Chapter 2. GAZ, Nizhni Novgorod

1. P. Aleshina et al., ed., *Gor'kovskii avtomobil'nyi* (Moscow: Profizdat, 1964), 17.

2. For another case of conversion from monastery to auto shop, this in downtown Moscow, see "From Monastery to Auto Magneto Shop," *Moscow Daily News,* Nov. 27, 1933, 3.

3. Osinskii wrote a fascinating "autobiography" covering the years from his birth into the Russian nobility (his real name was Obolenskii) until his appointment ("against my wishes") as director of the Central Statistical Administration in 1926. It is in Tsentral'nyi Gosudarstvennyi Arkhiv Moskovskoi Oblasti (TsGAMO), f. 320, op. 1, d. 73, ll. 21–32. I thank Alain Blum for sharing a copy with me.

4. For his account of his trip, see N. Osinskii, *Po tu storonu okeana: Iz amerikanskikh vpechatlenii i nabliudenii* (Moscow, 1926).

5. N. Osinskii, "Amerikanskii avtomobil' ili rossiiskaia telega?" *Pravda,* July 20, 1927, 2; July 21, 1927, 3; July 22, 1927, 3.

6. *Pravda,* Aug. 14, 1927, 4–5; Aug. 17, 1927, 4–5; Aug. 27, 1927, 5; Aug. 28, 1927, 5.

7. See S. S. Khromov, ed., *Industrializatsiia sovetskogo soiuza: Novye dokumenty, novye fakty, novye podkhody,* 2 vols. (Moscow: Institut rossiiskoi istorii RAN, 1997–99), 2:226.

8. The two debates ("disputy") can be found in Gosudarstvennyi Arkhiv Rossiiskoi Federatsii (GARF), f. 4426, op. 1, d. 59 and d. 317 (Stenographic reports of Avtodor debates on the question of "The Automobile or the Cart," November 28, 1927, and January 23, 1928).

9. See N. Osinskii, *Avtomobilizatsiia SSSR, stat'i, ocherki, rechi* (Moscow: Gosizdat, 1930), 35–62, 78, 88–93, 141–48, 162.

10. Kurt Schultz, "Building the 'Soviet Detroit': The Construction of the Nizhnii-Novgorod Automobile Factory, 1927–1932," *Slavic Review* 49, no. 2 (1990): 200–203. See also *Ekonomicheskaia zhizn',* Mar. 16, 1929, 3; Apr. 2, 1929, 3; Apr. 3, 1929, 1.

11. L. M. Shugurov, *Avtomobili Rossii i SSSR,* 3 vols. (Moscow: Prostreks, 1993–98), 1:65–69; GARF, f. 4426, op. 1, d. 3 (Protocols, resolutions, and stenographic reports of sessions of presidium of central committee, 1929), l. 5.

12. Boris Shpotov, "Ford in Russia, from 1909 to World War II," in *Ford: The European History, 1903–2003,* ed. H. Bonin et al., 2 vols. (Paris: P.L.A.G.E., 2003), 2:514–16. In a conversation with me (5.24.06) Shpotov claims that GM was unwilling to extend credits.

13. Yves Cohen, "The Soviet Fordson: Between the Politics of Stalin and the Philosophy of Ford, 1924–1932," in Bonin et al., *Ford: The European History,* 2:532; G. N. Sevost'ianov and E. A. Tiurina, eds., *Rossiia i SShA: Ekonomicheskie otnosheniia 1917–1933. Sbornik dokumentov* (Moscow: RAN, 1997), 406; and Mira Wilkins and Frank Ernest Hill, *American Business Abroad: Ford on Six Continents* (Detroit: Wayne State University Press, 1964), 208–15. See also I. A. Poliakov, "Dogovor s Fordom i nashe avtostroenie," *Ekonomicheskaia zhizn',* June 8, 1929.

14. René Fülöp-Miller, *The Mind and Face of Bolshevism* (London: G. P. Putnam's Sons, 1927), 22.

15. See Alan M. Ball, *Imagining America: Influence and Images in Twentieth-Century Russia* (Lanham, Md.: Rowman and Littlefield, 2003), 23–38.

16. Shpotov, "Ford in Russia," 516–17; Wilkins and Hill, *American Business Abroad,* 218–19. A typed copy of the contract is available online at http://www.users.bigpond.com/cpitman/contract.htm. (accessed 12.21.04).

17. For the Austin contract, dated Aug. 23, 1929, see RGAE, f. 7620, op. 1, d. 68, ll. 123–138. A copy is available at the Western Reserve Historical Society (WRHS), Richard Austin Files, "Autostroy-GAZ Miscellaneous contract documents, invoices and correspondence." A second supplemental agreement, dated July 18, 1930, is in RGAE, f. 7620, op. 1, d. 708, ll. 25–31.

18. For the factors favoring Nizhni Novgorod, see Lev Shugurov, "Rozhdenie rossiiskogo Detroita," *Gazeta,* Apr. 3, 2004, at http://www.gazeta.ru/2004/03/04/oa_113886.shtml (accessed 6.3.04).

19. Martin Greif, *The New Industrial Landscape: The Story of the Austin Company* (Clinton, N.J.: Main Street Press, 1978), 99.

20. Bay Brown, "Albert Kahn: The Russian Legacy," *Project Russia,* no. 7 (1997): 93–96. See also Milka Bliznikov, "The Realization of Utopia: Western Technology and Soviet Avant-Garde Architecture," in *Reshaping Russian Architecture: Western Technology, Utopian Dreams,* ed. William Blumfield (New York: Cambridge University Press, 1990), 157–73; and Frederico Bucci, *Albert Kahn: Architect of Ford* (New York: Princeton Architectural Press, 1993), 90–96 ("The Russian Adventure").

21. Shpotov, "Ford in Russia," 517.

22. Boris Shpotov, "Pereplatil li Sovetskii Soiuz kompanii Forda? (k voprosu o tsene industrializatsii)," *Ekonomicheskaia istoriia, ezhegodnik* (Moscow: ROSSPEN, 2004), 166–67. See also Allan Nevins and Frank Ernest Hill, *Ford: Expansion and Challenge, 1915–1933* (New York: Scribner's, 1957), 683.

23. Quotation from Greif, *New Industrial Landscape,* 97.

24. Richard Cartwright Austin, *Building Utopia: Erecting Russia's First Modern City, 1930* (Kent: Kent State University Press, 2004), 13–14.

25. Antony Sutton, *National Suicide: Military Aid to the Soviet Union* (Melbourne: Australian League of Rights, 1973); Shpotov, "Pereplatil li Sovetskii Soiuz," 180.

26. Schultz, "Building the 'Soviet Detroit,'" 206–12. See also Boris Shpotov, "'Ne dano nam istorii tishe idti' (tekhnicheskaia pomoshch' Zapada sovetskoi industrializatsii)," *Mir istorii,* no. 3 (2002), at http://www.historia.ru/2002/03/shpotov.htm (accessed 7.1.05).

27. Austin, *Building Utopia*, 98.

28. *Industrializatsiia sovetskogo soiuza*, 80–85. Osinskii referred to the automobile and tractor industry in the first-person plural ("we are not regarded as a fundamental industry of the country").

29. "Nizhegorodskii krai v istorii Rossii," *Istoricheskii arkhiv*, no. 6 (1999): 10.

30. Moshe Lewin, *The Making of the Soviet System: Essays in the Social History of Interwar Russia* (New York: New Press, 1994 [1985]), 265–66.

31. Karl Marx, *Capital: A Critique of Political Economy* (New York: International Publishers, 1967), 1:595.

32. Vladislav Todorov, *Red Square, Black Square: Organon for Revolutionary Imagination* (Albany: State University of New York Press, 1994), 10.

33. Boris Agapov, "Po bezdorozh'iu," *Za industrializatsiiu*, Aug. 2, 1930, 3. An English translation can be found in Austin, *Building Utopia*, 73–78. See also Greif, *New Industrial Landscape*, 101–2; and Schultz, "Building the 'Soviet Detroit'," 206. Greif incorrectly describes the article as "a manuscript, written in vividly colorful broken-English, by one of the Russian engineers" (100), and Schultz incorrectly cites the date of its publication. Agapov's article was reworked as "At the Frontier of the Future" in Boris Agapov, *Tekhnicheskie rasskazy* (Moscow: Khudozhestvennaia literatura, 1936), 65–73.

34. See editor's introduction and contributions by Moshe Lewin, Robert Sharlet, and S. Frederick Starr in Sheila Fitzpatrick, ed., *Cultural Revolution in Russia, 1928–1931* (Bloomington: Indiana University Press, 1978).

35. Chrysler quoted in David Halberstam, *The Reckoning* (New York: William Morris, 1986), 41.

36. Victor Terras, *A History of Russian Literature* (New Haven: Yale University Press, 1991), 387, 511–12. On the center's role in constructivism, see "Konstruktivizm (russkii)," in *Literaturnaia entsiklopediia*, 11 vols. (Moscow: Kommunisticheskaia akademiia, Institut literatury, iskusstva i iazyka, 1929–39), 5 (1931):450–53.

37. Agapov, "Po bezdorozh'iu." Agapov was one of the writers recruited to tour and write about the White Sea–Baltic Canal construction project in 1933. He contributed to three chapters in the lavishly published book, including one which concludes with the vision of a boy, now grown up, sailing through the canal: "Before him appear the Karelian lakes, the locks and dams. Everywhere he looks there are hotels, electric power stations, factories, farms, and, like a miracle, the surviving barracks that show him where those amazing builders used to live." *Belomorsko-Baltiiskii Kanal imeni Stalina, Istoriia stroitel'stva*, ed. M. Gor'kii, L. L. Averbakh, and S. G. Firin (Moscow: "Istoriia fabrik i zavodov," 1934), 320.

38. Sándor Horváth, "Everyday Life in the First Hungarian Socialist City," *International Labor and Working-Class History*, no. 68 (2005): 24–46 (quotation on 24).

39. Stephen Kotkin, *Magnetic Mountain: Stalinism as a Civilization* (Berkeley: University of California Press, 1995), 364–66.

40. See N. A. Miliutin, *Problema Stroitel'stva Sotsialisticheskikh Gorodov: Osnovnye voprosy ratsional'noi planirovki i stroitel'stva naselennykh mest SSSR* (Moscow: Gosizdat, 1930). This book, the vade mecum of constructivist architecture and urban planning, was lovingly translated and annotated by Arthur Sprague and published as *Sotsgorod: The Problem of Building Socialist Cities* (Cambridge: MIT Press, 1974). A French version, translated by Elizabeth Essaian and introduced by Jean-Louis Cohen, also was published as *Sotsgorod* in 2002.

41. Agapov, "Po bezdorozh'iu."

42. WRHS, Richard Austin Files, "Original Photos—GAZ," G-31, reproduced in Austin, *Building Utopia*, 18; *Pravda*, Nov. 1, 1931, 3, and Dec. 19, 1932, 2. See also *Istoriia geroicheskoi bor'by za nizhegorodskii Avtozavod (fotoalbom)* (Nizhni Novgorod, 1932): "There, where nothing was before."

43. Aleshina, *Gor'kovskii avtomobil'nyi*, 51–57; *New York Times*, Apr. 4, 1932; *Chicago Daily Tribune*, Apr. 4, 1932; *Trud*, July 10, 1932, 4; Jean-Paul Depretto, "Rabochie regiona i sovetskaia vlast' (1928–1832 gg.)," in *Obshchestvo i vlast': rossiiskaia provintsiia*, ed. A. N. Sakharov, 2 vols. (Moscow: RAN, 2005), 2:645–49; Schultz, "Building the 'Soviet Detroit'," 211. At least according to a summary report on Second Five-Year Plan results, GAZ's output of vehicles in 1937 exceeded 130,000. See *Istoriia industrializatsii Nizhegorodskogo-Gor'kovskogo kraia (1926–1941 gg.)*, ed. V. P. Fadeev et al. (Gor'kii: Vol'go-Viatskoe kn. Izd., 1968), 362.

44. Kotkin, *Magnetic Mountain*, 108–24 (quotations on 120, 118, 123).

45. John Scott, *Behind the Urals: An American Worker in Russia's City of Steel* (Bloomington: Indiana University Press, 1989 [1942]), 209–10.

46. *Nizhegorodskaia kommuna,* Jan. 3, 1930, 4.

47. Ibid., Jan. 19, 1930, 2; Jan. 30, 1930, 2; Kotkin, *Magnetic Mountain,* 114, 43–50. For details of the negotiations, see RGAE, f. 7620, op. 1, d. 633, ll. 191–211.

48. For critical evaluations of this and three other designs submitted to the competition, see V. Lavrov, "Avtostroi—sotsialisticheskii gorod," *Stroitel'stvo Moskvy,* no. 4 (1930).

49. Austin, *Building Utopia,* 45–56 (the article, "Communism Builds Its City of Utopia," was written in Nov. 1930, appeared in the *New York Times Magazine* on Aug. 9, 1931, and is reproduced in full on 51–56, 161–65). For another article by Allan Austin, see *Cleveland Press,* Apr. 25, 1931, 16. On communal apartments, see Katerina Gerasimova, "Public Privacy in the Soviet Communal Apartment," in *Socialist Spaces: Sites of Everyday Life in the Eastern Bloc,* ed. David Crowley and Susan E. Reid (Oxford: Berg, 2002), 207–30.

50. Austin, *Building Utopia,* 131–32, 166; I. M. Ashavskii, *Sotsgorod Nizhegorodskogo avtozavoda* (Nizhni Novgorod: OGIZ, 1932), 36–37, 41–42; A. Kadinskii, "Darovityi inzhener," in *Evrei Nizhnego Novgoroda,* ed. Z. Kh. Libinzon and D. I. Belkin (Nizhni Novgorod: DEKOM, 1993), 137–38. Also, *Ekonomicheskaia zhizn',* Sept. 18, 1931.

51. Scott, *Behind the Urals,* 211. For the recommendation of a norm of five square meters "in the first instance," see L. M. Sabsovich, *Sotsialisticheskie goroda* (Moscow: Moskovskii rabochii, 1930), 52. See also Ol'ga Orel'skaia, "1500–1917–1975," *Project Russia,* no. 4 (1997), 54–55.

52. RGAE, f. 7620, op. 1, d. 633, ll. 131–36 ("Avtozavod—Nizhni Novgorod," January 1932).

53. Austin, *Building Utopia,* 167–68; *Nizhegorodskaia kommuna,* Apr. 21, 1932, 1; Apr. 4, 1932, 3; *Otchet o rabote zavodskogo komiteta soiuza RATAP Gor'kovskogo Avtozavoda (za period s 15 iiunia 1932 g. po 15 dekabria 1932 goda* (Gor'kii: Profizdat, 1932), 31. On spontaneous occupation of apartments and efforts to control it, see Depretto, "Rabochie regiona," 655–58.

54. *Nizhegorodskaia kommuna,* July 23, 1930, 4; Walter L. Carver, "Amo and Nizhni-Novgorod Plants Lead," *Automotive Industries,* Mar. 12, 1932, 420–21; Philip K. Davis, "The Building of Molotov: Where Russian Fords Will Be Produced," *Journal of Worcester Polytechnic Institute,* Apr. 1932, 84–85; *Istoriia industrializatsii Nizhegorodskogo,* 151–52.

55. Anonymous [H. J. Heinz II], *Experiences in Russia 1931: A Diary* (Pittsburgh: Alton Press, 1932), 192–93, 197; Austin, *Building Utopia,* 96–101. For turnover, attributed largely to insufficiency of housing and its poor quality, see *Istoriia industrializatsii Nizhegorodskogo,* 195.

56. *Istoriia industrializatsii Nizhegorodskogo,* 510; Depretto, "Rabochie regiona," 643, 649. Nizhni Novgorod's boundaries expanded during these five years. For data on Detroit, see Campbell Gibson, "Population of the 100 Largest Cities and Other Urban Places in the United States: 1790 to 1990," Population Division Working Paper No. 27 (1998), U. S. Census Bureau, http://www.census.gov/population/www/documentation/twps0027.html (accessed 1.15.06).

57. Anatoli Ilyashov, "Victor Reuther on the Soviet Experience, 1933–35: An Interview," *International Review of Social History* 31 (1986): 305–6. In 1933, the year of the Reuthers' arrival, 67% of workers at GAZ consisted of former peasants of whom 60% were under twenty. See F. M. Bormotov, "Iz istorii bor'by Gor'kovskikh kommunistov za osvoenie novoi tekhniki v promyshlennosti v pervoi gody vtoroi piatiletki," *Uchenye zapiski Gor'kovskogo Universiteta,* no. 70 (1964): 7.

58. Lewin, *Making of the Soviet System,* 274.

59. Austin, *Building Utopia,* 106.

60. For a very positive assessment of Western and particularly American contributions, see Shpotov, "'Ne dano nam istorii.'"

61. Charles E. Sorensen with Samuel T. Williamson, *My Forty Years with Ford* (New York: W. W. Norton, 1956), 193–216; Nevins and Hill, *Ford,* 673–83.

62. Wilkins and Hill, *American Business,* 226, quoting from an interview in *Nation's Business* from June 1930.

63. Austin, *Building Utopia,* 86.

64. Andrea Graziosi, "Foreign Workers in Soviet Russia, 1920–40: Their Experience and Their Legacy," *International Labor and Working-Class History,* no. 33 (1988): 39.

65. Ibid., 56–58. At Magnitogorsk, the American village was known as the Amerikanka, later, Berezka (Birch Tree). When not calling it "Russia's Detroit," initial reports of the project in the U.S. press referred to the new city (that is, Sotsgorod) as Austingrad. See, for example, *New York Times,* Sept. 4, 1929, 39.

66. Austin, *Building Utopia,* 62–63, 68. This is P. Ia. Makarovskii, no relation to the Makarovskii who had been run out of the grounds of AMO in 1917.

67. WRHS, Austin-GAZ-Ford Papers, "Transcript of Allan S. Austin's interview with Martin Greif on August 4, 1976."

68. Austin, *Building Utopia,* 95, 111, 116–18, 123–24, 131, 133–34. Christmas, during which he played Santa Claus, brought out the "beautiful disposition."

69. WRHS, Richard Austin Files, "Americans and the Industrialization," RGAE, f. 7620, op. 1, d. 708, ll. 99–100.

70. RGAE, f. 7620, op. 1, d. 701, ll. 42–50.

71. RGAE, f. 7620, op. 1, d. 708, ll. 99–100.

72. For the American workers' statement, see *Trud,* Feb. 21, 1931, 1. VATO reported that there were ninety-nine foreign specialists and workers employed at Avtostroi as of Oct. 1, 1931. See *Industrializatsiia sovetskogo soiuza,* 242. A year later, there were a reported 181, of whom half were Russian re-emigrants from the United States. See *Istoriia industrializatsii Nizhegorodskogo,* 183.

73. Victor G. Reuther, *The Brothers Reuther and the Story of the UAW* (Boston: Houghton Mifflin, 1976), 88–103; Nelson Lichtenstein, *Walter Reuther: The Most Dangerous Man in Detroit* (Urbana: University of Illinois Press, 1995), 25–46; Frank Cormier and William J. Eaton, *Reuther* (Englewood Cliffs, N.J.: Prentice-Hall, 1970), 29–46.

74. More unusual were those who, generally out of political conviction, decided to stay and make a life for themselves and their families. See Victor Herman, *Coming Out of the Ice: An Unexpected Life* (New York: Harcourt Brace, 1979). Herman, who was seventeen at the time and working in the die room, is featured along with two other Americans from Detroit, Bill Tracy (a pattern maker) and John Rushton (a die maker, and initial host to the Reuthers) in Cyril Lambkin, "Americans at Gorky Auto Plant," *Soviet Russia Today* 2, no. 3 (1933): 6, 10.

75. Lichtenstein, *Walter Reuther,* 36–43; Cormier and Eaton, *Reuther,* 29–43; Reuther, *Brothers Reuther,* 97–113. Walter's relationship with "Lucy" became the subject of an international incident in 1959 when a Soviet newspaper (Trud) published what it claimed to be the woman's complaints against Reuther's moral turpitude. See also Reuther Library, Victor G. Reuther Collection, Box 71, folder 7–8, "The Long Way Home," 6–8. On foreign workers in general, see Graziosi, "Foreign Workers," quotation on cohabitation with Soviet women on 43.

76. Graziosi, "Foreign Workers," 53. For a survey of such literature in Russian, English, and German, see Sergei Zhuravlev, *"Malenkie liudi" i "bolshaia istoriia": inostrantsy moskovskogo Elektrozavoda v sovetskom obshchestve 1920–1930–kh gg.* (Moscow: ROSSPEN, 2000), 25–36.

77. See respectively, Cormier and Eaton, *Reuther,* 43; Jean Gould and Lorena Hickok, *Walter Reuther: Labor's Rugged Individualist* (New York: Dodd, Mead, 1972), 76; Lichtenstein, *Walter Reuther,* 44, 308. See also the copy of a letter from the Reuthers sent from "Samarkand, Central Asia" on June 20, 1935, to the labor lawyer Maurice Sugar (who had visited GAZ as a tourist in 1932), which refers to their stint at Gor'kii as an "inspiring contrast to what we knew as Ford wage slaves in Detroit." Walter P. Reuther Library, Wayne State University, Maurice Sugar Collection, Box 65, folder 1. See also Christopher H. Johnson, *Maurice Sugar: Law, Labor, and the Left in Detroit, 1912–1950* (Detroit: Wayne State University Press, 1988), 134, for the characterization of their attitude toward the Soviet Union as one of "starry-eyed appreciation."

78. Reuther, *Brothers Reuther,* 99, 101; Aleshina, *Gor'kovskii avtomobil'nyi,* 71.

79. See "Historie GAZ-fabriek," at http://www.volga.nl/GAZhistorieEN1930.htm (accessed 2.6.05); V. Ia. Dobrokhotov, *Gor'kovskii avtomobil'nyi* (Moscow: Mysl', 1981), 39; *Pravda,* Jan. 19, 1935, 6; Aleksei Smrelkov, "Emka, GAZ-M1," Motor, no. 8 (1999), at http://motor.ru/ archive.php?number=40&art=9 (accessed 2.1.06); and "Avtomobil' GAZ-M1 'Emka,'" at http:// easyget.narod.ru/tech/emka.html (accessed 1.31.06).

80. Dobrokhotov, *Gor'kovskii,* 39; Aleshina, *Gor'kovskii avtomobil'nyi,* 85–87; Shugurov, *Avtomobili Rossii,* 1:88–89; "Avtomobil' GAZ-M1 'Emka'"

81. Aleshina, *Gor'kovskii avtomobil'nyi,* 73–74; Dobrokhotov, *Gor'kovskii,* 41; A. Kh. Busygin, *Zhizn' moia i moikh druzei* (Moscow: Profizdat, 1939), 6, 13. On the Stakhanovite movement in general, see Lewis H. Siegelbaum, *Stakhanovism and the Politics of Productivity in the USSR, 1935–1941* (Cambridge: Cambridge University Press, 1988).

82. Bormotov, "Iz istorii bor'by Gor'kovskikh kommunistov," 22; *Istoriia industrializatsii Nizhegorodskogo,* 325, gives a slightly lower figure for the number of Busyginites.

83. Siegelbaum, *Stakhanovism,* 188, 231, 239; Soiuzkinozhurnal no. 1 (1936) at Rossiiskii gosudarstvennyi arkhiv kinofoto dokumentov (RGAKFD), Krasnogorsk, available at http://

www.soviethistory.org (accessed 2.10.06); V. A. Sakharov, "Zarozhdenie i razvitie stakhanovsk-ogo dvizheniia v avtotraktornoi promyshlennosti v gody vtoroi piatiletki" (Candidate's dissertation, Moscow Oblast Pedagogical Institute, named N. K. Krupskaia, 1979), 112–13.

84. Siegelbaum, *Stakhanovism*, 131–32. For more on Busygin's expeditions for supplies, see V. Lel'chuk, "Aleksandr Busygin," in *Novatory, sbornik*, ed. L. Rogachevskaia (Moscow: Molodaia gvardiia, 1972), 162–64. Sokolinskii had been instrumental in preparing the shop for Busygin's record.

85. Siegelbaum, *Stakhanovism*, 132.

86. R. W. Davies et al., *The Stalin-Kaganovich Correspondence, 1931–36* (New Haven: Yale University Press, 2003), 368–70.

87. Aleshina, *Gor'kovskii avtomobil'nyi*, 92–93; B. Dekhtiar, "Uchastie evreev v stroitel'stve i rabote Avtozavoda," in *Evrei Nizhnego Novgoroda*, 108–9. Not all arrested engineers were lost to Soviet industry. For example, Timofei Geller, the head of the wheel shop, was dispatched to an NKVD *sharashka* (research laboratory) outside Moscow that was directed by the pioneering aircraft designer Andrei N. Tupelev.

88. *Pravda*, Aug. 25, 1937, 3. On Osinskii's arrest, see the extract of his daughter's memoirs published as "Vospominaniia ob otse," *Za rulëm*, no. 4 (2000): 225.

89. Sergei Dyakonov, son of the director of the Soviet GAZ factory from 1932 to 1938, "Yanks for Stalin" interview transcript at http//abamedia.com/rao/catalogues/trans/yfs/yanks_serg_1.htm/ (accessed 9.7.05).

90. Graziosi, "Foreign Workers," 47. Herman, *Coming Out of the Ice.*

91. Graziosi, "Foreign Workers," 47; Scott, *Behind the Urals*, 288–89.

92. WRHS, Austin-GAZ-Ford Papers, Postcard to Mr. and Mrs. Phil Davis, August 30, 1939.

93. *Project Russia*, no. 4 (1997): 59–61.

94. Aleshina, *Gor'kovskii avtomobil'nyi*, 89–90; Shugurov, *Avtomobili Rossii*, 1:91–139. For having designed the GAZ-61 and the BA-64, an armored reconnaissance vehicle, Grachev was awarded a Stalin Prize in 1942. See A. N. Narbut, "V. A. Grachev (K 100-letiiu so dnia rozhdeniia)," *Avtomobil'naia promyshlennost'*, no. 2 (2003): 34–37.

95. *Istoriia industrializatsii Nizhegorodskogo*, 478–79.

96. N. S. Simonov, "Mobpodgotovka: Mobilization Planning in Interwar Industry," in *The Soviet Defence-Industry Complex from Stalin to Khrushchev*, ed. John Barber and Mark Harrison (Houndmills, England: Macmillan, 2000), 217; *Istoriia industrializatsii Nizhegorodskogo*, 482.

97. Mark Harrison and Nikolai Simonov, "*Voenpriemka*: Prices, Costs, and Quality Assurance in Interwar Defence Industry," in *Soviet Defence-Industry Complex*, 223; A. Dupouy, *L'automobile en URSS, chronologie de 1917 à 1990* (Grenoble: Alain Dupouy, 1991), 45; Shugurov, *Avtomobili Rossii*, 1:161, 166–70; Dobrokhotov, *Gor'kovskii*, 55–70.

98. Shugurov, *Avtomobili Rossii*, 1:169.

99. "The Russian GAZ Jeep, WW II Soviet 4 x 4 Military Vehicle," at http://members.aol.com/brimiljeep/WebPages/GAZWWIIJeepPage.html (accessed 2.8.06).

100. Austin, *Building Utopia*, 199–201; WRHS, Richard Austin's Files, "Original Photos—GAZ," G-13–G-15 (1943).

101. Dobrokhotov, *Gor'kovskii*, 72–77.

102. Shugurov, *Avtomobili Rossii*, 1:189. According to another account by Shugurov, Stalin unfavorably compared the car to the "long government limousines parked nearby." See "Soviet Classics," *Moscow Times Business Review*, Aug. 1999, at http://www.businessreview.ru/stories/07/12.html (accessed 2.12.06). The cartoon is in *Krokodil*, no. 30–31 (1946): 3. Along with the automobile, a popular watch, a powerful locomotive, a brand of cigarette, a dirigible, and a mountain peak all bore the name of Pobeda.

103. Iu. A. Dolmatovskii, *Povest ob avtomobile* (Moscow: Molodaia gvardiia, 1950), 7; M. Burenkov, *Vremia, zavod, liudi* (Gor'kii: Gork. obl. gos. izd., 1950), 31; *Pravda*, Nov. 24, 1945, 2 (article by Akopov); Apr. 6, 1946, 1.

104. At sixteen thousand (post–currency reform) rubles it was beyond the reach of workers whose average wage was about six hundred rubles per month, leaving aside gaining access to the restricted queue. Price information from "Soviet Classics" and "Oldtimer picture gallery. Cars. GAZ-M20," at http://www.autogallery.org.ru/gaz20.htm. (accessed 2.12.06).

105. Shugurov, *Avtomobili Rossii*, 1:190–91. Between 1951 and 1974 a Polish version of the Pobeda was produced, with modifications, by the Fabryka Samochodów Osobowych (FSO) under the Warsaw trademark.

106. V. N. Nosakov and N. V. Kolesnikova, "Pokoleniia avtomobilei 'GAZ' i ikh sozdateli," *Avtomobil'naia promyshlennost'*, no. 7 (1996): 12.

107. A. A. Lipgart et al., *Avtomobil' ZIM* (Moscow, 1954); Nikolai Belousov, "Istoriia sozdaniia GAZ-12 ZIM," at http://www.autobook.by.ru/stat_010.shtml (accessed 2.11.06)

108. See Shugurov, *Avtomobili Rossii*, 1:197, and Belousov, "Istoriia sozdaniia."

109. Ruth Brandon, *Auto Mobile: How the Car Changed Life* (London: Macmillan, 2002), 304–5; John Jerome, *The Death of the Automobile: The Fatal Effect of the Golden Era, 1955–1970* (New York: W. W. Norton, 1972), 26–27; Halberstam, *Reckoning*, 45–47.

110. K. A. Sharapov, "Amerikanskie legkovye avtomobili 1956 g.," *Avtomobil'naia i traktornaia promyshlennost'*, no. 8 (1956): 39–46.

111. V. V. Bekman, "Osnovnye tekhnicheskie parametry zarubezhnykh legkovykh avtomobilei," *Avtomobil'naia i traktornaia promyshlennost'*, no. 10 (1956): 43–46.

112. Jelle Jan Gerrits, "The development of the Volga," at http://www.volga.nl/ontwikkeling EN.htm. (accessed 10.19.05). This Dutch enthusiast notes similarities with the 1953 Ford Custom. See the comment on GAZ's official website: "The designers . . . found a successful compromise between European and American schools of design." "Istoriia gor'kovskogo avtozavoda" at http://www.gaz.ru/ist/history (accessed 10.5.05).

113. Quoted in Iu. Klemanov, "Blizhaishie perspektivy," *Za rulëm*, no. 6 (1956): 15.

114. Aleshina, *Gor'kovskii avtomobil'nyi*, 278–80; Dobrokhotov, *Gor'kovskii*, 149; "Istoriia gor'kovskogo avtozavoda."

115. "Istoriia gor'kovskogo avtozavoda;" Dobrokhotov, *Gor'kovskii*, 128, 130–31, 133.

116. RGAE, f. 398, op. 1, d. 19 (Basic technical-economic indices of work at automobile factories for 1958–65), l. 18.

117. Pavel Anisimov, "Istoriia modeli 'Chaika'," at http://www.autobook.by.ru/stat_006. shtml (accessed 2.19.06); Shugurov, *Avtomobili Rossii*, 2:47–49.

118. Steven E. Harris, "Moving to the Separate Apartment: Building, Distributing, Furnishing, and Living in Urban Housing in Soviet Russia, 1950s–1960s," PhD diss., University of Chicago, 2003, 137–40.

119. Ibid., 141–77; Aleshina, *Gor'kovskii avtomobil'nyi*, 210.

120. *Pravda,* June 10, 1957, 1; June 11, 1957, 2; Harris, "Moving to the Separate Apartment," 150–52, 177–84.

121. Wyndham Mortimer, "My Trip to the Soviet Union," memoir dated Jan. 13, 1962, in Reuther Library, Maurice Sugar Collection, Box 3, folder 27. Mortimer was a former vice president of the UAW and member of the CPUSA's National Committee, living in retirement in California.

122. Shugurov, *Avtomobili Rossii*, 2:11; *Pravda,* July 28, 1965, 2.

123. See capsule biographies of V. A. Grachev (1903–78), G. V. Evart (1913–77), N. A. Iushmanov (1913–85), A. A. Lipgart (1898–1980), G. G. Mikhailov (1902–83), A. N. Ostrovtsev (1902–88), B. A. Shaposhnik (1902–85), Konstantin Sharapov (1899–1980), and A. P. Zigel' (1908–94) in N. N. Shcherbakov, ed., *Entsiklopediia Avtoznamenitostei. Konstruktory. Dizainery. Predprinimateli* (Moscow: Za rulëm, 2000).

124. Charles Maier, *Dissolution: The Crisis of Communism and the End of East Germany* (Princeton: Princeton University Press, 1997), 81–82, 105.

125. Joe Kerr, "Trouble in Motor City," in *Autopia: Cars and Culture,* ed. Peter Wollen and Joe Kerr (London: Reaktion Books, 2002), 125–38; Peter Gavrilovich and Bill McGraw, ed., *The Detroit Almanac: 300 Years of Life in the Motor City* (Detroit: Detroit Free Press, 2000), 289, 294–95, 301–2.

126. Micheline Maynard, *The End of Detroit: How the Big Three Lost Their Grip on the American Car Market* (New York: Currency/Doubleday, 2003), 43–50; Keith Bradsher, *High and Mighty: SUVs—The World's Most Dangerous Vehicles and How They Got That Way* (New York: Public Affairs, 2002), xiii–xviii, 263–65.

127. Maynard, *End of Detroit,* 55–88, 308 (quotation); Leslie S. Hiraoka, *Global Alliances in the Motor Vehicle Industry* (Westport, Conn.: Quorum, 2001), 60–84.

128. Roman Zhuk, "Komu prinadlezhit Rossiia? (Avtomobil'naia promyshlennost')," *Kommersant. Vlast',* Oct. 2, 2001: 52; Trevor Buck, Igor Filatotchev, Mike Wright, and Vladimir Zhukov, "Russian Mass Privatization: What Has Been Achieved?" *International Journal of Business* 4, no. 2 (1999): 33–34, 37. The authors, citing GAZ as one of three cases, conclude that "privatization has so far yielded little evidence of progress" in terms of shifts in managerial strategy.

129. "Avtomobili GAZ," Auto-motor.ru at http://www.auto-motor.ru/gaz.html (accessed 2.19.06); Austin, *Building Utopia*, 203–6; *International Herald Tribune*, Feb. 11, 1998, 19; Bob Sherman, "Fiat and GAZ Announce JV," *Automotive Industries*, Sept. 1998. The deal was worth $850 million, nearly the same amount in nominal dollars as Fiat's "deal of the century" in 1966.

130. Gregory Feifer, "Russia's Economic Crisis," Johnson's Russia List #3101, Mar. 21, 1999, at http://www.cdi.org/russia/johnson/3101.html (accessed 3.1.06); "Istoriia Avtozavodskogo raiona," at http://www.admcity.nnov.ru/goradm/distr/art/history.html (accessed 2.6.06).

131. Austin, *Building Utopia*, 208; Athan Koutsiouroumbas and Trevor Gunn, "Post-Crisis Auto Prospects in Russia," Bisnis Online, at http://www.bisnis.doc.gov/bisnis/bulletin/99-9bull5.htm (accessed 3.3.06).

132. Press release, "GM-Avtovaz Automotive Factory in Togliatti," June 15, 2001, at http://www.ebrd.com/new/pressrel/2001/01jun15x.htm (accessed 3.3.06); Ford Motor Company, "Ford Reaches Investment Agreement in Russia," at http://media.ford.com/newsroom/release_dispaly.cfm?release=2162 (accessed 3.3.06); Sergei Smirnov, "'Otvertku' pridumal Ford," *Nasha gazeta*, May 26–28, 2003, 9.

133. Zhuk, "Komu prinadlezhit Rossiia?" 58; Maria Rozhkova and Vladislav Maximov, "Aluminum Giant and Gaz in Auto Deal," *St. Petersburg Times*, Nov. 28, 2000, 6.

134. David Mandel, *Labour after Communism: Auto Workers and Their Unions in Russia, Ukraine, and Belarus* (Montreal: Black Rose Books, 2004), 64 (quoting the vice president of the Union of Auto and Farm-Machine Workers of Russia). The ratio among U.S. carmakers was approximately 80–1.

135. Mandel, *Labour after Communism*, 151; Austin, *Building Utopia*, 209–10; Jeremy Page, "Soviet Car Drives into Sunset," *Times* Online at http://www.timesonline.co.uk/article/0,13509-1915163,00.html (accessed 2.24.06).

136. Basic Element Company/Social Development Programmes, at http://www.sibal.ru/kbe/kbe.nsf/epages/echarity.html. (accessed 3.4.06). On the number of workers, cf. "Gaz tsentr," at http://www.gaz-center.com/index.php?c=5262 (accessed 3.6.06) and "'Gaz' Segodnia," at http://www.gaz.ru/gaz/gaz.htm (accessed 3.6.06). To be fair, these websites indicate a rise in average monthly wages from 7,229 rubles ($250) in 2004 to "more than" 9,800 rubles ($337) in 2006.

137. Micheline Maynard and Erin E. Arvedlund, "The Russians Are Coming to Take Over Rouge Steel," *New York Times*, Oct. 25, 2003, B1.

138. Bill Vlasic and Brett Clanton, "Staggering Blow: Delphi's Bankruptcy Ominous Sign for Fading Auto Industry," *Detroit News*, Oct. 9, 2005, 1A; David Shephardson, Gary Heinlein, and Ron French, "Shell-Shocked Workers Fear for Future: Job and Pay Cuts Will Change a Way of Life," *Detroit News*, Oct. 9, 2005, 9A; Bill Vlasic and Brett Clanton, "Black October: How One Month Changed the Course of the Auto Industry," *Detroit News*, Nov. 13, 2005, IA; Danny Hakim, "For a G.M. Family, the American Dream Vanishes," *New York Times*, Nov. 19, 2005, A1; Chris Andrews, "Area Workers Afraid for Their Jobs, Children," *Lansing State Journal*, Mar. 2, 2006, 1A.

139. Jeffrey McCracken, "Detroit's Symbol of Dysfunction: Paying Employees Not to Work," *Wall Street Journal*, Mar. 1, 2006, A1.

140. Administratsiia Avtozavodskogo raiona, Avtozavodskii raion v tsifrakh at http://www.avtozavod.nnov.ru/region/r_zifr.htm (accessed 10.9.05).

141. Marina Kulakova, "Gimn avtozavoda," in *Reka po imeni master* (Nizhni Novgorod: Dekom, 1995), 32–36.

Chapter 3. VAZ, Togliatti

1. For different ways of conceptualizing Soviet Russian cities, see R. Antony French, *Plans, Pragmatism, and People: The Legacy of Soviet Planning for Today's Cities* (Pittsburgh: University of Pittsburgh Press, 1995), and A. S. Seniavskii, *Rossiiskii gorod v 1960-e—80-e gody* (Moscow: RAN, 1995).

2. The best-known accounts in English (or any other language) of the building of these cities are devoted to Magnitogorsk. See John Scott, *Behind the Urals: An American Worker in Russia's City of Steel* (Bloomington: Indiana University Press, 1989 [1942]), and Steven Kotkin, *Magnetic Mountain: Stalinism as a Civilization* (Berkeley: University of California Press, 1995). See also on Komsomol'sk-na-Amur, Thomas Lahusen, *How Life Writes the Book: Real*

Socialism and Socialist Realism in Stalin's Russia (Ithaca: Cornell University Press, 1997); and Marina Kuz'mina, *Komsomol'sk-na-Amure: Legendy, mify, i real'nost'* (Komsomol'sk-na-Amure: "Memorial," 2002).

3. The company has gone through a series of name changes over the more than forty years of its existence and especially since 1993. For the sake of simplicity, I refer to VAZ during the Soviet era and AvtoVAZ after 1992.

4. I take the phrase from Robert Jay Lifton, *Revolutionary Immortality: Mao Tse-Tung and the Chinese Cultural Revolution* (New York: Random House, 1968). Even Andropov and Chernenko posthumously lent their names to Soviet towns (which quickly reverted to their antecedents after 1991).

5. Torez ("Thorezgrad") is listed as one of several cities having "international relations" with the Pas de Calais mining town of Avion at http://villedavion.free.fr/avionpresent.htm (accessed 12.13.04). Pas de Calais was the département in which Maurice Thorez was born and raised.

6. For text of Togliatti's "Yalta memorandum," see William E. Griffith, ed., *Sino-Soviet Relations, 1964–1965* (Cambridge: MIT Press, 1967), 373–83. See also Joan Barth Urban, *Moscow and the Italian Communist Party: From Togliatti to Berlinguer* (Ithaca: Cornell University Press, 1986), 246–51. For alternative evaluations of Togliatti's career, cf. Giorgio Bocca, *Palmiro Togliatti* (Rome-Bari: Laterza, 1973), and Aldo Agosti, *Palmiro Togliatti* (Turin: UTET, 1996).

7. See, for example, Paul W. Werth, *At the Margins of Orthodoxy: Mission, Governance, and Confessional Politics in Russia's Volga-Kama Region, 1827–1905* (Ithaca: Cornell University Press, 2002), 3–8, 108–10; Willard Sunderland, *Taming the Wild Field: Colonization and Empire on the Russian Steppe* (Ithaca: Cornell University Press, 2004), 48–53.

8. Michael Khodarkovsky, *Where Two Worlds Met: The Russian State and the Kalmyk Nomads, 1600–1771* (Ithaca: Cornell University Press, 1992), 208–9.

9. On the revolution and civil war in the middle Volga region, see Orlando Figes, *Peasant Russia, Civil War: The Volga Countryside in Revolution, 1917–1921* (Oxford: Clarendon Press, 1989), and S. V. Starikov, *Vlast Sovetam, a ne partiiam! Sovetskaia revoliutsiia v Samare v 1917–1918 gg.* (Ioshkar-Ola: Min. obshchego i prof. obraz., 1999). Among those who left Stavropol in 1921 was Klavdiia Gavrilina, mother of the composer Valerii Gavrilin (1939–99). See V. I. Belov, "Golos, rozhdenyi pod Vologdoi: Povest' o kompozitore Valerii Gavriline," *Nash Sovremennik*, no. 9 (2004): 21.

10. N. F. Semizorov, "Stroiteli shli pervymi," in *VAZ: Stranitsy istorii, 1991–1996*, ed. A. Shavrin, 5 vols., rev. ed. (Togliatti: OAO Avtovaz, 1997), 1:49.

11. I. A. Prokhorenko, "Zhilishchno-grazhdanskoe stroitel'stvo v period vozvedeniia volzhskoi GES im. V. I. Lenina (1950–1958 gg.)," in *Istoriia OAO "Avtovaz": Uroki, problemy, sovremennost'. Materialy I Vserossiiskoi nauchnoi konferentsii, 26–27 noiabria 2003 g.*, ed. A. E. Livshits and P. A. Nakhmanovich (Togliatti: OAO Avtovaz, TGU, 2003), 176–78 (hereafter, *Istoriia OAO AvtoVAZ*, 1). Among the ammonia plants is OAO Togliattiazot, the world's largest exporter. See Jeanne Whalen, "'Red Director' Cultivates Prosperity While Scoffing at Stocks and Bonds," *Wall Street Journal*, Apr. 18, 2001: 6.

12. *Za kommunizm* (Togliatti), May 22, 1966, 2; June 8, 1966, 1; July 3, 1966, 2.

13. Rossiiskii gosudarstvennyi arkhiv Ekonomiki (RGAE), f. 398 (Ministry of Automobile Production), op. 1, d. 5, ll. 149–50 ("Information on the question of developing automobile construction in the USSR," Dec. 11, 1965).

14. Cited in Central Intelligence Agency, Directorate of Intelligence, *USSR: About to Enter the Automotive Age?* (Washington, D.C., 1966), 9. Vladimir Nikolaevich Novikov, former assistant chairman of the Council of Ministers, claimed to recall in a 1991 interview that Khrushchev had told him "now is not the time for passenger cars; we must organize public transportation, throw our resources into the production of buses and trolley buses that are needed by the people. Cars can wait." V. N. Novikov, "Vzgliad na VAZ s vysot Sovmina i ne tol'ko," in *VAZ: Stranitsy istorii*, 1:6.

15. See, for example, Vladimir Andrianov, *Kosygin* (Moscow: Molodaia gvardiia, 2003), 200–201; Vladimir Kadannikov, "VAZ: ideia I voploshchenie," in *Fenomen Kosygina, zapiski vnuka, mneniia sovremennikov*, ed. V. I. Desiaterik, Iu. V. Firsov, B. I. Stukalin (Moscow: Ekaterina, 2004), 254–60.

16. See V. I. Azar, *Otdykh trudiashchikhsia SSSR* (Moscow: Statistika, 1972), 6–18; B. A. Grushin, *Chetyre zhizni Rossii v zerkale oprosov obshchestvennogo mneniia: Ocherki massovogo-soznaniia rossiian vremen Khrushcheva, Brezhneva, Gorbacheva i El'tsina*, 2 vols. (Moscow:

Progress-Traditsiia, 2001-), 1:438–43; I. M. Daksergof, ed., *Avtomobilist-liubitel'* (Moscow: Fizikul'tura i sport, 1963).

17. A. Romanov and A. Chemonin, "Pni na shosse," *Izvestiia,* May 20, 1965, 6.

18. "Bureau of Transportation Statistics, Table 1–15: Annual U. S. Motor Vehicle Production and Factory (Wholesale) Sales," http://www.bts.gov/publications/national_transportation_statistics/2003/html/table_01_15.html (accessed 12.19.04); and TsSU SSSR, *Narodnoe khoziaistvo SSSR v 1975 godu* (Moscow, 1976), 265. Approximately one quarter of Soviet cars produced were exported.

19. RGAE, f. 398, op. 1, d. 5, ll. 152, 155.

20. RGAE, f. 398, op. 1, d. 12, l. 81 ("On planning for the development of the automobile industry in 1966–70," Nov. 24, 1965).

21. L. M. Shugurov, *Avtomobili Rossii i SSSR,* 3 vols. (Moscow: Prostreks, 1994–1998), 2:28–30; "ZAZ," Wikipedia, http://en.wikipedia.org/wiki/ZAZ (accessed 12.19.04). Khrushchev is quoted in Kommersant—New Russia's First Independent Newspaper (online), http://www.kommersant.com/tree.asp?rubric=2&node=19&doc_id=365959 (accessed 12.19.04). Ironically, Kommersant reports that the privatized legatee of ZAZ, known as ZAO ZAZ, was assembling E- and M-class series Mercedes Benzes.

22. Robyn Dixon, "Soviet-Era Automobile Still Revs Up Passion in Russia," *Los Angeles Times,* Apr. 10, 2002, 3.

23. As with the Zaporozhets, Volga, and other Soviet and East European cars, specs and a capsule history of the Moskvich are available from http://www.autosoviet.altervista.org.

24. RGAE, f. 398, op. 1, d. 1, l. 9 (Protocol No. 3 of session of ministry's board, Dec. 18, 1965); d. 2, ll. 6–29 (Materials relating to protocols of the board's sessions, Dec. 1965); d. 466, l. 208 (Protocol no. 31, Dec. 13, 1966); d. 470 (Materials relating to protocols N26–32 of sessions of the ministry's board), ll. 145–48. Five years later, suppliers were still being blamed by the firm's administrators for poor quality. See *Pravda,* Nov. 17, 1971, 3.

25. RGAE, f. 398, op. 1, d. 490, ll. 1–6 (Proposed resolution "on measures for the further development of production of the Moskvich 408").

26. RGAE, f. 398, op. 1, d. 653, ll. 76–89 (Protocol of June 10, 1966); ll. 143–47 (Minister of Foreign Trade to Minister of Automobile Production, Nov. 5, 1966); d. 490, l. 4 (Draft of resolution on measures for further development of production of Moskvich 408). According to Vladimir Novikov, the proposal was a sop to defense minister Dmitri Ustinov, who opposed any deal with Fiat on the grounds that the defense industry could handle increased car production. Kosygin is said to have played the role of Solomon. See *VAZ: Stranitsy istorii,* 1:26.

27. Nearly indistinguishable from the 408 in appearance, the 412 had a more powerful (75 hp) engine. Although it compared favorably in acceleration, tractability, and luggage space when tested alongside similarly sized West European cars, it did not rate well in braking, road handling, and steering at high speeds; its ventilation, heating, and finish were considered "poor"; and its interior was described as "cheap and nasty." See B. V. Vlasov et al., *Ekonomicheskie problemy proizvodstva avtomobilei* (Moscow, 1971), 47; Ronald Amann, Julian Cooper, and R. W. Davies, *The Technological Level of Soviet Industry* (New Haven: Yale University Press, 1977), 550–56.

28. See Shugurov, *Avtomobili Rossii,* 1:47, 54–59.

29. Valerio Castronovo, *Fiat 1899–1999, un secolo di storia italiana* (Milan: Rizzoli, 1999), 449–52, 907. The Zastava (which incidentally means "turnpike" in Russian!) was sold in the United States as the Yugo in the 1980s.

30. See contributions by A. K. Sokolov, "Rozhdenie volzhskogo avtogiganta v kontekste vnutrennego i vneshnego polozheniia SSSR," and K. Mangarino, "VAZ-FIAT: Tappe fondamentali di collaborazione," in *Istoriia OAO "AVTOVAZ": Uroki, problemy, sovremennost'. Materialy II Vserossiiskoi nauchnoi konferentsii, 26–27 oktiabria 2005 g.,* ed. R. G. Pikhoia (hereafter *Istoriia OAO AvtoVAZ,* 2) (Togliatti: OAO AVTOVAZ, 2005), 45, 60–61.

31. For a biography of Valletta published in the series on "the social life of new Italy," see Piero Bairati, *Vittorio Valletta* (Turin: Unione tipografico-editrice torinese, 1983). On the succession of 1945 and the fascinating politics of the firm in general, see the truly gargantuan centennial book by Castronovo, *Fiat 1899–1999.* "Ostpolitik" is a term borrowed by Castronovo (1103) from the West German Social Democratic Party's policy under Chancellor Willi Brandt of reconciliation with the Communist East.

32. Leonid Kolosov, *Sobkor KGB, zapiski razvedchika i zhurnalista* (Moscow: Tsentrpoligraf, 2001), 223–24.

33. For details, see Castronovo, *Fiat 1899–1999*, 725–89.

34. "U.S. Department of State: Foreign Relations of the United States 1964–1968, XII, Western Europe" (doc. 114), http://www.state.gov/r/ho/frus/johnsonlb/xii/2243.htm. (last accessed 1.7.05); Castronovo, *Fiat 1899–1999*, 1105–6.

35. The factory was to become one of the hot spots of labor unrest during the "hot autumn" of 1969. See Giuseppe Berta, *Mirafiori* (Bologna: Il Mulino, 1998), 63–69, and Carlo Maria Olmo, *Mirafiori* (Turin: U. Allemandi, 1997). For Marietta Shaginian's glowing description of the factory ("gleaming Italian marble" and all), see "Tri dnia na 'Fiate'," *Izvestiia*, Jan. 24, 1967, 5.

36. Bairati, *Valletta*, 344–47; Castronovo, *Fiat 1899–1999*, 1109–10.

37. "Foreign Relations of the United States, XII" (doc. 114).

38. RGAE, f. 398, op. 1, d. 93 ("Report of the director of ZIL, comrade Borodin, on his trip to Italy to inspect Fiat," Nov.–Dec. 1965), ll. 10, 101–3. The description is no less applicable to AvtoVAZ's headquarters today.

39. RGAE, f. 398, op. 1, d. 648 ("Report of group of Soviet specialists on trip to Italy," May 18, 1966), ll. 1–15.

40. *Vneshnaia torgovlia*, no. 8 (1966): 43–44.

41. Boris M. Katsman, *Zavod bez kompromissov: Ocherk istorii Volzhskogo ordena Trudovogo Krasnogo Znameni avtomobil'nogo zavoda im. 50-letiia SSSR 1966–1975 gody* (Togliatti: AVTOVAZ, 2005), 34–40. Katsman was the first director of the economic-planning administration of the factory. The publication of his manuscript, incomplete and unpublished at the time of his death in 1976, was undertaken by a "creative collective" under L. S. Pakhuta.

42. Manfred Grieger, "Cooperation in the Area of Technology: The Volkswagen Group and the Countries of Eastern Europe," paper presented at conference on "The Automobile Revolution: The Automobile and Society after 1945," Moscow, Feb. 16–17, 2007. Grieger, citing Volkswagen documents, claims the Soviet side rejected the proposal in part because the start-up time was too long.

43. Kolosov, *Sobkor KGB*, 226–32; Castronovo, *Fiat 1899–1999*, 1119–20. For the financial arrangements, see RGAE, f. 398, op. 1, d. 653, ll. 4–17 (Agreement between Bank for Foreign Trade of the USSR and Istituto Mobiliare Italiano, 4 May 1966). See also Vladimir Nikolaevich Sushkov, *Zakliuchennyi po klichke "Ministr"* (Moscow: Sovershenno sekretno, 1995), 104–11.

44. For the photograph, see *Illustrato Fiat* (Apr.–May 1966); Harriman quoted in Castronovo, *Fiat 1899–1999*, 1120; Agnelli quoted in Luca Ciferri, Automotive News Europe, at http://www.autonews.com/files/euroauto/inductees/agnelli.htm (accessed 1.9.05).

45. "To Russia—without Love," *Forbes*, Oct. 1, 1966: 19–20. Gleason would produce gear-cutting, testing, and measuring machines valued at $8.9 million. See "U.S. Department of State: Foreign Relations of the United States 1964–1968, XIV, Soviet Union" (doc. 269) http://www.state.gov/r/pa/ho/frus/johnsonlib/xiv/1406.htm (accessed 7.13.07).

46. "To Russia without Love," *Forbes*, Oct. 1, 1966, 19–20.

47. *The Fiat-Soviet Auto Plant and Communist Economic Reforms. A Report pursuant to House Resolution 1043, 89th Congress, 2d session for the Subcommittee on International Trade, Committee on Banking and Currency, House of Representatives (March 1, 1967)* (Washington, D. C.: U.S. Government Printing Office, 1967), 1–3.

48. V. K. Isakov, "Italiia—Rossiia: Voskhozhdenie k VAZu (o nekotorykh istoricheskikh predposylkakh sozdaniia Volzhskogo avtomobil'nogo zavoda)," in *Istoriia* 1:165.

49. *Pravda*, Aug. 22, 1966, 4. The last sentence of the quotation was not included in *Pravda;* it is taken from the Togliatti-based newspaper, *Za kommunizm*, Aug. 24, 1966, 1. Alicata is better known among cinéastes as the screenwriter for Luchino Visconti's film *Ossessione* (1943).

50. Ugo lo Conte, "Shkola zhizni, shkola raboty," in *VAZ: Stranitsy istorii*, 1:164.

51. S. P. Polikarpov, "A nachinalos' vse s proekta," in *VAZ: Stranitsy istorii*, 1:42. See *Pravda*, Sept. 26, 1968, 2, for the claim that "54 sites and 30 populated places" were in contention. The earliest date for which I found evidence of site consideration is Jan. 19, 1966. See RGAE, f. 398, op. 1, d. 495, l. 15 (Tarasov to A. A. Goregliad, assistant chairman of Gosplan).

52. RGAE, f. 398, op. 1, d. 496, l. 196. This is a memorandum from the RSFSR Council of Ministers to the USSR Council of Ministers, dated Apr. 18, 1966. See also Sokolov, "Rozhdenie volzhskogo avtogiganta," 45–46, and E. V. Kravtsova, "Volzhskii avtomobil'nyi zavod: nekotorye aspekty sozdaniia predpriiatiia," in *Istoriia OAO AvtoVAZ*, 2:136–39.

53. Moshe Lewin, *The Soviet Century* (London: Verso, 2005), 334–41.

54. The report signed by Fedorenko and N. G. Nekrasov, chairman of Gosplan's Council on Productive Forces, is in RGAE f. 4372, op. 66. d. 1079, ll. 65–69. It has been published in

Aleksandr Stepanov, *Osennii debiut: Materialy k nachal'noi istorii AVTOVAZa* (Togliatti: AV-TOVAZ, 2005), 263–65. For commentary, see V. A. Ovsiannikov and V. E. Borovik, "K voprosu ob istoriografii stroitel'stva volzhskogo avtomobil'nogo zavoda v 70-e gody XX stoletiia," in *Istoriia*, 1:155; *VAZ: Stranitsy istorii*, 1:42; and Sokolov, "Rozhdenie volzhskogo avtogiganta," 48–50.

55. For a photoreproduction of the original document, see E. A. Bashindzhagian, *Trudnyi put' k "Zhiguliam"* (Togliatti: AVTOVAZ, 2006), between 64 and 65.

56. Ibid., 172–249. See also Bashindzhagian's recollections in R. A. Kiseleva, *Boris Pospelov* (Togliatti: AVTOVAZ, 2006), 76–79. Pospelov was assistant chief designer and also part of the delegation in Turin.

57. RGAE f. 398, op. 1, d. 507 (Materials relating to the construction of the Volga auto plant, vol. 1: 2 May—24 Nov., 1966), ll. 77, 83–87, 109–115, 141–46; Polikarpov in *VAZ: Stranitsy istorii*, 1:43–44.

58. RGAE, f. 398, op. 1, d. 507, l. 219; d. 508 (Materials relating to the construction of the Volga auto plant, vol. 2: 25 Nov.—31 Dec. 1966), l. 1; Iu. M. Bogomolova, "'Avtograd'—Sputnik volzhskogo avtomobil'nogo zavoda," in *Istoriia OAO AvtoVAZ*, 1:179–81. For the two plans, see B. R. Rubanenko, A. S. Obraztsov, and M. K. Savel'ev, *Gorod Tol'iatti: General'nyi plan novoi chasti goroda, proekt i ocheredi stroitel'stva (1968–1971 gg.)* (Togliatti, 1968); and Rubanenko, Obraztsov, and Savel'ev, *Gorod Tol'iatti—general'nyi plan na 25–30 let* (Moscow: Znanie, 1971). I read these in the Togliatti State Archive (TGA), also known as Upravlenie po delam arkhivov g. Tol'iatti (TGA), f. R-17 (Main office of architecture and urban planning of the executive committee of the Togliatti city soviet), where they are cataloged respectively as op. 1, d. 287b and d. 287a.

59. TGA, f. R-17, op. 1, d. 287a, ll. 10–11.

60. V. M. Pravosud, "Rol' i znachenie sotsial'noi politiki VAZa kak gradoobrazuiushchego predpriiatiia. Uroki, problemy, sovremennost'," in *Istoriia OAO AvtoVAZ*, 1:246; A. K. Sinel'nik, *Istoriia gradostroitel'stva i zaseleniia Samarskogo kraia* (Samara: Agni, 2003), 186.

61. TGA, f. R-17, op. 1, d. 287b, ll. 1–17. For the assertion that Togliatti was given (by whom, one wonders) the "privilege" to construct tall buildings—otherwise limited to Moscow, Leningrad, and the Union republic capitals—see I. M. Popova, "Proektirovanie novogo zhilogo raiona v g. Tol'iatti i ego osobennosti," in *Istoriia OAO AvtoVAZ*, 1:192. On trends in domestic architecture, see Blair Ruble, "From Khrushcheby to *Korobki*," in *Russian Housing in the Modern Age: Design and Social History*, ed. William Brumfield and Blair Ruble (Washington, D.C.: Woodrow Wilson Center Press, 1993), 232–70.

62. See, for example, V. A. Shkvarikov et al., *Zastroika zhilykh mikroraionov* (Moscow: Sos. izd-vo lit. po stroitel'stvu arkhitekture i stroitel'nym materialam, 1959); and N. V. Baranov, *Sovremennoe gradostroitel'stvo, glavnye problemy* (Moscow: Gosstroiizdat, 1962). Shkarikov was one of the architects recruited by Rubanenko to work on Togliatti.

63. TGA, f. R-17, op. 1, d. 287a, ll. 1–32.

64. Ruble, "From Khrushcheby," 248–52.

65. On car ownership in the country, see TsSU SSSR, *Narodnoe khoziaistvo SSSR v 1985* (Moscow, 1986), 446. See E. I. Kutyrev and M. K. Saveljev, *New Town of Togliatti* (Moscow: Central Scientific Research and Design Institute of Town Planning of Gosgrazhsanstroy, 1973), 8. It was anticipated that 25% of commuters would use their own cars.

66. N. A. Egortseva, "Blagotvoritel'naia deiatel'nost' OAO 'Avtovaz,'" in *Istoriia OAO AvtoVAZ*, 1:317–18; TGA, f. R-17, op. 1, d. 287a, ll. 25–26. Popova in *Istoriia OAO AvtoVAZ*, 1:191, 193.

67. Cited in Ruble, "From Khrushcheby," 251.

68. *Pravda*, Sept. 25, 1968, 2; Sept. 26, 1968, 2; Mar. 16, 1969, 2; Mar. 17, 1969, 2; June 3, 1970, 2; June 11, 1970, 3. The classic novel that employs both themes was Valentin Kataev's *Time Forward!* from 1932. Much of the pathos of construction is conveyed via the use of military metaphors in Katsman, *Zavod bez kompromissov*.

69. Shugurov, *Avtomobili Rossii*, 2:39–40. Shugurov tastefully notes that Zhiguli was not exactly an ideal name outside of Russia because "in a number of foreign languages it had double meanings."

70. *Volzhskii avtostroitel'*, Oct. 25, 2005, 1–2.

71. Elena Varshavskaia, "Vy vybrali VAZ 2101," *Za rulëm*, no. 1 (2000): 4–6. Over eighty thousand readers voted, of whom a mere 6% were women. A fictitious—and bawdy—account of the life of the first Zhiguli over a thirty-year period was the subject of Ivan Dykhovichnyi's

2001 film, *Kopeika*. For a photograph of the first (real) owner of a Zhiguli, V. M. Penkin of Togliatti, see the original edition of *VAZ: Stranitsy istorii*, ed. A. Shavrin (Samara: KLASS, 1991), 1:166. For the nostalgic appeal of the model among post-Soviet Russians, see *Argumenty i fakty*, May 2, 2001, 8. One of the original "kopeiki" occupies a place of distinction in AvtoVAZ's museum.

72. Katsman, *Zavod bez kompromissov*, 361; *VAZ: Stranitsy istorii*, ed. A. Shavrin (Togliatti: AVTOVAZ, 2005), 5:188.

73. These and other events are commemorated in the company's museum that Poliakov signed into existence on his very last day as general director. T. L. Ralka, "O roli i meste istoriko-tekhnicheskogo muzeia OAO 'Atvovaz' v zhizni i deiatel'nosti zavoda i goroda," in *Istoriia OAO AvtoVAZ*, 1:336. On Poliakov, see A. A. Shavrin, "Pervye rukovoditeli VAZa: Rol' i mesto v istorii avtomobilestroeniia, VAZa, regiona i strany," in *Istoriia OAO AvtoVAZ* 1: 205–6.

74. V. Ia. Romaniuk, *VAZ—sem'ia rabochaia* (Kuibyshev: Knizh. Izd., 1979), 4–5. BAM is the acronym of the Baikal-Amur Mainline railroad and was the last of the hero construction projects of the Brezhnev era.

75. Boris Agapov, *Tekhnicheskie rasskazy* (Moscow: Khudozhestvennaia literatura, 1936), 87–88; Semizorov, *VAZ: Stranitsy istorii*, 1:53.

76. T. Zherbatsskas, "KamAZ stroit vsia strana," *Za rulëm*, no. 3 (1973): 1.

77. See Anna Louise Strong, *From Stalingrad to Kuzbas: Sketches of the Socialist Construction in the USSR* (London: Modern Books, 1932); Scott, *Behind the Urals;* and I. L. Pecheniuk, ed., *BAM, doroga sozidaniia* (Moscow: Sovetskaia Rossiia, 1983).

78. On the GDR, Kurt Möser, personal conversation, Feb. 17, 2007; on Finland, Jukka Gronow, "Vzlet i padenie Lada ('Zhiguli') v Finliandii. Prodazhi, imidzh i otnoshenie k sovetskim avtomobiliam v Finliandii v 1970–1990-kh gg.," in *Istoriia OAO AvtoVAZ*, 2:268–70; and on Britain, Peter Hamilton, "The Lada: A Cultural Icon," in *Autopia: Cars and Culture,* ed. Peter Wollen and Joe Kerr (London: Reaktion Books, 2002), 191–98. Ladas and Nivas arrived in South Africa and Chile in the early 1990s, hard on the heels of the end of authoritarian rule in those countries. After some initial popularity among younger drivers, the reputations of both cars went south. In Chile, the expression "peor que nada" (worse than nothing) became "peor que Lada."

79. Reuther Archives of Labor and Urban Affairs, Wayne State University, Herman Rebhan Collection, Box 6–11—Soviet Union, 1970–76. *Congressional Record,* June 3, 1975: E2789 citing articles in the *Washington Star* and *Detroit News* from May 31, 1975.

80. *VAZ: Stranitsy istorii,* ed. A. Shavrin (Togliatti: AO Avtovaz, 1993), 2:253. Iurii Stepanov describes Sapsai as a "specialist from God" in *VAZ: Stranitsy istorii,* 5:188.

81. *Volzhskaia kommuna,* May 26, 1967, 2–3; *Pravda,* Sept. 25, 1968, 2; Agapov, *Tekhnicheskie,* 91; Romaniuk, *VAZ,* 24; A. Brodskii, "I znaiu—gorod budet," *Za rulëm,* no. 5 (1968): 8–11.

82. *Pravda,* Sept. 26, 1968, 2.

83. T. I. Adaevskaia, "Trudovye konflikty i korporativnye formy ikh razresheniia na Volzhskom avtomobil'nom zavode," in *Istoriia OAO AvtoVAZ*, 2:178–79. On the people's construction projects at GAZ, see Stephen Harris, "Moving to the Separate Apartment: Building, Distributing, Furnishing, and Living in Urban Housing in Soviet Russia, 1950s–1960s," PhD diss., University of Chicago, 2003, 128–85. For more on this incident, sparked by a letter signed by 138 people, see *AVTOVAZ mezhdu proshlym i budushchim. Istoriia Volzhskogo avtomobil'nogo zavoda 1966–2005 gg.,* ed. R. G. Pikhoia (Moscow: RAGS, 2006), 101–2.

84. TGA, f. R-352 (Volga conglomerate for production of light automobiles—AvtoVAZ, 1966–76), op. 1, d. 320 (Materials on composition and turnover of workers for 1970), l. 2. For June 1970 figures, see l. 24.

85. N. N. Borodina, "Zhenshchiny v proizvodstvennom protsesse volzhskogo avtozavoda (1970–1980)," in *Istoriia OAO AvtoVAZ*, 2:171–72.

86. TGA, f. R-352, op. 1, d. 128 (Materials on number, composition, and education of cadres in directorate for 1968), ll. 3, 13; V. V. Riabov et al., *VAZ—istoriia v dokumentakh* (Kuibyshev: Knizhnoe izd-vo, 1985), 108; O. K. Vologina in *VAZ: Stranitsy istorii,* 1:151.

87. See Gail Lapidus, "The Female Industrial Labor Force: Dilemmas, Reassessments, and Options," in *Industrial Labor in the USSR,* ed. Arcadius Kahan and Blair Ruble (New York: Pergamon Press, 1979), 247: "The large-scale movement of women into white-collar and professional occupations...has been associated with a profound decline in their average status and pay relative to skilled blue-collar employment."

88. Borodina, "Zhenshchiny," 171–72. The proportion of women among production personnel rose from 35.2% to 38.5% between 1976 and 1981; for nonindustrial workers the corresponding proportions were 67.1% and 80.8%.

89. E. I. Kuzmicheva and T. Iu. Kramarova, "Sistema doshkol'nogo obrazovaniia OAO 'Avtovaz' v sotsial'noi politike zavoda," in *Istoriia OAO AvtoVAZ*, 2:277–79. In 1976 the number of children accommodated by VAZ programs was 18,577, which represented an excess of more than four thousand.

90. Pravosud in *Istoriia*, 1:248–49; *Literaturnaia gazeta*, Oct. 3, 1979: 12; Sinel'nik, *Istoriia gradostroitel'stva*, 191.

91. See Barbara Garson, "Lordstown: Work in an American Auto Factory," in *Work in Market and Industrial Societies*, ed. Herbert Applebaum (Albany: State University of New York Press, 1984); Heather Ann Thompson, "Auto Workers, Dissent, and the UAW: Detroit and Lordstown," in *Autowork*, ed. Robert Asher and Ronald Edsforth (Albany: State University of New York Press, 1995), 200–206; Larry W. Isaac and Larry D. Christiansen, "Degradations of Labor, Cultures of Cooperation: Braverman's 'Labor,' Lordstown, and the Social Factory," in *Rethinking the Labor Process*, ed. Mark Wardell, Thomas L. Steiger, and Peter Meiksins (Albany: State University of New York Press, 1999), 123–38.

92. Adaevskaia, "Trudovye konflikty," 179–80. Adaevskaia uses the feminine *truzhenitsy* (female laborers). On a tour of the shop in October 2005, I saw only women on the shop floor. On work stoppages and other disputes elsewhere in Soviet Russia, see Mary McAuley, *Labour Disputes in Soviet Russia, 1957–1965* (Oxford: Clarendon Press, 1969).

93. Popova in *Istoriia OAO AvtoVAZ*, 1:194.

94. A. K. Sokolov, "Kolletiv AvtoVAZa i ego osobennosti v sovetskii period (1970–1980-e gg.)," 3, paper presented at conference on "The Automobile Revolution: The Automobile and Society after 1945," Moscow, Feb. 16–17, 2007.

95. TGA, f. R-300 (Auto factory district soviet of people's deputies and its executive committee), op. 1, d. 50 (Protocols of sessions and reports of sitting commission on socialist legality and maintenance of public order, 1974, vol. 1), ll. 4, 13–18.

96. Ironically, at least in France, factory industry was supposed to be a solution to the problem of theft of materials put out by merchants for "protoindustrial" production. See Ronald Aminzade, "Reinterpreting Capitalist Industrialization," in *Work in France: Representations, Meaning, Organization, and Practice*, ed. Steven Laurence Kaplan and Cynthia J. Koepp (Ithaca: Cornell University Press, 1986), 402–3, 408.

97. Hedrick Smith, *The Russians* (London: Sphere Books, 1976), 279; Konstantin Simis, "The Machinery of Corruption in the Soviet Union," *Survey* 23, no. 4 (1977–78): 55.

98. TGA, f. R-94 (Togliatti City Soviet and its Executive Committee), op. 1, d. 417 (Protocols of sessions and reports of sitting commission on socialist legality and maintenance of public order, 1971–72), ll. 51, 110.

99. TGA f. R-300, op. 1, d. 51 (Protocols of sessions and reports of sitting commission on socialist legality and maintenance of public order, 1974, vol. 2), l. 150. Among the latter, 1,372 (86%) were classified as workers, 1,247 (78%) were over the age of twenty-five, and 261 (16%) were either party or Komsomol members.

100. Ibid., l. 122.

101. TGA f. R-300, op. 1, d. 127 (Protocols of sessions and reports of sitting commission on socialist legality and maintenance of public order, 1975–77), l. 9. On comrades' courts in the early Soviet era, see Lewis H. Siegelbaum, "Narratives of Appeal and the Appeal of Narratives: Labor Discipline and Its Contestation in the Early Soviet Period," *Russian History* 24, nos. 1–2 (1997): 65–87.

102. TGA, f. R-17, op. 1, d. 287a, l. 63.

103. Ruble, "From Khrushcheby," 242, notes higher average housing allocations for new apartments in Moscow.

104. *Pravda*, Sept. 26, 1968, 2.

105. TGA, f. R-300, op. 1, d. 50, l. 31.

106. Ibid., ll. 32–34.

107. Many of Sheila Fitzpatrick's recent works are devoted to this theme. See her collection of essays, *Tear Off the Masks: Identity and Imposture in Twentieth-Century Russia* (Princeton: Princeton University Press, 2005).

108. *AVTOVAZ mezhdu proshlym i budushchim*, 194.

109. Ibid., 193.

110. Ibid., 198–232.

111. Ibid., 250–51.

112. Ibid., 252–56.

113. Ibid., 232–36; Walter D. Connor, *The Accidental Proletariat: Workers, Politics, and Crisis in Gorbachev's Russia* (Princeton: Princeton University Press, 1991), 52–91. On Vietnamese at VAZ, see photographs in *AVTOVAZ: Istoriia millionov 1966–2006*, ed. Vladimir Isakov et al. (Togliatti: Lada-Imidzh, 2006), 140–41.

114. *AVTOVAZ mezhdu proshlym i budushchim*, 204–14; Anders Åsland, *Gorbachev's Struggle for Economic Reform: The Soviet Reform Process, 1985–88* (Ithaca: Cornell University Press, 1989), 93–96.

115. *AVTOVAZ mezhdu proshlym i budushchim*, 206.

116. Ibid., 257.

117. Councils of labor collectives were introduced throughout the Soviet Union by the Law on State Enterprises of July 1987. They monitored fulfillment of labor contacts and otherwise duplicated functions of trade unions. See Donald Filtzer, *Soviet Workers and the Collapse of Perestroika: The Soviet Labour Process and Gorbachev's Reforms, 1985–1991* (Cambridge: Cambridge University Press, 1994), 90–92.

118. *AVTOVAZ mezhdu proshlym i budushchim*, 399. VAZ cited these figures to justify its new regulations.

119. Ibid., 266.

120. Ibid., 399–402.

121. Ibid., 318–22; Filtzer, *Soviet Workers and the Collapse of Perestroika*, 90–92; David Mandel, *Labour after Communism: Auto Workers and Their Unions in Russia, Ukraine, and Belarus* (Montreal: Black Rose, 2004), 132.

122. Mandel, *Labour*, 131–32.

123. Ibid.

124. Mandel, *Labour*, 132–50; *AVTOVAZ mezhdu proshlym i budushchim*, 450, 517.

125. Renfrey Clarke, "Russian Car Lockout Signals New Conflicts," *Green Left Weekly*, online edition, #164, Oct. 26, 1994, at http.greenleft.org.au (accessed 9.6.05); and "U.S. State Department 1994 Human Rights Report: Russia," at http://dosfan.lib.uic.edu (accessed 9.6.05); Alla Startseva, "AvtoVAZ Strike Goes against Union," *Moscow Times*, Oct. 11, 2000.

126. Adaevskaia, "Trudovye konflikty," 183; Mandel, *Labour*, 148–51. See also N. M. Kapagin, "Profsoiuznaia organizatsiia OAO 'Avtovaz' kak factor stabilizatsii sotsial'nykh otnoshenii v krupnoi promyshlennoi strukture," in *Istoriia OAO AvtoVAZ*, 2:207–13.

127. "Togliatti Referendum Fails to Change Name," *Russian Regional Report*, Apr. 12, 1996, in http://www.isn.ethz.ch/researchpub/publihouse/rr/docs/rrr961204.pdf (accessed 1.26.05); Utkin quoted in "Verlag eerste bezoek Bart Staes aan Russische Federatie 14–17 April 2002," http://www.bartstaes.be (accessed 1.26.05).

128. For this term and what it describes, see Johanna Granville, "'Dermokratizatsiya' and 'Prikhvatizatsiya': The Russian Kleptocracy and the Rise of Organized Crime," *Demokratizatsiya*, no. 3 (2003): 449–57. For one of the better analyses of the process, see Vadim Volkov, *Violent Entrepreneurs: The Use of Force in the Making of Russian Capitalism* (Ithaca: Cornell University Press, 2002).

129. *AVTOVAZ mezhdu proshlym i budushchim*, 30.

130. On Berezovsky's dealings with OAO AvtoVAZ, see Paul Klebnikov's rather sensationalist and libelous article, "Godfather of the Kremlin?" *Forbes*, Dec. 30, 1996, 90–96, and his book, *Godfather of the Kremlin: Boris Berezovsky and the Looting of Russia* (New York: Harcourt, 2000), esp. 70–71, 75–76, 88–89. See also Roman Zhuk, "Komu prinadlezhit Rossiia? (Avtomobil'naia promyshlennost')," *Kommersant. Vlast'*, Oct. 2, 2001, 51–60, and David E. Hoffman, *The Oligarchs: Wealth and Power in the New Russia* (New York: Public Affairs, 2003), 135–49.

131. Klebnikov, *Godfather*, 140–43; Hoffman, *Oligarchs*, 215–18, 226–28. For a fictionalized account of these dealings by one of its participants, see Iu. A. Dubov, *Bol'shaia paika: Roman* (Moscow: Vagrius, 2000), 247–75. For a succinct overview, see *AVTOVAZ mezhdu proshlym i budushchim*, 286–89.

132. Klebnikov, *Godfather*, 92.

133. *St. Petersburg Times*, May 26, 2000, 12; *St. Petersburg Times*, Oct. 25, 2002: 1; Archie Brown, "Vladimir Putin and the Reaffirmation of Central State Power," *Post-Soviet Affairs* 17, no. 1 (2001): 45–55. The Russian government has proven unsuccessful in its efforts to extradite Berezovsky from Britain to face the charges.

134. *New York Times,* July 23, 1992, A1; S. Iu. Tselikov, "Avtomobil'nyi rynok Rossii," in *Istoriia OAO AvtoVAZ,* 1:265–66; VAZ (Russia), http://www.autoindex.org/maker.plt?no=1820 (accessed 4.27.04); *AvtoSreda* (Togliatti), no. 6 (2004): 4–5; "GM-AvtoVAZ Increases Production," *Russian Journal,* Jan. 11, 2005, http://www.russiajournal.com/russian/news_46947. html. (accessed 1.27.05).

135. Sergei Zhuravlev, "Khozaeva i naemnye rabotniki: sotsial'naia istoriia postsovetskogo AvtoVAZa," paper presented at conference on "The Automobile Revolution: The Automobile and Society after 1945," Moscow, Feb. 16–17, 2007.

136. M. A. Kudinov, "Molodezh' v usloviiakh industrial'nogo goroda (na primere g. Tol'iatti)," in *Istoriia OAO Avtovaz* 2: 294–95; *Volzhskii avtostroitel',* Apr. 11, 1997, 4.

137. Liam Pleven, "2003 Generation Afflicted: HIV Spreads Quickly in Russia, Particularly among the Young," Transatlantic Partners against AIDS, http://www.tpaa.net/articles/reg_ 080403_generation.html; USAID Europe and Eurasia, "New USAID-Sponsored Twinning Healthcare Partnership to Create Model HIV/AIDS Programs in Russia," http://www.usaid.gov/loca tions/europe_eurasia/press/success/twinning_healthcare_partnership.html (accessed 11.02.07).

138. Personal correspondence with B. Krotov, Togliatti; and Anna Smolchenko, "State Managers Take over AvtoVAZ," *Moscow Times,* Dec, 23, 2005, 1.

139. "The Automobile Revolution: The Automobile and Society after 1945," Moscow, Feb. 16–17, 2007.

Chapter 4. Roads

1. See United States Federal Highway Administration, *America's Highways, 1776–1976: A History of the Federal-Aid Program* (Washington, D.C.: U. S. Department of Transportation, 1977), and Tom Lewis, *Divided Highways: Building the Interstate Highways, Transforming American Life* (New York: Viking, 1997).

2. For different perspectives, see Henry Moon, *The Interstate Highway System* (Washington, D.C.: Association of American Geographers, 1994); Owen D. Gutfruend, *Twentieth-Century Sprawl: Highways and the Reshaping of the American Landscape* (Oxford: Oxford University Press, 2004); Andrew Cross, "Driving the American Landscape," in *Autopia: Cars and Culture,* ed. Peter Wollen and Joe Kerr (London: Reaktion, 2002), 249–58; and Jane Holtz Kay, "The Asphalt Exodus," in ibid., 266–76.

3. Central Intelligence Agency, Directorate of Intelligence, *USSR: About to Enter the Automotive Age?* (Washington, D.C., 1966), 19–20.

4. Holland Hunter, *Soviet Transport Experience, Its Lessons for Other Countries* (Washington, D.C.: Brookings Institution, 1968), 50, 91–92; Elizabeth Clayton, *Soviet Rural Roads: Problems and Prospects,* Soviet Transportation Research Project Working Paper #7 (Philadelphia: Wharton Econometric Forecasting Associates, 1984), 9. The reasons for Russia's use of broad-gauge rails are in dispute.

5. For the USSR, TsU SSSR, *Narodnoe khoziaistvo SSSR v 1970* (Moscow: Gos. stat. izd-vo, 1971), 153. Comparable figures from the United States for 1994 were 200 million vehicles and 3.75 million kilometers of paved road, a ratio of 53.3 vehicles per kilometer. See Department of Transportation, Federal Highway Administration, at http://www.fhwa.dot.gov/ ohim/1994/section5.htm. (accessed 1.13.05).

6. To take another example, in Australia there were 12.7 million registered vehicles in 2003 and 337,400 kilometers of paved (bitumen and cement) roads, yielding a ratio of 37.6. See "Year Book, Australia, Transport Infrastructure," at http://www.abs.gov.au/Ausstats/abs@.nsf (accessed 2.28.05).

7. Belorusskaia Assotsiatsiia Mezhdunarodnykh Avtomobil'nykh Perevozchikov— "Novosti" at http://www.bairc.org/index.shtml. (accessed 5.12.05).

8. Allen C. Lynch, "Roots of Russia's Economic Dilemmas: Liberal Economics and Illiberal Geography," *Europe-Asia Studies* 54, no. 1 (2002): 34. For the argument that Russia is uniquely cursed by the combination of harsh climate and predominantly clay soils, see Aleksandr Nikonov, "Ukhaby na dorogakh," *Novaia gazeta,* Aug. 21, 2003, 16.

9. *Krokodil,* July 30, 1946.

10. Lynch, "Roots," 36.

11. O. V. Skvortsov, ed., *Dorogi Rossii: Stranitsy istorii dorozhnogo dela* (St. Petersburg: Liki Rossii, 1996), 108; on Glavkomtrud, see E. H. Carr, *The Bolshevik Revolution, 1917–1923* 3 vols. (Harmondsworth: Penguin, 1966), 2:211–12; Thomas F. Remington, *Building Socialism*

in *Bolshevik Russia: Ideology and Industrial Organization, 1917–1921* (Pittsburgh: University of Pittsburgh Press, 1984), 82–92.

12. Cited in *Komsomol'skaia pravda*, Aug. 27, 1931, 3. According to a report from 1930, "from the first days of the Imperialist War to 1923–24, not one kopeck from the state budget was invested in road maintenance." Gosudarstvennyi arkhiv rossiiskoi federatsii (GARF), f. 4426, op. 1, d. 5 (Protocols of sessions of presidium of Avtodor Central Council, 1930), l. 55.

13. A. A. Nadezhko, ed., *Dorogi Rossii, istoricheskii aspekt.* (Moscow: Kruk, 1996), 73; for Siberia, see Tat'iana Belova, "Dorogi tridtsatogo goda," *Vechernii Novosibirsk*, Mar. 22, 2003, at www.vn.ru/22.3.2003/ (accessed 05.17.05).

14. Nadezhko, *Dorogi*, 72–75, 77.

15. GARF, f. 4226, op. 1, d. 5, l. 55 ob.

16. Walter Benjamin, *Moscow Diary* (Cambridge: Harvard University Press, 1986), 9, 66–67.

17. B. P. Orlov, *Razvitie transporta SSSR, 1917–1962* (Moscow: AN, 1963), 93–94.

18. A. S. Kudriavtsev, "Razvitie dorozhnogo stroitel'stva v SSSR za 20 let," *Doroga i avtomobil'*, no. 11 (1937): 9–10.

19. See M. Kol'tsov, "Koleso na pamiat'," *Za rulëm*, no. 1 (1928): 27–28, for a reference to a driver in Stalingrad Oblast who "had heard that somewhere there are excellent asphalted roads, but one could only imagine in one's dreams such a road here in Russia, on the Volga!"; see also Viktor Shklovskii, "Dorogi Kazakhstana," *Za rulëm*, no. 5 (1928): 31, namely, "as far as roads are concerned,...there are none." In October 1928 it was reported that of 8,935 kilometers of roads in Novosibirsk Okrug, three kilometers were stone covered; the remainder were dirt. Belova, "Dorogi tridtsatogo goda."

20. N. Osinskii, *Po tu storonu okeana, iz amerikanskikh vpechatlenii i nabliudenii* (Moscow-Leningrad: Gosizdat, 1926), 61–63.

21. N. Osinskii, "Amerikanskii avtomobil' ili rossiiskaia telega?" *Pravda*, July 22, 1927, 3. See also *Pravda*, Aug. 14 and 17, 1927.

22. GARF, f. 4426, op. 1, d. 59 (Stenographic report of Avtodor on question of "The Automobile or the Cart," 28 Nov. 1927), ll. 16, 26.

23. GARF, f. 4426, op. 1, d. 317 (Stenographic report of debate on theme "Automobile or Cart," 23 Jan. 1928), ll. 13–16, 17, 26, 39–40, 44–50.

24. Rossiiskii Gosudarstvennyi Arkhiv Ekonomiki (RGAE), f. 4372, op. 31, d. 998 (Five-Year Plan of development of auto route transport proposed by Tsudortrans), ll. 76–84.

25. *Trud*, Apr. 17, 1930, 6; GARF, f. 4426, op. 1, d. 5, l. 55 ob. To take the province of Riazan' as an example, it was estimated that surfacing (*shossirovka*) its roads would cost R 450 million. Even if the budget were raised from R 600,000 to R 2 million, it would have taken 225 years. N. Beliaev, "O pochetnykh prezidiumakh i dorozhnoi revoliutsii," *Za rulëm*, no. 3 (1929): 6–7.

26. Matthew J. Payne, *Turksib: Stalin's Railroad and the Building of Socialism* (Pittsburgh: University of Pittsburgh Press, 2000), 1. In the year before the Turksib project got under way (1926–27), state investment in railroad construction and reconstruction was R 315 million (18).

27. Orlov, *Razvitie transporta*, 168.

28. M. Ilin, *New Russia's Primer: The Story of the Five-Year Plan*, trans. George S. Counts and Nucia P. Lodge (Boston: Houghton Mifflin, 1931), 126.

29. Kuibyshev quoted in *Za rulëm*, no. 21 (1933): 3; *Pravda*, June 13, 1933, 1; *Trud*, Apr. 17, 1930, 6.

30. V. D. Batiushkov and N. S. Vatiushkin, *Tverdye gruntovye dorogi* (Petrograd, 1915), 3.

31. RGAE, f. 4372, op. 31, d. 998, l. 76.

32. George S. Counts, *A Ford Crosses Soviet Russia* (Boston: Stratford, 1930), 34–35, 41. Counts was a long-time professor of education in the Teachers College at Columbia University.

33. Transcript of David Kempler's interview with Martin Greif, Nov. 8, 1976, in Austin— G.A.Z. papers, Western Reserve Historical Society (Cleveland, Ohio); Gosudarstvennyi Arkhiv Nizhni Novgorod Oblast (GANO), f. 2431, op. 2, d. 7, ll. 14, 55 (letters from Palmer to Mr. Zenziper at Avtostroi, November 5 and 23, 1929) in File 41, Richard Austin's Files at Western Reserve Historical Society.

34. *Za industrializatsiiu*, Aug. 2, 1930, 3. For a photograph of a Ford truck laying concrete on what is described in the caption as "heavily reinforced" and the "first in Russia outside any city," see GAZ Photos R Series Set #2, R-10, Western Reserve Historical Society.

35. V. I. Lenin, *Polnoe sobranie sochineniia*, 5th ed. (Moscow: Politizdat, 1964), 45:86.

36. N. I. Bukharin, *Put' k sotsializmu v Rossii*, ed. Sidney Heitman (New York: Omicron Books, 1967), 262–72, 284, 288–89; I. V. Stalin, *Sochineniia* (Moscow, 1949), 2:247–52. In his

biography of Bukharin, Stephen Cohen accords this and related works tremendous importance, entitling the chapter wherein they are discussed "Bukharinism and the Road to Socialism." See Stephen Cohen, *Bukharin and the Bolshevik Revolution: A Political Biography, 1888–1938* (New York: Knopf, 1973), 160–212.

37. *Komsomol'skaia pravda*, Aug. 27, 1931, 3.

38. *Ekonomicheskaia zhizn'*, Aug. 26, 1931, 3.

39. K. Krüger, *Motorising Russia and Asia (Incorporating German Autobahns)* (Berlin: Verlag der Neue Orient, 1934), 10. On "Moscow's street landscape" and the city council's "huge" investment in paving, widening, and constructing new roads during these years, see Stephen V. Bittner, "Green Cities and Orderly Streets: Space and Culture in Moscow, 1928–1933," *Journal of Urban History* 25, no. 1 (1998): 40–51.

40. To be sure, the numbers were still small. In Moscow, there were a reported 3,203 vehicles in 1927; by 1932 the number had increased to 7,887 of which 4,310 (54%) were trucks. See *Za rulëm*, no. 6, 1936: 5.

41. L. M. Kaganovich, *Socialist Reconstruction of Moscow and Other Cities in the USSR* (New York: International Publishers, 1931), 90. On Moscow's General Plan, see R. Antony French, *Plans, Pragmatism, and People: The Legacy of Soviet Planning for Today's Cities* (Pittsburgh: University of Pittsburgh Press, 1995), 62–65; Timothy Colton, *Moscow: Governing the Socialist Metropolis* (Cambridge: Harvard University Press, 1995), 272–81.

42. Nadezhko, *Dorogi*, 78. Another source cites figures of ninety-three thousand kilometers, or one quarter of the planned target, and as far as hard surfacing was concerned, only twelve thousand kilometers, or a mere 9% of the planned target of 139,000 kilometers. *Doroga i avtomobil'*, no. 11 (1937): 11. These figures coincide with Gosplan's retrospective analysis presented in RGAE 4372, op. 31, d. 998, ll. 68–67.

43. National Archives (College Park, Maryland), Records of the Department of State Relating to the Internal Affairs of the Soviet Union, 1930–1939, 861.5017, Living Conditions/567.

44. Arne Strøm, *Uncle Give Us Bread* (London: Allen and Unwin, 1936), 113.

45. *Sotsialisticheskoe stroitel'stvo SSSR, Ezhegodnik* (Moscow: TsUNKhU Gosplana SSSR, 1935), 451–52. By the mid-1940s, at least for transport purposes, a third category (republic, krai, and oblast roads) was inserted between "union" and "local." See A. S. Kudriavtsev, *Avtoguzhevye dorogi i tekhnika uskorennogo vosstanovleniia proezda na nikh* (Moscow: AN SSSR, 1944), 9.

46. On the *amerikanka*, see Colton, *Moscow*, 323, 346. For upkeep and reconstruction of Moscow's thoroughfares including Gork'ii Street and the Mozhaisk Highway, see RGAE, f. 4372, op. 38, d. 1839 (Notes by employees of Gosplan's municipal department), ll. 3–74.

47. For the 1928 decree, see *Za rulëm*, no. 9 (1929): 32. This contains the RSFSR version. Analogous measures were passed by other union republics.

48. Tracy Nichols Busch, "'A Class on Wheels': Avtodor and the 'Automobilization' of the Soviet Union, 1927–1935," PhD diss., Georgetown University, 2003, 25–26 (also 221). In her authoritative history of "Stalin's peasants," Sheila Fitzpatrick subsumes her several references to the phenomenon under the category of corvée. See Sheila Fitzpatrick, *Stalin's Peasants: Resistance and Survival in the Russian Village after Collectivization* (Oxford: Oxford University Press, 1994), 69, 99, 111, 128–29, 133–34, 179.

49. *Za rulëm*, no. 6 (1928): 28. See also Hunter, *Soviet Transport Experience*, 95.

50. For the figure of 15%, see *Komsomol'skaia pravda*, Aug. 27, 1931, 3; for 25%, see GARF, f. 4426, op. 1, d. 5, l. 323 (Road section report on total labor participation in road work in 1929–30 in RSFSR); for 30%, see d. 6, l. 57 (Stenographic report of session of presidium of Central Council, March 21, 1931). One wonders how these percentages were arrived at.

51. See GARF, f. 4426, op. 1, d. 488 (Stenographic report of First All-Union Conference on Road Construction, May 15, 1932), ll. 15, 23, 56. Eventually, the length of roads built and improved and number of participants became the standard criteria. See, for example, GARF, f. 4426, op. 1, d. 525 (Stenographic report of session of road council under Central Council, Dec. 15, 1934), ll. 1–2.

52. Fitzpatrick, *Stalin's Peasants*, 133–34, 179–80; Belova, "Dorogi tridtsatogo goda."

53. *Izvestiia*, Apr. 25, 1932, 3. According to this report, the total number of labor days "given" to this task in the RSFSR in 1931 was 25.366 million. If, as indicated in another source, some nineteen million people were eligible for such service, that would mean an average of 1.33 labor days.

54. *Doroga i avtomobil'*, no. 7 (1931): 7; Tsudortrans, *Avtodorozhnoe khoziaistvo SSSR v tsifrakh: Statisticheskii sbornik* (Moscow, 1935), 44–45.

55. *Istoriia kolkhoznogo prava: Sbornik zakonodatel'nykh materialov SSSR i RSFSR, 1917– 1958 gg.*, 2 vols. (Moscow: Gosizdiuridlit, 1959), 1:329–30.

56. GARF, f. 4426, op. 1, d. 488, l. 24; d. 10, ll. 298–313 (Report by A. Blium on the question of budgetary assignments for mastering labor participation of the population in road construction, Dec. 13, 1932); *Istoriia kolkhoznogo prava* 1: 478–79.

57. Charles Hachten, "Separate Yet Governed: The Representation of Soviet Property Relations in Civil Law and Public Discourse," in *Borders of Socialism: Private Spheres in Soviet Russia*, ed. Lewis H. Siegelbaum (New York: Palgrave, 2006), 73. For the claim that in the Georgian SSR "the general plan for labor participation in road construction…was fulfilled by 175%" in 1936 because "the majority of kolkhozes established specially selected kolkhoz road brigades," see N. Vasil'evich, "Ot bezdorozh'ia—k kul'turnym dorogam," *Doroga i avtomobil'*, no. 11 (1937): 44.

58. *Komsomol'skaia pravda*, Aug. 27, 1931, 3.

59. GARF, f. 4426, op. 1, d. 5, ll. 131, 206–14; d. 6, 49ob–50. Kulaks were rural dwellers identified as exploiters and (therefore) enemies of collectivization. Pioneers was a mass youth organization founded in 1922 for those aged ten to fifteen, patterned on the Boy Scouts.

60. Nichols Busch, "Avtodor and the 'Automobilization,'" 40–55. Timothy Paynich, "Mastering Technology for the 'Future War': Para-militarism and Popular Science in the 1930s," unpublished paper presented at American Association for the Advancement of Slavic Studies annual convention, Salt Lake City, Nov. 6, 2005. On air-mindedness, see Scott W. Palmer, *Dictatorship of the Air: Aviation Culture and the Fate of Modern Russia* (Cambridge: Cambridge University Press, 2006), 2–3.

61. GARF, f. 4426, op. 1, d. 499, ll. 148, 197; d. 489, ll. 1, 8. For Avtodor's involvement with socialist competition and the like, see GARF, f. 4426, op. 1, d. 475, 487, 493, 494, 496, 513, 521, 522, 529.

62. Daniel Peris, *Storming the Heavens: The Soviet League of the Militant Godless* (Ithaca: Cornell University Press, 1998). Avtodor's rural membership was not too plentiful. As late as June 1932, of a reported membership in the RSFSR of nearly nine hundred thousand only some 124,000 (14%) were rural based. In terms of individual branches ("collectives"), one in five was located in the countryside. *Izvestiia*, June 23, 1932, 2.

63. Nichols Busch, "Avtodor and the 'Automobilization,'" 231.

64. GARF, f. 4426, op. 1, d. 13, l. 10; *Za rulëm*, no. 19 (1931): 1.

65. *Sotsialisticheskoe stroitel'stvo* (1935), 451. Georgia may have benefited from the perceived strategic importance and value as a conduit for tourists of the 220-kilometer-long Georgian Military Highway (today, A301). I thank Diane Koenker for this observation.

66. Sheikovskii, "Chto meshaet uspekhu dorozhnoi povinnosti," *Za rulëm*, nos. 17–18 (1930): 26; GARF, f. 4426, op. 1, d. 5, l. 324.

67. GARF, f. 4426, op. 1, d. 43 (Stenographic report of meeting of central council employees with Tsudortrans, 1935), l. 72.

68. Ibid., l. 69.

69. Gushosdor, *Instruktsiia po zapolneniiu raiispolkomami otchetnoi kartochki (forma No. 100) o vypolnenii plana truduchastiia i dorozhnykh rabot po mestnym dorogam na 1937 god* (Moscow: Mosoblgorlit, 1937).

70. Vasil'evich, "Ot bezdorozh'ia," 46; Valery Lazarev and Paul R. Gregory, "The Wheels of a Command Economy: Allocating Soviet Vehicles," *Economic History Review* 55, no. 2 (2002): 343; Fitzpatrick, *Stalin's Peasants*, 216–17; *Pravda*, Aug. 25, 1937, 2. The number of trucks "in agriculture" increased from 26,600 at the end of 1933 to 195,800 at the end of 1938, according to *Sotsialisticheskoe stroitel'stvo Soiuza SSR (1933–1938 gg.), Statisticheskii sbornik* (Moscow: Gosplanizdat, 1939), 8.

71. N. Osinskii, "Dve tysiachi kilometrov na avtomobile," *Za rulëm*, no. 15 (1929): 12. He also wrote an account for *Pravda* (July 16, 1929) that appeared as well in a collection of his articles and speeches. See N. Osinskii, *Avtomobilizatsiia SSSR: Stat'i, ocherki, rechi (1927–1929)* (Moscow: Gosizdat, 1930), 225–35.

72. Osinskii, "Dve tysiachi kilometrov," 17.

73. GARF, f. 4426, op. 1, d. 328, ll. 1–14 (Report on the Viatka provincial rally, June–July 1929).

74. GARF, f. 4226, op. 1, d. 320 (Report on results of rally along the route Moscow—Volga German Republic, Nov. 1928), ll. 1–19.

75. Il'ia Ilf and Evgenii Petrov, *Dvenadtsat' stul'ev; Zolotoi telenok* (Kiev: Radianskii pis'mennik, 1957), 376–78. On satire reinforcing what it seemingly is subverting, see Northrop Frye, "The Nature of Satire," *University of Toronto Quarterly* 14 (1944–45): 75–89; Edward

Bloom and Lillian Bloom, *Satire's Persuasive Voice* (Ithaca: Cornell University Press,1979), 19 ("The affirmative impulse...is the seal of satire at its best"); and Fredric V. Bogel, *The Difference Satire Makes* (Ithaca: Cornell University Press, 2001), 32, 62.

76. *Za rulëm,* no. 17 (1929): 19; no. 18 (1929): 13.

77. GARF, f. 4426, op. 1, d. 342 (Report of member of the organization commission, Engineer N. M. Zaborovskii, May 19, 1930), ll. 14–15; d. 5, l. 90.

78. GARF, f. 4426, op. 1, d. 342, ll. 40–46. Indeed, whenever in subsequent years the possibility of reviving the Vladivostok–Moscow (or, alternatively, Moscow–Vladivostok) rally came before Avtodor's central council, someone would refer to "the sad history of 1930" or the "mistake of the 1930 rally," and the proposal would be shelved. Such proposals came before Avtodor's central council in 1933, 1934, and 1935. For details see GARF, f. 4426, op. 1, d. 363, l. 3; d. 23, ll. 82 ob., 105; and d. 405, ll. 14–71.

79. *Pravda,* July 23, 1933, 4.

80. I. Ustrinenko, "Paralleli," *Za rulëm,* no. 20 (1933): 13; El-Registan and L. Brontman, *Moskva–Kara-Kum–Moskva* (Moscow: Sovetskaia literatura, 1934), 26. See also "Sovkino zhurnal," no. 23 (1933); State Archive of Cinema and Photographic Documents, Krasnogorsk (GAKFD), 0–2436. The newsreel, shot as the rally passed through the Chuvash Republic, contained titles such as "Thousands of kilometers without bumps," "Everywhere new bridges," and "You won't spill the milk!," the latter preceding a clip of a peasant woman carrying a pail in a truck.

81. *Pravda,* July 23, 1933, 4.

82. El-Registan and Brontman, *Moskva–Kara-Kum–Moskva,* 105.

83. Ibid., 200–218; *USSR in Construction,* no. 2 (1934).

84. GARF, f. 4426, op. 1, d. 405 (Stenographic report of session of committee to organize Far East–Siberian rally, 17 January 1935), ll. 18, 28, 38, 54–55. Tatiana Fedorova, who worked on the Moscow metro and was interviewed for the "Red Flag" episode of the PBS series, *People's Century* (1999), recalls John Morgan as "an American consultant and a very good, solid engineer." *Man with a Movie Camera* was the title of Vertov's documentary from 1929.

85. N. S. Vetchinkin, "Iakutsko-Chukotskaia Avtomagistral' dlia velikogo severnogo vozdushnogo puti," *Doroga i avtomobil',* no. 10 (1937): 2–3. On the transpolar flights of the mid-1930s, see John McCannon, *Red Arctic: Polar Exploration and the Myth of the North in the Soviet Union, 1932–1939* (New York: Oxford University Press, 1998), esp. 65–72.

86. See *Pravda,* July 25, 1934, 6; and Sergei D'iakonov, "Istoriia odnogo motora, k 70-letiiu mezhdunarodnogo dizel'nogo konkursa," *Avtomobili i tseny,* no. 38 (2004): 18–21. On the latter two rallies, see *Za rulëm,* no. 18 (1938): 11–17; *Pravda,* July 4, 1939, 6.

87. *Pravda,* July 31, 1936, 6; July 30, 1936, 4. See also *Za rulëm,* no. 17 (1936): 10; *Pravda,* Sept. 30, 1936, 6; *Izvestiia,* Sept. 9, 1936, 4; *Trud,* Sept. 30, 1936, 3; Oct. 1, 1936, 1 (editorial); A. P. Volkova, *Zhenshchina za rulëm, zapiski komandora 1-go zhenskogo avtoprobega imeni Stalinskoi konstitutsii* (Moscow: Profizdat, 1937).

88. Il'ia Ilf and Evgenii Petrov, *Odnoetazhnaia Amerika* (Moscow: Tekst, 2003), 8, 86, 92–93. The book was originally published in 1937 by Khudozhestvennaia literatura. The English-language version appeared in an authorized translation by Charles Malamuth as *Little Golden America* (New York: Farrar and Rinehart, 1937).

89. R. Krasnov, "Bakinskie Amerikantsy," *Za rulëm,* no. 10 (1929): 27; I. Feld'man, "Amerika s tochki zreniia Avtodorovtsa," *Za rulëm,* no. 14 (1930): 12.

90. For the origins and building of the autobahns, see M. Kornrumpf, *HAFRABA E. v.— Deutsche Autobahn-Planung 1926–1934* (Berlin: Kirschbaum, 1990); Erhard Schütz and Eckhard Gruber, *Mythos Reichsautobahn: Bau und Inszenierung der "Strassen des Führers"* (Berlin: Ch. Links, 1996); and Karl Lärmer, *Autobahnbau in Deutschland 1933 bis 1945: Zu d. Hintergründen* (Berlin: Akademie Verlag, 1975).

91. I. I. Diumulen, "Ford 1934 g. v probege," *Za rulëm,* no. 20 (1934): 6; N. Osinskii, "Dve tysiachi," 17. Dumoulin also accompanied Osinskii on the 1929 auto trip.

92. *Pravda,* May 10, 1933, 5.

93. *Pravda,* May 12, 1933, 5; *Doroga i avtomobil',* no. 8–9 (1933): 13. For more on the reasons for Avtodor's dissolution, see Nichols Busch, "Avtodor and 'Automobilization,'" 111–13, 185–87.

94. *Pravda,* Oct. 29, 1935, 1. Serebriakov seems to have been demoted in connection with the shift to first deputy director. He was arrested in August 1936.

95. *Pravda,* Mar. 4, 1936, 2; *Za rulëm,* no. 7 (1936): 25.

96. *Pravda,* Jan. 26, 1937, 2; Jan. 30, 1937, 2. Cf. testimony of Narkomput deputy commissar Livshits in which he recounts that Serebriakov had told him to undermine the railroads because "the railroad is the basic nerve of the country." Jan. 28, 1937, 2.

97. A. S. Kudriavtsev, "K vysotam sovremennoi dorozhnoi tekhniki," *Doroga i avtomobil',* no. 7 (1937): 2–3. See also no. 4 (1937): 24–25. Kudriavtsev survived to become a prolific author on road construction. See his *Ocherki istorii dorozhnogo stroitel'stva v SSSR* (Moscow: Dorizdat, 1957) and note 45 above.

98. See Moshe Lewin, *The Soviet Century* (London: Verso, 2005), 108.

99. "Soobshchenie Mikhaila Isaakovicha Gokhfel'da," in Krasnoiarskoe obshchestvo "Memorial," at http://www.memorial.krsk.ru/svidet/Mhochfgr.htm (accessed 4.4.05). Gokhfel'd reportedly believed that his nonparty status saved him. Memorial, a voluntary organization created in the late 1980s, is dedicated to documenting Stalin-era repression and memorializing its victims.

100. Perepëlkin was the commander of the Moscow–Tiflis diesel engine rally of 1934. See his report in *Za rulëm,* no. 19 (1934): 3–6. For his brief biography, composed by friends some time in the 1950s after his posthumous rehabilitation, see Stepan Stepanovich Perepëlkin, in "Iz istorii avtomobilia v Rossii," at http://www.imwerden.de/autohistory.htm/ (accessed 4.4.05).

101. "Stalinskie spiski—Spisok 28.03.1941 (AP RF f. 3, op. 24, d. 421, l. 185)," at http://www.memo.ru/history/vkvs/spiski/pg13068.htm/ (accessed 4.7.05).

102. Vladimir Papernyi, *Kultura Dva* (Moscow: Novoe lit. obozrenie, 1996), 60–143.

103. The memorandum, dated Nov. 25, 1935, can be found in V. Kozlov, ed., *Istoriia stalinskogo Gulaga: Konets 1920-kh—pervaia polovina 1950-kh godov,* 7 vols. (Moscow: ROSSPEN, 2004), 3 (*Ekonomika Gulaga,* ed. O. V. Khlevniuk):136–44.

104. Ibid., 138–39. On Moscow-centeredness, see James van [von] Geldern, "The Centre and the Periphery: Cultural and Social Geography in the Mass Culture of the 1930s," in *New Directions in Soviet History,* ed. Stephen White (Cambridge: Cambridge University Press, 1992), 62–80.

105. N. V. Petrov, "Istoriia Imperii 'Gulag'," at http://www.pseudology.org/GULAG?Glava06.htm, chap. 6, 3 (accessed 4.5.05). This is an immensely detailed account of the Gulag system by a staff member of Memorial in Moscow. It is available, to my knowledge, only online. Subsequent citations will be to the same site, followed by chapter and page numbers.

106. R. J. Overy, "Cars, Roads, and Economic Recovery in Germany, 1932–38," *Economic History Review,* n.s. 28, no. 3 (1975): 473–74, 480. See also Rudy Koshar, *German Travel Cultures* (Oxford: Berg, 2000), 118–19.

107. Dm. B., "Germanskie avtostrady," *Za rulëm,* no. 6 (1936): 13–14. For similar assumptions among contemporary commentators in France, Britain, and the United States, see James D. Shand, "The Reichsautobahn: Symbol for the Third Reich," *Journal of Contemporary History* 19, no. 1 (1984): 196–97. Shand rejects these assumptions, arguing that "geographic, demographic, and economic factors, not military considerations, dictated the placement of the *Autobahnen.*"

108. Detlev Peukert, *Inside Nazi Germany: Conformity, Opposition, and Racism in Everyday Life* (New Haven: Yale University Press, 1987), 39. On Germany's promotion of its highway construction, see esp. speeches by Rudolf Hess and Fritz Todt in Permanent International Association of Road Congresses, *VIIth International Road Congress: Report of the Proceedings of the Congress* (Rennes-Paris: Imprimeries Oberthur, 1935), 52–70. In addition to a reception hosted by Josef Goebbels, delegates participating in the congress had the opportunity to attend the Nazi Party rally in Nuremberg, of which some 450 reportedly availed themselves. The "statistical table of members of the [seventh] congress" (9) listed twelve individual members from the USSR, down from sixteen whose names appeared in the proceedings of the Washington congress. See Permanent International Association of Road Congresses, *Sixth International Road Congress: Proceedings of the Congress* (Washington, D.C.: United States Government Printing Office, 1931), 6.

109. Overy, "Cars, Roads, and Economic Recovery," 480. For quotation, see Shand, "Reichsautobahn," 192. How free the labor that autobahn construction absorbed actually was is another matter. On this point, see Schütz and Gruber, *Mythos Reichsautobahn,* 66–93; Wolfgang Ayaß, *"Asoziale" im Nationalsozialismus* (Stuttgart: Klett-Cotta, 1995), 20–32, 118–23.

110. See Todt's speech to the 1936 Nazi Party Congress in *Der Parteitag der Ehre vom 8. bis 14. September 1936. Offizieller Bericht über den Verlauf des Reichsparteitages mit sämtlichen Kongreßreden* (Munich: Zentralverlag der NSDAP, 1936), 268–71. See also his speeches to subsequent party conventions in *Die Straße,* 18 (1937): 518–20; 19 (1938): 600–603.

111. Petrov, "Istoriia Imperii 'Gulag'," 6:3.

112. Oleg Khlevnyuk, "The Economy of the OGPU, NKVD, and MVD of the USSR, 1930–1953: The Scale, Structure, and Trends of Development," in *The Economics of Forced Labor: The Soviet Gulag*, ed. Paul R. Gregory and Valery Lazarev (Stanford: Hoover Institution Press, 2003), 44, 46, 48.

113. O. Esterkin, "Avtomobil'naia magistral' Moskva–Minsk," *Pravda*, July 18, 1936, 4.

114. See *Belomorsko–Baltiiskii Kanal imeni Stalina: Istoriia stroitel'stva 1931–1934 gg.*, ed. M. Gor'kii et al. (Moscow: "Istoriia fabrik i zavodov," 1934); and for analysis, Cynthia A. Ruder, *Making History for Stalin: The Story of the Belomor Canal* (Gainesville: University of Florida Press, 1998).

115. O. Mikhailov, "Na magistrali Mosvka–Kiev," *Pravda*, Aug. 9, 1936, 4. Evoking such flights of fancy was not unique to Soviet *avtomagistral'* construction; in this respect as well it mimicked the autobahn whose planners occasionally dreamed of building not seven thousand but as many as eleven thousand kilometers of highway.

116. Petrov, "Istoriia Imperii 'Gulag'," 6:8.

117. M. B. Smirnov, ed., *Sistema ispravitel'no-trudovykh lagerei v SSSR* (Moscow: Zven'ia, 1998), 199.

118. "Avtomagistral' Moskva–Minsk," at http://www.rosavtodor.ru/doc/history/minsk.htm (accessed 4.4.05); and "Avtodoroga Moskva–Minsk: Byloe i vekhi," at http://www.m1-uprodor.ru/xml (accessed 4.4.05).

119. Petrov, "Istoriia Imperii 'Gulag'," 5:5; "Ukazatel' imen," at http://www.memo.ru/memory/communarka/komm_in1.htm (accessed 4.8.05). All of these men were posthumously exonerated in 1956. Three of the first five directors of Gushosdor were arrested and executed between May 1937 and March 1939. See N. V. Petrov and K. V. Skorkin, *Kto rukovodil NKVD, 1934–1941: Spravochnik* (Moscow: Zven'ia, 1999), 109–10, 133–34, 176, 283, 417.

120. Iu. Mitsel'skii, "O khode stroitel'stva avtomagistrala Moskva—Kiev," *Doroga i avtomobil'*, no. 2 (1937): 5; S. A. Kornienko and V. A. Gaiduk, "Avtomagistrali Sovetskogo Soiuza," *Stroitel'stvo dorog*, no. 2 (1938): 5–6.

121. The director and chief engineer were blamed for a host of problems—a typhus outbreak, failure to fulfill the plan, overexpenditure of funds. Two months after a new director had taken over, things were, if anything, worse: in addition to typhus, cases of scurvy and pellagra were reported. See *Istoriia stalinskogo Gulaga, 2 (Karatel'naia sistema: Struktura i kadry*, ed. N. V. Petrov), 134–35, 139, 147–49.

122. For technical details about the Moscow–Minsk highway, see Nadezhko, *Dorogi*, 95–97; for details on Kaluga, see http://www.memo.ru/history/nkvd/gulag/maps/184.htm., and Smirnov, *Sistema*, 280.

123. Nadezhko, *Dorogi*, 98–99; *Pravda*, Aug. 24, 1938, 6; Smirnov, *Sistema*, 122. It also appeared on the list of suspended projects issued by MVD chief Beria after the Nazi invasion. See A. I. Kokurin and N. V. Petrov, *GULAG (Glavnoe upravlenie lagerei) 1917–1960* (Moscow: Materik, 2000), 781–82.

124. Walter S. Dunn Jr., *The Soviet Economy and the Red Army, 1930–1945* (Westport: Praeger, 1995), 210, 216–18, 221; Dunn, *Soviet Blitzkrieg: The Battle for White Russia, 1944* (Boulder: Lynne Rienner, 2000), 216–26.

125. Catherine Merridale, *Ivan's War: Life and Death in the Red Army, 1939–1945* (New York: Metropolitan Books, 2006), 101, citing frontline general I. I. Fedyuninsky; *Istoriia Velikoi Otechestvennoi voiny Sovetskogo Soiuza, 1941–1945*, ed. P. N. Pospelov, 6 vols. (Moscow: Voen. Izd-vo, 1960–65), 2:172.

126. Dunn, *Soviet Economy*, 217. See also David M. Glantz, *Colossus Reborn: The Red Army at War, 1941–1943* (Lawrence: University Press of Kansas, 2005), 353–56.

127. *Doroga v russkom iskusstve*, ed. Anna Laks (St. Petersburg: Palace Editions, 2004), 5.

128. V. M. Koval'chuk, N. A. Lomagin, and V. A. Shishkin, eds., *Leningradskaia epopeia: Organizatsiia oborony i naselenie goroda* (St. Petersburg: RAN, 1995), 85–87; V. M. Koval'chuk et al., eds., *Nepokoronnyi Leningrad: Kratkii ocherk istorii goroda v period Velikoi Otechestvennoi voiny* (Leningrad: Nauka, 1970), 198–208.

129. Koval'chuk et al., *Leningradskaia epopeia*, 87–100; *Leningrad v osade: Sbornik dokumentov*, ed. A. R. Dzeniskevich (St. Petersburg: Liki Rossii, 1995), 194–97, 246–48; David Glantz, *The Battle for Leningrad, 1941–1944* (Lawrence: University Press of Kansas, 2002), 140–45.

130. Vera Inber cited in Harrison Salisbury, *The 900 Days: The Siege of Leningrad* (New York: Harper and Row, 1969), 422; also Vera Inber, *Pochti tri goda, Leningradskii dnevnik*

(Moscow: Sovetskaia Rossiia, 1968), 232; A. Fadeev, "Gorod velikikh zodchikh," *Slaviane,* nos. 5–6 (1942): 59.

131. Nina Tumarkin, *The Living and the Dead: The Rise and Fall of the Cult of World War II in Russia* (New York: Basic Books, 1994), 142–45.

132. See http://www.museum.navy.ru/f4.htm (accessed 4.21.05). The museum is one of six branches of the Central Naval Museum. On the theme of the war and generational indebtedness to its participants, see Tumarkin, *Living and the Dead,* 125–57.

133. Examples include Helen Dunmore, *The Siege* (London: Viking, 2001), Paullina Simmons, *The Bronze Horseman* (London: William Morrow, 2001), and Gillian Slovo, *Ice Road* (London: Little Brown, 2004).

134. Richard Bidlack, foreword to Cynthia Simmons and Nina Perlina, *Writing the Siege of Leningrad* (Pittsburgh: University of Pittsburgh Press, 2002), xv.

135. John Barber and Andrei Dzeniskevich, ed., *Life and Death in Besieged Leningrad, 1941–44* (Houndsmills: Palgrave, 2005), 6. These are the words of John Barber. Emphasis mine.

136. See, respectively, Nadezhda Cherepenina, "The Scale of Famine in the Besieged City," in Barber and Dzeniskevich, *Life and Death,* 55; Boris Belozerov, "Crime during the Siege," in Barber and Dzeniskevich, *Life and Death,* 226; Vladimir Daev, *S distantsii poluveka, ocherki blokadnogo Leningrada* (St. Petersburg: Sudarynia, 1998), 82.

137. D. S. Likhachev, "Kak my ostalis' zhivy," *Neva,* no. 1 (1991): 18.

138. Petrov, "Istoriia imperii 'Gulag'," 11:2.

139. *Avtomobil'noi doroge Moskva–Samara 50 let, 1946–1996, Istoricheskii ocherk* (Penza: B.izd. 1996), 8.

140. *Arteri zhizni: Proshloe i nastoiashee dorozhnoi stroitel'noi sluzhby Ivanovskoi oblasti* Ivanovo: Ivanovskaia gazeta, 2000), 31.

141. Smirnov, *Sistema,* 122. See also L. Kogan, "Iz istorii gradostroitel'stva Novograda–Volynskogo," at http://www.novograd.com.ua/content/view/65/60/ (accessed 5.2.05).

142. See Jan T. Gross, *Revolution from Abroad: The Soviet Conquest of Poland's Western Ukraine and Western Belorussia* (Princeton: Princeton University Press, 1988).

143. "Holocaust in Romania," in "The Raport [sic] of the International Commission on the Holocaust in Romania," 187–89, at http://www.ispaim.ro (accessed 5.03.05); Matatias Carp, *Holocaust in Romania: Facts and Documents on the Annihilation of Romania's Jews, 1940–1944,* trans. Sean Murphy (Budapest: Primor, 1994), 217.

144. It is claimed that as of April 1944 over four thousand kilometers of hard-surfaced roads were destroyed. Kudriavtsev, *Ocherki istorii dorozhnogo stroitel'stva* 223.

145. This is the estimate given by Golfo Alexopoulos, "Amnesty 1945: The Revolving Door of Stalin's Gulag," *Slavic Review* 64, no. 2 (2005): 282. Alexopoulos notes that "anywhere from one-fifth to two-thirds of gulag prisoners left various important economic sectors of the NKVD, such as the Main Administration for Road Construction, the Department of Industrial Construction, and the Main Administration of Camps for Mining and Metallurgy" (284).

146. Cf. Stefan Karner, *Im Archipel GUPVI: Kriegsgefangeneschaft und Internierung in der Sowjetunion 1941–1956* (Vienna: Oldenbourg, 1995); M. M. Zagorul'ko, ed., *Voennoplennye v SSSR 1939–1956* (Moscow: Logos, 2000); S. G. Sidorov, *Trud voennoplennykh v SSSR, 1939–1956 gg.* (Volgograd: Izd-vo VGU, 2001). See, for example, the considerable difference between the figures for the distribution of prisoners of war in 1947 given in Zagorul'ko (655–65) and Donald Filtzer, *Soviet Workers and Late Stalinism: Labour and the Restoration of the Stalinist System after World War II* (Cambridge: Cambridge University Press, 2002), 23. Filtzer cites special files of Stalin and Beria (GARF f. 9401).

147. Smirnov, *Sistema,* 123.

148. Zagorul'ko, *Voennoplennye,* 696–98, 712.

149. *Avtomobil'noi doroge,* 9.

150. GARF, f. 9419, op. 1, d. 7 (Plans for labor at enterprises of Gushosdor for 1948), ll. 8, 30, 48, 69, 70–71. See also the testimony of G. P. Privalova in *Avtomobil'nye dorogi i dorozhniki Vologodchiny,* ed. A. N. Plekhanov (Vologda, 2000), 80. Privalova worked alongside German POWs on the Vologda–Griazovets road in 1948.

151. GARF, f. 9419, op. 1, d. 3 (Plans of administrations of Corrective Labor Camps and Gushosdor construction sites for labor for 1947), ll. 8, 18, 21, 24; d. 7 (Annual plans for labor for 1948 at enterprises of Gushosdor), l. 32.

152. Filtzer, *Soviet Workers,* 235. Filtzer characterizes the wages as "almost universally low...with a large minority of workers not even managing to maintain basic levels of subsistence" (234).

153. Nadezhko, *Dorogi,* 136.

154. GARF, f. 9419, op. 1, d. 13 (Stenographic report of meeting with Deputy Minister of Internal Affairs on Moscow–Khar'kov–Simferopol' road project, Feb. 15, 1949), ll. 102, 119, 124.

155. Zagorul'ko, *Voennoplennye,* 696–98, 712, 719–20.

156. Patrick Sergeant, *Another Road to Samarkand* (London: Hodder and Stoughton, 1955), 24.

157. Heinz Lathe and Günther Meierling, *Return to Russia,* trans. Charlotte Dixon (London: Galley Press, 1961), 71. The postwar highway projects also gave some Soviet citizens opportunities to advance their careers in civil engineering. For the case of one who supervised the laying of asphalt and cement, primarily by German prisoners of war, on the Moscow–Minsk highway, see Ia. Z. Shirniuk, *Stranitsy zhizni dorozhnika,* 2nd ed. (Brest, 1997), 25–46.

158. Nadezhko, *Dorogi,* 140–41.

159. Smirnov, *Sistema,* 375, 424, 458–59.

160. Nikolai Zabolotskii, "Makers of Highways," *Reporter,* Aug. 16, 1949, 20–21. On the poem and its reception, see Nikita Zabolotsky, *The Life of Zabolotsky,* ed. R. R. Milner-Gulland (Cardiff: University of Wales Press, 1994), 246–48; Gara Goldstein, *Nikolai Zabolotsky, Play for Mortal Stakes* (Cambridge: Cambridge University Press, 1993), 101, 264.

161. See Alex Lichtenstein, *Twice the Work of Free Labor: The Political Economy of Convict Labor in the New South* (London: Verso, 1996); Timothy Dodge, "State Convict Road Gangs in Alabama," *Alabama Review* 53, no. 4 (2000): 266–68; *New York Times Magazine,* Sept. 17, 1995: 62–63.

162. GARF, f. 9419, op. 1., d. 57 (Directives of MVD and its chief departments on questions of labor utilization and securing special contingents, 1951), ll. 7, 24; d. 84 (Directives of MVD and its chief departments on questions of security, labor utilization, and special contingents, 1952), ll. 6, 13, 19–21, 26.

163. GARF, f. 9419, op. 1, d. 84, ll. 19–21. Khlevniuk, "Economy of the OGPU, NKVD, and MVD," 57. Road workers were hardly unique in organizing escapes. G. N. Safonov, USSR procurator general, referred to a "systematic increase" in escapes in a letter to G. M. Malenkov dated 17 August 1948. "Mass disorders," "riots," and "group escapes" were widely reported. See *Istoriia stalinskogo Gulaga,* 6 (*Vosstaniia, bunty i zabastovki zakliuchennykh,* ed. O. V. Lavinskaia): 186, 196, 198–99, 221–32 (quotation at 198). See also Marta Kraveri and Oleg Khlevniuk, "Krizis ekonomiki MVD (konets 1940-kh—1950–e gody)," *Cahiers du Monde russe* 36, nos. 1–2 (1994): 182–83.

164. GARF, f. 9419, op. 1, d. 57, ll. 51–52. Dolgikh's recommendation is consistent with the Gulag's tendency to advocate the downsizing of camp operations in the late Stalin era, according to Aleksei Tikhonov, "The End of the Gulag," in *Economics of Forced Labor,* 67–73. On the MVD officials, see Kokurin and Petrov, *GULAG,* 614, 831, 832–33.

165. Tikhonov, "End of the Gulag," 67–68; Khlevniuk, "Economy of the OGPU, NKVD, and MVD," 54–55. For the decree, see Kokurin and Petrov, *GULAG,* 792. For lower estimate of one million released, see Kraveri and Khlevniuk, "Krizis ekonomiki," 182.

166. Kudriavtsev, *Ocherki,* 273. For equivalent increases in mechanized timber cutting and haulage, see Khlevniuk, "Economy of the OGPU, NKVD, and MVD," 56. Another source claims that such high percentages were obtained by restricting the survey to "special roads" rather than those of "mass construction." N. N. Fedorovskii, *Usloviia proezzhaemosti gruntovykh dorog SSSR* (Munich: Institute for the Study of the History and Culture of the USSR, 1954), 10.

167. For more details on the administrative musical chairs, see Nadezhko, *Dorogi,* 137–40.

168. Kudriavtsev, *Ocherki,* 280–81; *Arteri zhizni,* 34–35.

169. Kudriavtsev, *Ocherki,* 295–307 (quotation at 302).

170. Nadezhko, *Dorogi,* 161–62. These figures would be more persuasive if dates and sources were provided.

171. Ibid., 161, 163. Another source quotes Khrushchev as telling a meeting in Alma-Ata that "roads do not raise the productive potential of the country," which allegedly led to a cessation of many road construction projects. See V. Kostylev, "Dobri sled na zemle: Ministr Nikolaev (k 90-letiiu so dnia rozhdeniia)," *Rossiiskii Dorozhnik,* no. 35 (2003): 2.

172. Pierre Pruvost, *L'envers du Spoutnik,* 4th ed. (Paris: Nouvelles Editions Debresse, 1960), 60, 178.

173. Kostylev, "Dobri sled," 2; *Arteri zhizni,* 34–35; *Avtomobil'nye dorogi Vologodchiny,* 83.

174. "Offitsial'nyi sait Ministerstva promyshlennosti, transporta i sviazi Stavropol'skogo kraia," at http://www.stavminprom.ru/roads/ (accessed 5.11.05); *Narodnoe khoziaistvo SSSR*

v 1968 g. (Moscow: Gos. statisticheskoe izd-vo, 1969), 487; *Narodnoe khoziaistvo SSSR v 1970 g.* (Moscow: Gos. statisticheskoe izd-vo, 1971), 451.

175. Roger R. Reese, *The Soviet Military Experience: A History of the Soviet Army, 1917–1991* (London: Routledge, 2000), 160.

176. Ministerstvo avtodorog RSFSR, *Maiaki dorozhnogo stroitel'stva* (Moscow: Transport, 1982), 11–13; *Avtomobil'nye dorogi i dorozhniki Vologodchin,* 69–70, 83–85.

177. Z. M. Gal'perina, *Bezdorozh'e ili platnye dorogi v Rossii?* (Novosibirsk: EKOR, 1995), 33.

Chapter 5. One of the Most "Deficit" of Commodities

1. I am quoting from the "slightly shortened version" in George Katkov, *Russia 1917: The February Revolution* (London: Longmans, 1967), 177–79. See also Orlando Figes, *A People's Tragedy: The Russian Revolution, 1891–1924* (New York: Viking, 1996), 276.

2. M. Gorelov, *Chort za rulëm! (Zametki o bol'shevizme)* (Berlin: Tip. Evgeniia Aleksandrovicha Gutnova, 1920), 31–32.

3. Iurii Leving, *Vokzal–Garazh–Angar: Vladimir Nabokov i poetika russkogo urbanizma* (St. Petersburg: Izd. Ivana Limbakha, 2004), 204–5, 263, 271–73.

4. Brian Boyd, *Vladimir Nabokov: The Russian Years* (Princeton: Princeton University Press, 1990), 102.

5. Leving, *Vokzal,* 207–9, 215, 221, 251. Quotations are from Vladimir Nabokov, *Sobranie sochinenii russkogo perioda v piati tomakh* 5 vols. (St. Petersburg: Sympozium, 2000), 5:263.

6. Leving, *Vokzal,* 252; V. D. Nabokov, "Vremennoe pravitel'stvo," in *Arkhiv russkoi revoliutsii,* ed. G. V. Gessen 10 vols. (Berlin: Slowo Verlag, 1921), 1:84–85. For an English edition, see V. D. Nabokov, *The Provisional Government* (Brisbane: University of Queensland Press, 1970), 106.

7. George F. Kennan, *Russia Leaves the War* (Princeton: Princeton University Press, 1956), 72–73. The fullest account is that of the former U.S. ambassador, David R. Francis, who reported that the car belonged to his secretary, Sheldon Whitehouse, and "virtually had been commandeered." David R. Francis, *Russia from the American Embassy, April 1916—November 1918* (New York: Charles Scribner's Sons, 1921), 179–80.

8. John Reed, *Ten Days That Shook the World* (New York: International Publishers, 1967), 79, 336; Louise Bryant, *Six Red Months in Russia* (New York: George H. Doran, 1918), 151.

9. Semen Iushkevich, *Avtomobil', rasskazy* (Berlin: Izd. Grzhebin, 1923), 38–43.

10. In fact, as Allen Samuels notes, "there is hardly a page without some car reference. Cars tell you about people's sexual morés and define their characters.... And it is the mix-up over cars...that provides the necessary plot and the accident which brings about Gatsby's demise." Allen Samuels, "Accidents: The Car and Literature," in *Autopia: Cars and Culture,* ed. Peter Wollen and Joe Kerr (London: Reaktion, 2002), 57.

11. Cited in Leving, *Vokzal,* 264.

12. Ilya Ehrenburg, *The Life of the Automobile,* trans. Joachim Neugroschel (New York: Urizen Books, 1976), 135, 139. The book was originally published as *Desiat' l.s.: Khronika nashego vremeni* (Berlin: Petropolis, 1929).

13. Ibid., 149–56. Ehrenburg flirts here with anthropomorphism of the car as he does earlier, namely, "Car no 180–74—iron splinters, glass shards, a lump of warm flesh—lay unstirring beneath the solemn midday sun" (5).

14. Filippo Tommaso Marinetti, *Selected Writings,* trans. and ed. R. W. Flint (New York: Farrar, Straus and Giroux, 1972), 41–42; Wolfgang Sachs, *For Love of the Automobile: Looking Back into the History of Our Desires,* trans. Don Reneau (Berkeley: University of California Press, 1992), 79, 123.

15. Edward Brown, *Mayakovsky: A Poet in the Revolution* (Princeton: Princeton University Press, 1973), 90–93. See V. V. Maiakovskii, *Sobranie sochinenii v vos'mi tomakh* 8 vols. (Moscow: Ogonek, 1968), 1:28, 31.

16. Vladimir Mayakovsky, *Mayakovsky Plays,* trans. Guy Daniels (Evanston, Ill.: Northwestern University Press), 39–139; Maiakovskii, *Sobranie sochinenii,* 1:240–43; 3:82; 5:32; Brown, *Mayakovsky,* 203. For the importance of time in Mayakovsky, see Victor Terras, *Vladimir Mayakovsky* (Boston: Twayne, 1983), 140–43.

17. V. O. Pertsov, *Maiakovskii, zhizn' i tvorchestvo (1893–1917)* (Moscow: Nauka, 1969), 330; Vladimir Mayakovsky, *My Discovery of America,* trans. Neil Cornwell (London: Hesperus Press, 2005), 93–99.

18. Brown, *Mayakovsky,* 136; Aleksandr Mikhailov, *Zhizn' Maiakovskogo: Ia svoe zemnoe ne dozhil* (Moscow: Tsentrpoligraf, 2001), 402, 451, 455, 463; Bengt Jangfeldt, ed., *V. V. Maiakovskii i L. Iu. Brik: Perepiska 1915–1930* (Stockholm: Almqvist and Wiksell, 1982), 178–181, 272. See also the extremely moving account of Mayakovsky and Iakovleva by Francine du Plessix Gray, "Mayakovsky's Last Loves," *New Yorker* 77, no. 42 (2002): 38–56.

19. Brown, *Mayakovsky,* 342. For the poems and related matters, see Ann and Samuel Charters, *I Love: The Story of Vladimir Mayakovsky and Lili Brik* (New York: Farrar, Straus and Giroux, 1979), 302–13.

20. *Za rulëm,* no. 1 (1929): 15. This was the second poem by Mayakovsky published by the journal. The first, "Story about a Daydream," about winning the Avtodor lottery, appeared in no. 6 (1928): 22–23.

21. Charters, *I Love,* 322. Lily drove the car herself, claiming to be the only woman in Moscow other than the French ambassador's wife who had a driver's license. See Vasilii V. Katanian, *Lilia Brik, Vladimir Maiakovskii i drugie muzhchiny* (Moscow: Zakharov, 1998), 79–80.

22. Charters, *I Love,* 322. No source is cited for the statement by Bedny. For Lily's driving, see Katanian, *Lilia Brik,* 80–81. Nine of these photographs are displayed by the Gary Tatintsian Gallery website at http://www.tatintsian.com/inventory.html (accessed 3.26.06).

23. Elias Canetti, *The Torch in My Ear,* trans. Joachim Neugroschel (New York: Farrar, Straus and Giroux, 1982), 275–76.

24. See Aleksandr Pikulenko, "Muzei Renault," Nov. 28, 2005, Auto-Dealer.ru, at http://adlr.ru/articles/event.php?id=7093 (accessed 4.4.06).

25. For numbers of cars, see Tsudortrans, *Avtodorozhnoe khoziaistvo SSSR v tsifrakh, statisticheskii sbornik* (Moscow, 1935), 139; T. Nikol'skaia, "Samodvizhushchiesia ekipazhi," in *Moskovskii Arkhiv. Istoriko-kraevedcheskii al'manakh,* ed. V. F. Kozlov (Moscow: Mosarkhiv, 1996), 506; Boris Shpotov, "Ford in Russia, from 1909 to World War II," in *Ford: The European History, 1903–2003,* ed. H. Bonin et al., 2 vols. (Paris: P.L.A.G.E., 2003), 2:528. On Moscow businesses, see Lev Shugurov, *Avtomobil'naia Moskva: Stoletie 1902–2001* (Moscow: TsDTS, 2004), 9–10.

26. Shugurov, *Avtomobil'naia Moskva,* 25–32. For ownership and driving elsewhere, see Sachs, *For Love of the Automobile,* 3–31 ("Pleasures for the Wealthy, 1890–1914"), and Ruth Brandon, *Automobile: How the Car Changed Life* (London: Macmillan, 2002), 11–62. For (largely rural-based) opposition to cars and car owners, see Uwe Fraunholz, *Motorphobia: Anti-Automobiler Protest in Kaiserreich und Weimarer Republik. Kritische Studien zur Geschichtswissenschaft* (Göttingen: Vandenhoeck and Ruprecht, 2000).

27. "Avtomobil' v okt. 1917 goda," *Za rulëm,* no. 8 (1928): 28; "Avtomobil'naia khronika," *Za rulëm,* nos. 21–22 (1937): 47; Shugurov, *Avtomobil'naia Moskva,* 34–35; L. M. Shugurov, *Avtomobili Rossii i SSSR,* 3 vols. (Moscow: Prostreks, 1993–98), 1:47–48; Patrick Wright, *Tank: The Progress of a Monstrous War Machine* (London: Faber and Faber, 2000), 198.

28. Wright, *Tank,* 198–99. The armored car is mentioned in E. H. Carr, *The Bolshevik Revolution, 1917-1923,* 3 vols. (Harmondsworth: Penguin, 1966), 1:89. It is depicted in "Desiat' let sovetskogo avtomobil'ia," *Motor,* no. 11 (1934): inside cover, and commemorated in S. Savel'ev, "Legendarnye broneviki," *Za rulëm,* no. 4 (1973): 4–7.

29. Shugurov, *Avtomobil'naia Moskva,* 37–38. Until he was no longer capable of traveling, Lenin had the same chauffeur, Stepan Kazimirovich Gil'. Gil', who previously had worked in the tsar's garage, wrote a brief memoir of his "six years with V. I. Lenin." Full of the reverence and formulaic language required of such Stalin-era literature, the memoir describes a few adventures on the road including an attempted hijacking in January 1919 of the car in which Lenin, his sister, and another passenger, Fritz Platten, were being conveyed. S. K. Gil', *Shest' let s V. I. Leninym: Vospominaniia lichnogo shofëra Vladimira Il'icha Lenina* (Moscow: OGIZ, 1947), 48–53. See also "Iz vospominanii shofëra Vladimira Il'icha, tov. Stepan Kazimirovich Gil'," *Za rulëm,* no. 5 (1928): 3; A. Shaparo, "Shofër iz Smol'nogo," *Za rulëm,* no. 4 (1959): 5.

30. "Desiat' let," 6; A. D. Rubets, "Gruzovye avtomobil'nye perevozki (1917–1940 gg.)," *Avtomobil'nyi transport,* nos. 10–12 (1995): 12.

31. Gil', *Shest' let,* 7–8; Zinaida Gippius, *Dnevniki,* ed. A. K. Nikoliukina, 2 vols. (Moscow: Intelvak, 1999), 2:157.

32. Shugurov, *Avtomobil'naia Moskva,* 36–41, 43.

33. Gosudarstvennyi Arkhiv Rossiiskoi Federatsii (GARF), f. 5454, op. 4, d. 69 (Correspondence of Central Committee with provincial departments on condition of auto transport in 1921), ll. 21–22.

34. For 1928 estimates, see, respectively, "S chego nachinat'," *Za rulëm*, no. 1 (1928), 2; E. Chudakov, "Budushchee avtomobil'noi promyshlennosti v SSSR," ibid., 3; and Ia. Gol'dberg, "Nashe avtomobil'noe khoziaistvo," ibid., 14.

35. Goldberg, "Nashe avtomobil'noe khoziaistvo," 14; Moskavtoklub, *Avtomobil', spravochnik* (Moscow: Motor, 1926), 11. Exceptions were fire engines and vehicles belonging to the diplomatic service, Sovnarkom, TsIK, the Council of Labor and Defense, and organs of the Commissariat of Post and Telegraph.

36. Compared with 196 in Germany, 46 in France, 34 in England, and 5 in the already automobile-driven United States. Chudakov, "Budushchee," 3. In 1913 there were 7,308 cars; on Jan. 1, 1927, the number was 7,003. Tsudortrans, *Avtodorozhnoe khoziaistvo*, 139.

37. *Dekrety Sovetskoi vlasti*, 16 vols. (Moscow: Gos.izd.polit. litry, 1957–99), 9:76–80.

38. *Avtomobil', spravochnik*, 33; Shugurov, *Avtomobil'naia Moskva*, 46–47; L. V., "Razvitie avtomobilizma v Moskve," *Za rulëm*, no. 3 (1929): 23. On taxis, see A. Rubets, "Taksi dvadtsatykh i tridtsatykh godov," *Avtomobil'nyi transport*, no. 4 (1996): 10–12. The introduction of the Renault taxis is commemorated in Ilf and Petrov's *The Little Golden Calf (New York: Farrar and Rinehart, 1932)*, chap. 3.

39. Vassily Aksyonov, *Generations of Winter*, trans. John Glad and Christopher Morris (New York: Random House, 1994), 5.

40. Mikhail Prezent, "Uporiadochenie ulichnogo dvizheniia," *Za rulëm*, no. 9 (1928): 24–27; Boris Zil'pert, "O russkom shofëre," *Za rulëm*, no. 2 (1929): 13.

41. *Trud*, July 5, 1928, 3. The investigation was conducted by the Commissariat of Labor and the Central Committee of the Transport Workers Union of Moscow Province.

42. Katanian, *Lilia Brik*, 80.

43. This is a standard trope of Marxism. The phrase cited here is from V. I. Lenin, "Capitalism in Agriculture," *Collected Works*, vol. 4 (London: Lawrence and Wishart, 1960).

44. Rossiiskii gosudarstvennyi arkhiv Ekonomiki (RGAE), f. 1884 (USSR Ministry of Transport), op. 5, ed. kh. 93 (Protocols of sessions 1–17 of the All-Russian Experimental Auto Rally Committee), ll. 34, 36, 56, 58, 83, 103; *Pravda*, Sept. 16, 1923, 3; Sept. 18, 1923, 3; Sept. 26, 1923, 6.

45. Perovskii's reports were published in *Pravda*, Aug. 22–Sept. 10, 1925; Vl. Kononov, "Avtomobil'-derevne," *Pravda*, Aug. 26, 1925, 3.

46. Fraunholz, *Motorphobia*.

47. George S. Counts, *A Ford Crosses Soviet Russia* (Boston: Stratford, 1930), 66–68. On Pilnyak's journey, see Eugene Lyons, *Assignment in Utopia* (New York: Harcourt, Brace, 1937), 441–42. For similar encounters in other parts of the world, see Richard Schweid, *Che's Chevrolet, Fidel's Oldsmobile: On the Road in Cuba* (Chapel Hill: University of North Carolina Press, 2004), 17; Fraunholz, *Motorphobia*, 101–2, 119–23.

48. Counts, *A Ford*, 69–71. On peasants playing up their image as ignorant rubes, see Daniel Field, *Rebels in the Name of the Tsar* (Boston: Houghton Mifflin, 1976), and James C. Scott, *Weapons of the Weak: Everyday Forms of Peasant Resistance* (New Haven: Yale University Press, 1985).

49. El-Registan and L. Brontman, *Moskva—Kara-Kum—Moskva* (Moscow: Sovetskaia literatura, 1934), 218; Lewis H. Siegelbaum and Andrei Sokolov, *Stalinism as a Way of Life: A Narrative in Documents* (New Haven: Yale University Press, 2000), 174 (Document 59); Gennady Andreev-Khomiakov, *Bitter Waters: Life and Work in Stalin's Russia*, trans. Ann E. Healy (Boulder: Westview Press, 1997), 62.

50. Valery Lazarev and Paul Gregory, "The Wheels of a Command Economy: Allocating Soviet Vehicles," *Economic History Review* 55, no. 2 (2002): 324–48; Lazarev and Gregory, "Commissars and Cars: A Case Study in the Political Economy of Dictatorship," *Journal of Comparative Economics*, vol. 31 (2003): 1–19. The authors are the source for the title of this chapter.

51. Lazarev and Gregory, "Commissars and Cars," 4–5.

52. GARF, f. 5446, op. 14a, d. 628 (Plan for the distribution of automobiles for the first and second quarters of 1933), ll. 46, 42; d. 635 (Plan for distribution of automobiles for the fourth quarter of 1933), l. 55.

53. GARF, f. 5446, op. 14a, d. 628, ll. 13–17 (Narkomvneshtorg); l. 20 (Osoaviakhim); l. 107 (Middle Volga Krai); d. 634, l. 56 (Osoaviakhim); op. 14, d. 2029b, ll. 40–41 (Narkomput').

54. Lazarev and Gregory, "Commissars and Cars," 12–13; GARF, f. 5446, op. 14a, d. 634, l. 5; d. 635, ll. 31–33. The most puzzling reason for treating cars and trucks as substitutable is that "the output of the automobile industry was always given in public reports as the number of

vehicles, rather than separated into cars and trucks." This simply is not so. See, for example, Tsudortrans, *Avtodorozhnoe khoziaistvo*, 139–40.

55. Lazarev and Gregory, "Wheels," 343; *Izvestiia*, Mar. 15, 1935, cited in Sheila Fitzpatrick, *Tear Off the Masks! Identity and Imposture in Twentieth-Century Russia* (Princeton: Princeton University Press, 2005), 275. Fitzpatrick quoted on p. 271. For another scam that involved fleecing several cars from the "Auto Trust" (evidently, VATO), see *An American Engineer in Stalin's Russia: The Memoirs of Zara Witkin, 1932–1934*, ed. Michael Gelb (Berkeley: University of California Press, 1991), 211–12.

56. *Trud*, Mar. 1, 1930, 4; Lazarev and Gregory, "Wheels," 343.

57. RGAE, f. 4372, op. 31, d. 36 (Copies of letters sent by Gosplan to Sovnarkom and Council of Labor and Defense, April 1933), l. 228; GARF f. 5446, op. 14, d. 2029 g(1) (Information on release of automobiles in 1933), l. 79; d. 2042 (On exhaustion of auto promissory notes of 1930 and subsequent years), ll. 1–2. The scale of purchases of promissory notes never came close to that of the KDF wagon, which attracted 380 million reichsmarks from 336,668 Germans, not one of whom ever received a car. See Rudi Volti, *Cars and Culture: The Life Story of a Technology* (Westport, Conn.: Greenwood Press, 2004), 78.

58. GARF, f. 5446, op. 14, d. 2029g (1) (Information on delivery of automobiles in 1933), ll. 15–18. The informant, who worked in the machine shop of GAZ's parts division, wrote to Molotov "because the factory is named after you."

59. *Za rulëm*, no. 4 (1928): 42; GARF, f. 4426, op. 1, d. 561 (Second All-Union Avtodor Lottery), ll. 4–41; *Za rulëm*, no. 5 (1934): 25.

60. GARF, f. 5446, op. 14, d. 2029g(3), ll. 356–63. According to a recent history of Soviet Jewish agricultural colonization, "annual, nationwide lotteries—their earnings dedicated to Jewish colonization—became the focus of [OZET's] activity from the late 1920s." Jonathan L. Dekel-Chen, *Farming the Red Land: Jewish Agricultural Colonization and Local Soviet Power, 1924–1941* (New Haven: Yale University Press, 2005), 53.

61. *Za rulëm*, no. 6 (1940): inside cover.

62. RGAE, f. 4372, op. 38, d. 1416 (2) (Government instructions and copies of agreements on the work of auto transport for 1940), ll. 1–3.

63. The Economic Council was set up in November 1937 to fulfill administrative functions with respect to the economy previously performed by the Council of Labor and Defense. It survived until March 1941. Its first chair, Anastas Mikoian, was replaced by Molotov in early 1940. See Derek Watson, *Molotov and Soviet Government: Sovnarkom, 1930–41* (New York: St. Martin's Press, 1996), 133–35. I was not able to determine how much earlier EKOSO assumed responsibility for automobile distribution.

64. RGAE, f. 4372, op. 38, d. 1419 (Correspondence with Commissariats on distribution of automobiles, use of empties, and repair, January–October 1940), ll. 10, 19, 21. The Winter War against Finland was fought from November 1939 to March 1940.

65. *Za rulëm*, no. 3 (1937): 30; no. 4 (1937): 9; no. 16 (1937): 9.

66. A. Samoilov, "O tak nazyvaemykh vladel'tsakh avtomashin," *Pravda*, May 19, 1937, 5.

67. RGAE, f. 4372, op. 38, d. 1419, l. 38.

68. Kevin Borg, "'The Chauffeur Problem' in the Early Auto Era: Structuration Theory and the Users of Technology," *Technology and Culture* 40, no. 4 (1999): 797–832; Lesley Hazleton, *Confessions of a Fast Woman* (Reading, Mass.: Addison-Wesley, 1992), 120–24. Hazleton, a journalist who spent a summer as a mechanic's apprentice, notes "the moment the mechanic fulfills his role, he loses his aura, his mystique, his magical powers, and becomes once again a working-class man to be paid off and forgotten—until the next time."

69. Lyons, *Assignment in Utopia*, 444.

70. Andreev-Khomiakov, *Bitter Waters*, 57–58.

71. *Za rulëm*, no. 3 (1937): 30.

72. GARF, f. 5454, op. 1. See also *Putevoditel' Fondy Gosudarstvennogo arkhiva Rossiiskoi Federatsii po istorii SSSR*, ed. S. V. Mironenko, 3 vols. (Moscow: GARF, 1997), 3:583–84.

73. GARF, f. 5454, op. 7, d. 151, l. 1.

74. GARF, f. 5454, op. 12, d. 232 (Statistical information of the Central Committee of the Transport Workers Union on the number, sex, and age composition of members, 1930), ll. 3, 5.

75. *Krasnyi transportnik*, no. 1 (1932): 10; F. Kallianidi, "Gotovit' kadry po-bol'shevistski," *Za rulëm*, no. 10 (1932): 14.

76. Arsen Tumanian, "Dlia chego proizvoditsia obmen shofërskikh knizhek," *Za rulëm*, no. 6 (1935): 10–11; *Za rulëm*, no. 3 (1934): 10.

77. GARF, f. 5454, op. 16, d. 1 (Materials prepared for First All-Union Congress of Union of Drivers, 1933), l. 43.

78. GARF, f. 5454, op. 12, d. 233 (Statistical summaries of national composition of members of union of transport workers, 1929), ll. 12–13.

79. Data for 1928–30 show women making up 3.2–3.6% of union membership. No separate figures for drivers were given. GARF, f. 5454, op. 12, d. 232 (Statistical information of the central committee on the number, sex, and age of union members), l. 4. Women made up a "modest" 3% of Avtodor's members as of 1932, according to its president. *Za rulëm*, no. 5 (1933): 1. By Jan. 1, 1934, there were 917 women drivers registered in Moscow. *Za rulëm*, no. 5 (1935): 5.

80. *Trud*, Oct. 1, 1936, 1. The rally was covered extensively by all the main newspapers (*Pravda, Izvestiia, Trud*). For subsequent coverage of women competitors, some replete with photographs, see *Za rulëm*, no. 1 (1937): 12; no. 5 (1937): 5–9; nos. 21–22 (1937): 30–31; no. 18 (1938): 11–14; *Pravda*, Aug. 31, 1938, 6.

81. *Pravda*, June 6, 1935, 1; *Za rulëm*, no. 13 (1935): 2, 11; no. 19 (1935): 1.

82. *Za rulëm*, no. 3 (1934): 24–25; no. 21 (1935): 21; no. 1 (1937): 13–14; A. G. Tumanian, *Avarii na avtotransporte* (Moscow: Zhur-obe"d, 1936), 22–26. Tumanian was *Za rulëm*'s special correspondent on accidents and accident prevention.

83. *Za rulëm*, no. 6 (1934): 19; Tumanian, *Avarii*, 28–37. A new driver is told by another auto depot worker that "the first thing you do around here is provide a bottle" to the mechanic who is his "main man, now" in Anatolii Rybakov, *Fear*, trans. Antonina W. Bouis (Boston: Little, Brown, 1992), 556.

84. Lawrence J. Ouellet, *Pedal to the Metal: The Work Lives of Truckers* (Philadelphia: Temple University Press, 1994), 11, 219–20.

85. *Prozhektor*, no. 30 (1928): 25; *Za rulëm*, no. 1 (1937): 15.

86. *Za rulëm*, no. 6 (1935): 10.

87. Stephen Meyer, "Work, Play, and Power: Masculine Culture on the Automotive Shop Floor, 1930–1960," in *Boys and Their Toys? Masculinity, Technology, and Class in America*, ed. Roger Horowitz (New York: Routledge, 2001), 13–32.

88. Ouellet, *Pedal to the Metal*, 105. "The trucker's subculture itself excites a certain romanticized public interest because it is somewhat mysterious and deviant. The members of this subculture . . . do much of their work at night, which can be understood as a frontier where one finds greater solitude and tranquility, a camaraderie with fellow night workers, the loosening of social rules and more danger and outlawry." See also James H. Thomas, *The Long Haul: Truckers, Truck Stops, and Trucking* (Memphis: Memphis State University Press, 1979), 5–7: "The trucker and the cowboy have an independence not enjoyed—but sought—by most members of American society."

89. Rybakov, *Fear*, 457, 484. Rybakov knew of what he wrote. He too had spent three years living in Siberia, returning in 1936 to get a job as a driver after having studied the textbook and passing the driver's exam. See his *Roman-vospominanie* (Moscow: Vagrius, 1997), 55–56.

90. S. A. Moiseev and A. A. Danilov, *GAI-GIBDD UVD Ivanovskoi oblasti 65 let. Ocherk istorii* (Ivanovo: Ivanovskii gos. universitet, 2001), 29.

91. *Za rulëm*, no. 18 (1935): 12–13; no. 1 (1935): 21. Both Koshkin and Vshivkov were sentenced to be executed.

92. *Pravda*, June 6, 1935, 1; *Za rulëm*, no. 6 (1935): 10. On the party's verification of documents, see J. Arch Getty, *Origins of the Great Purges: The Soviet Communist Party Reconsidered, 1933–1938* (Cambridge: Cambridge University Press, 1985), 58–89.

93. *Za rulëm*, no. 3 (1936): 6; no. 6 (1935): 25; no. 9 (1936): 1–6; no. 11 (1936): 12–13.

94. Ibid., no. 6 (1936): 25.

95. Nina Lugovskaya, *The Diary of a Soviet Schoolgirl 1932–1937*, trans. Joanne Turnbull (Moscow: Glas, 2003), 63–65.

96. For the epigraph, see Vassily Aksyonov, *The Winter's Hero*, trans. John Glad (New York: Random House, 1996), 3. For the poem, Boris Slutskii, *Sobranie sochinenii v trekh tomakh* 3 vols.(Moscow: Khud. lit-ra, 1991), 1:170.

97. Thaddeus Wittlin, *Commissar: The Life and Death of Lavrenty Pavlovich Beria* (New York: Macmillan, 1972), 250; Amy Knight, *Beria, Stalin's First Lieutenant* (Princeton: Princeton University Press, 1993), 97, 241; Richard Lourie, *The Autobiography of Joseph Stalin: A Novel* (Washington, D.C.: Counterpoint, 1999), 108; Anton Antonov-Ovseenko, *Beriia* (Moscow: ACT, 1999), 350–52; Andrei Makine, *Dreams of My Russian Summers*, trans. Geoffrey Strachan (New York: Arcade, 1997), 144–45.

98. Valentina Bogdan, "Memoirs of an Engineer," in *In the Shadow of Revolution: Life Stories of Russian Women from 1917 to the Second World War,* ed. Sheila Fitzpatrick and Yuri Slezkine (Princeton: Princeton University Press, 2000), 408. Bogdan's reference to the GPU (State Political Directorate) is anachronistic.

99. Alexander Solzhenitsyn, *The Gulag Archipelago, 1918–1956,* trans. Thomas P. Whitney (London: Collins/Fontana, 1974), 528.

100. RGAE, f. 2352, op. 1, d. 169 (Correspondence with administration of Moscow Soviet of Workers' and Peasants' Deputies on sale of "Packard" truck for conveying prisoners, 1923–24), ll. 5–6, 56, 73, 76–80.

101. See also Dmitry Shepilov, "The Kremlin's Scholar: A Memoir of Soviet Politics under Stalin and Khrushchev," unpublished manuscript edited and annotated by Stephen V. Bitner, trans. by Anthony Austin (New Haven: Yale University Press, 2007), 160, 239.

102. Eugenia Semyonovna Ginzburg, *Journey into the Whirlwind,* trans. Paul Stevenson and Max Hayward (San Diego: Harcourt Brace, 1967), 43–44, 100. Ginzburg was the wife of Pavel ("Paul") Aksyonov, head of the Kazan city party organization and a member of TsIK. Their son, Vassily, became a writer.

103. Olga Velikanova, "The Myth of the Besieged Fortress: Soviet Mass Perception in the 1920s–1930s," Working Paper No. 7 in *The Stalin-Era Research and Archives Project* (Toronto: University of Toronto, 2002), 4–5.

104. Tim Edensor, *National Identity, Popular Culture, and Everyday Life* (Oxford: Berg, 2002), 118.

105. Veniamin Braslavskii, "Sviazi vremeni," *Zhurnal Vestnik* online, no. 17 (302), Aug. 21, 2002, at http://www.vestnik.com/issues/2002/0821/win/braslavsky.htm (accessed 3.27.06). Aleksandr Vertinsky (1889–1957) was a popular singer who returned to live in Russia in 1943 after a twenty-three-year absence. Braslavsky recalls a line from the song "Hispano-Suiza."

106. Mikhail German, *Slozhnoe proshedshee* (St. Petersburg: Iskusstvo Spb, 2000), 32. The accompanying text by Iurii Dolmatovskii suggested that readers send drawings of cars they saw. For a story about the friendship between a car and a tractor, see L. Kassil', "Druzhnaia semeika," *Murazilka,* no. 6 (1933): 4–6.

107. V. Tambi, *Avtomobil'* (Moscow: Gosizd., 1930). M. Il'in was the penname of Il'ia Iakovlevich Marshak (1896–1953), the younger brother of the better-known children's writer, Samuil Marshak.

108. German, *Slozhnoe proshedshee,* 33. Compare to Braslavsky: "Among the boys of my age, the automobile was an object of heightened interest. Nobody among us gave a thought about the possibility of ever having a car of one's own. It was considered an event if one was given the chance to go for a drive, sit behind the wheel, look under the hood, or simply see a new model." Braslavskii, "Sviazi vremeni."

109. In the ordinary world, even nonflying convertibles were few and far between, though for a frequently reproduced photograph from 1940 of a GAZ-61–40 all-terrain vehicle (a modified Emka designed by Vitalii Grachev) climbing the broad steps of the river station at Khimki outside Moscow, see Shugurov, *Avtomobil'naia Moskva,* 76. Nearly forty years later, a decidedly non–socialist realist American fantasy film, *Grease* (dir. Randal Kleiser, 1978), would end happily with the two high school sweethearts ascending in a convertible.

110. Article 10, *Constitution (Fundamental Law) of the Union of Soviet Socialist Republics* (Moscow: Gosizdat, 1969), 15.

111. Ars. Tumanian, "O shofërov-liubiteliakh," *Za rulëm,* no. 8 (1936): 21.

112. GARF, f. 5446, op. 14a, d. 635, ll. 31–33.

113. Ginzburg, *Journey into the Whirlwind,* 37.

114. Inna Shikheeva-Gaister, "A Family Chronicle," in *In the Shadow,* 372, 375.

115. M. Iunprof, "Pervyi sezon sovetskogo avto-mototurizma," *Za rulëm,* no. 23 (1935): 18–19.

116. M. Iunprof, "Sovetskii avtoturizm," *Za rulëm,* no. 11 (1937): 12–13. For Ilf and Petrov's account of their trip, see *Odnoetazhnaia Amerika, pis'ma iz ameriki* (Moscow: Tekst, 2003).

117. *Pravda,* July 30, 1936, 4, 6; July 31, 1936, 6; M. Iunprof, "Avtomotosport," *Za rulëm,* no. 23 (1936): 14–15.

118. Iunprof, "Avtomotosport," 15; Vladimir Zakharov, *Vsego odin kilometr . . . o sovetskikh avtogonshchikakh i sozdateliakh skorostnykh avtomobilei* (Kiev: Molod, 1984), 3. See also A. Kurdzikauskas and L. Shugurov, *Avtomobil'nyi sport v SSSR, spravochnik* (Vilnius: MINTIS, 1976), 11–14.

119. *Za rulëm,* no. 2 (1937): 18–19; no. 7 (1937): 2.

120. *Za rulëm,* no. 14 (1937): 13; no. 15 (1937): 14; no. 17 (1937): 19; no. 8 (1998): 128–29. For the sake of comparison, Campbell's Bluebird traveled at just over 500 km/h at the Bonneville Salt Flats in September 1935.

121. Diane Koenker, personal communication, July 7, 2006. On alpinism, see Eva Maurer, "*Al'pinizm* as Mass Sport and Elite Recreation," in *Turizm: The Russian and East European Tourist under Capitalism and Socialism,* ed. Anne E. Gorsuch and Diane P. Koenker (Ithaca: Cornell University Press, 2006), 141–62. Maurer notes that "mountaineers never achieved the same individual hero status awarded to pilots…contrary to some authors' assumptions" (147). Much the same could be said of auto-racing champions.

122. Diane Koenker, "The Proletarian Tourist in the 1930s: Between Mass Excursion and Mass Escape," in *Turizm,* 128.

123. A. Grechanik, "Avtomobil'nye perevozki voisk," *Za rulëm,* no. 4 (1937): 7–9. See also S. Pugachev, "Voina i transport," *Pravda,* Mar. 6, 1937, 3. On the training of drivers and mechanics by the U.S. Army during the war, see Kevin L. Borg, *Auto Mechanics: Technology and Expertise in Twentieth-Century America* (Baltimore: Johns Hopkins University Press, 2007), 65–71.

124. I. Khalepskii, "Molodezh', na avtomobil'!" *Pravda,* Mar. 4, 1937, 3.

125. Liapidevskii (1908–83) was one of the rescuers of the ice-bound Cheliushkin crew in 1934 for which he was awarded a Hero of the Soviet Union medal. His article directed especially at Soviet youth was published in *Pravda,* Mar. 3, 1937.

126. *Pravda,* Mar. 10, 1937, 6.

127. *Za rulëm,* no. 5 (1937): 7; no. 17 (1937): 17; no. 11 (1937): 21.

128. *Za rulëm,* no. 2 (1938): 25; no. 6 (1938): 19; no. 7 (1938): 12; no. 13 (1938): 14; *Rezoliutsiia po otchetnomu dokladu Orgbiuro sportivnogo Dobrovol'nogo Obshchestva "Avtomotor" za oktiabr' 1936—1 aprelia 1938 g.* (Khar'kov: Soiuz shoferov Iuga, 1938).

129. *Za rulëm,* no. 15 (1937): 14.

130. "Zhizn' zamechatel'nykh mashin," "Avtopilot," no. 6 (1997), at http://autopilot.kom mersant.ru/issues/Auto/1997/06/inde(accessed 7.9.06).

Chapter 6. Cars, Cars, and More Cars

1. Hans Koningsberger, *Along the Roads of the New Russia* (New York: Farrar, Straus and Giroux, 1968), 176. Koningsberger did a lot of traveling through time and space, authoring books on his native Amsterdam, Vermeer's world, Christopher Columbus, China, 1968, and several novels. After 1972 he published under the name of Hans Koning.

2. Ibid., 16, 31, 79, 176, 181, 186. Note that this relatively carless utopia was accessible only because Koningsberger had "his own car." For other car-centric utopias, see Peter Wollen and Joe Kerr, ed., *Autopia: Cars and Culture* (London: Reaktion, 2002).

3. David Willis, *Klass, How Russians Really Live* (New York: St. Martin's, 1985), 131.

4. *Stalin and the Soviet-Finnish War, 1939–1940,* ed. E. N. Kulkov and O. A. Rzheshevsky (London: Frank Cass, 2002), 16, 226–27.

5. Antony Beevor and Luba Vinogradova, ed., *A Writer at War: Vasily Grossman with the Red Army 1941–1945* (London: Harvill Press, 2005), 50, 57.

6. Ibid., 131.

7. Cf. George C. Herring Jr., *Aid to Russia 1941–1946: Strategy, Diplomacy, and the Origins of the Cold War* (New York: Columbia University Press, 1973); Albert Weeks, *Russia's Life-Saver: Lend Lease Aid to the USSR* (Lanham, Md.: Lexington, 2004), chap. 7 and table 4; *Velikaia Otechestvennaia voina: Voenno-istoricheskie ocherki,* ed. V. A. Zolotarev et al., 4 vols. (Moscow: Nauka, 1998–99), 1:85; Mikhail Suprun, *Lend-liz i severnye konvoi, 1941–1945 gg.* (Moscow: Andreevskii flag, 1997).

8. G. V. Kirilenko, "Ekonomicheskoe protivoborstvo storon," and G. A. Kumanev and L. M. Chzavkov, "Sovetskii Soiuz i Lend Liz, 1941–1945," in *Voina i obshchestvo, 1941–1945,* ed. G. N. Sevost'ianov, 2 vols. (Moscow: Nauka, 2004), 1:346, 370–72.

9. On these and other Hollywood films and their reception by Soviet audiences, see Todd Bennett, "Culture, Power, and *Mission to Moscow:* Film and Soviet-American Relations during World War II," *Journal of American History* 88, no. 2 (2001): 512–15; Lev Navrozov, *The Education of Lev Navrozov: A Life in the Closed World Once Called Russia* (New York: Harper's Magazine Press, 1975), 364–65. Navrozov claims that Soviet audiences "perceived Steinbeck's wrathful message of *poverty* as a futuristic fantasy."

10. Anatolii Rybakov, *Roman-vospominanie* (Moscow: Vagrius, 1997), 86–100.

11. Veniamin Braslavskii, "Sviazi vremeni," *Zhurnal Vestnik* online, no. 17 (302), Aug. 21, 2002, at http://www.vestnik.com/issues/2002/0821/win/braslavsky.htm (accessed 3.27.06); Dmitrii Mal'kov, "'Innostrantsy' na ulitsakh Krasnoiarske," *Ekonomika i zhizn' Sibir,* Oct. 25, 2004 (no. 216), at http://www.ekolife.krsk.ru/content.asp?id=4375 (accessed 7.23.06).

12. Gosudarstvennyi Arkhiv Rossiiskoi Federatsii (GARF), f. 9401, op. 7, d. 586 (Memoranda and reports of Assistant Commissar of Internal Affairs on automobile and tractor fleet, 1944), l. 46; d. 590 (Cumulative reports on presence of automobiles and tractors for 1945), l. 6; d. 594 (Presence of automobiles and tractors for 1946), ll. 19, 40, 59; d. 601 (Repair of automobiles for 1947), ll. 3, 8, 13; d. 605 (Report to the leadership of MVD on production of parts for automobiles and tractors, 1948–1950), ll. 63, 65, 68. Attempts to transfer to other institutions an additional 1,250 via the State Supply Commission (Gossnab) proved unsuccessful because of a lack of interest.

13. Rybakov, *Roman-vospominanie,* 114, 128.

14. Rossiiskii Gosudarstvennyi Arkhiv Noveishei Istorii (RGANI), f. 6, op. 6, d. 1587, ll. 106–12. I thank James Heinzen for providing me with a copy of this document.

15. Lev Shugurov, *Avtomobil'naia Moskva: Stoletie 1902–2001* (Moscow: TsDTS, 2004), 81; "Wartburg," at http://www.team.net/www/ktud/wartburg.html (accessed 7.29.06); "The Production at IFA WERK in Eisenach East Germany after 2nd World War," at http://home.no.net/eisenach/production_at_ifa_werk_in_eisenach.htm (accessed 7.29.06).

16. Shugurov, *Avtomobil'naia Moskva,* 82; "M-20 Pobeda—istoriia—mashiny tret'ei serii: 1955–1958," at http://www.gaz20.spb.ru/history_1955–1958.htm (accessed 7.16.06); David Holloway, *Stalin and the Bomb: The Soviet Union and Atomic Energy, 1939–1956* (New Haven: Yale University Press, 1994), 148.

17. Braslavskii, "Sviazi vremeni," 3; "M-20 Pobeda."

18. *Avtomobil',* no. 3 (1950): 22; no. 7 (1950): 23; no. 6 (1951): 27; no. 7 (1951): 47.

19. Vera Dunham, *In Stalin's Time: Middleclass Values in Soviet Fiction,* rev. ed. (Durham: Duke University Press, 1990), 46–47.

20. TsSU, *Narodnoe khoziaistvo SSSR v 1964 g.* (Moscow: Gos. stat. izd-vo, 1965), 632.

21. Braslavskii, "Sviazi vremeni," 3.

22. Patrick Sergeant, *Another Road to Samarkand* (London: Hodder and Stoughton, 1955), 24; Heinz Lathe and Günther Meierling, *Return to Russia,* trans. Charlotte Dixon (London: Galley Press, 1961), 55.

23. L. M. Shugurov and V. P. Shirshov, *Avtomobili strany sovetov* (Moscow: DOSAAF, 1983), 62–74; TsSU, *Narodnoe khoziaistvo SSSR v 1970 g.* (Moscow: Gos. stat. izd-vo, 1971), 452.

24. GARF, f. 9401, op. 2, d. 169, l. 243 (report from Ministry of Internal Affairs on technical condition of auto fleet, 24 April 1947). I thank James Heinzen for bringing this document to my attention.

25. *Za rulëm,* no. 3 (1979): 28; E. B. Gruzdeva and E. S. Chertikhina, *Trud i byt sovetskikh zhenshchin* (Moscow: Politizdat, 1983), 21.

26. Lathe and Meierling, *Return to Russia,* 72.

27. Anatolii Rybakov, "Voditeli," *Oktiabr',* no. 1 (1950): 27. The novel was serialized in nos. 1–3.

28. Rybakov, *Roman-vospominanie,* 144, 162; *Avtomobili,* no. 7 (1950): 32. Without consulting a transcript it is impossible to know whether these criticisms were voiced by the audience or by engineer M. Shulov, who summarized the discussion.

29. The film was derived from a popular song, "The Ballad of a Driver" (Shofërskaia ballada), which was about the friendly rivalry between two drivers, Kol'ka and Raika, that ends tragically. See *Gazeta,* Sept. 17, 2004, 15; "Ekkhali dva shofëra," *Nastoiashchee kino,* Mar. 2002, at www.filmz.ru/film/1200.htm (accessed 8.8.06).

30. Rybakov, "Voditeli," *Oktiabr',* no. 3 (1950): 83.

31. For a story that refers to truck drivers who *intentionally* transport illegal goods, see the novel *Olenka* by Mikhail Zhestev (1955) as summarized in Ann Livschiz, "De-Stalinizing Soviet Childhood: The Quest for Moral Rebirth, 1953–58," in ed. Polly Jones, *The Dilemmas of De-Stalinization: Negotiating Cultural and Social Change in the Khrushchev Era* (Abingdon: Routledge, 2006), 125–26.

32. Kathleen Parthé, "Shukshin at Large," in *Vasily Shukshin: Stories from a Siberian Village,* trans. Laura Michael and John Givens (De Kalb: Northern Illinois University Press, 1996), x.

33. See, respectively, Vasilii Shukshin, *Sobranie sochinenii v trekh tomakh* 3 vols.(Moscow: Molodaia gvardiia, 1985), 2:120–36, 108–20, 79–90. For the film script, see Vasilii Shukshin,

Kinopovesti, 2nd ed. (Moscow: Iskusstvo, 1988), 5–47. "Ballad of a Driver" contains the lines "There is a road in the Chuiskii *trakt* / Traveled by many a driver."

34. For swearing "like a driver," see the complaint of first-class driver M. M. Kalik in *Za rulëm*, no. 3 (1956): 9.

35. I am grateful to Andrey Shlyakhter for sharing with me his paper, "Manning (and Mining) the Arteries of Soviet Trade: Recollections of a Soviet Truck Driver," which incorporates the interview with Goldshteyn in Chicago in November 2003. All quotations are from that interview.

36. *Za rulëm*, no. 12 (1960): 10–11, 16.

37. *New York Times*, Oct. 1, 2005, Λ4.

38. *Amerika, Illustrirovannyi zhurnal*, no. 16 (1958): 23; no. 19 (1958): front cover; no. 23 (1958): 17. The journal was inaugurated in 1944 and suspended publication in 1952.

39. Joseph S. Nye, *Soft Power: The Means to Success in World Politics* (New York: Public Affairs, 2004). Nye, who introduced the concept in 1990, defined it as "the ability to get what you want through attraction rather than through coercion."

40. *Avtomobil'naia i traktornaia promyshlennost'*, no. 8 (1956): 39–46; no. 10 (1956): 43–46.

41. "V nachale byl Moskvich," *Za rulëm*, no. 3 (2002): 132. The author is Vladimir Arkusha, assistant chief editor.

42. Walter L. Hixson, *Parting the Curtain: Propaganda, Culture, and the Cold War, 1945–1961* (New York: St. Martin's, 1997), 199, 202–3; for a photograph from the exhibit, see Shugurov, *Avtomobil'naia Moskva*, 117.

43. Aline Mosby, *The View from No. 13 People's Street* (New York: Random House, 1962), 91.

44. For a similar point made with respect to the GDR's Socialist Unity Party (SED), see Jonathan Zatlin, "The Vehicle of Desire: The Trabant, the Wartburg, and the End of the GDR," *German History* 15, no. 3 (1997): 363–66.

45. *Za rulëm*, no. 3 (1960): inside cover. See also p. 13 for the claim that ten thousand Moskviches were being exported to the United States, a claim I have been unable to substantiate.

46. Kommunisticheskaia partiia Sovetskogo Soiuza, S"ezd 1956, Moscow, *Stenograficheskii otchet*, 2 vols. (Moscow: Gosizdat, 1956), 1:51.

47. A. Taranov, "Avtomobil'-massam," *Za rulëm*, no. 4 (1960): 10–11; no. 12 (1959): 8–9, inside cover.

48. *Shofer ponevole* (dir. Nadezhda Kosheverova, 1958, Lenfil'm). The screenplay was by Sergei Mikhalkov, children's story writer, coauthor of the words to the Soviet national anthem, and father of the future film director, Nikita.

49. More perceptive viewers might have regarded the switch in identities—a classic device for exploring and questioning social boundaries that in the film is precipitated by an inadvertent appropriation of clothing—as an extreme case of homosocial (if not homoerotic) bonding.

50. Muriel Reed, "Avec la nouvelle société russe en vacances j'ai goûté aux délices de Sotchi," *Réalités*, no. 213 (1963): 59–60.

51. "Problemy prokata," *Za rulëm*, no. 8 (1960): 17–19.

52. I. Starshinov, "Nereshennye problemy prokata," *Za rulëm*, no. 3 (1962): 12–13.

53. On the "colossal" urban growth under Khrushchev and its implications for public transport, see R. Antony French, *Plans, Pragmatism, and People: The Legacy of Soviet Planning for Today's Cities* (Pittsburgh: University of Pittsburgh Press, 1995), 159–67; O. P. Litovka, *Problemy prostranstvennogo razvitiia urbanizatsii* (Leningrad: Nauka, 1976), 4–5, 53–62.

54. *Za rulëm*, no. 5 (1959): 20–21; no. 1 (1960): 20; no. 4 (1960): 11; Irving R. Levine, *Main Street, USSR* (New York: Doubleday, 1959), 236–37.

55. *Za rulëm*, no. 3 (1956): 1; N. B. Lebina and A. N. Chistikov, *Obyvatel' i reformy: Kartiny povsednevnoi zhizni gorozhan v gody nepa i khrushchevskogo desiatiletiia* (St. Petersburg: Dmitrii Bulanin, 2003), 284. Leningraders with their own cars were targeted in advertisements for Black Sea resorts that the Ministry of Trade's resort office placed in the city's newspapers. The authors cite *Leningradskaia Pravda* from Mar. 19, 1955.

56. *Za rulëm*, no. 4 (1959): 30; no. 5 (1960): 22. Some of this information also could be found in guidebooks that, replete with maps, were issued by physical culture and sports associations. See, for example, I. M. Daksergof, ed., *Avtomobilist-liubitel'* (Moscow: Izd. Fizikul'tura i sport, 1963).

57. "Na gornykh dorogakh" (music by Aleksandr Voronov, words by Vadim Malkov), *Za rulëm*, no. 11 (1960): inside cover.

58. S. I. Keangeli et al., *Spravochnik avtoturista* (Moscow: Transport, 1969), 4. On Soviet and East European tourism, see Anne E. Gorsuch and Diane P. Koenker, eds., *Turizm: The*

Russian and East European Tourist under Capitalism and Socialism (Ithaca: Cornell University Press, 2006).

59. Keangeli, *Spravochnik,* 38, 162–63, 168; *Za rulëm,* no. 7 (1956): 9; *Za rulëm,* no. 4 (1966): 28; no. 11 (1966): 20.

60. Christian Noack, "Coping with the Tourist: Planned and 'Wild' Mass Tourism on the Soviet Black Sea Coast," in *Turizm,* 301.

61. S. V. Mikhalkov, *Teatr dlia vzroslykh* (Moscow: Iskusstvo, 1979), 329–78. In the film version the women drive a Zaporozhets.

62. Petr Vail' and Aleksandr Genis, *60-e: Mir sovetskogo cheloveka* (Ann Arbor, Mich.: Ardis, 1988), 105–16; quotation on 105. Diane Koenker, who is writing a history of Soviet tourism, points out that people did wander before the 1960s but did so for the most part surreptitiously (personal communication).

63. *Za rulëm,* no. 5 (1966): 18–19.

64. Levine, *Main Street, USSR,* 240. Levine accurately describes Soviet gas station protocol as follows: "Often customers take the hose themselves; the attendant simply watches and collects the coupons. The patron may fill his tires with air if he wishes, but like windshield cleaning, it's self-service." This, of course, anticipates by some twenty-five years U.S. practices, as did the right turn on red that according to Levine "presents a hazard for pedestrians" (241). See also Mosby, *View from No. 13 People's Street,* 95. Mosby similarly noted the prevalence of women attendants and the self-service system.

65. Almost every imaginable kind of vehicle visits the gas station, including a black Cadillac that disgorges an American family easily identifiable by the car, a hula hoop–twirling girl, and a boy sporting shorts and a cowboy hat. For another film with the same message, see *The Green Light* (*Zelenyi ogonëk,* dir. V. Azarov, 1964), whose main character, a taxi driver named Sergei, says at one point, "Everyone can be outstanding in his own place." Sergei's taxi, the only Moskvich in a garage full of Volgas, seems to have a mind of its own and also is capable of speech.

66. Howard Norton, *Only in Russia* (Princeton: Van Nostrand, 1962), 117.

67. *Krokodil,* no. 15 (1960): 8.

68. Ibid., no. 29 (1947): 10.

69. *Za rulëm,* no. 15 (1959): 20; no. 2 (1959): 20.

70. G. Charnetskii and L. Panov, "Garazhi v zhilykh kvartalakh," *Arkhitektura SSSR,* no. 4 (1958): 16–20; Steven E. Harris, "Moving to the Separate Apartment: Building, Distributing, Furnishing, and Living in Urban Housing in Soviet Russia, 1950s–1960s," PhD diss., University of Chicago, 2003, 398.

71. Harris, "Moving to the Separate Apartment," 438–39.

72. Quoting from the Sovnarkom resolution of July 3, 1936, in *Dirizhery Moskovskikh magistralei, sbornik vospominanii, ocherkov i rasskazov o sotrudnikakh Gosavtoinspektsii,* ed. V. A. Iur'ev (Moscow: Robin, 1996), 55–57. To date, no independent, comprehensive history of the Soviet traffic police exists.

73. A. M. Kormilitsyn (director of GAI from 1956 to 1960), "Po zovu dolga," in *GAI 60 let. Istoriia, vospominaniia, ocherki,* ed. A. G. Gorlov (Moscow: MVD Rossii, 1996), 47–69; *Sbornik zakonodatel'stva po avtomobil'nomu transportu,* ed. D. I. Polovinchik (Moscow: Iurid. lit., 1964), 298–305.

74. Konstantin Simis, *USSR, the Corrupt Society: The Secret World of Soviet Capitalism* (New York: Simon and Schuster, 1982), 186. "Vadim" (see below) brought two bottles of cognac and his driving instructor, a lieutenant colonel in the army, to the test site. "He knew GAI, and they drank together. I paid the lieutenant colonel a small amount of money."

75. Cited in "Istoriia stanovleniia GIBDD v Kirovskoi oblasti," 31, at http://gibdd.kirov.ru/History.files/History/History.htm (accessed 8.25.06). This anonymously written forty-two-page account is rich in detail about the automobile inspectorate of Kirov Oblast.

76. See Vil' Lipatov, "Starshii avtoinspektor," *Izvestiia,* Apr. 18, 1971, 3; "Biografiia muzhestva," in *GAI 60 let,* 243–54; "Istoriia stanovleniia," 40–42.

77. *Pravda,* Oct. 10, 1961, 6.

78. "Istoriia stanovleniia," 35–36; Fyodor Abramov, *The New Life: A Day on a Collective Farm,* trans. George Reavey (New York: Grove Press, 1963), 132, originally published in *Neva* in January 1963.

79. *Izvestiia,* Jan. 28, 1965, 3. For a satirical treatment of excessive concern about the acquisition and ownership of cars, see El'dar Riazanov's film, *Beregis' avtomobilia!* (Mosfil'm, 1966).

80. *Izvestiia,* Mar. 4, 1966, 3; Mar. 5, 1966, 3.

81. *Izvestiia,* Aug. 18, 1966, 5.

82. The proportion of Soviet households reported as owning televisions and refrigerators rose respectively from 24% and 11% in 1965, to 74% and 65% in 1975, and 92% and 89% in 1982. See table 2.6 in David Lane, *Soviet Economy and Society* (New York: Blackwell, 1985), 58. For references to these items in connection with automobile ownership, see D. P. Velikanov, "Avtomobil' i my," *Literaturnaia gazeta,* Mar. 19, 1971, 12; *Pravda,* July 24, 1971, 3; Leonid Likhodeev, *Ia i moi avtomobil'* (Moscow: Sovetskii pisatel', 1972), 17–19 ("Do you have a TV, do you have a refrigerator? So, there will be a car."), and G. N. Andrienko, "Legkovoi avtomobil' v sem'e," in *Ekonomika i organizatsiia promyshlennogo proizvodstva,* vol. 21 (1985): 106.

83. Grace Lees-Maffei, "Men, Motors, Markets and Women," in Wollen and Kerr, *Autopia,* 363, 70, and Roland Barthes, "La voiture, projection de l'égo," *Réalités,* no. 213 (1963). See also Wolfgang Sachs, *For Love of the Automobile: Looking Back into the History of Our Desires* (Berkeley: University of California Press, 1992); D. Gartman, *Auto Opium: A Social History of Automobile Design* (London: Routledge, 1994).

84. A. Plakhkov, *Kommersant,* Nov. 18, 1997, 13, cited in David MacFadyen, *The Sad Comedy of El'dar Riazanov: An Introduction to Russia's Most Popular Filmmaker* (Montreal: McGill-Queen's University Press, 2003), 113.

85. I am citing here the version in Emil' Braginskii and El'dar Riazanov, *Tikhie omuty* (Moscow: Vagrius, 2000), 41.

86. Ibid., 113. For a different interpretation, see MacFadyen, *Sad Comedy,* 116–17.

87. *Izvestiia,* Mar. 4, 1966, 3.

88. Donald D. Barry and Carol Barner Barry, "Happiness Is Driving Your Own Moskvich," *New York Times Magazine,* Apr. 10, 1966, 48.

89. See, respectively. E. I. Aiueva, "Sdelki grazhdan po rasporiazheniiu legkovymi avtomobiliami," *Sovetskoe Gosudarstvo i Pravo,* no. 9 (1974): 109–14; V. V. Zhigulenkova and K. B. Iaroshenko, "Judicial Practice in Cases Involving the Alienation of Automobiles Belonging to Citizens according to the Right of Personal Ownership," *Soviet Statutes and Decisions* 22, no. 1 (1985): 33–45; John Hazard, William E. Butler, and Peter B. Maggs, *The Soviet Legal System: Fundamental Principles and Historical Commentary* (Dobbs Ferry, N.Y.: Oceana Publications, 1977), 406; *Soviet Statutes and Decisions* 22, no. 3 (1986): 54–57.

90. For the contrast between Khrushchev's "populist approach" and Brezhnev's "managerial approach," see George W. Breslauer, "Khrushchev Reconsidered," in *The Soviet Union since Stalin,* ed. Stephen F. Cohen, Alexander Rabinowitch, and Robert Sharlet (Bloomington: Indiana University Press, 1980), 50–70.

91. John Thompson, *A Vision Unfulfilled: Russia and the Soviet Union in the Twentieth Century* (Lexington, Mass.: D. C. Heath, 1996), 423; James Millar, "The Little Deal: Brezhnev's Contribution to Acquisitive Socialism," *Slavic Review* 44, no. 4 (1985): 694–706.

92. *Pravda,* Apr. 9, 1966, 6. See also Feb. 20, 1966, 2. Truck production was to increase by a relatively modest 1.6–1.7 times, with the result that more passenger cars than trucks would be produced by 1970. In actuality this did not occur until 1972.

93. TsSU SSSR, *Narodnoe khoziaistvo SSSR v 1975* (Moscow: Gos. stat. izd-vo, 1976), 265. Output hardly grew thereafter, reaching 1.3 million in 1980 and remaining at more or less that level throughout the decade. For VAZ's annual production (1970–2005), see the in-house *Rubezhi,* July 20, 2006, 4.

94. TsSU SSSR, *Narodnoe khoziaistvo SSSR v 1985* (Moscow: Gos. stat. izd-vo, 1986), 446. Toli Welihozkiy, "Automobiles and the Soviet Consumer," in *Soviet Economy in a Time of Change: A Compendium of Papers Submitted to the Joint Economic Committee, Congress of the United States* (Washington, D.C.: U.S. Government Printing Office, 1979), 818, cites a figure of 7.3 million vehicles by 1979, of which 80% (5.8 million) were owned by individuals.

95. Welihozkiy, "Automobiles," 819; *MVMA Motor Vehicle Facts and Figures '80* (Detroit: Motor Vehicle Manufacturer Association, 1980), 37. At the other end of the spectrum in Eastern Europe was the German Democratic Republic where, in the late 1980s, 40–50% of households had a car. Zatlin, "Vehicle of Desire," 361.

96. D. P. Velikanov, "Vazhneishie voprosy razvitiia avtomobil'nogo transporta v SSSR," in *Voprosy razvitiia avtomobil'nogo transporta,* ed. D. P. Velikanov (Moscow: Transport, 1971), 20–21; Velikanov, "Avtomobil' i my," 12; V. T. Efimov and G. I. Mikerin, "Avtomobilizatsiia v razvitom sotsialicheskom obshchestve," *Sotsiologicheskie issledovaniia,* no. 1 (1976): 134; A. Arrak, "Ispol'zovanie avtomobilei lichnogo pol'zovaniia," *Voprosy ekonomiki,* no. 7 (1978): 134.

97. See, for example, Max Carasso, *People vs. Cars: The Rising Resentment against the Automobile* (New York: Autofacts, 1970); Kenneth R. Scheider, *Autokind vs. Mankind* (New York: W. W. Norton, 1971); John Jerome, *The Death of the Automobile: The Fatal Effect of the Golden Era, 1955–1970* (New York: W. W. Norton, 1972); and Emma Rothschild, *Paradise Lost: The Decline of the Auto-Industrial Age* (New York: Random House, 1973).

98. Velikanov, "Vazhneishie voprosy," 20–21.

99. *Izvestiia*, Aug. 14, 1988, 3.

100. John M. Kramer, "Soviet Policy towards the Automobile," *Survey* 22, no. 2 (1976): 20.

101. Kramer, "Soviet Policy"; Welihozkiy, "Automobiles," 822; Lane, *Soviet Economy and Society*, 60.

102. Andrienko, "Legkovoi avtomobil'," 111. Zatlin, "Vehicle of Desire," 367–68, suggests three factors accounting for the high prices of autos in the GDR: high production costs, the need of the state to recoup some of the cost of subsidizing basic material needs, and as a means of soaking up extra cash. These factors pertained in the USSR as well.

103. Welihozkiy, "Automobiles," 822; A. Iarovikov et al., "V prodazhe—avtomobil'," *Sovetskaia torgovlia*, no. 5 (1974): 26. Was this any worse, the authors of this article asked, than the opposite phenomenon of two million cars produced by Detroit in 1972 lacking customers because of the "deep crisis of the automobile industry in the U.S."?

104. Welihozkiy, "Automobiles," 820.

105. For the regulations governing sales of used cars that were introduced in 1971, see M. Teliushkin, "Pravovye voprosy komissionnoi torgovli legkovymi avtomobiliami," *Sovetskaia iustitsiia*, no. 9 (1972): 15–17.

106. For some examples, see Welihozkiy, "Automobiles," 823–24.

107. For a fascinating analysis of "second economy activity in the market for the used cars" based on a survey of some seventy respondents, see William Pyle, "Private Car Ownership and Second Economy Activity," *Berkeley-Duke Occasional Papers on the Second Economy in the USSR*, no. 37 (Washington, D.C., 1993), 42–45; quotation on 42.

108. In the GDR, for example, a new Lada cost 28,500 marks, but used ones were selling for 80,000 in the late 1980s. Zatlin, "Vehicle of Desire," 373.

109. Andrienko, "Legkovoi avtomobil'," 111.

110. L. A. Gordon and A. K. Nazimova, *Rabochii klass SSSR, tendentsii i perspektivy sotsial'no-ekonomicheskogo razvitiia* (Moscow: Nauka, 1985), 30. See also M. E. Podzniakova, "Obespechennost' naseleniia predmetami kul'turno-bytovogo naznacheniia," *Sotsiologicheskie issledovaniia*, no. 3 (1987): 60, based on an all-Union survey of 1981. It would be useful to know to what extent men were overrepresented, but unfortunately data relating to gender were not included in the literature at my disposal.

111. Ch. A. Mansimov, "Izmeneniia v zhiznennom uklade semei lenkoranskogo raiona," *Sotsiologicheskie issledovaniia*, no. 3 (1981): 105. The sample was six hundred people.

112. See Ferenc Fehér, Agnes Heller, and György Márkus, *Dictatorship over Needs: An Analysis of Soviet Societies* (Oxford: Blackwell, 1983).

113. Iarovikov, "V prodazhe," 26; Andrienko, "Legkovoi avtomobil'," 112.

114. Vladimir Voinovich, *The Anti-Soviet Soviet Union* (San Diego: Harcourt Brace, 1985), 5–6.

115. Willis, *Klass*, 8.

116. Cited in Julian Pettifer and Nigel Turner, *Automania: Man and the Motor Car* (Boston: Little, Brown, 1984), 30. For a conveniently assembled compendium of reminiscences about Brezhnev's fondness for cars and fast driving, see V. Shelud'ko, ed., *Leonid Brezhnev v vospominaniiakh, razmyshleniiakh, suzhdeniiakh* (Rostov-on-Don: Feniks, 1998), 108–17.

117. A. Druzenko, "Odinokii kilometr," *Izvestiia*, Aug. 23, 1966, 4.

118. The fear was expressed by B. T. Efimov, professor at the Moscow Automobile and Highway Institute (MADI), in Efimov and Mikerin, "Avtomobilizatsiia," 130.

119. Pettifer and Turner, *Automania*, 167.

120. See http://www.caroftheyear.org. (last consulted 6.30.04). For a more jaundiced but not unaffectionate view, see Peter Hamilton, "The Lada: A Cultural Icon," in Wollen and Kerr, *Autopia*, 191–98.

121. Barry and Barry, "Happiness," 48; Willis, *Klass*, 126. For an estimate of 250,000 privately owned cars by 1978, see *Za rulëm*, no. 1 (1978): 17. By comparison, in the United States there was one repair station for every eight hundred cars in 1972. *MVMA Motor Vehicle Facts and Figures '78*, 68.

122. *Za rulëm,* no. 3 (1968): back page; no. 4 (1968): 17; "Skol'ko zhit' avtomobiliu?" no. 5 (1968): 12. The shortage of spare parts topped the list of eight items mentioned.

123. Andrienko, "Legkovoi avtomobil'," 115.

124. Welihozkiy, "Automobiles," 828–29.

125. *Izvestiia,* May 20, 1973, 3; L. Agalakov, "Pochemu ne stroit'sia garazh," *Za rulëm,* no. 1 (1978): 17.

126. Moshe Lewin, *The Soviet Century* (London: Verso, 2005), 342–60.

127. *Pravda,* July 24, 1971, 3; *Izvestiia,* Apr. 13, 1972, 4.

128. *Pravda,* Oct. 14, 1971, 2; *Izvestiia,* Aug. 5, 1973, 3; Feb. 4, 1974, 3; Aug. 24, 1974, 2. The USSR paradoxically was the world's leading producer of cement.

129. GARF-2, f. 398, op. 9., d. 9 (Correspondence with Gosplan USSR on work of automobile transport, July–Dec. 1969), l. 335. In 1965, the Moscow Likhachev factory reported having produced 377 domestic refrigerators above plan. See Rossiiskii Gosudarstvennyi arkhiv Ekonomiki (RGAE), f. 398, op. 1, d. 56 (Annual Report of the Moscow Automobile Factory named after Likhachev—ZIL, 1965), l. 74.

130. *Pravda,* July 24, 1971, 3; *Literaturnaia gazeta,* no. 19 (1973): 10–11; ibid., no. 38 (1978): 12.

131. Andrienko, "Legkovoi avtomobil'," 109. This same source claims that spare parts production declined by 9% between 1980 and 1982.

132. V. E. Louis and J. M. Louis, *Louis Motorist's Guide to the Soviet Union,* 2nd ed. (Oxford: Pergamon, 1987), 12. Interestingly, the first edition, published in 1967, did not contain such advice. Meanwhile, customers in both the United Kingdom and Canada "reported satisfaction with the services provided by Lada dealers, including a ready supply of spare parts." Welihozkiy, "Automobiles," 826.

133. *Literaturnaia gazeta,* no. 38 (1978): 12; Andrienko, "Legkovoi avtomobil'," 112. For the sake of (an inexact)comparison, do-it-yourself auto repairs were estimated at 24 percent of total volume in the U.S. in 1964. Kevin L. Borg, *Auto Mechanics: Technology and Expertise in Twentieth-Century America* (Baltimore: The Johns Hopkins University Press, 2007), 128.

134. *Pravda,* Nov. 12, 1983, 3.

135. M. Alexeev, "Underground Market for Gasoline in the USSR," *Berkeley-Duke Occasional Papers on the Second Economy in the USSR,* no. 9 (Washington, D.C., 1987), 1–25. Alexeev estimates that at least 75% of all gasoline used by private car owners in 1982 was obtained illegally (17).

136. Efimov and Mikerin, "Avtomobilizatsiia," 134.

137. *Literaturnaia gazeta,* no. 38 (1978): 12. For other experiences with mechanics, see Likhodeev, *Ia i moi avtomobil',* 9 ("Ah, Genka, my angel-savior from the municipal garage. How did you know that I wallow in a maelstrom of helplessness?"), and *Literaturnaia gazeta,* no. 8 (1973): 12.

138. *Izvestiia,* Aug. 6, 1977, 2. The items listed under "repair" were automobiles, motorcycles, motor scooters, mopeds, motorized wheelchairs, bicycles, televisions, loudspeakers, watches, fountain pens, "and others."

139. Likhodeev, *Ia i moi avtomobil'; Garazh* (1979, dir. El'dar Riazanov); *Soviet Statutes and Decisions* 22, no. 3 (1986): 54–57.

140. Kazbek Ismagilov [Stanislav Malozemov], *Roskoshnyi avtomobil': Povest'-fel'ton i iumoristicheskie rasskazy* (Tashkent: Zazushy, 1984), 105–6.

141. Arrak, "Ispol'zovanie avtomobilei," 136.

142. Telephone interview with "Vadim" (Vladimir Cherkassky), June 9, 2004. For this sense of "private," see Jeff Weintraub, "The Theory and Politics of the Public/Private Distinction," in *Public and Private in Thought and Practice: Perspectives on a Grand Dichotomy,* ed. Jeff Weintraub and Krishan Kumar (Chicago: University of Chicago Press, 1997), 4–5.

143. Ulf Mellström, *Masculinity, Power and Technology: A Malaysian Ethnography* (Aldershot, Hampshire: Ashgate, 2003), 115.

144. As Jean Baudrillard observed in a very different cultural context, "The car rivals the house as an alternative zone of everyday life: the car, too, is an abode, but an exceptional one; it is a closed realm of intimacy, but one released from the constraints that usually apply to the intimacy of the home, one endowed with a formal freedom of great intensity." See *The System of Objects* (London: Verso, 1996), 67.

145. "In Pictures: Murmansk's Gorgeous Garages, Beauty or Beast?" BBC News at http://news.bbc.co.uk/2/shared/spl/hi/pop_ups/06/business_murmansk0s_gorgeous_garages/html/1.stm (accessed 2.8.07). My thanks to Andrew Paul Janco for drawing my attention to this source.

146. I am grateful to Steven Harris for urging me to 'make this point more explicit.

147. I. Kiselev, "Avtoliubitel' priekhal v magazin," *Za rulëm*, no. 4 (1978): 36–37.

148. Interview with "Sasha" (Aleksandr Blinov), Sept. 13 and 18, 2004, in Moscow.

149. Telephone interview with "Vadim" (Vladimir Cherkassky), June 9, 2004.

150. Michael R. Leaman, "Riding the Survivors of the Soviet Union," in Wollen and Kerr, *Autopia,* 160–62. Although Leaman is writing about post-Soviet Moscow, personal experience confirms that such driving was common in the 1970s and '80s.

151. *Za rulëm,* no. 5 (1986): 5. See also no. 4 (1986): 6; no. 12 (1986): 4–5.

152. *Izvestiia,* Sept. 7, 1988, 6.

Conclusion

1. R. M. Gasanov, *Baloven' veka: Avtomobil' i biznes* (Moscow: Molodaia gvardiia, 1990), 188.

2. See, respectively, William Abernathy, *The Productivity Dilemma: Roadblock to Innovation in the Automobile Industry* (Baltimore: Johns Hopkins University Press, 1978); Emma Rothschild, *Paradise Lost: The Decline of the Auto-Industrial Age* (New York: Random House, 1973); John Jerome, *The Death of the Automobile: The Fatal Effect of the Golden Era, 1955–1970* (New York: Norton, 1972).

3. See, for example, Marcia D. Lowe, *Alternatives to the Automobile: Transport for Livable Cities* (Washington, D.C.: Worldwatch Institute, 1990); James J. MacKenzie, *Driving Forces: Motor Vehicle Trends and Their Implications for Global Warming, Energy Strategies, and Transportation Planning* (Washington, D. C.: World Resources Institute, 1990); Steve Nadis and James J. MacKenzie, *Car Trouble* (Boston: Beacon Press, 1993).

4. Robert Argenbright, "Cars, Class, and Space in Post-Soviet Moscow: The First Decade," paper presented at American Association for the Advancement of Slavic Studies conference, Washington, D.C., Nov. 18, 2006. For the sake of comparison, Paris in 1950 had about six hundred thousand cars, a number that doubled in ten years and doubled again by 1965. Kristin Ross, *Fast Cars, Clean Bodies: Decolonization and the Re-ordering of French Culture* (Cambridge: MIT Press, 1995), 42.

5. "Federal'naia trassa 'Amur'," at http://www.rosavtodor.ru/doc/history/chyta1.htm (accessed 9.19.06).

6. S. Iu. Tselikov, "Avtomobil'nyi rynok Rossii, istoriia formirovaniia i perspektivy razvitiia: Positsionirovanie AVTOVAZa v usloviiakh rasushchei konkurentsii," *Istoriia OAO Avtovaz: Uroki, problemy, sovremennost'. Materialy I Vserossiiskoi nauchnoi konferentsii, 26–27 noiabria 2003 g.,* ed. A. E. Livshits and P. A. Nakhmanovich (Togliatti: OAO Avtovaz, TGU, 2003), 263–65; Stanley Root, PwC, "Russian Automotive Industry 2003—An Industry in Transition," presentation to AUTOCEE 2003 Conference, Prague, Oct. 2003, at http://www.pwc.com/gx/eng/about/ind/auto/2003stanleyroot.pdf (accessed 12.13.03).

7. *Le Monde,* Mar. 6, 2007, 15; *New York Times,* Feb. 12, 2003, national ed., C1; Oct. 13, 2005, national ed., C4. Parts manufacturers such as Delphi, Robert Bosch, and Michelin also have production facilities in Russia.

8. "Estimating Global Road Fatalities," at http://www.factbook.net/EGRF_Regional_analyses_CEE.htm (accessed 2.11.05); "Multi-Country Per Capita Fatality Data for 2003," Drive and Stay Alive, Inc., at http://www.driveandstayalive.com/info%20section/statistics/stats-multicountry-percapita-2003.htm (accessed 9.21.06); Julius Strauss, "Russians Shrug Off Road Carnage," Jan. 15, 2004, news.telegraph at http://www.telegraph.co.uk/news/main.jhtml?xml (accessed 2.10.05).

9. See Lewis H. Siegelbaum, "The Case of the Phantom Soviet Truck," *Radical History Review,* no. 90 (2004): 142–49.

index